The Best American History Essays 2008

The Best American Essays 2008

The Best American History Essays 2008

Edited by
David Roediger
for the
Organization of American Historians

First published in 2008 by
PALGRAVE MACMILLAN™
175 Fifth Avenue, New York, N.Y. 10010 and
Houndmills, Basingstoke, Hampshire, England RG21 6XS
Companies and representatives throughout the world.

PALGRAVE MACMILLAN is the global academic imprint of the Palgrave Macmillan division of St. Martin's Press, LLC and of Palgrave Macmillan Ltd. Macmillan® is a registered trademark in the United States, United Kingdom and other countries. Palgrave is a registered trademark in the European Union and other countries.

ISBN-13: 978–0–230–60590–9 (hardcover)
ISBN-10: 0–230–60590–7 (hardcover)
ISBN-13: 978–0–230–60591–6 (paperback)
ISBN-10: 0–230–60591–5 (paperback)

Library of Congress Cataloging-in-Publication Data is available from the Library of Congress.

A catalogue record for this book is available from the British Library.

Design by Newgen Imaging Systems (P) Ltd., Chennai, India.

First edition: April 2008

10 9 8 7 6 5 4 3 2 1

Printed in the United States of America.

Contents

List of Illustrations

Acknowledgments

Each year the ten-member *Best American History Essays* editorial board reads thousands of articles in the process of narrowing down the list of best American history essays. Under the leadership of editor David Roediger, University of Illinois, the following board members each read more than two hundred articles and essays before making their initial round of cuts resulting in the short list of thirty-six articles from which the ten best were selected: Anthony J. Badger, Cambridge University; John M. Belohlavek, University of South Florida; John Saillant, Western Michigan University; Ellen Carol DuBois, University of California, Los Angeles; Eric Foner, Columbia University; Sharon Harley, University of Maryland; Jane Kamensky, Brandeis University; Jackson Lears, Rutgers University; and Elliott West, University of Arkansas. On behalf of the Organization of American Historians, I would like to congratulate the authors whose works are represented in this volume, and to thank the editorial board's dedication, professionalism, and energy spent on this important endeavor.

In addition to the editorial board's labor, there was a lot of hard work behind the scenes performed by the executive office staff of the Organization of American Historians. Those who helped to bring this 2008 edition of *Best American History Essays* to print are publications director Michael Regoli, *OAH Magazine of History* editor Phillip M. Guerty, *OAH Magazine of History* assistant editor Keith Eberly, OAH Meetings director Amy Stark, and administrative associate Ashley Howdeshell.

Finally, we want to thank our colleagues at Palgrave Macmillan, especially editors Alessandra Bastagli and Christopher Chappell, whose efforts made this volume possible.

—*Lee W. Formwalt*
Executive Director, Organization of American Historians

Introduction

Rebranding History? The Best History Essays and the Popular Appeals of the Past

David Roediger

Recently while getting a haircut on a research trip, I quizzed the barber on her working life, which had taken her from earning a living as a flight attendant, to being a women's hairstylist, to the shop where she then worked. She asked about my job and on hearing that I was a historian unexpectedly rhapsodized about the field, her hobby. She went to every historical lecture that she could attend, watched the History Channel in order to find books to then read, and took community college history classes for fun. Like most modest day-to-day expressions of approval for history, her remarks ended characteristically. She confessed surprise at her own interest, having hated history in high school. I, in turn, confessed my surprise at meeting someone quite so enamored of history.

For most of the past three decades I have taught a big lecture class on U.S. history every spring. Sometimes it has surveyed the first "half" of that history—through 1877—and usually the shorter second half. Sometimes it has had three hundred students, usually seven hundred. If the pattern holds, and my math is right, I'll soon teach my fifteen thousandth student in such a class. A few are history majors, but the class is pitched to the big majority who are not, and who may take no other class in the field. It surprises me how energizing the classes always are, repeated in so many incarnations. In part, the challenge of telling such a big story in thirty hours explained its initial appeal, but I long ago gave up on pretending that the whole story was being told.

The pleasures of the survey course come instead from a decision to use it to teach something of what historians actually do, of how they argue about evidence, of how they revise, and on which wavelengths the passions of a historian are shared by those who have their own histories and passions. The course insists that even the facts and dates are objects of debate. The greatest account of mid-nineteenth-century U.S. history, W.E.B. Du Bois's *Black*

Reconstruction, has the Civil War lasting almost a quarter of a century, after all.[1]

Meetings with the small army of graduate assistants who teach the various sections of the course, and who are usually much closer to students in age and educational experiences, end in wide-ranging discussions of what young people have learned about history and of what they are ready to learn. When I thought that I knew most of the answers to such questions, students received a guarantee at the class's beginning: If you hated the way history was taught in high school, you will really like this class. That is, if the idea that history packages for memorization by students the facts and dates concerning great men and big events held little appeal in high school, then the idea of history as an interpretation and even an imagination of the past should hold greater attraction.

Eventually, the guarantee had to be dropped. It too much implied a corollary that pessimistically predicted that those students most liking their prior education in history would then hate the course. In fact they sometimes liked both styles of teaching history. Alas, a few in the class reported finding little but tedium in either approach. Moreover, students increasingly come to college having learned, often from superb high-school teachers, a history based on a combination of memorization and interpretation so that their love–hate relationships with the discipline were anything but simple. Some have reported liking the class because it continued creative approaches with which they were already familiar. Still the most common comment on course evaluations expressed surprise that a history course could be engaging—that it could be the perfect discipline for those who like to argue and who shun the cut-and-dried.

Such long-standing reflections on the appeals of history have assumed sharper and somewhat different contours for me as this volume has taken shape. The process involved my chairing a committee of nine historians, distinguished as prizewinning academic authors, as writers for a popular audience, as leaders of professional organizations, and as influential editors. The committee included Jane Kamensky, Eric Foner, Ellen Dubois, John Saillant, John Belohlavek, Jackson Lears, Sharon Harley, Elliott West, and Anthony Badger. Each member read an astounding number of essays—essentially one-ninth of the massive bibliography of history essays compiled by the Organization of American Historians for the year under consideration. Each forwarded a handful of nominees for the group's consideration. The essays chosen in that first set of selections were then read by all members, with a series of votes producing the ten choices for publication. A list of the essays that were nominated but not included in the final ten can be found on page 265.

Our charge from the OAH and from the publisher guiding the process was deceptively simple. We were to value soundness, excellence, and accessibility to a broad audience. The last of those criteria opened onto, and in some ways changed my mind about, the questions raised by teaching large introductory classes: What do people bring with them as they encounter historical works? Why do they seek out history or avoid it like the plague? What claims for the attention and engagement of educated listeners and readers can academic history make? What makes people like and read history? At times in our e-mail conversations and especially in a single fascinating committee meeting, wonderful discussions of accessibility, excellence, and the current state of history as a discipline occurred. This brief introduction makes no claim to speak for the committee or to summarize its discussions, but my idiosyncratic remarks here did benefit from the collective process that went into producing the book.

History is perhaps the discipline most misunderstood as the very result of its being taught. If a child takes several art classes, he generally comes away with some experience trying to produce art. If enrolled in band, she learns more or less the problems and joys faced by musicians. Science classes have their hands-on labs, and in composition, students compose. But in many history classes only that most atypical of the writings that historians produce, the textbook, gets assigned and sometimes read. When alarmist cries about the state of history education occur, the charge is that too few basic facts have stuck in the heads of students, not that they cannot use historical documents to make a convincing argument. Indeed the number of history classes taken by school children can, if they are of a certain type, almost predict the level of their misunderstanding of what historians do. Much-schooled students have more reasons to believe, however wrongly, that doing history means mastering those facts that historians have concluded are uncontroversially true—not coming to understand how historians disagree, reason, and typically fail to conclude. Students inevitably imagine a history conference as a kind of large-scale *Jeopardy* competition, though nerdier, in which the best scholars have the most ready answers, not the best questions.

One promising way to address such a misapprehension is that suggested by my survey course: to rebrand history completely, defining it as an argument, using the best available evidence, for a particular imagination of the past and of change over time. Besides being more or less true as a description of what most historians actually do, such a definition has the advantage of making history an act of creativity, without losing the central role of evidence and reasoned argument, in its production. Such a definition usefully separates our historical thinking about the past from the past itself. The latter remains too undocumented, unwieldy, and inevitably controversial to submit to being memorized. The definition also makes some of the intellectual skills involved in thinking historically much more familiar and concrete. Comparisons of athletes across generations, for example, consistently show sports talk radio, of all places, to be a repository of the best in historical thinking, with partisans arguing closely from evidence, producing new data and even drawing lines between historical periods to set evidence in context. (The "dead-ball era" is an example).

The importance of arguing even over facts and names becomes crystal clear when students think about the difference between our naming the almost twenty-year conflict still raging in Iraq as one ongoing war with several phases, or more typically identifying several wars and at least two U.S. victories. Such current controversies cause them to know that when Du Bois makes us think about the Civil War as stretching out over decades, rather than four years, he is making critical interpretive points about its origins, outcomes, and meanings. They notice how impassioned the debates become over whether the Iraq conflict ought to be named a civil war. Indeed the role of the present in shaping our decisions about what to stress, and even to see, in the past becomes more clear once we define history as reasoned marshalling of evidence by historians who react variously to their own present and argue for certain imaginations of the past.

There is then a temptation to claim a popular audience for history by bringing more and more people into its mysteries, by expanding the circle, the mission, and the sophistication of those whom television programming calls "history detectives." But as important and potentially democratizing as such approaches to reconceptualizing history may be, they also present difficult problems. One set of such problems is frankly political and is often perceived as coming from "outside" of the historical profession. As the debates over the process of formulating national history standards showed more than a decade ago, innovations have been much more subject to political attack, usually but not always from the right, when they have strayed from a great man, just-the-facts approach and into approaches requiring interpretation of evidence.[2]

To the extent that they use awareness of the present to frame and to make familiar questions regarding the past, history educators open themselves to charges that they are being "political" in ways that their critics allegedly are not. The current U.S. president George W. Bush, although a history major when at Yale as an undergraduate, has disparaged disagreements with his Iraq policies as "revisionist history," as if history were possible without revising interpretations of the past in light of new evidence and ideas.[3] Former Republican speaker of the House of Representatives Newt Gingrich is one of the most-publicized historians in the United States, offering his own televised and mass-marketed survey course designed to use history for "renewing American civilization" around such "pillars" as entrepreneurship and faith. The course argues for its own necessity on the grounds that it combats a drift to political uses of the past.[4] Such drift is often associated with the rise of putatively "disuniting" interdisciplinary initiatives such as ethnic studies, women's studies, and queer studies, said to undermine the idea of a received national story for their own political purposes, if not by their very existence.[5]

But as much as such political pressures are real, it must be said the hesitancy to base the popular appeals of history on introduction to it as a craft comes, for better and for worse, as much from within history as from without. There is first of all the practical problem exemplified by the fact that a student may well take only one survey history course. How much of a history detective can she become in fifteen weeks? At what point is it better to assign an astonishing tour-de-force historical book, showing how history at its best is really done, and trusting students will make the connections between their own efforts at interpretation of sources and the book's genius. If, as is sometimes argued, the past is "another country," is not some detailed knowledge of that country necessary before interpretation and analysis can begin? What authority can the teaching assistant claim when a student slips from the idea of history as a well-supported argument for an imagination of the past into "my opinion" (or even "feeling") about the past, one that is ipso facto as good as anyone else's?

Beyond such logistical, but still daunting, problems lies a further set of difficulties, one perhaps especially relevant to trying to reach an audience outside of classrooms. In attempting to show to others what it is that makes historical research and writing so exciting to its practitioners, historians can end up like the magician whose act consists of exposing how the trick works, creating not so much awe for their craft as the undermining of such awe. The worried responses over recent years of historians to the "death of the narrative" in the face of challenges portrayed as ranging from postmodernist theory, to social science methods, to multiculturalism to MTV, betray the anxiety that the thing we do best—telling meaningful stories—is in peril.[6]

Moreover, a case could be made that losing an emphasis on the narrative of past would divorce history from the considerable popular readership that it already commands, with no guarantee of creating a new base of history lovers. There is already a substantial audience for the finished products of historians and in many cases the bigger the better, with giant books often becoming bestsellers, especially if they concentrate on wars, politics, disasters, and/or eventful individual lives. Such popular work is sometimes suspected by academic historians for its very success at selling books, but it represents a real achievement by which historians such as the late Stephen Ambrose, Barbara Tuchman, David Levering Lewis, David McCulloch, Douglas Brinkley, James McPherson, and Doris Kearns Goodwin could capture the imagination of readers. In doing so, popular works of history sometimes are adventuresome in interpretation—think of classics such as Fawn Brodie's precocious life of Jefferson, or Erik Erikson on Gandhi—but they are also "traditional" in form, offering supersized and often much-footnoted accounts with a more-or-less omniscient authorial perspective.[7] To give up the audience, not to say market, cultivated by such historians in order to invite readers into learning a little about the craft of history asks a lot.

That is, when lay readers say that they love history, they often mean that they love traditional narrative history that presents conclusions confidently. It may be that they learn later in life to appreciate history because it covers a "new" topic, one textbook history had convinced them was taboo. The barber at the beginning of this introduction, for example, pinpointed the finding of her passion for history as when she learned that accounts of crime and criminals existed, that history was not all about presidents and elections. Nonetheless, the books that she said she liked were sweeping, traditionally narrated histories of such mayhem. The best recent popular writers of history reflect the attractions of new subjects generated by the trend of writing "history-from-below" in the late 1960s and the 1970s. The common soldier and railroad workers, for example, can find prominent places alongside generals, magnates, and presidents. But they typically do so in long-established ways.

Nor does a desire for change in society necessarily undermine the appeals of historical writing based on narratives, facts, and dates. The two million, often young, buyers of Howard Zinn's *A People's History of the United States* (1980) sometimes express rebellion by carrying it to coffee shops, but the book itself is sized, structured and even sold in ways very like the big books on John Adams or Harry Truman that the parents of the rebels might carry around. Working in 1990 on a people's history project in South Africa, then on the verge of its liberation, brought this point home for me. I noticed that one of our sons, although attending the wonderful parish school of the antiapartheid archbishop Desmond Tutu, suffered four days a week through learning the deeds of great white "heroes" in order to prepare for standardized exams still controlled by the old regime. Only on Fridays could the truth come out. On meeting with a group of African educators likely to become primary and second-ary school administrators after freedom, I remarked on the situation and asked whether the future curriculum should simply replace apartheid's great men with the heroines and heroes of the freedom struggle or try to change the whole way that history was learned and tested. The discussion was fascinating, but most participants firmly opted for a new nationalist narrative history curriculum and for keeping the old school style of the test with new heroes.

Reading the best essays on U.S. history in a given year offers an oppor-tunity to see the redefinition of history that I still would advocate in a class-room as something likely to emerge gradually and to consider the various kinds of existing love for history and what supports them. As a form, the essay cannot rely on the monumentality that characterizes popular works of history generally. It cannot offer the appeal of being able to spend some minutes each day in the company of a John Adams or a Thomas Jefferson for weeks on end. The essay often instead lays out its sources, problem, and strategy in a way much more conducive to showing what historians do than the mega-book, and is therefore more likely to introduce readers to the craft of history. But a collection of the very best essays like this one can illustrate much else that grounds compelling cases for history's claim to a broad readership.

First of all, the finest essays show that we need not accept a stark choice between defending narrative approaches to history or undertaking search-ing analyses of historical events. Du Bois closed *Black Reconstruction* with a searing indictment of those white supremacist historians of slavery, the Civil War, and Reconstruction who had given us a "propaganda of his-tory." He challenged their racial assumptions and their isolation of U.S. events from the rest of world history as well as their tendency to misuse some sources and to ignore others altogether. Near the end of his bitter bill of particulars, Du Bois arrived at perhaps his most devastating criticism. Blind to the humanity of black Southerners, such historians kept readers from seeing the *drama* of the events they rehearsed and distorted. They erred not only on this point and that, but also, and spectacularly, in making readers fully miss the "most magnificent drama in the last thousand years of human history...a tragedy that beggared the Greek."[8]

We would be much better off if we joined Du Bois in insisting on defending the historian's capacity to capture drama, not just his or her mere ability to narrate, as the key virtue of the discipline. Indeed the best big books by popular authors often hinge on just that virtue. As Du Bois's own example so well shows, drama and a commitment to interpret are far from necessarily at odds with each other. Indeed the capturing of an historical drama necessitates arguing, at least implicitly, for a particular imagination of the past.

Such drama animates many of the pieces included in this volume. Anna Pegler-Gordon's marvelous *American Quarterly* essay on photography and Chinese exclusion, for example, takes us into a process in which every advance in photographic surveillance was matched by new strategies among immigrants, who attempted to use photographs to document the sometimes fictive family relationships that would legalize their residency and work in the United States. At its climax, the essay shows authorities grilling applicants who had created their own "provisional family archives," turning the very technologies deployed to exclude them into whatever advantage that they could obtain.

Coming from the discipline whose business it is to attend to change over time, historians often describe in these essays dramatic transformations occurring in a relatively short time. Pegler-Gordon thus writes of a period in which photographs changed from mainly providing "honorific self-presentations" of the middle class to "the repressive documentation of inmates and the urban poor." Monica Richmond Gisolfi portrays the change in the space of a generation from an upcountry Georgia economy based on the "fleecy lock" of cotton to one based on the "fuzzy down" of chicks, a transformation made still more dramatic by the ways in which she connects the backward-looking crop-lien system of the old cotton sharecropping order with the enduring and modern-seeming contract-farming operations in the poultry industry.

The dramas depicted are not infrequently laced with irony, as when Gloria L. Main describes, and painstakingly reconstructs, the success of New Englanders at limiting family size despite the absence of effective birth control technologies. Their decisions to do so required a new mutuality, if not equality, so that for a time "the need for sexual restraint would become patriarchy's gentle solvent." David M. Wrobel richly reconstructs the extent to which published accounts by travelers to the United States energized and rendered as exceptional the impulse toward American empire. He finds space to linger briefly over the irony that the greatest celebrant of U.S. democracy, Alexis de Tocqueville, also enthused over Indian removal policies by the U.S. state, projecting their applications to French colonialism in Algeria. Michael McDonnell's study of class in revolutionary Virginia takes off from the irony, and the contradiction, of the most advanced freedom fighters in the world offering a slave, along with land, as the bounty to induce enlistments in the fight against British oppressors.

That historians revise views of the past, partly in view of the present, emerges in these pages as a far more benign process than when such processes are vilified on Fox News Channel or by the White House. Sometimes, as in the case of Beth English's impressive and understated study of the lives and culture of cotton-mill women, the rewriting of history proceeds from the discovery of compelling new sources. In McDonnell's case, the target of revision is one of the most esteemed contributions to U.S. history over the last several decades, Edmund Morgan's studies of the connections between slavery and freedom in the American past. But McDonnell's call for a greater attention to class differences among whites is delivered not to score politically correct points, nor with the back-and-forth among scholars crowding out the drama of revolution, but rather as a part of giving us access to a new drama and to a new sense of the revolution.

Clearly many of the essays you are about to read could take some of their inspiration from today's headlines. They concern, for example, capital punishment, empire, immigration, and how to make sense of a war amidst contradictory reports and uncertain outcomes. But they use the present as a source of intellectual curiosity, to pose new questions and to open new areas of inquiry into the past, rather than bending the past to justify a set of policy prescriptions in the present. Jeffrey Adler's arresting and scenic account of the startling rate at which Chicago jurors in the Progressive Era turned accused murderers loose provides the best example on this score. It speaks to present concerns, but with no claims of correspondence between the present and a very different past. If Adler's work is liberating, and for me it is decidedly so, this is because it so brilliantly shows change over time, both within the Progressive Era and between then and now. The knowledge that things were not ever thus—that history moves and responds to human action—is what makes the past worth studying by those who care for the present and the future, far more than any "lessons" that history directly holds.

Similarly, the essays as a whole suggest that interdisciplinary approaches, and specifically those grounded in the interdisciplinary fields of ethnic studies and of gender and women's studies, are not what is keeping us from telling dramatic human stories commanding a broad readership. The late Thomas B. Alexander, an old friend, used to charmingly express his hopes for the spread of social science methods among historians by counting and charting how many tables appeared within history journals over time. Tom would have been pleased to see an average of nearly one table per article here. He would have been more pleased at the ways in which they lead into an understanding of human relationships, not simply into more tables. Carma R. Gorman's essay deftly brings together insights and evidence from areas as different as art history, physical education, marketing, postmodernist theory, and management. Her doing so is precisely what makes Gorman's study of how bodies and commodities both came to be the objects of streamlining in the second quarter of the twentieth century so remarkably able to get at what Neil Harris has called "the drama of consumer desire."[9]

Multicultural and feminist approaches also lead in these essays to deeper and better dramas, not to truncated and disparate stories. Such is strikingly the case even at the level of method when Jason Phillips explores the intriguing role of rumors, circulating through the Confederacy on the "grape vine telegraph," in keeping Southern hopes alive, in some cases even after surrender. The essay addresses a topic, Civil War history, that has perhaps commanded the widest popular audience and greatest historical attention of any within the U.S. past. Phillips says something new and fascinating on that topic not only because of the quality of his evidence—one Virginia soldier skewers the many rumors killing off the Union's greatest general by observing that "Grant is **still** dead; but comes to life occasionally" in a remark I'll now always think of when hearing of Fidel Castro's many prematurely reported demises—but also because he draws on inspirations from important studies of rumor within African American history and African American studies. At key junctures, for example, in McDonnell's accounts of manliness and class, or in Adler's discussions of jurors acquitting abused wives accused of killing their husbands, gender becomes a critically important category of analysis even when it is not the subject of the essay.

In one exasperated moment, the poet Amiri Baraka responded to attacks on African American authors for allegedly remaining confined to writing about their "own people." What did critics think that James Joyce's *The Dubliners* were, Baraka sharply asked, "abstract literary categories?"[10] Paul Rosier's brilliant essay on American Indians and the Cold War shows that the history, like the literature, of a racialized group is unlikely to be narrow. Like the important recent work on African American civil rights and the Cold War, Rosier's contribution finds internally colonized people in the United States attempting to use liberal anticommunist rhetoric, and the pressures created by Soviet media portraying U.S. racism to the whole watching world, to defend themselves. The subtly rendered ways in which campaigns to support self-determination fostered activism among Indians as members of a specific nation, as participants in pan-Indian coalitions, and as defenders of the U.S. nation remind us that scholarship in ethnic studies, far from being narrow and inward looking, has from its inception, and necessarily, pioneered in adopting transnational approaches. Rosier's contribution provides an apt place to end an introduction that has stressed the need not so much to "rebrand" published history wholesale as to gradually develop a firmer sense of what historians do, while drawing on and deepening the multiple appeals and promising connections that the field possesses. Enjoy what follows, for all of the reasons you choose.

Notes

David Roediger is the Babcock Professor of History at the University of Illinois. His recent books include *Working toward Whiteness* (Basic Books, 2005), *History Against Misery* (Kerr), *Colored White* (University of California Press, 2002), and a new edition of *The Wages of Whiteness* (Verso, with an introduction by Kathleen Cleaver, 2007). Among his recent edited books are the Modern Library edition of W.E.B. Du Bois's *John Brown* (Random House, 2001), *Black on White* (Schocken, 1998), and, with Archie Green, Franklin Rosemont, and Salvatore Salerno, *The Big Red Songbook* (Kerr, 2007).

1. W.E.B. Du Bois, *Black Reconstruction in America* (New York: Atheneum, 1992, originally 1935), 30, dates the Civil War as lasting from 1854 until 1876.
2. See, e.g., C. Frederick Risinger, "The National History Standards: A View from the Inside," *The History Teacher*, 28 (May 1995), 387–93; and Gary Nash, "Lynne Cheney's Attack on the History Standards, Ten Years Later," *History News Network* (November 8, 2004) at http://hnn.us/essays/8418.html.
3. "Bush Raps Revisionist Historians on Iraq," *CNN.com/Inside Politics* (June 16, 2003) at http://www.cnn.com2003/ALLPOLITICS/06/16/bush.iraq/; and David E. Sanger, "After the War: Intelligence," *New York Times* (June 9, 2003), Section A, p. 14.
4. Allan J. Lichtman, "History According to Newt: Newt Gingrich as a History Teacher," *Washington Monthly*, 27 (May 1995), 48–9.
5. For an account particularly focused on ethnicity and race, see Arthur Schlesinger, Jr. *The Disuniting of America: Reflections on a Multicultural Society* (New York: W.W. Norton, 1998).
6. See Jeffrey N. Wasserstrom, "The Ends of History," *Common-Place*, 2 (January 2002) at http://www.historycooperative.org/journals/cp/vol-02/no-02/wasserstrom/; and James M. McPherson, "History: It's Still about the Stories," *New York Times* (September 19, 1999) at http://nytimes.com/books/99/09/19/bookend/bookend.html.
7. Fawn Brodie, *Thomas Jefferson: An Intimate History* (New York: W.W. Norton, 1973); and Erik Erikson, *Gandhi's Truth: On the Origins of Militant Nonviolence* (New York: W.W. Norton, 1993, originally 1970).
8. Du Bois, *Black Reconstruction*, 727 and 710–29.
9. Neil Harris, "The Drama of Consumer Desire," in his *Cultural Excursions: Marketing Appetites and Cultural Tastes* (Chicago: University of Chicago Press, 1990), 174–97.
10. Amiri Baraka, *Home: Social Essays* (Hopewell. NJ: Ecco Press, 1998), 163.

Chinese Exclusion, Photography, and the Development of U.S. Immigration Policy

Anna Pegler-Gordon

In her fictionalized history of the Chinese in America, Maxine Hong Kingston describes how the Chinese immigrants who worked to build the transcontinental railroad were not included in the photograph commemorating its completion in 1869. "While the demons posed for photographs, the China Men dispersed," Kingston writes. "It was dangerous to stay. The Driving Out had begun." As Kingston suggests, many Chinese immigrants who had found work on the railroads soon found themselves unemployed. Although they had never been fully welcome, they had been encouraged to migrate by the promise of work in the United States as well as by social upheaval in China. More than ten thousand strong, Chinese laborers formed as much as 90 percent of the Central Pacific Railroad workforce. However, not one appeared in the photograph documenting the meeting of the rails at Promontory Point, Utah. This photograph is a graphic metaphor for the ways that the Chinese were excluded from the United States and the ways that their long-standing presence in this country has been erased.[1]

However, the driving out was not only a process of erasure. After 1882, as most Chinese were excluded from the United States, the exclusion laws also heralded the introduction of identity documentation for the few Chinese who were exempt from exclusion. Elite Chinese diplomats and merchants, students and travelers, native-born U.S. citizens, some laborers, and some wives were exempted from exclusion laws, allowed to enter or

From *American Quarterly*. Anna Pegler-Gordon, "Chinese Exclusion, Photography and the Development of U.S. Immigration Policy," *American Quarterly* 58:1 (2006), 51–77. © The American Studies Association. Reprinted with permission of The Johns Hopkins University Press.

remain in the United States. This essay will argue that rather than being erased, the exempt Chinese were more closely observed, documented, and photographed than any other immigrant group.

Historians of immigration have long claimed that Chinese exclusion marked a new development in immigration policy as the first law to discriminate against a group of immigrants on the basis of race and class. In recent years, scholars have also drawn attention to the ways that Chinese immigration restrictions were central to the development of general immigration policy. Among others, Lucy Salyer has shown how Chinese challenges to exclusion shaped the judicial review of immigration law, and Erika Lee has explored how the administration of exclusion was pivotal in the development of the United States as a "gatekeeping nation."[2]

The Chinese exclusion laws also mark another critical development: the formal emergence of visual regulation within immigration policy. From 1875 through the 1920s, as the federal government increased restrictions on immigration, it also expanded the use of visual regulation as a central component of immigration administration. This regulation took varied forms, ranging from photographic identification to medical inspections based on visual readings of immigrants' bodies. Together, these intersecting practices increasingly privileged visual knowledge within immigration law.

In particular, the Federal Immigration Bureau used the early photographic identification of the Chinese as a model for the bureau's expansion of photographic documentation to other immigrant groups. Starting with Chinese women, then all Chinese immigrants, and finally U.S. citizens of Chinese descent, photographic immigration identification was extended to regulate the Chinese community, and only the Chinese community, long before it was applied to other immigrant groups. With the inclusion of Mexican immigrants under general immigration laws in 1917 and the implementation of quotas favoring north-western European immigration in the 1920s, Mexican and European immigrants were gradually incorporated into an expanding system of racialized immigration restrictions. At the same time, they were also integrated into the system of visual and photographic regulation that underpinned these laws. Starting in 1917, Mexican border-crossers and agricultural laborers were issued photographic identification cards. All immigrants, including Europeans, were required by U.S. law to provide photographic identification to immigration officers in 1924, and were issued immigration identification in 1928. The 1924 requirement that immigrants provide photos on their visas represented the first time that photographic identity documentation became part of general immigration law, more than thirty years after the first statutory requirement that Chinese immigrants provide photographic documentation.[3]

The role of photography within immigration policy has been overlooked by most historians both because of their focus on written records and because of their traditional attention to European immigration as central to immigration history. However, European immigrants were not central to the development of photographic immigration documentation and were largely untouched by official photographic practices until they were restricted as part of the racially based National Origins Act of 1924. The experiences of the Chinese under exclusion show both that Chinese exclusion was central to the development of general immigration policy and that visual identity documentation was a key component of immigration restriction.[4]

The stringent visual regulation of the Chinese reflected widespread American beliefs about Chinese racial inassimilability, inferiority, and inherent criminality. These beliefs included concerns that most Chinese immigrants entered the United States illegally, aided by the fact that— according to exclusionists—all Chinese looked alike and were inherently inscrutable.[5]

However, both excluded and exempt Chinese fought against policies of Chinese exclusion, representation, and regulation by the United States.[6] They did so through three key strategies. First, elite Chinese community leaders launched diplomatic, legal, and political challenges to the implementation of new photographic documentation policies. When these challenges were unsuccessful, documented Chinese took control over their own photographic images, presenting themselves as respectable individuals in their identity documentation. This self-control was always partial and provisional, since it accepted conventional American understandings of respectability and depended on the immigration inspectors' reading of the immigrant's appearance. Finally, excluded Chinese resisted their rejection under the exclusion laws by manipulating photographs and photographic documentation to enter the United States. They substituted photographs on identity documents, exchanged certificates, and altered photographs through retouching and deliberate aging. In contrast to efforts to control photographic documentation through legal means, these extralegal uses of photography ultimately undermined both the purposes of documentation and the apparent objectivity of image. In the process, the Chinese not only challenged discriminatory immigration policies but also questioned the photograph's emerging authority as evidence.

"Facts Necessary for Identification": The Introduction of Photographic Documentation

Three years after the passage of the 1882 Chinese exclusion law, the San Francisco customs collector responsible for administering exclusion called for a new rule requiring photographs on Chinese laborer certificates. The collector, William Sears, noted that Judge Ogden Hoffman, a federal judge who dealt extensively with the Chinese, required Chinese plaintiffs to submit photographs of themselves when they appeared in court. In addition to this requirement, Judge Hoffman repeatedly recommended photographs on Chinese identification certificates. Although the 1882 exclusion law did not refer to photographs, Sears cited the law when he argued that it required information about the applicant's "*name, age, occupation, last place of residence, physical marks or peculiarities and all facts necessary for the identification of each of such chinese laborers."* "The photograph," wrote Sears, "would be a very important 'fact necessary' for their identification, and to prevent the transfer of certificates, and the traffic in them at Hong Kong, and other ports."[7] Although it appears that Sears was looking for a loophole in the law that would allow his office to require photographs from Chinese immigrants, it is significant that he refers to the photograph as a "fact." At this point, early in the development of visual identity documentation, immigration officials seemed confident in the empirical power of photography. However, after photographs had been introduced on Chinese documentation and found less than effective in reducing the circulation of fraudulent certificates, immigration officials adopted a more cautious and complex understanding of photography.

The first Chinese Exclusion Act, passed in 1882, prohibited almost all Chinese migration to the United States. Only a few groups of Chinese were exempt from the law: they included diplomats, merchants and their families, college students, and travelers. American citizens of Chinese descent and laborers who were already in the United States were also allowed to stay. Chinese women were allowed to enter the United States only if they were themselves native-born U.S. citizens or if they were married to diplomats, merchants, or U.S. citizens.[8] As the Chinese exclusion acts were renewed and revised in the following years, they implemented a series of increasingly stringent identification requirements covering those Chinese who were exempt from exclusion. By 1909, almost all people of Chinese descent in the United States, including U.S. citizens, were required to possess photographic documentation.[9] These photographic identity documents were checked upon entry into the United States and could be demanded at any time by immigration or other U.S. officials conducting raids or investigations. The only group not required to obtain U.S. identity documentation consisted of Chinese diplomats, although they needed Chinese passports stating that they were part of the Chinese legation. These exclusion laws remained in force until 1943.

Throughout the passage of the exclusion acts, the use of photography was debated. Although photographs were not required by statute until 1893, government rules and even individual inspectors often required photographic identification that exceeded statutory mandates. As early as the first federal immigration act, the 1875 Page Law prohibiting the immigration of prostitutes, Chinese women had been obliged to supply photographs with their applications for admission because of concerns that they were being imported for immoral purposes. Prior to their departure, Chinese women were questioned about their morality by U.S. officials. If provisionally approved, they were issued a "certificate of good moral character" that was forwarded to their port of entry with their photographs. Upon arrival, these women were questioned again and compared with their photographs to ensure that they were the same individuals who had been previously approved. After passage of the Scott Act in 1888, which prohibited Chinese laborers from returning to the United States, departing merchants and U.S. citizens of Chinese descent were issued photographic identity certificates, which were checked against the Immigration Bureau's records upon their return.[10]

In 1892, ten years after its passage, the first Chinese exclusion act came up for reauthorization. The new act was known as the Geary Act, and it was far harsher than the original exclusion law. In addition to continuing exclusion, the Geary Act required that Chinese laborers register for certificates of residence proving their right to remain in the United States. The Chinese community mounted significant opposition to the law, refusing to register and challenging its constitutionality in the U.S. Supreme Court. After the law was ruled constitutional in 1893, the Geary Act was amended to extend Chinese registration for an additional six months. This extension was known as the McCreary amendment and, although it has received little attention from historians, it marked a significant expansion of existing policy by requiring photographs on identity certificates. The McCreary amendment contained the first statutory requirement of photographic identification on immigration documentation, a statutory requirement that has always remained part of subsequent immigration policy.[11]

Early debates about the use of photography on Chinese certificates revealed a range of assumptions about both the nature of the Chinese and the nature of photography. In congressional and diplomatic circles, the debate quickly solidified around two primary positions: the practical necessity of requiring photographs versus the emotional and financial cost such a requirement would impose upon the Chinese. Exclusionists and photography proponents argued that photographs were legally allowed and justified by widespread document fraud. Supporters of Chinese immigration and opponents of photographic documentation claimed that the practice was a humiliating form of unequal treatment that violated both the United States' treaty obligations with China and the U.S. Constitution.

In support of the statutory photograph requirement, the primary sponsor of the 1892 and 1893 legislation, Representative Thomas Geary (Calif.) argued that "all Chinamen look alike, all dress alike, all have the same kind of eyes, all are beardless, all wear their hair in the same manner."[12] Verbal descriptions alone are insufficient, he maintained, and therefore photographs are required to provide a more detailed form of description. The apparent objectivity and detailed likeness of photographic image was intended to link each individual to his or her identity documentation, making it impossible for the Chinese to sell, exchange, or create fraudulent documents.

Arguments in favor of registration centered on fears of Chinese immigration fraud. But proponents argued that registration was not enough to stop fraud without photography. "The registration of a Chinaman without a photograph is not worth the paper it is written on," Representative Eugene Loud (Calif.) maintained while introducing the 1893 McCreary amendment. "Unless you have a photograph, every registration certificate of men between the ages of 20 and 40 will command in the markets of China or in Victoria from \$200 to \$400 or \$500."[13] The hyperbole of Loud's argument, that "every" certificate was susceptible to being sold, revealed a deeper belief that every Chinese immigrant was suspect.

Exclusionists often suggested that the entire Chinese community was engaged in criminal activities, even that criminality and immorality were part of the Chinese racial character. According to Representative Henry Blair (N.H.), the Chinese had created "a Sodom in San Francisco and a Gomorrah in New York." The popular conception of Chinese criminality was multifaceted and has been well documented by scholars. It included gambling, prostitution, opium smuggling, and gang warfare. But one of the most common and least studied aspects of Chinese criminality was the assumption that all Chinese were illegal immigrants using fake immigration documents and that their presence in America was itself criminal.[14] This idea, enshrined in the Geary Act, represented the most fundamental concerns about Chinese criminality. According to this understanding, the very existence of the Chinese in America was not only assumed to be economically, morally, and racially dangerous; it was also assumed to be criminal.

"The Law Itself Makes All Guilty": Legal and Political Opposition to Photographic Documentation

In contrast to the exclusionists who assumed that all Chinese were tainted by criminality, supporters of Chinese immigration were concerned that photographic documentation marked innocent Chinese residents as criminals. Identity photographs were strongly associated with criminality at this time because, prior to Chinese registration, suspected and convicted criminals formed the primary group of people being photographed by the state for identification purposes. Photographic historians have argued that, during the latter half of the nineteenth century, the purpose of photographic portraiture changed from the honorific self-presentation of European and American middle classes to the repressive documentation of inmates and the urban poor, who fell outside the middling range of respectability.[15]

In the American context, racial minorities and urban immigrants figured prominently in this process of documentary representation.[16] However, until immigration documentation was required of Mexican agricultural workers in 1917, Chinese residents were the only racial group subject to photographic documentation requirements by the U.S. government. Further, these requirements were not based on their actions but on their racial identity: as immigrants and U.S. citizens of Chinese descent, they were required to have photographic documentation simply to prove their right to reside in the United States.

In part because of concerns about Chinese criminality, the San Francisco Police Department was a pioneer in the field of photography, compiling identity photographs of all people arrested in the city starting in 1854. These photographs were used in large "mug book" albums and wall-mounted displays known as rogues' galleries. At the police station, crime victims could peruse the photographs to look for possible suspects and police officers could check the faces of people in their custody to see whether they had previously committed crimes under different names. The racial dimensions of photographic regulation are highlighted by the fact that, from the 1860s through the 1940s, the San Francisco Police Department kept its mug books of Chinese criminals separate from other criminals. This division was clearly racial rather than national, as photographs of Chinese suspects were kept separate from others regardless of their country of birth or place of residence.[17]

Opponents of Chinese registration compared registration photographs to rogues' galleries because these archives were the only American counterpart to the systematic documentation of Chinese residents. Chinese consul Wu Ting Fang, for example, complained that a respectable student who wanted to study in the United States "must submit to be photographed as if he were a criminal and candidate for the rogues' gallery."[18]

The registration requirement of the Geary Act and photography requirement of the McCreary amendment did more than create the appearance of Chinese criminality. These laws literally criminalized Chinese residents: they required the Chinese to obtain documentation and then established the presumption of guilt for all Chinese without it. According to Representative Robert Hitt (Ill.), "the law itself makes all guilty."[19] Although the registration and photography requirements were compared to the rogues' gallery, in many ways they were more denigrating and controlling. Criminal suspects were photographed for the rogues' gallery only after they had been accused of wrongdoing; Chinese were photographed upon their entry into the United States. The rogues' gallery was located at the police station; archives of Chinese photographs were not only held in a central location but also marked each individual who was required to carry an identity certificate at all times.

Although initial opposition to identity documentation focused on its unfairness to all Chinese, official protests gradually shifted their focus to the implementation of photographic documentation and exempting "respectable" Chinese from these requirements. In 1908, Chinese newspaper editor and community leader Ng Poon Chew argued that, while laborers may be excluded, exempt classes "must no longer be detained, photographed and examined as if they were suspected of crime." Of course, white exclusionists did not acknowledge class distinctions between Chinese; they suspected all Chinese of having committed the crime of illegal entry. It was this pervasive suspicion that undergirded the construction of a photographic identification policy. In short, the visual identification and registration system was the concrete implementation of exclusionists' beliefs that all Chinese were suspect at all times.

As restrictionists worked to expand the scope of Chinese exclusion, they relied on photographic documentation to enhance the government's efforts at enforcement. However, the expansion of photography also offered a forum for the Chinese to control their own representation of themselves, challenge dominant stereotypes, and assert their place in the United States.

A Favorable Appearance: Strategies of Self-Representation

After the certification provisions of the Geary Act were upheld by the Supreme Court in 1893 and the photographic requirement of the McCreary amendment was passed, there was a rush on portrait galleries as immigrants registered and had their photographs taken for the certificates.[20] Although Chinese fought against photograph requirements, once such legislation was enacted, they chose the ways in which they represented themselves in their identity photographs. Early application forms specified that "the photographs shall be sun pictures, such as are usually known as card photographs of sufficient size and distinctness to plainly and accurately represent the entire face of the applicant, the head not to be less than 1½ inches from the base of the hair to the base of the chin."[21]

Following these requirements, the vast majority of identity photographs were simple, frontal portraits that focused on the subject's facial features. Photographic historians have argued that, in contrast to the "cultivated asymmetries," soft lighting, and partial shading of the honorific studio portrait, these repressive photographs subscribed to conventions of frontality and clear lighting, revealing the details of the subject's features and eliminating all outside detail.[22] However, Chinese applicants for admission supplied their own photographs to the Immigration Bureau, allowing significant variation in their portraits that blurred the boundaries between the honorific and repressive functions of photography. This variation can be interpreted in many ways: as evidence that the conventions of identity portraiture were contested, as a sign of resistance to dominant representations of the Chinese, and as a graphic representation of the different ways that these immigrants negotiated their place in America.

In presenting themselves to immigration officials, Chinese immigrants defied American stereotypes by making themselves appear respectable. This is not to suggest that Chinese were not respectable, but that respectability is always a process of appearances. Chinese honorific identity portraits were both a conscious counterrepresentation to popular stereotypes and a succinct visual argument in support of their application to enter the United States. By presenting themselves as conventionally respectable, Chinese immigrants opposed exclusion through seeking acceptance.

Although most photographic portraits were very similar, some strategies of self-presentation worked differently for different Chinese groups. These differences reflected the subjects' varied relations to both Chinese and American portraiture traditions, as well as their legal status within U.S. exclusion policies. Almost all Chinese American portraits display some intermingling of Chinese and American portraiture practices, but they do so in diverse ways. These approaches often split along the fault lines of immigration status created by exclusion: native-born citizens and merchants, men and women, often presented themselves in ways that reflected their group status. However, within the constraints of Immigration Bureau policies and portraiture conventions, individuals also chose to present themselves in their own ways.

In contrast to diplomats and merchants who typically presented themselves in Chinese clothes, some native-born U.S. citizens emphasized their Americanness by favoring more Western conventions. In one case, a man of Chinese descent, Lee Gum Yoke, was required to prove his birth in the United States in order to claim his U.S. citizenship and his right to reenter the United States. The immigration inspector noted the reputable nature of Lee's white witnesses and concluded that "his appearance is decidedly in favor of his claims."[23] The photograph Lee submitted (figure 1.1) also supported this appearance and his claims of respectability and U.S. citizenship. In this photograph, Lee wears Western clothing: a stylish well-fitting suit jacket, starched shirt, and elegant tie. The jacket is unbuttoned to reveal a watch chain hanging from his waistcoat. Lee's clothes, the length of the portrait (reaching almost to his waist, instead of just his head and shoulders), and the gentle fading at the lower edge of the photograph reveal this to be more than an identity photograph: it is a studio portrait.

Although Lee presents himself within the tradition of bourgeois American portraiture, he looks directly at the camera in a pose more often associated with identity photographs. Frontality was common in Chinese portraiture, but Lee's face reveals another possible reason for this pose. While he is wearing American clothes, Lee's hair is shaved in the front and longer in the back, probably braided in a queue. By looking directly at the camera, Lee hides the evidence of this Chinese cultural practice and presents himself as a short-haired American man dressed in Western clothes. It may be that the suit that appears to fit him so well was loaned to him by the photo studio for the occasion: such practices were fairly common, as people borrowed clothes to dress up for their portraits.[24] Or it could be that the photograph represents the dual aspects of Lee's life, living as a Chinese man in America. Regardless, Lee presented himself to the immigration authorities as a respectable, appropriately dressed American citizen.

Like Chinese men, the vast majority of women presented simple identity photographs to immigration officials. However, whereas men's varied exemption status often influenced their presentation of themselves in their applications and their photographs, women were primarily concerned with presenting themselves as respectable, traditional, and chaste. Whether Chinese women sought entry as wives of merchants, as wives of native-born citizens, or as citizens themselves, inspectors typically assumed that most Chinese women were prostitutes imported for immoral purposes.[25]

United States of America,)
State of Utah,) SS.
County of Summit.)

_James Don_____, being first duly sworn, on oath deposes and says: That he is a citizen of the United States, over the age of twenty one years; that he is a resident of Park City, Utah, and has resided in said City ever since the year _1882___; that he knows Lee Gum Yoke, whose picture is hereto attached and made a part hereof, ever since his birth; that said Lee Gum Yoke was born in Park City, Utah, sometime during the year 1884 and has resided in Park City during all of the time since his birth except about the last four years.

_James Don_____

Subscribed and sworn to before me this _28th_ day of March, A.D. 1904.

Tho. Cubit
Notary Public for Summit County, Utah.

Picture Identified
C. M. Wilson
Mayor of Park City

Exhibit a

HENDERSON, PIERCE, CRITCHLOW & BARRETTE
ATTORNEYS-AT-LAW
SALT LAKE CITY

Figure 1.1 Affidavit of James Don in support of native-born U.S. citizen Lee Gum Yoke, 1904.

Source: National Archives and Records Administration—Pacific Region (San Francisco).

Outside of immigration records, photographs of Chinese women often portrayed them surrounded by Chinese props in elegant settings that emphasized high class status and suggested home life. In addition to submitting conventional identity photographs, some Chinese women also submitted these elaborate studio photographs of themselves to the Immigration Bureau.

In the matter of Young Fou, for example, a Chinese American merchant and his wife sought to gain entry to the United States for their son. The photograph of Young Fou shows the upper body of a small boy seated in a large ornate Chinese chair. The boy looks straight ahead. The affidavit of his father contains a simple identify photograph of a man facing the camera in plain black Chinese clothes and a black hat. Only his face and shoulders are shown. However, the photograph of his wife, Low Shee, is a full-length studio portrait of a woman seated in a chair similar to her son's, but surrounded by familiar symbols of Chinese culture and tradition (figure 1.1). The photograph is placed sideways on the affidavit and still barely fits in the space available. It could have been cut down to a smaller size, as the son's portrait was, but instead it is used in its entirety in order to include the wealth of detail in the apparently Chinese context.[26]

This photograph is not uncommon. It looks very much like many other studio portraits of Chinese women taken in America at the turn of the century (figure 1.2). This photograph may well have been the only one that the family had available; however, its use as an identity portrait is still significant. The surplus of props, for example, is especially noticeable when the image becomes an identity photograph since such images are usually devoid of extraneous detail. The Chinese props and background place Low Shee, like other female subjects, into an unmistakably Chinese context. Their respectability is represented as an adherence to Chinese traditions through the Chinese-style setting. This visual adherence to traditional Chinese respectability, however, is not complete. Low Shee's feet—just visible and placed firmly together on a footstool—appear to be unbound. The footstool is a traditional feature of Chinese portraits, but women's feet were rarely represented in respectable portraiture, since they were considered erotic. "For reasons still unexplained," art historians Jan Stuart and Evelyn Rawski have noted, "the introduction of the camera ushered in the innovation of...Chinese women displaying their feet in photographs." Immigration officials often looked favorably on applicants with bound feet, recognizing the practice as a marker of high class position and respectability within Chinese society. However, officials also may have noticed markers of Western respectability. Although Low Shee's feet are not bound, her left hand is carefully positioned on the edge of the table to display what appears to be a wedding band. In traditional commemorative portraiture, women's hands were often more carefully hidden in the sleeves of their garments than men's.[27] However, although wedding rings were not customary in China, women in this photographic portrait and others may have presented ringed fingers to register their married status and respectability to a Western viewer. Unlike the many uniform immigration identity portraits, these photographs

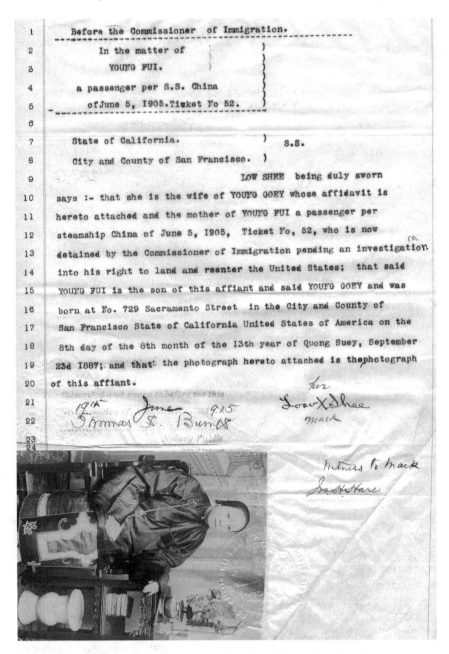

1	Before the Commissioner of Immigration.
2	In the matter of)
3	YOUNG FUI.))
4	a passenger per S.S. China)
5	of June 5, 1905. Ticket No 52.)
6	
7	State of California.) S.S.
8	City and County of San Francisco.)
9	LOW SHEE being duly sworn
10	says :- that she is the wife of YOUNG GOEY whose affidavit is
11	hereto attached and the mother of YOUNG FUI a passenger per
12	steamship China of June 5, 1905, Ticket No, 52, who is now
13	detained by the Commissioner of Immigration pending an investigation
14	into his right to land and reenter the United States; that said
15	YOUNG FUI is the son of this affiant and said YOUNG GOEY and was
16	born at No. 729 Sacramento Street in the City and County of
17	San Francisco State of California United States of America on the
18	8th day of the 8th month of the 13th year of Quong Suey, September
19	23d 1887; and that the photograph hereto attached is the photograph
20	of this affiant.
21	Subscribed and sworn to before me this
22	19th day of June 1905
23/24	Thomas F. Bunn Notary Public

Figure 1.2   Affidavit of Low Shee in support of Young Fou, 1905.

Source: National Archives and Records Administration—Pacific Region (San Francisco).

encased their female subjects within Chinese settings. In contrast to the native-born U.S. citizen Lee Gum Yoke, these visual strategies made few claims on America. Nevertheless, these photographs still presented women as accepting some of the immigration officials' American expectations of respectability.

Although Chinese immigrants resisted both exclusion and American stereotyping by representing themselves in photographic portraits, this resistance was never fully effective. While they were sometimes successful in using photographs to persuade immigration officials of their rights to enter the United States, they could not control the ways that these officials viewed them. In the end, immigration inspectors looked at the Chinese in America and saw what they wanted to see.

As photographs became increasingly important to the administration of exclusion, the Immigration Bureau also expanded its control over the production of images and attempted to standardize the range of acceptable images. This codification of identity photograph conventions gradually limited the opportunities for Chinese immigrants' representations of themselves in their immigration portraits.[28] However, it did not affect their ability to use photographs to enter the country in spite of exclusion, since self-representation was only one method of Chinese resistance. As the following section shows, substantial numbers of Chinese immigrants entered the United States illegally and their presence itself undermined the purpose of exclusion. The success of these illegal efforts depended significantly on the weakness of U.S. registration policies and the vulnerability of photographic documentation.

Coaching Photos: Resisting and Enforcing Exclusion through Photography

Alongside the public politics of protests and photographic representations of respectability, the Chinese evaded exclusion successfully through a different path: the open secret of illegal immigration. They entered and lived in the United States illegally in large numbers, undermining the government's attempts to exclude all Chinese. In fact, their informal acts of evasion were intimately connected to more formal aspects of opposition and were ultimately more effective. In one letter, for example, a man involved in an illegal immigration scheme provided instructions to bribe immigration officials and requested more information about protests against exclusion.[29]

Despite the effectiveness of Chinese illegal immigration strategies in undercutting exclusion, these successes also offered opportunities for immigration inspectors to increase the stringency of their examinations and expand their regulation of the Chinese. In addition, the Chinese community's successful evasion of exclusion and documentation ultimately reinforced ideas of Chinese criminality, ideas that had originally undergirded the establishment of exclusion and documentation policies. Like formal protests and strategies of self-representation, the success of illegal immigration was always provisional.

It is impossible to know the exact numbers of Chinese who entered the United States illegally during the period of exclusion. But it is generally accepted that the numbers were substantial, with estimates ranging from a conservative 25 percent of the Chinese American population to as much as 90 percent. As early as 1892, government documents estimated that 95 percent of all Chinese entrants were illegal. Most historians accept that government estimates were exaggerated, noting that many inspectors seemed to assume that all applicants were fraudulent. However, this assumption was based not only on the racism of those who believed that Chinese were inherently duplicitous and criminal. It also reflected the effectiveness with which excluded Chinese laborers used fabricated photographs, documents, and relationships to evade the racist exclusion laws and make their way in the United States.[30]

As already noted, photographs were introduced to control the expansion and circulation of fraudulent documents. Proponents of photographic documentation argued that, although the similar appearance of all Chinese facilitated the circulation of certificates, photographs would reveal the slight differences between Chinese not evident in written descriptions. From the moment of their invention, photographs had been praised for revealing minute details that were often overlooked by the naked eye. This thoroughgoing accuracy was attributed to the indexical quality of photography: since photographs were the result of the direct impression of light upon the light-sensitive photographic paper, they represented everything, including apparently insignificant details. At the same time and for the same reasons, photographs were assumed to be objective. They necessarily represented whatever was placed before them. Photography's indexicality apparently secured a complete and objective accuracy that could never be achieved by other forms of representation such as written descriptions.

However, this understanding of photography viewed the image in isolation. It imagined the photographic production process as a closed system of disinterested mechanical reproduction. In fact, in contrast to the ideal of the objective image promoted by supporters of photographic identification, photographic prints could be manipulated through various means, including re-touching, blurring, and deliberate aging.

Perhaps most significant in the case of photographic identification, the image was meaningless unless it was captioned with the name of the person depicted in the photograph. The caption and the image together formed the identification photograph: the visual representation and the written identification of a given individual. An identity photograph was reliable only if neither the image was retouched nor the caption rewritten. However, the caption was easier to falsify than the image. False captions or names could be adopted without affecting the photograph's indexicality and without leaving a trace on the image itself.

In contrast to the assumptions of members of Congress who had supported photographic identification, immigration officials gradually realized that photography was not entirely reliable. Although inspectors initially praised photographs for providing detailed transcriptions of masses of supposedly similar faces, Chinese oppositional practices raised significant questions about the reliability of the photographic image as documentary evidence.

As photographic historian Derrick Price has noted, "When it became plain that the technologies of photography were not automatic transcribers of the world, other questions about the nature of authenticity began to be raised and other guarantors of photography's fidelity were advanced. Among these was the notion that we need to trust, not the mechanical properties of the camera, but the personal integrity of the photographer."[31] In immigration photography, the integrity of the image was not limited to the photographer. It also depended on the conditions of photographic production. Although indexical integrity continued to be conferred upon apparently disinterested photographs (such as documentary representations of immigrants taken by respectable white photographers), photographs paid for and taken under the direction of immigrants as part of their immigration cases became considered less reliable.

This was particularly true for Chinese because of the way in which they were racialized: immigration inspectors viewed both Chinese immigrants and Chinese photographs as untrustworthy. In fact, inspectors seemed to believe that Chinese photographs and Chinese witnesses shared a particularly treacherous artifice: on the surface both appeared honest, but this apparent honesty concealed a deeper duplicity. Chinese immigrants' successful use of photographs to evade exclusion and immigration inspectors' stereotypes about the Chinese worked together to destabilize the credibility of photographic identification.

Chinese immigrants developed numerous ways to evade exclusion using photography, and immigration officials developed many forms of investigation in response. One of the systems through which many Chinese entered the United States was the "slot" or "paper son" system. Under this system, exempt Chinese created fictional families by claiming that they had fathered children on visits to China, creating a slot for a person to immigrate in the future. Typically, young men known as paper sons then purchased these slots and used coaching papers to learn about their adopted identities. Although these entrants were almost exclusively men, young women were also occasionally brought to the United States as paper daughters or paper wives.

Histories of Chinese immigration and exclusion have typically described the practice of paper sons through coaching papers. However, photographs were just as significant as papers to the successful entry of many sons. As photographic documentation became central to the enforcement of Chinese exclusion, photographs became central to the evasion of these laws. In one case, for example, the judge noted that two Chinese men had brought a woman into the country for immoral purposes: "They were successful in imposing upon the immigration officers by means of false representations, and skilful use of photographs identifying the girl as a daughter of the accomplice, and a native of this country." Just as the presence of the Chinese in America challenged the purposes of exclusion, the Chinese manipulation of photographic documentation challenged one of the key technologies for implementing exclusion.[32]

In addition to the paper son system, some Chinese became part of complex schemes involving corrupt immigration officials that changed the legal status of large numbers of immigrants. In one scheme, Chinese men obtained their identity photographs from Fong Get's Portrait Studio. The short-haired men arrived at the studio in American clothes and proceeded to don Chinese clothes and wigs with queues before sitting for their portraits. These prints, taken in 1916, were then aged and substituted on certificates from the 1890s with the help of immigration officials. The doctored certificates gave the impression that the Chinese applicants had previously lived in the United States and were entitled to reenter. As photographic critic Roland Barthes has written, the photograph always represents "that the thing has been there." However, these Chinese laborers exploited the fact that the thing that appears before the camera is not necessarily what it appears to be. Carefully placed by corrupt immigration officials on genuine immigration certificates, the faked photographs appeared to represent that the immigrants had been there, before the camera, in the United States at an earlier time. However, in the subsequent investigation into official corruption, it became apparent that—through the photograph—the past and the apparent presence of the immigrants had been manipulated.[33]

In contrast to these complex schemes, some immigrants simply took advantage of certificates with faded or indistinct photographs or images of people who happened to look like them. In Walla Walla, Washington, an inspector located 110 pawned certificates, which were presumably sold if their original holders defaulted on their loans.[34] These documents were presented to immigration authorities when the photograph represented a much younger individual or after the photograph had aged or been damaged, making it difficult to compare the image to the individual now holding the document. These actions exploited the imperfect indexicality of many early images that had been incidentally (rather than deliberately) blurred and made indistinct with age.

Photographs had been introduced to ensure the correlation between the document and the immigrant: the photographic portrait was intended as the link between the information contained in the document and the individual who stood before the immigration inspector. But, as these practices reveal, Chinese immigrants broke this link in numerous ways. Although these tactics varied, they shared the same effect: they challenged the assumptions of accuracy and objectivity that underpinned Chinese exclusion photographic policy.

Ironically, the introduction of documentation probably made it easier for Chinese to enter the United States illegally. Although exclusionists and immigration officials believed that documents would authenticate real identity claims, Chinese applicants used documents to fabricate new identities and relationships. The widely reported problem of fraudulent documentation, which had been one of the main reasons for the introduction of photographs, continued. Only now it included concerns about photographs as well as documents. Chinese oppositional practices had far-reaching consequences for the shaping of exclusion laws: throughout the exclusion era, the curtailment of fraudulent documents and photographs became central to exclusion's primary aim of curtailing Chinese immigration.[35]

As a result of these practices, immigration inspectors never assumed that the photograph represented the applicant before them. However, they continually attempted to reassert their authority through two related approaches. First, they attempted to regain control of Chinese immigrants and their documents, in part by controlling the conditions under which immigration photographs were produced and circulated. In addition to hiring their own photographers, inspectors conducted increasingly detailed investigations into identity photographs and created an extensive national archive of Chinese identity documents. Second, immigration inspectors emphasized their own power, particularly their ability to see through fraudulent applications. However, despite their own claims of authority, they were unable to develop a system of photographic identification that successfully controlled Chinese immigrants and the multifaceted ways that they evaded and undermined exclusion.[36]

As problems with fraudulent applications increased, the Immigration Bureau developed an increasingly detailed system of examining Chinese applicants. Since many Chinese based their claims to U.S. residence on their father's status as a laborer exempt from exclusion, a merchant, or a native-born citizen, most investigations explored family relationships in detail. During the immigration investigation, applicants would first be asked to identify their own photograph, then the photographs of their family and friends. If they could not identify all of these images, their application for admission was generally rejected. As part of the investigation, applicants were not only asked detailed questions about their villages, homes, and families; they were also commonly asked about any photographs used to authenticate these relationships. They were asked when and where these photographs were taken, whether they had seen photographs of family members before or had sent photographs to the United States, and whether there were photographs of relatives in their homes in China. "When did you first see the photograph of Quong Chong," his alleged brother was asked during one investigation. "Have you a copy of that photograph?"[37] These questions were an attempt to confirm whether the applicant was really related to the father, brother, or uncle as he claimed, or whether this relationship had been established only through photographs. They also reflected the officials' awareness of the ways that some Chinese used photographs to create paper families. The photographs themselves, which had been introduced to help officials in their investigation, became one of the subjects of investigation.

The Immigration Bureau's increasingly detailed case files and their accompanying photographs formed a vast archive of Chinese living in America. Each applicant typically had to provide images in triplicate, with one photograph placed on the identity certificate, one remaining at the immigration station, and one being sent to the national offices of the Immigration Bureau in Washington, D.C. This system created a truly national archive in which different immigration stations actively coordinated to share their images with one another. This archive was cross-referenced to allow the bureau to check the stories of Chinese against one another whenever they chose to enter, leave, or return to the United States or when they were arrested without a certificate. The photographs of applicants attempting to enter, for example, might be checked against the photographs of deported applicants if they were deemed suspicious. However, this archive wasn't limited to the files of the Immigration Bureau. As photographs began to be placed in passports and court records of cases involving immigrants, these were also made available to the Immigration Bureau. Significantly, only the Chinese were required to provide their photographs. Whites obtaining passports, appearing in court, or testifying in support of a Chinese applicant were not subject to the photography requirement.[38]

In response to this regulation, some Chinese also created their own provisional family archives, which were very effective at enabling them to evade the exclusion laws. Exploiting the photograph's mass reproducibility, Chinese applicants retained identical copies of images submitted to the Immigration Bureau. In this way, paper sons could recognize the photos of family members on file with the bureau and paper fathers could recognize their sons. The coaching letters that paper fathers supplied frequently included portraits that enabled the young men to learn the identities of their paper family members and witnesses. The fathers warned their wards to destroy not only their coaching papers once they had memorized them, but also the photographs that accompanied these papers. After providing a detailed description of Chang Sam's paper brother and "a photograph of him as he looks," From Yook urged Chang to "take the coaching paper and the photograph and burn them, so that the immigration officers cannot find them."[39]

Paper relatives were also familiar with the Immigration Bureau's photographic archives. They often knew whose photographs would be shown to the paper sons during the immigration interrogation because they originally supplied the photographs on file with the Immigration Bureau. "Bing Suey's photograph is in the Detention House," wrote one paper uncle in a secret coaching note. "If they again ask you if you know Bing Suey's photograph, say that you know him and talked to him when he was in China."[40] In other cases, paper relatives decided who would be called as witnesses and sent photographs to enable the paper son to identify their alleged acquaintances. "For the present Lee Gim Jem is not to be used for your witness," wrote a paper father. "The inspectors do not have his photograph to give you to identify. If Lee Gim Jem should be used for your witness later, you will then be notified."[41]

Although the photograph played a critical role in identifying fraudulent applicants, it was not always the final arbiter in immigration decisions. Mr. Tsang, a native-born citizen, relayed his experience of almost being rejected upon his return to the United States because immigration officials said he didn't look like his baby picture. He was allowed to enter only after a doctor confirmed that his appearance had been altered by a cut under his left eye-brow. The Immigration Bureau also ruled against Yee Kim Sue because he appeared younger than the person named on his identity certificate. Although the photograph on record "resembles him considerably," the inspector stated that this was not because they were the same person but because "the person interested in the case of this applicant would pick out a boy to resemble as nearly as possible the person who departed in 1902."[42]

This logic was difficult to escape. While looking different from your identity photograph was typically sufficient reason for deportation, looking like your photograph was not always good enough for admission. In the first case, immigration inspectors relied on the photograph as effective evidence. In the second, they distrusted the photograph because they distrusted the Chinese. These rulings moved in contradictory directions, but usually favored denial and deportation. These outcomes were consistent with government rules that required that if inspectors had any doubt about the case, they rule "in favor of the exclusion of the alien."[43]

Conclusion

Chinese immigrants not only chose how they represented themselves and how they used photographs to evade exclusion. They also made their own meanings out of identity photographs. By 1911, Immigration Bureau policy required that identity certificates be canceled upon the holder's death so that they could not be fraudulently circulated. However, family members asked to keep the official photographs as mementos of their loved ones. In Hastings, Minnesota, the white widow of a Chinese laundryman requested that her husband's identity photograph be removed and returned to her "as it was the only one she had of her husband, and she and the children are very desirous of keeping it." A Chinese son in Boston made the same request and had his father's photograph returned to him.[44] In regaining possession of the photograph and the image of their father, family members reclaimed its meaning. They changed the purpose of the photograph from the identification of an unknown laborer to the intimate recognition of a familiar face. However, the photograph always contained both possibilities. Its meaning always depended on its viewer.

The Chinese community strenuously fought the introduction and expansion of exclusion using diplomacy, political protests, and legal challenges to the laws. These challenges were successful in reducing the scope of exclusion and providing some protections for Chinese living in America. However, legal strategies for opposing exclusion were consistently less effective at undermining exclusion than extralegal efforts. The Chinese immigrants who entered America illegally during exclusion not only successfully undermined the restrictive purpose of the laws: they challenged common ideas about photographic representation and made immigration inspectors question their own eyes.

Notes

My thanks to the following friends and colleagues for their insightful readings and invaluable research assistance: Kim Alidio, Kirsten Fermaglich, Michael Frush, John McKiernan Gonzalez, William Greene, Richard Kim, Brian Locke, Nhi Lieu, Susette Min, Mindy Morgan, Tom Nehil, Wei Chi Poon, Stephen Rohs, George Sánchez, Richard Cándida Smith, Marian Smith, Neil Thomsen, Judy Yung, Rebecca Zurier, and two anonymous readers at *American Quarterly*.

1. Maxine Hong Kingston, *China Men* (1980; New York: Vintage International, 1989), 145; Ronald Takaki, *Strangers from a Different Shore: A History of Asian Americans* (New York: Penguin Books, 1989), 85; Sucheng Chan, *Asian Americans: An Interpretive History* (Boston: Twayne Publishers, 1991), 30; Frank Chin, *Donald Duk* (Minneapolis: Coffee House Press, 1991), 131–32; David L. Eng, "I've Been (Re)Working on the Railroad: Photography and National Memory in *China Men* and *Donald Duk*," in *Racial Castration: Managing Masculinity in Asian America* (Durham, N.C.: Duke University Press, 2001), 35–103.

2. Lucy Salyer, *Laws Harsh as Tigers: Chinese Immigrants and the Shaping of Modern Immigration Law* (Chapel Hill: University of North Carolina Press, 1995); Erika Lee, *At America's Gates: Chinese Immigration During the Exclusion Era, 1882–1943* (Chapel Hill: University of North Carolina Press, 2003), 19.

3. Act of March 3, 1875, 18 Stat. 477; Act of November 3, 1893, sec. 2, 28 Stat. 7; Chinese and Hawaiian Certificates of Identity, 1908–1938, Records of the Immigration and Naturalization Service, Record Group 85, National Archives and Records Administration—Pacific Region (San Francisco); U.S. Department of Commerce and Labor, Bureau of Immigration, *Treaty, Laws and Regulations Governing the Admission of Chinese* (Washington, D.C.: GPO, 1910); U.S. Department of Labor, Bureau of Immigration, *Immigration Laws, Rules of May 1, 1917* (Washington, D.C.: GPO, 1922), rule 12, subd. 9; Circular from William B. Wilson, Secretary of Labor, to Commissioners of Immigration, Inspectors in Charge, and Others Concerned, May 23, 1917, File 54,261-202, Entry 9, Records of the Immigration and Naturalization Service, Record Group 85, National Archives, Washington, D.C.; Executive Order No. 2932 of August 8, 1918, title 1, sec. 5; Immigration Act of 1924, sec 2b, 43 Stat. 153; U.S. Department of Labor General Order, July 1, 1928, cited in *New York Times*, June 16, 1928. On the introduction of passports in the United States, see John Torpey, *The Invention of the Passport: Surveillance, Citizenship and the State* (Cambridge: Cambridge University Press, 2000), 93–103, 117–21.

4. Recently, a few historians have begun to address the importance of visuality within immigration policy, specifically Chinese exclusion. Nayan Shah has explored the visual aspects of Chinese medical inspections at Angel Island and Eithne Luibhéid has shown how Chinese women were regulated through photography because of concerns that they might be prostitutes. Nayan Shah, *Contagious Divides: Epidemics and Race in San Francisco's Chinatown* (Berkeley: University of California Press, 2001), 179–203; Eithne Luibhéid, *Entry Denied: Controlling Sexuality at the Border* (Minneapolis: University of Minnesota Press, 2002), 41–54.

5. See, for example, Alexander Saxton, *The Indispensable Enemy: Labor and the Anti-Chinese Movement in California* (Berkeley: University of California, 1971); Andrew

Gyory, *Closing the Gate: Race, Politics, and the Chinese Exclusion Act (Chapel Hill: University of North Carolina Press, 1998).*

6. Charles McClain, *In Search of Equality: The Chinese Struggle Against Discrimination in Nineteenth-Century America (Berkeley: University of California Press, 1994); Salyer, Laws Harsh as Tigers; K. Scott Wong and Sucheng Chan, eds., Claiming America: Constructing Chinese American Identities During the Exclusion Era* (Philadelphia: Temple University Press, 1998); Xiaojian Xhao, *Remaking Chinese America: Immigration, Family, and Community, 1940–1965* (New Brunswick, N.J.: Rutgers University Press, 2002); and Lee, *At America's Gates.*

7. Letter from William Sears, Collector of Customs to Daniel Manning, Secretary of the Treasury, July 23, 1885, Copies of letters sent to the Secretary of the Treasury, 1869–1912, Records of the U.S. Customs Service (Port of San Francisco), Record Group 36, National Archives Records Administration—Pacific Region (San Francisco). Author's italics. I am grateful to Neil Thomsen for bringing this letter to my attention.

8. Sucheng Chan, "The Exclusion of Chinese Women," in *Entry Denied: Exclusion and the Chinese Community in America, 1882–1943,* ed. Sucheng Chan (Philadelphia: Temple University Press, 1991), 109–23.

9. U.S. Department of Commerce and Labor, Bureau of Immigration, *Treaty, Laws and Regulations Governing the Admission of Chinese* (Washington, D.C.: GPO, 1910).

10. George Anthony Peffer, *If They Don't Bring Their Women Here: Chinese Female Immigration Before Exclusion* (Urbana: University of Illinois Press, 1999), 43–49, 60–101; Luibhéid, *Entry Denied,* 41– 43; Act of October 1, 1888, 25 Stat. 504; Statement of S.J. Ruddell, Inspector of Customs, U.S. Congress, House Report no. 4048, 51st Cong., 2nd sess. (1890), 280.

11. Act of May 5, 1892, 27 Stat. 25; McClain, *In Search of Equality,* 207; Salyer, *Laws Harsh as Tigers,* 46–52, 56; *Fong Yue Ting v. United States,* 149 U.S. 698 (1893); Act of November 3, 1893, sec. 2, 28 Stat. 7.

12. *Congressional Record,* 53rd Cong., 1st sess. (1893), 25, pt. 3, appendix: 231.

13. Ibid., pt. 2: 2440–41.

14. Ibid., 2554; Ivan Light, "From Vice District to Tourist Attraction: The Moral Career of American Chinatowns, 1880–1940," *Pacific Historical Review* 43 (1974): 367–94; Lee, *At America's Gates,* 147.

15. John Tagg, *The Burden of Representation: Essays on Photographs and Histories* (Minneapolis: University of Minnesota, 1988). See also Allan Sekula, "The Body and the Archive," in *The Contest of Meaning: Critical Histories of Photography,* ed. Richard Bolton (Cambridge, Mass.: MIT Press, 1989), 342–88; and Simon Cole, *Suspect Identities: A History of Fingerprinting and Criminal Identification* (Cambridge, Mass.: Harvard University Press, 2001).

16. See, for example, Shawn Michelle Smith, *American Archives: Gender, Race, and Class in Visual Culture* (Princeton, N.J.: Princeton University Press, 1999); Laura Wexler, *Tender Violence: Domestic Visions in an Age of U.S. Imperialism* (Chapel Hill: University of North Carolina Press, 2000); and Anthony W. Lee, *Picturing Chinatown: Art and Orientalism in San Francisco* (Berkeley: University of California Press, 2001).

17. Donald Dilworth, *Identification Wanted: Development of the American Criminal Identification System, 1893–1943* (Gaithersburg, Md.: International Association of Chiefs of Police, 1977), 1; vol. 30, p. 6, Jesse Brown Cook Scrapbooks Documenting San Francisco History and Law Enforcement, ca. 1895–1936, Bancroft Library, University of California, Berkeley; Mug Book Collection, San Francisco Police Department, San Francisco History Center, San Francisco Public Library.

18. "Wu Ting Fang on Exclusion," *Salt Lake City News*, April 4, 1902.

19. *Congressional Record*, 53rd Cong., 1st sess. (1893), 25, pt. 2: 2435.

20. "What the Chinese Think About the Chinese Exclusion Act. Wong Kai Kah, Former Minister to England Points Out Some Objections to the Way It Is Enforced," *Spokane [Washington] Press*, May 23, 1905; Ng Poon Chew, "The Treatment of the Exempt Classes of Chinese in the United States" (San Francisco, January 1908): 14, Box 3, Folder 15, Ng Poon Chew Collection, Asian American Studies Collection, Ethnic Studies Library, University of California, Berkeley; James G. McCurdy, "Use of Photographs as Evidence," *Scientific American* 87 (November 15, 1902): 328.

21. Form of Application, Act of May 5, 1892, Scrapbook 4 (Chinese Exclusion), n.p., Box 6, Ng Poon Chew Collection, Asian American Studies Collection, Ethnic Studies Library, University of California, Berkeley.

22. Tagg, *The Burden of Representation*, 36; David Green, "Veins of Resemblance: Photography and Eugenics," *Oxford Art Journal* 7.2 (1984): 8.

23. Letter from H.C. Kennah, Chinese Inspector, to Chinese Inspector in Charge, June 22, 1905, File 10061/28, Immigration Arrival Case Files, 1884–1944, Records of the Immigration and Naturalization Service, Record Group 85, National Archives Records Administration—Pacific Region (San Francisco) [hereafter IACF, INS].

24. Richard Vinograd, *Boundaries of the Self: Chinese Portraits, 1600–1900* (Cambridge: Cambridge University Press, 1992), 85; Jan Stuart and Evelyn S. Rawski, *Worshiping the Ancestors: Chinese Commemorative Portraits* (Stanford, Calif.: Stanford University Press, 2001), 168; Claudia Brush Kidwell with Nancy Rexford, Foreword, in Joan L. Severa, *Dressed for the Photographer: Ordinary Americans and Fashion, 1840–1900* (Kent, Ohio: Kent State University Press, 1995), xiii.

25. Sucheng Chan, "The Exclusion of Chinese Women," 97, 132; Lee, *At America's Gates*, 94. See also the relationship between respectable appearance and suspicion of prostitution in: Letter from John Dunn, Chinese Inspector, to Chinese Inspector in Charge, File 10059/6390, IACF, INS.

26. In the Matter of Young Fou, File 10059/52, IACF, INS.

27. Stuart and Rawski, *Worshiping the Ancestors*, 58, 114, 172; Lee, *At America's Gates*, 95.

28. Anna Pegler-Gordon, "In Sight of America: Photography and U.S. Immigration Policy, 1880–1930" (Ph.D. diss., University of Michigan, 2002), 113–17.

29. Letter from (Wong) Bing Foon to Wong Som Gar, January 24, 1916, translated by Interpreter H.K. Tang, no file number, "San Francisco District INS, Coaching Letters," Entry 232, Case Files of Immigration Fraud Investigations (12016), 1914–24, INS, RG 85, National Archives Records Administration—Pacific Region (San Francisco) [hereafter CFIFI, INS].

30. For a range of estimates, see Lee, *At America's Gates*, 190–91; and Mae Ngai, *Impossible Subjects: Illegal Aliens and the Making of Modern America* (Princeton, N.J.: Princeton University Press, 2004), 204. For government estimates, see U.S. Congress, House, Committee on Immigration and Naturalization, *Chinese Immigration*, 52nd Cong., 1st sess. (1892), H. Rept. 255, serial 3042:1.

31. Derrick Price, "Surveyors and Surveyed," in *Photography: A Critical Introduction*, ed. Liz Wells (London: Routledge, 1997), 66.

32. On coaching papers, see Him Mark Lai et al., *Island: Poetry and History of Chinese Immigrants on Angel Island, 1910–1940* (San Francisco: Chinese Culture Foundation/HOC DOI, 1980), 20; Lee, *At America's Gates*, 193–97. On the role of photographs, see Letter from H[arold] Edsell, Chinese Inspector in Charge,

to Commissioner-General of Immigration, February 1, 1907, 1–3, File 14610/183, Entry 132, Records of the Immigration and Naturalization Service, Record Group 85, National Archives, Washington, D.C. [hereafter Entry 132, INS]; Letter from H[arold] Edsell, Chinese Inspector in Charge, to Commissioner-General of Immigration, February 2, 1907, 1–2, File 14610/184, Entry 132, INS; *United States v Ah Sou*, 132 F 878 (N.D. DC 1904).

33. File 12016/1076, CFIFI, INS; File 9564/10 and File 9560/49, IACF, INS; File 12017/31836, Return Certificate Application Case Files of Chinese Departing, 1912–1944 (12017), INS, RG 85, National Archives Records Administration—Pacific Region (San Francisco); Roland Barthes, *Camera Lucida: Reflections on Photography*, trans. Richard Howard (New York: Hill and Wang, 1981), 76. Author's italics.

34. U.S. Treasury Department, *Annual Report of the Commissioner-General of Immigration* (Washington, D.C.: GPO, 1901), 47–48. See also *Reisterer v Lee Sum*, 94 F 343 (2d Cir 1899); Letter from Inspector in Charge, Ketchikan, Alaska, to Commissioner-General of Immigration, Washington, D.C., December 17, 1903, File 11099, Entry 9, INS, RG 85, National Archives, Washington, D.C.; Letter from John Dunn, Chinese Inspector, to Chinese Inspector in Charge, June 13, 1905, p. 1, File 10055/ 117, IACF, INS; Mr. Lai, Box 1, Folder 28, Judy Yung Collection, Asian American Studies Collection, Ethnic Studies Library, University of California, Berkeley.

35. Salyer, *Laws Harsh as Tigers*, 61, 150; *Annual Report of the Commissioner-General of Immigration* (1901), 46–47.

36. Pegler-Gordon, "In Sight of America," 113–17, 122–35, 141–43.

37. Testimony of Quong Sam Fat, January 12, 1925, 4, File 23847/5-3, IACF, INS. See also Case of Lee Choy, 1910, File 10395/36, IACF, INS; Case of Yee Kim Sue, 1911, File 53329-111, Accession 60A600, INS, RG 85, National Archives, Washington, D.C. [hereafter Accession 60A600, INS]; Case of Jew Lan Wah, 1924–25, File 23847/5-14, IACF, INS. Witnesses for the applicant were also asked these questions. See, for example, Testimony of Louie Ak, July 7, 1905, File 10055/117, IACF, INS.

38. On the use of passport photographs, see Letter from Chinese Inspector to Chinese Inspector in Charge, Angel Island Station, April 3, 1912, 3, File 10739/10862, IACF, INS. On the use of photographs from court cases, see Case of Wong Sear Oun, 1910, File 10395/26, IACF, INS. See also Letter from Joseph Scully, Immigrant Inspector, to Inspector in Charge, Chinese Division, Angel Island, April 3, 1912, File 10740/3, IACF, INS. On whites not being required to submit photographs, see File 55,598-130 (1926), IACF, INS.

39. Coaching paper from From Yook to Chang Sam, translated by Chinese Inspector and Interpreter John Endicott Gardner, File 12907/5-1, IACF, INS. See also Coaching paper from Dong Hung to Dong Loon, mailed April 18, 1925, translated by Interpreter H.K. Tang, May 1, 1925, File 23847/5-7, 49–50, IACF, INS. See, generally, "San Francisco District INS, Coaching Letters," CFIFI, INS.

40. Translation of coaching letter from Bing Ying to Shew Non, 1907, File 14610/179, Entry 132, INS.

41. Coaching paper from Dong Hung to Dong Loon, mailed April 18, 1925, translated by Interpreter H.K. Tang, May 1, 1925, File 23847/5-7, 50, IACF, INS.

42. Mr. Tsang, Box 1, Folder 30, Judy Yung Collection, Asian American Studies Collection, Ethnic Studies Library, University of California, Berkeley; Letter from Inspector Albert Long to Inspector in Charge, Chinese Division, Angel Island, July 31, 1911, File 53329-111, Accession 60A600, INS.

43. "Rules for the Government of United States Immigrant Inspectors and Boards of Special Inquiry," January 20, 1903, File 5738 (1905–1906), Entry 10, Central Files, 1897–1923, Records of the Public Health Service, Record Group 90, National Archives Records Administration—College Park.

44. Letter from Charles W. Seaman, Inspector in Charge, Minneapolis, Minn., to Commissioner-General of Immigration, February 15, 1912, File 53416-39, located with File 53329-111, Accession 60A600, INS; Letter from George Billings, Commissioner, Chinese Division, Boston, Mass., to Daniel J. Keefe, Commissioner-General of Immigration, November 7, 1911, File 53329-111, Accession 60A600, INS.

2

From Crop Lien to Contract Farming: The Roots of Agribusiness in the American South, 1929–1939

Monica Richmond Gisolfi

In 1929 rural sociologist Rupert Vance surveyed the southern landscape, seeing no end in sight to the cotton production that impoverished the South. In search of ways for cotton farmers to diversify, Vance noted that "whether equitable or not, a system of division of the product by shares between landlord and tenant has been worked out by custom and law for cotton." Indeed, there was a credit system in place that facilitated cotton production, a system that dated back to Reconstruction. Lamenting that "no generally accepted system of share cropping has been worked out for more complex forms of farming," Vance could not foresee that soon furnishing merchants would refashion the crop lien to facilitate poultry production. For some time, politicians, Vance, and a host of rural reformers waged an unsuccessful war against the crop lien, and its close relatives sharecropping and tenancy, which they considered to be the basis of southern problems. The poultry industry—today the model for contract farming and a multi-million-dollar business—grew out of the crop lien system, an institution thought to be the root of southern poverty.[1]

As the country entered the Great Depression, few Upcountry Georgians could imagine an end to cotton farming. Cotton dictated the rhythm of their lives and had dominated the Upcountry since the end of the Civil War, but this would soon change. Over the course of the 1930s, cotton farmers in Georgia's Upcountry began trading cotton production for poultry growing and planted the seeds of a multi-million-dollar industry. Proprietors of

From *Agricultural History*. This article first appeared in *Agricultural History* 80 (Spring 2006), 167–89.

country stores adapted the crop lien system, the farm credit system that had facilitated cotton production since the end of the Civil War, to poultry growing. Soon spring chickens or "fryers" that once ran about yards and were considered a seasonal crop were renamed "broilers" and were grown year-round in enclosed houses under tightly regulated conditions. What had been once the domain of women and children—who patched together makeshift chicken coops, read up on artificially heated incubators or "wooden hens," and became devotees of the county agent and home demonstration service—became the domain of hatchery-men, feed-dealers, poultry growers, poultry processing plants, poultry integrators, poultry scientists, and national corporations.[2]

Over the course of the twentieth century, in the Upcountry and beyond, farmers shifted from labor-intensive to capital-intensive production and came to depend on a host of costly products: pesticides, machinery, and other technological innovations in breeding, feeding, and disease control. The shift to capital-intensive production led to increasing dependence on crop liens and, later, contract farming. The movement toward contract farming started in the 1930s, when merchants began to extend credit for poultry growing to cotton farmers. They advanced chicks and feed to farmers, much in the same way that they had loaned seed and fertilizer to cotton farmers. By the time the United States entered World War II, merchants had laid the foundation of contract farming. With credit identified as the most important factor in its growth, the Georgia poultry industry after World War II was characterized as the quintessential agribusiness and economists recommended that other agricultural enterprises follow the lead of Upcountry Georgia. By the 1950s poultry, once a sideline activity that buffered farmers against the whims of the cotton market, had become Georgia's most important farm product. Georgians came to depend on chicken in the way that they and their ancestors had depended upon cotton, a dependence that begot poverty and indebtedness.[3]

Cotton farming and the crop lien system had not always dominated Upcountry Georgia. Prior to the Civil War, Upcountry farmers produced little to no cotton on diversified farms. These farmers constituted 25 percent of Georgia's white population and produced less than 10 percent of the state's cotton before the Civil War. In this area characterized by white landowning farmers and small farms, farmers generally grew enough grain and meat to feed their families and rarely relied on country stores for essential food supplies. Until the Civil War, these farmers, in the words of historian Steven Hahn, "remained on the periphery of the export economy."[4]

The Civil War, however, devastated the Upcountry. When troops returned home they found weed-filled fields, broken fences, and empty storehouses. Confederate soldiers seeking provisions, followed by General William Tecumseh Sherman's troops, wreaked havoc across the region as they stole livestock and destroyed crops. These conditions chipped away at the self-sufficiency that had once characterized life in the Upcountry. Farmers increasingly turned to country merchants for credit for the supplies needed to plant crops. Merchants soon demanded a lien or a mortgage on the crop in exchange for credit and required that farmers grow cotton, a crop that could be sold in northern markets. The cotton crop served as security for the credit the merchant extended to the farmer. Since farmers were forced to produce cotton to secure credit, they reduced acreage planted in corn, wheat, and other foodstuffs, increasingly relying on merchants not only for fertilizer and cottonseed but also for bacon, corn, and other necessities. Hahn explains that this "new and exploitative credit system...tied small-holders firmly to staple agriculture," and by 1890 "the Upcountry stood fully transformed, wrenched from the margin into the mainstream of the cotton market."[5]

From the end of the Civil War through the Great Depression, farmers in Upcountry Georgia grew record amounts of cotton, and little else, on infertile land. In the first decades of the twentieth century, cotton produc-tion expanded and conditions among farmers worsened, as they lost their land and slipped into the ranks of tenants and sharecroppers. A region once inhabited by small landowning farmers became a land dominated by furnishing merchants and cotton farming, plagued by soil erosion, tenancy, and sharecropping.[6]

Cotton production obstructed diversification and impoverished Georgia farmers. In 1914 a Georgia businessman painted a bleak portrait of farm-ers' heavy reliance on cotton cultivation. A man could "ride a hundred miles without seeing a herd of livestock," he observed, adding, "When you do see cattle they are little tick infested creatures that no more resemble real cows than a tubercular cotton factory operator resembles an athlete.... There is no grain, no hay, no poultry, no vegetable gardens, no orchards—except the peach orchards belonging to non-resident corporations—nothing that goes to make up a real farmer's home." A Georgia farmer reiterated the same concerns and insisted that "what is hurting poor people here the worst of anything is trying to raise cotton to buy supplies with." If farmers diversified and produced a range of food crops in addition to cotton, this farmer reasoned, Georgia farmers and their families would be "the happi-est people in the world," but the credit system tethered Upcountry farmers to cotton and prevented them from growing a variety of crops.[7]

Writing in 1929 rural sociologist Rupert Vance criticized the South's one-crop system and argued that "financial interests," not "agricultural interests," were to blame for the South's reliance on cotton. Farmers did not choose to grow cotton year after year; rather their creditors required them to do so. Furnishing merchants advanced farmers seed, fertilizer, and neces-sities on credit and refused to loan credit on any crop but cotton. Likewise, landed farmers often owned commissary stores where they sold foodstuffs to their tenants and sharecroppers and earned handsome profits. Country stores depended upon the sale of foodstuffs to farmers and therefore had little to gain and much to lose if farmers could produce food for themselves. The interests of farmers directly competed against the interests of creditors. Vance argued that "there exists a fundamental conflict between the public needs of the region and the vested interests of those engaged in supplying the various forms of cotton credit."[8]

Cotton farmers could not change the system. They could neither opt to plant sweet potatoes and corn nor expand their flock of laying hens and spring chickens and expect to receive goods on credit. Change, Vance argued, "will have to be engineered from above by bankers, landlords, and supply merchants." Those in power would have to undergo "a social crisis such as a continued depression in the cotton market." Only after a period of "continued loss," he reasoned, would bankers, merchants, and landlords allow farmers to cease cultivating cotton.[9]

The period of continued loss that Vance predicted began in 1920 when cotton prices plummeted. During the roaring 1920s Georgia farmers, and southern farmers more generally, slipped deeper and deeper into debt. In 1919 cotton sold for thirty-five cents a pound and cottonseed sold for seventy dollars a ton. The following year, in 1920, the price of cotton dropped to sixteen cents a pound, and cottonseed sold for thirty-one dollars a ton. Even though cotton prices reached a record high during World War I, a 1918 survey determined that 44 percent of farms lost money on cotton despite high prices. Surveys conducted during the 1920s concluded that the situation continued to worsen. A 1925 study reported that the average Georgia cotton farmer lost $4.80 per acre. Eventually merchants, bankers, and large landowners began to fall into poverty as well.[10]

A plague of insects and the adoption of new technology compounded rural poverty in the Upcountry. The boll weevil brought devastation in the mid-1920s. Between 1921 and 1923 the Georgia cotton yield dropped from two hundred pounds to eighty pounds per acre. Just south of the Upcountry, in Georgia's Greene County, farmers who routinely produced nearly 20,000 bales a year harvested a paltry 333 bales in 1922. The agricultural depression and drops in crop yields devastated farmers, who began to leave the land. Between 1920 and 1925 roughly 3.5 million acres of arable land were removed from production in Georgia. One government study found that Georgia and South Carolina led the way in the decline in crop acreage.[11]

As Georgia cotton farmers decreased the amount of land in production, Oklahoma and Texas farmers forged ahead in acres planted. Between 1919 and 1926 Texas farmers increased acreage under cotton cultivation from over ten million acres to more than eighteen million acres. The high altitudes and dry climates of the southern plains prevented boll weevil infestation. Moreover, Oklahoma and Texas cotton farmers worked flat, large plots of land and relied on the use of tractors and cotton-picking machinery. With their increased production and low overhead costs, western cotton farmers drove down cotton prices, placing Upcountry cotton farmers at a crippling disadvantage.[12]

With the agricultural depression, the demographic composition of Upcountry Georgia changed dramatically. Abandoned farms began to dot the hills where the farm population dropped precipitously. The president of the Georgia State College of Agriculture estimated that 100,000 of the farm population left Georgia in the first six months of 1922, and county agents found that 11,000 farms were abandoned in that same period. The Agricultural Census of 1930 confirmed these estimates, showing that since 1920 Georgia had lost 55,000 farms, 3,400,000 acres of farmland were laid fallow, and 266,000 of the rural population had left the country-side. With the stock market crash of 1929, the nation entered the Great Depression, which further shocked an already impoverished rural South. Cotton prices continued to tumble, and Upcountry farmers fell deeper into poverty. In Georgia, the gross income for farmers dropped from $206 in 1929 to $83 in 1932. In that same year, cotton prices reached an all-time low of 4.6 cents per pound.[13]

As lean year followed lean year with no end in sight, merchants, bankers, and large landowners in the South were no longer immune to the poverty that surrounded them. Furnishing merchants went bankrupt, and banks failed as low cotton prices prevented clients from paying bills. One study of the credit system in Georgia explained that increasingly growers were unable to pay debts in unrelentingly poor crop years. The logic of the lien entailed that a year of loss would be followed by a profitable year, allowing creditors to collect old debts. However, in the 1920s, creditors found it increasingly difficult to collect debts and watched their clientele shrink, as farmers left the land. This inability to collect, in the words of one survey, impaired "the lending power of local banks and credit merchants" leading to "a general restriction of credit."[14]

In the late summer of 1933, at the behest of the newly formed Agriculture Adjustment Administration (AAA), landowners measured their crops and plowed up a third of their cotton, directing tenants and sharecroppers to do the same. In the years that followed, cotton farmers took acreage out of production and required smaller amounts of cottonseed and fertilizer than in years past. Rupert Vance's prediction—that cotton cultivation in the South would decline only when merchants and landlords had undergone a period of "continued loss" that was "painful and of long duration"—was fast becoming a reality. In Georgia alone, ninety-seven thousand farmers plowed up seven hundred thousand acres of cotton for which the government paid them roughly eight million dollars. This cut production by roughly 360,000 bales. Seeking to control crop surpluses that were glutting markets and driving down prices, the government used allotments to control crop production. The government paid farmers to take land out of production, effectively "renting" land to lay fallow.[15]

The plow-up of 1933 has been remembered as a dramatic moment that signaled great change in the South, a moment in which the federal government changed the order of things and stepped in to dethrone tyrannical King Cotton. Throughout the South, farmers and AAA agents exchanged words and sometimes blows over allotments, measurements, and the fact that the federal government was taking a central role in the lives of farmers. As a young man, president-to-be Jimmy Carter measured cropland for the AAA to determine if farmers were planting their allotted acreage. "Meticulous in [his] work," Carter nonetheless found that his calculations sometimes contradicted those of landowners, a discrepancy that could erupt in violence. Carter remembered one farmer who stormed into the Carter family store, grabbed him, and shouted, "Why the hell are you trying to cheat me out of my government payments?" When Carter attempted to explain his calculations, the farmer remained unconvinced, threw Carter to the ground, and began punching him.[16]

A New York Times reporter, Charles Puckette, who headed south in the summer of 1933 to investigate the plow-up, also noted opposition to the measure. One important group that deserved mention, in the journalist's view, was an essential part of the South's workforce: mules. The journalist explained, "the mule has been trained to walk between the rows and not to tread on the cotton plants." However, New Dealers had "asked this conservative [the mule] to change his ways, to trample on the rows as he dragged the destroying plow."[17]

Farmers balked just as hard at the thought of intentionally destroying fields of cotton. It just seemed "wrong before God to plow up a crop," admitted one. A friend of the Carter family remembered that he "couldn't keep [his] mule up on the row, where she had never been before without being whipped." He explained, "I had to let her walk near the middle, and hold the plow way over sidewise to reach the cotton stalks," adding "It was hard work, and I almost cried." In Georgia's Greene County, sociologist Arthur Raper overheard tenants discussing the plow-up. One remarked, "I ain't never pulled up no cotton stalks befo', and somehow I don't like the idea." Another tenant proposed the following, "Let's swap work that day; you plow up mine, and I'll plow up yours." In fact, swapping became common practice throughout the South, where farmers could not bear the thought of plowing up their own rows of cotton, destroying the fruits of their labor.[18]

Despite human and animal opposition, federal support of reduced production continued. In April 1934 Congress passed the Bankhead Cotton Control Act to thwart the efforts of farmers who evaded allotments. The act set marketing quotas, limiting the amount of cotton farmers could sell. In 1936, when the Supreme Court invalidated key provisions of the AAA, the Roosevelt administration fired back with the Soil Conservation and Domestic Allotment Act, which paid farmers for shifting land from cotton to soil-conserving crops. In Georgia cotton acreage fell precipitously from 3.4 million acres in 1929 to under 2.2 million acres in 1939. As cotton farmers began plowing up portions of their crops in return for government payments, they bought fewer and fewer sacks of cottonseed and fertilizer, and furnishing merchants found once-bustling stores as empty as surrounding cotton fields.[19]

The drama surrounding the plow-up and the subsequent allotment policy may cloud the fact that New Deal reforms reinforced the power structure in Georgia and the South. County elite sat on the committees that oversaw the distribution of AAA allotments, and they administered AAA policies in a manner that strengthened their power. This meant that payments intended for tenants and sharecroppers found their way back to landlords. One report explained the "wholesale neglect of the tenant" by pointing to the fact that the AAA "organized its program under the direction of the planters themselves." In his study on two Georgia counties, Arthur Raper explained "practically all of [AAA money] found its way into the hands of the landlord. One-half of it belonged to him as rent, while the other half was used to reduce the tenants' indebtedness to him for furnishings." It would be wrong to assume that landlords even felt the need to justify taking their tenants' or croppers' payments. In the early stages, many tenants and sharecroppers did not know that they were entitled to payments, and those who were aware of the program could not easily demand their checks from their landlords.[20]

Not only did renters and croppers lose out on government payments, but small landowners lost as well. County agricultural agent H.A. Maxey explained the plight of small farmers who, prior to New Deal reforms, produced "just enough cotton to supply their necessary things of life." When small farmers were forced to reduce their acreage planted in cotton, Maxey stated, "it dug into their very existence." In contrast, large farmers reduced acreage, turned profits, and received large allotment checks from the government. According to Upcountry cotton farmer Guy Castleberry, large farmers were fine, but small farmers suffered: "the man like me that just had a few acreage, [sic] he just had to get out of it." For small farmers, taking land out of production left them with minimal acreage on which to grow a cotton crop. One study concluded that ultimately the AAA served as "merely a subsidy to planters."[21]

The AAA policies further hurt tenants and sharecroppers, who were cast off the land as landowners removed acreage from production. Some allowed their tenants to stay, but benefit payments encouraged landowners to demote croppers and tenants to wage hands. Raper observed that AAA allotments "made it advantageous for the landlord to use wage hands instead of croppers." Census figures from Upcountry Georgia's Hall County testify to these practices. In 1930, 924 owners and 1,805 tenants farmed in Hall County. By 1940 the number of tenants in Hall County had fallen to 1,351. A handful of these 454 tenants who left the ranks of the tenant class secured land, but the vast majority became wage laborers or left the land altogether. Surrounding counties watched their tenant farmer populations decline as well.[22]

Landowners voiced ardent opposition to relief measures that provided croppers and tenants with food and other necessities, purportedly fearing that government handouts would make tenants and sharecroppers unwilling to work for their keep. Landlords opposed relief measures because sharecroppers' dependence upon landlords for work made for loyal workers. Relief measures, landlords claimed, would make already lazy tenants and sharecroppers even more shiftless. One report explained, "There is a considerable feeling among landlords that anything which disturbs this dependent status of the cropper is undesirable." Landlords explained their opposition to relief in moral terms; they feared the "demoralizing effect" of relief on farm laborers. After the season was over, however, landlords conveniently forgot their concern for the morality of their workers and eagerly supported federal relief measures, largely because they no longer wished to provide for their workers.[23]

As landowners cast aside tenants and sharecroppers, they began to purchase automobiles and farm machinery using federal money. "The cotton reduction program and other federal emergency agencies...have caused a kind of boom," Raper observed. With cash in hand, landowners went out and purchased cars and tractors. Amid the Depression, the number of automobiles in Georgia climbed. In 1932 there were 310,684 automobiles in the state. Two years later, after landowners had received their allotment checks, the number climbed to 397,685.[24]

Landowners used government payments not only to purchase automobiles, but also to improve farm buildings, which would soon house the Upcountry's new cash crop: chickens. Some cotton farmers took their allotments and used them to convert cotton ginning houses to chicken houses, and others tore down tenant houses, building chicken houses in their place. When they married in 1933, Tom and Velva Blackstock—both natives of Hall County, Georgia—tore down a tenant house on Tom Blackstock's family's property and built a chicken house in its place. Like many farmers who received allotment checks, the Blackstocks used the money to improve farm buildings. It is likely that the tenant house they tore down was vacated after the Blackstocks cast off their tenant farmers when the government began paying farmers to take land out of production.[25]

As cotton acreage declined in the Upcountry, furnishing merchants, who in most cases did not receive allotment checks, also found themselves in a predicament. Their market for cottonseed and fertilizer was steadily shrinking, and they needed to find another way to earn their keep. New Deal cotton allotments forced merchants to face the fact that continued cotton production was quickly becoming untenable. "The collapse of the regnant cotton culture of the old Southeast" was at hand, declared reformer Will W. Alexander in 1936. "Cotton farming in this area," he wrote soberly, "is doomed." Soon merchants realized that poultry could replace cotton production, and they facilitated the shift from cotton to poultry, turning poultry, once a sideline activity, into Georgia's new cash crop.[26]

The stalwart mythology that explains the rise of the Upcountry's poultry industry credits divine intervention and human ingenuity. In 1936 a tornado swept through Gainesville, Georgia, the soon-to-be self-proclaimed capital of the poultry industry. The tornado killed 227 people and left only the statue of Johnny Reb standing in the town square. Following the tornado, furnishing merchant Jesse Dixon Jewell "surveyed the wrecked population center" and considered the economic plight of the region. Taking in the battered landscape, Jewell had an idea: he would promote poultry growing. Soon residents of Gainesville and the surrounding areas followed Jewell's lead into poultry growing. Bolstering this mythology, one journalist explained that Jewell's "idea changed the course and history of the region, the state's agriculture and the eating and purchasing habits of the nation."[27]

Acts of God and indomitable human ingenuity undoubtedly make a much better story than government bureaucrats paying cotton farmers not to plant cotton. This version of the poultry industry's beginnings omits AAA policy and its impact on furnishing merchants like Jewell. The tornado and Jewell's entrepreneurial talents were powerful forces that shaped the region. However, they coincided with the advent of cotton allotments that left furnishing merchants like Jewell with limited options. Merchants could develop new markets for products or go bankrupt. Furnishing merchants adapted the credit system used to finance cotton farming to poultry growing and introduced the region's new cash crop. "The extensive use of credit," a government report later declared, "has been responsible for the continued expansion of the [poultry] industry."[28]

By the time Jewell and other merchants began to promote poultry growing, Upcountry Georgians already had extensive knowledge of raising chickens. For generations, chicken and egg raising had been the domain of farm women and children, who tended yard flocks on farms throughout the South and traded eggs and chickens to supply their families' needs. Jimmy Carter recalled that his family "always had a yard full of chickens." A couple of times a year, Carter's father ordered hundreds of baby chicks from Sears and Roebuck, which the family ate and used for trading. While tenants and sharecroppers could not afford to purchase biddies in such bulk, they too had yard flocks. Ruby Faye Smith, the child of tenant farmers, reminisced that her family "always had a yard flock," adding, chickens were "a part of life all the way."[29]

As long as general stores had existed in the Upcountry, farmers used chickens and eggs to barter for goods. "There wasn't any money along there from the late twenties on till about the late thirties," Upcountry farmer Spurgeon Welborn recalled, so his family, like many others, swapped chickens and eggs for sugar, coffee, and flour. "Chicken eggs were a readily accepted form of currency," Jimmy Carter remembered, adding, "it was a matter of honor for a seller to assure their freshness, and there was an automatic replacement guarantee." Ruby Faye Smith's mother traded eggs and chickens for soap and coffee. Smith rebuffed the notion that the egg money belonged solely to her mother and was her "pin money." "There wasn't no 'my money and your money.' It was just lucky if we had money," she said.[30]

Many people considered poultry raising the domain of farm women. Women, often with the help of their children, had raised chickens and eggs to supplement the family income, and in the mid-1930s women began to watch incomes rise. Describing herself as "not the clinging vine type," Mrs. O.H. Cooper expanded her flock and started raising broilers in 1930.

"I get tired and discouraged, sure. No, everything don't run smoothly all the time by no means," she admitted in 1937, "but the joy and happiness of being the means of saving our home which we surely would have lost without my help, and my family having a decent living in the meantime, pays for all the discouragement." However, the division of labor on the farm challenged the neat categories of men's work and women's work and the notion of separate spheres.[31]

In the mid-1930s Jewell and an army of other furnishing merchants secured credit from feed companies and local bankers to purchase feed and baby chicks. Using connections to northern seed and fertilizer companies, they sought the backing of northern feed mills and promised to create a wholly new market for animal feed: credit flooded into the Upcountry. Lines of credit extended from northern feed companies such as Ralston-Purina and Quaker Oats Company down to local stores such as Martin Feed & Poultry Company and Hall Brothers Hatchery. The University of Georgia's Experiment Station studied the origins of the industry, and researchers discovered that "feed mills were particularly generous in extending credit to feed dealers." In interviews, feed dealers added that in some cases, "feed mills started dealers in business, with no capital being furnished by the dealer."[32]

With customers who had little capital, furnishing merchants advanced farmers baby chicks and feed on credit, much in the same way that they had advanced farmers cottonseed, fertilizer, and other farm supplies. Farmers settled their accounts, paying merchants for the chicks and feed, when the merchant or another distributor purchased the grown broilers. Farmers housed, fed, and cared for the chickens for twelve–sixteen weeks; this became known as the "grow-out period," and the farmers who cared for the poultry became known as "poultry growers." Before formal contracts were introduced in the 1940s, farmers sold their broilers in markets of their choosing. For example, a grower could receive birds and feed from Jewell, but then sell the grown broilers to another distributor who might offer a higher price than Jewell. Upcountry farmer Arthur Flemming recalled that he chose when and where to market his broilers. While his furnishing merchant supplied him with chicks, feed, and medication, Flemming was not required to market his broilers through his dealer.[33]

When furnishing merchants began encouraging farmers to raise poultry for sale, many families initially expended very little money to enter the business. They drew upon knowledge of poultry raising accrued over generations and expanded their current chicken coops, using materials found on the farm to build chicken houses. Some landed farmers tore down vacant tenant houses, reusing the materials to build chicken houses. Other farmers used whatever materials were available. One young boy gathered bricks in his pockets, "picking them up where he could find them discarded" and built a brooder from these found materials. In the mid-1930s farmers mixed their own feed. There was "no science" to it, one farmer recalled. He fed his chickens a mixture of corn, wheat, and salt. Flemming reminisced that his family made their own feeders out of lumber found on the farm, built their own coal brooders, and mixed their own feed. His grandparents purchased a drinker, and he recalled how this eased his workload a bit. The drinker "held five gallons of water," and Flemming thought his family "had it made when we got that five gallon of water in place of going in there and filling up them little, old can and things."[34]

Family members divided their time between row crops and their growing chicken flocks and finally watched incomes rise. "Pretty soon that jingle of money down the streets of Gainesville got others interested" in poultry, Jewell recalled. Sanford Byers recollected the first time his feed dealer came by to gather the first batch of grown broilers. The feed dealer drove a Ford truck, a symbol of wealth and portent of good things to come, and sold the chickens in Atlanta. His feed dealer returned from Atlanta and wrote Byers a check for $165. "That was the most money I'd ever seen in my life." Byers quickly reinvested it in expanding his chicken houses. In 1936 Ruby Faye Smith's father, an Upcountry tenant farmer, entered poultry growing at the encouragement of his landlord and furnishing merchant. To Smith, the benefits of poultry growing seemed numerous: "when we got to raising chickens and got feed sacks, our problems were solved." Smith's mother used the feed sacks to make "panties, and slips, shirts, table cloths, sheets, pillow cases, dish towels." Her family was one of the lucky few that made the transition from tenants to landowners, at a time when many tenant families were leaving farming altogether. Poultry offered a way for farmers to stay on the land, and the number of poultry growers grew.[35]

As broilers became the main source of family income, pushing aside cotton, women ceased being the lords of their flocks, but they by no means ceased working with broilers. As the industry grew, poultry did not shift from women's work to men's work, rather men took control of decision making, and while women and children continued to work alongside their husbands, fathers, and brothers. "This poultry business got big," Spurgeon Welborn explained, and men, in his estimation, did the majority of the work, but the work of women and children remained indispensable. Family labor was so essential that Ruby Byers remembered the height of the industry as "the egg years," a stretch of years in which the poultry business so consumed her and her family's time that she could neither attend church nor visit extended family. Women remained vital to the industry, although they lost control of their flocks. Historian Lu Ann Jones notes "Women's loss of autonomy prefigured the erosion of independence that their men folks, in turn, would experience when they began growing broilers on contract."[36]

As the 1930s wore on, husbands cut cotton acreage, expanded chicken houses, built new ones, and began investing in feeding, watering, and brooding devices. As early as 1927, Georgia State College of Agriculture Professor J. H. Wood argued that the poultry industry "is destined to become one of the state's main industries at an early date." After all, he wrote, poultry "offers the most desirable avenues for investment and hence provides an opportunity for diversification which should not be overlooked or neglected any longer by our people." However, contract poultry farming was not the route to diversification that Wood envisioned.[37]

"We depend a lot on our chickens," Cora Tull announces toward the beginning of William Faulkner's *As I Lay Dying*, reiterating the sentiments of Ruby Byers—the daughter of tenant farmers—who recalled that "eggs was a precious commodity," explaining that "as long as the old hen laid you could kinda count on falling back on that." By the end of the 1930s, many farm men and women might have uttered the same words as Faulkner's Cora Tull, but their meaning would have been entirely different. Farmers were no longer dependent upon their yard flocks for supplemental income; indeed, increasingly integrators barred poultry growers from keeping yard flocks, fearing that they might infect the commercial flock. At the end of the decade, many Upcountry Georgians had traded cotton farming for poultry growing, but this shift neither amounted to diversified farming nor guaranteed an end to the problems that accompanied cotton production and the crop lien. Indeed, poultry growing began to reinforce and even heighten the problems of a one-crop economy. Upcountry Georgians increased their poultry production but could not imagine the shape and degree of dependence and indebtedness that lay ahead.[38]

By the early 1940s successful furnishing merchants had begun to purchase hatcheries, distribution facilities, and processing plants. Soon they owned every stage of the process, except the poultry houses in which the broilers were raised, which were fast becoming the most expensive and most risky part of the business. Essentially, furnishing merchants vertically integrated the industry, becoming known as "poultry integrators." They began to enter into fixed contracts with poultry growers. Integrators began retaining title to the birds and paid poultry growers based on how efficiently they produced broilers; the dominant model became known as the "feed-conversion plan." Integrators furnished the chicks and the feed, and growers supplied broiler houses, all equipment, all labor, heat, and the litter that lined the houses. By the mid-1950s the vast majority of growers grew broilers under contract, and Jewell boasted that his operation was "practically 90, 95, maybe 100 percent" contracts. Informal arrangements and independent poultry growers became a thing of the past.[39]

Under the feed-conversion model, integrators paid growers based on how efficiently they turned chicken feed into broiler meat, and poultry growers began to invest in mass-produced equipment and housing to insure the greatest efficiency and output. Jewell explained that integrators paid growers "according to the number of pounds of chickens they get out of the number of pounds of feed they use." Integrators not only demanded standardized equipment but also began to require that growers increase their chicken-house capacity, telling growers to abandon newly built houses deemed too small. Growers, who had assembled makeshift houses, feeding devices, and brooders, were forced to abandon homemade devices and invest in costly new machinery. The cost of growing chickens began to rise, but grower autonomy did not.[40]

As the industry grew, poultry growers reported that they had less and less independence; among many changes, integrators increasingly dictated how to raise the birds and how many flocks each grower would produce per year. Field agents, employed by integrators, monitored each grower's progress and reprimanded those who had not followed company policies. Like cotton farming decades before, poultry growing became increasingly expensive. As integrators began to demand that poultry houses meet exact requirements to maximize efficiency, growers had to invest in a range of automatic feeding and watering devices to expand their broiler capacity. Poultry growers began to mortgage their homes and incur large debts to secure the capital necessary to meet these demands. Increasingly, growers were subject to the whims of integrators. Under the feed-conversion model, integrators could refuse to do business with any grower for any reason at any time, thus leaving poultry growers with large debts incurred to build broiler houses that could be used for no other purpose than poultry growing.[41]

Upcountry farmer Spurgeon Welborn lamented the loss of grower autonomy. He recalled that in the early years the farmer retained a degree of control, overseeing when and where his broilers were sold. Things began to change, and these changes did not sit well with Welborn, who recalled that "if you didn't have a contract and they didn't furnish you feed and chicken.... You couldn't sell your chickens." The feed dealers "put the chickens in when they wanted them in. They took them out when they wanted them out." They told the grower what to feed the chickens. Like many observers of the industry, Welborn feared that poultry growers were becoming hired hands. Farmers who sought to retain some independence were shut out of the industry and often could not find a market for grown broilers.[42]

As chicken houses spread across the hillsides, the farmers who built them imagined that they were securing independence for their families. Poultry growing allowed farmers to remain on their farms and remain their own bosses, at least in day-to-day operations. Poultry growing meant that farmers, for a time, were not reduced to seeking out wage work in factories. As farmers built the multi-million-dollar poultry industry, they reshaped their landscapes, replacing cotton fields with poultry houses and clearing their land of yard flocks and spring chickens. They ousted cotton, doing away with fertilizer bills and a cotton market that brought them meager returns. They imagined that they were restoring depleted soils with an endless supply of chicken manure, which was silently making its way into streams, rivers, and lakes and before long would contaminate the water supply, kill wildlife, and cause illness. By the late 1930s the demands of industrialized agriculture began to bear down on Upcountry farmers. They began to realize that they had traded one cash crop for another. In doing so, farmers had not escaped their creditors nor had they solved the problems associated with a one-crop system.[43]

On the eve of World War II, a local newspaper triumphantly announced, "The fuzzy down of the baby chick has all but ousted the fleecy lock of the cotton boll from its pedestal as chief money crop of Hall County." This enthusiasm was especially justified at the end of the war. Before the war, poultry products in Hall County, the center of Georgia's poultry industry, valued roughly one hundred and twenty thousand dollars, which represented about 14 percent of all the farm products sold from the county that year. Ten years later, poultry products in Hall County were valued at almost six million dollars, representing 86 percent of all the farm products sold from the county that year. In 1935 Georgia farmers produced five hundred thousand broilers. Fifteen years later Georgia farmers produced sixty-three million broilers, making poultry one of the state's most important farm products and making Georgia the nation's second largest broiler-producing state. As the industry grew, American consumption of chicken swelled. In 1930 Americans consumed roughly half a pound of chicken a year; thirty years later, Americans ate about twenty-four pounds of chicken a year, and today Americans consume over seventy pounds of chicken a year.[44]

A tough bargain was reached in the Upcountry. Poultry growers stayed on their land and to a degree remained independent farmers. Unlike the pattern of development found on southern neoplantations and in midwestern and western agribusiness, heads of industry in the Upcountry neither consolidated land nor forced Georgia farmers into wage work. Poultry firms did not strip farmers of their means of production. Indeed, they took the reverse course and began demanding that farmers invest in poultry houses and poultry feeding machinery. As contract farming became the norm, integrating firms set the precedent that poultry growers would assume much of the capital investments for the expansion of the industry. Ironically, poultry growers' dependence became rooted in the very fact that they owned the means of production.[45]

Contract farming persists in the poultry industry, and today poultry integrators—like Tyson and Perdue—require poultry growers to invest in and maintain poultry houses, which cost roughly $120,000 per house, with most growers generally owning four houses. One scholar estimates that "grower investments in fixed capital represent more than half of the total investment in fixed capital in the industry." Under this business model, poultry integrators have shifted a substantial portion of the financial risk to poultry growers. Since the mid-twentieth century the poultry industry and poultry integrators specifically have benefited from technological advances, and the industry can be easily characterized as a model of efficiency. The industry's feed conversion rate has rapidly declined since 1940; the grow-out period has been reduced from twelve to six weeks; and an average processing plant turns out eight thousand birds per hour. Advances came at a cost: today, workers in poultry-processing plants experience high injury rates and receive some of the lowest factory wages in the country. Most poultry growers invest $150,000 per poultry house, typically own three houses, and generally earn a return of $12,000 per year.[46]

Notes

1. Rupert Bayless Vance, *Human Factors in Cotton Culture: A Study in the Social Geography of the American South* (Chapel Hill: University of North Carolina Press, 1929), 185.

2. On Georgia's Upcountry, see, Steven Hahn, *The Roots of Southern Populism: Yeoman Farmers and the Transformation of the Georgia Upcountry, 1850–1890* (New York: Oxford University Press, 1983); Wallace Hugh Warren, "Progress and Its Discontents: The Transformation of the Georgia Foothills, 1920–1970" (master's thesis, University of Georgia, 1997); Numan V. Bartley, *The Creation of Modern Georgia* (Athens: University of Georgia Press, 1983); and Ann Short Chirhart, *Torches of Light: Georgia Teachers & the Coming of the Modern South* (Athens: University of Georgia Press, 2005). On northwest Georgia, which became dominated by the textile industry, see, Douglas Flamming, *Creating the Modern South: Millhands and Managers in Dalton, Georgia, 1884–1984* (Chapel Hill: University of North Carolina Press, 1992); and Michelle Brattain, *The Politics of Whiteness: Race, Workers, and Culture in the Modern South* (Princeton: Princeton University Press, 2001). Other relevant studies of Georgia include Jonathan M. Bryant, *How Curious a Land: Conflict and Change in Greene County, Georgia, 1850–1885* (Chapel Hill: University of North Carolina Press, 1996) and Mark Schultz, *The Rural Face of White Supremacy: Beyond Jim Crow* (Urbana: University of Illinois Press, 2005).

   Industry histories, biographies, and autobiographies of the poultry industry include: Gordon Sawyer, *The Agribusiness Poultry Industry: A History of its Development* (New York: Exposition Press, 1971); Oscar August Hanke, *American Poultry History, 1823–1973* (Lafayette, Ind.: American Poultry Historical Society, 1974); Marvin Schwartz, *Tyson: From Farm to Market* (Fayetteville: University of Arkansas Press, 1991); David W. Brooks, *D.W. Brooks, Gold Kist, and Seven U.S. Presidents: An Autobiography* (Atlanta: D. W. Brooks Family, 1993); Huey Crisp, *Lloyd Peterson and Peterson Industries: An American Story* (Little Rock: August House, 1989); Harold H. Martin, *A Good Man, A Great Dream: D.W. Brooks of Gold Kist* (Atlanta: Gold Kist, Inc., 1982); William H. Williams, *Delmarva's Chicken Industry: 75 Years of Progress* (Georgetown, Del.: Delmarva Poultry Industry, 1998); Mitzi and Frank Perdue, *Fifty Years of Building on a Solid Foundation: In Celebration of Frank Perdue's 50th Anniversary with the Company Founded by His Father, Arthur W. Perdue* (Baltimore: Lucas Press, 1989); and Stephen F. Strausberg, *From Hills and Hollers: Rise of the Poultry Industry in Arkansas* (Fayetteville: Arkansas Agricultural Experiment Station, University of Arkansas, 1995). For a critical assessment of the industry, see Steve Striffler, *Chicken: The Dangerous Transformation of America's Favorite Food* (New Haven: Yale University Press, 2005).

3. Walton W. Harper and O.C. Hester, "Influence of Production Practices on Marketing of Georgia Broilers," University of Georgia College of Agriculture Experiment Stations (1956): 9. See also, Walton W. Harper, "Marketing Georgia Broilers," University of Georgia College of Agriculture Experiment Stations, *Bulletin* 281 (July 1953); O.T. Hester and Walton W. Harper, "The Function of Feed-Dealer Suppliers in Marketing Georgia Broilers," University of Georgia College of Agriculture Experiment Stations, *Bulletin* 283 (Aug. 1953); Sawyer, *The Agribusiness Poultry Industry*, 205.

   Regional histories on the industrialization of southern agriculture include Pete Daniel, *Breaking the Land: The Transformation of Cotton, Tobacco, and Rice Cultures since 1880* (Urbana: University of Illinois Press, 1985); Gilbert Fite, *Cotton Fields*

No More: Southern Agriculture, 1865–1980 (Lexington: University Press of Kentucky, 1984); and Jack Temple Kirby, *Rural Worlds Lost: The American South, 1920–1960* (Baton Rouge: Louisiana State University Press, 1987). On the growth of pesticide use, see Pete Daniel, *Toxic Drift: Pesticides and Health in the Post-World War II South* (Baton Rouge: Louisiana State University Press, 2005); Bernard F. Tobin and Henry B. Arthur, *Dynamics of Adjustment in the Broiler Industry* (Boston: Harvard University, Graduate School of Business Administration, 1964). John H. Davis, a professor of agriculture and business at Harvard Business School, coined the term "agribusiness" in 1955. He believed that a new term was needed to describe the evolution of American agriculture that was taking place. He defined agribusiness as "the sum of all farming operations, plus the manufacture and distribution of all farm production supplies provided by business, plus the total of all operations performed in connection with the handling, storage, processing, and distribution of farm commodities. In brief, agribusiness refers to the sum-total of all operations involved in the production and distribution of food and fiber." John H. Davis, "Business Responsibility and the Market for Farm Products," speech given Oct. 17, 1955, quoted in Alan E. Fusonie, "John H. Davis: His Contributions to Agricultural Education and Productivity," *Agricultural History* 60 (Spring 1986): 108–109.

4. Hahn, *The Roots of Southern Populism,* 9, 4.
5. Ibid., 152, 166.
6. For growth in cotton production after the Civil War throughout the South, see Gavin Wright, *Old South, New South: Revolutions in the Southern Economy since the Civil War* (Baton Rouge: Louisiana State University Press, 1996) and Harold D. Woodman, *King Cotton and His Retainers: Financing and Marketing the Cotton Crop of the South, 1800–1925* (Washington, DC: Beard Books, 2000); Warren, "Progress and its Discontents"; David F. Weiman, "Farmers and the Market in Antebellum America: A View from the Georgia Upcountry," *Journal of Economic History* 47 (Sept. 1987): 627–47; and Willard Range, *A Century of Georgia Agriculture, 1850–1950* (Athens: University of Georgia Press, 1954), 90–166.
7. J.T. Holleman, "Is the South in the Grip of a Cotton Oligarchy?" 9–10, pamphlet, quoted in Vance, *Human Factors in Cotton Culture,* 188; G.W. Wharton, *Economic Needs of Farm Women* (Washington, DC: USDA, Office of Information, 1915), 50.
8. Vance, *Human Factors in Cotton Culture,* 187, 189, 190. See also Rupert Bayless Vance, *Human Geography of the South: A Study in Regional Resources and Human Adequacy* (Chapel Hill: University of North Carolina Press, 1932). On the credit system, see Woodman, *King Cotton and His Retainers* and Wright, *Old South, New South.*
9. Vance, *Human Factors in Cotton Culture,* 190.
10. Range, *A Century of Georgia Agriculture,* 267–68, 175.
11. Arthur F. Raper, *Preface to Peasantry: A Tale of Two Black Belt Counties* (New York: Atheneum, 1936), 202–203. Rural sociologist Arthur F. Raper's *Preface to Peasantry* is a study of Greene and Macon Counties in Georgia. For the study, Raper gathered data in these counties between 1927 and 1934. Greene and Macon Counties lie south of the Upcountry; Range, *A Century of Georgia Agriculture,* 174.
12. US Bureau of the Census, "Special Cotton Report," in *Sixteenth Census of the United States, 1940* (Washington, DC: GPO, 1943); Arthur N. Moore, J.K. Giles, and Roy C. Campbell, "Credit Problems of Georgia Cotton Farmers," Georgia Experiment Station, *Bulletin* 153 (June 1929): 4; Vance, *Human Factors in Cotton Culture,* 128–30,132; Charles S. Johnson, Edwin R. Embree, and Will W. Alexander, *The Collapse of Cotton Tenancy: Summary of Field Studies & Statistical Surveys, 1933–1935* (Freeport, NY: Books for Libraries Press, 1935), 46–47. For more on

competition from western cotton producers, see Daniel, *Breaking the Land;* Fite, *Cotton Fields No More;* and Kirby, *Rural Worlds Lost.*

13. Vance, *Human Factors in Cotton Culture,* 138; Range, *A Century of Georgia Agriculture,* 176, 270, 271; Johnson, *Collapse of Cotton Tenancy,* 47.

14. Range, *A Century of Georgia Agriculture,* 272; Raper, *Preface to Peasantry,* 6, 77–78, 233, 256; Woodman, *King Cotton and His Retainers;* Harold Hoffsommer, "Survey of Rural Problem Areas: Morgan County, Georgia, Cotton Growing Region of the Old South," 1935, pp. iv–v; Federal Emergency Relief Administration State Reports on Rural Problem Areas, 1934–35; Records of the Division of Farm Population and Rural Life and its Predecessors, Bureau of Agricultural Economics, RG 83, National Archives and Records Administration, College Park, Md. [hereafter NARA II]; Moore et al.," Credit Problems of Georgia," 8.

15. Raper, *Preface to Peasantry,* 245; Vance, *Human Factors in Cotton Culture,* 190. On the plow-up, see also Daniel, *Breaking the Land,* 258; Kirby, *Rural Worlds Lost,* 58–65; Fite, *Cotton Fields No More,* 123, 129–130; Range, *A Century of Georgia Agriculture,* 178.

16. Jimmy Carter, *An Hour before Daylight: Memories of a Rural Boyhood* (New York: Simon & Schuster, 2001), 70–71. Jimmy Carter's boyhood memoir chronicles his childhood in southwest Georgia. Even though Carter did not come of age in the Upcountry, the agricultural phenomena upon which he comments occurred throughout the South.

17. Charles McD. Puckette, "King Cotton's New Adventure: The South Watches With Hope Here and Misgiving There the Great Experiment in Which the First Step, Just Completed, Was the Plowing Under of Millions of Cultivated Acres," *New York Times Magazine,* Aug. 27, 1933, Section 6, 1.

18. Carter, *An Hour before Daylight,* 64; Raper, *Preface to Peasantry,* 245.

19. AAA, USDA, "Agricultural Adjustment: A Report of Administration of the Agricultural Adjustment Act May 1933 to February 1934" (Washington, DC: GPO, 1934); Theodore E. Whiting and Thomas Jackson Woofter, *Summary of Relief and Federal Work Program Statistics, 1933–1940* (Washington, DC: GPO, 1941); Miriam S. Farley, *Agricultural Adjustment under the New Deal* (New York: American Council, Institute of Pacific Relations, 1936), 12–13; Fite, *Cotton Fields No More,* 132–33; Range, *A Century of Georgia Agriculture,* 179; U.S. Bureau of the Census, "Special Cotton Report," xiv–xv.

20. Johnson, *The Collapse of Cotton Tenancy,* 51–53; Kirby, *Rural Worlds Lost,* 59; Raper, *Preface to Peasantry,* 245; Daniel, *Breaking the Land,* 105–108; Records of the USDA's Extension Service confirm elite control. See, e.g., T.L. Asbury, "Annual Report of the District 1 Agricultural Agent, 1935," pp. 4–5, M855, Roll 71, Georgia, 190944, Extension Service Annual Narrative and Statistical Reports, RG 33.6, NARA II.

21. H.A. Maxey, "Annual Report of Extension Activities, Cherokee County, December 31,1934–December 31, 1935," p. 8, M855, Roll 72, Georgia, 1909–44, Extension Service Annual Narrative and Statistical Reports, RG 33.6,NARA II; Guy Castleberry, interview by Lu Ann Jones, Apr. 24, 1987, transcript, p. 22, An Oral History of Southern Agriculture, National Museum of American History, Washington, DC [hereafter SAOHP]; Johnson, *The Collapse of Cotton Tenancy,* 52.

22. Range, *A Century of Georgia Agriculture,* 274; Pete Daniel, "The Legal Basis of Agrarian Capitalism: The South Since 1933," in *Race and Class in the American South since 1890,* ed. Melvyn Stokes and Rick Halpern (Providence, RI: Berg, 1994), 79–102; Raper, *Preface to Peasantry,* 252. Between 1930 and 1940, in nearby Cherokee County, the number of tenant farms fell from 1,405 to 1,298.

Over the same ten years, Forsyth County witnessed a similar decline as its tenant farms fell from 1,320 to 1,247. To access statistics on state and county population and other census material, see University of Virginia Library, "Historical Census Browser," http://fisher.lib.virginia.edu/collections/stats/histcensus/. The database allows you to examine state and county data for individual census years and to examine data over time. The data and terminology are drawn from the U.S. Census, *Agricultural Adjustment: A Report of Administration of the Agricultural Adjustment Act May 1933 to February 1934*, 272.

23. Harold Hoffsommer quoted in Johnson, *The Collapse of Cotton Tenancy*, 58–59. See also Lee J. Alston and Joseph P. Ferrie, "Labor Costs, Paternalism, and Loyalty in Southern Agriculture: A Constraint on the Growth of the Welfare State," *Journal of Economic History* 45 (Mar. 1985): 95–117; Lee J. Alston and Joseph P. Ferrie, "Paternalism in Agricultural Labor Contracts in the U.S. South: Implications for the Growth of the Welfare State," *American Economic Review* 83 (Sept. 1993): 852–76; Lee J. Alston and Joseph P. Ferrie, "Resisting the Welfare State: Southern Opposition to the Farm Security Administration," *Research in Economic History* Supplement 4 (1985): 83–120; Lee J. Alston and Joseph P. Ferrie, *Southern Paternalism and the American Welfare State: Economics, Politics, and Institutions in the South, 1865–1965* (New York: Cambridge University Press, 1999).

24. Raper, *Preface to Peasantry*, 85, 251–52.

25. U.S. Bureau of the Census, "Special Cotton Report"; Tom Blackstock, interview by Lu Ann Jones, Apr. 22, 1987, transcript, pp. l0, 45, SAOHP.

26. Farley, *Agricultural Adjustment under the New Deal*, 21; "An Interview with Jesse D. Jewell," *Broiler Industry* (Mar. 1959): 3–15; William Alexander in the foreward to *Preface to Peasantry*, xv.

27. James Aswell, "Chickens in the Wind," *Colliers*, Sept. 9, 1950, 31–48; Ted Oglesby, "Poultryland's Salute to Jesse Jewell," special supplement to *The Gainesville Ga. Times*, Nov. 7, 1971; see also Sawyer, *The Agribusiness Poultry Industry*, 85–96.

28. Harper and Hester, "Influence of Production Practices," 9; Harper, "Marketing Georgia Broilers," 25; Sawyer, *The Agribusiness Poultry Industry*, 205.

29. Carter, *An Hour before Daylight*, 89; Ruby Byers, interview by Lu Ann Jones, Apr. 23, 1987, transcript, p. 9, SAOHP.

30. Spurgeon Welborn, interview by Lu Ann Jones, Apr. 27, 1987, transcript, pp. 11, 16, SAOHP; Carter, *An Hour before Daylight*, 90; Ruby Byers, interview by Lu Ann Jones, Apr. 23, 1987, transcript, p. 11, SAOHP.

31. "How I Developed My Market Project and What it has meant to me by Mrs. O.H. Cooper, a testimonial of a club woman, Walton county, Georgia," unpaginated appendix, reproduced in Leila R. Mize, "Marketing (Women) Annual Report, 1937," M855, Roll 87, Georgia, 1909–44, Extension Service Annual Narrative and Statistical Reports, RG 33.6, NARA II. See also "How I Developed My Market Project and What it has meant to me by Mrs. W.D. Watson, Monroe County, Georgia," unpaginated appendix, reproduced in Leila R. Mize, "Marketing (Women) Annual Report, 1937"; Ray Marshall and Allen Thompson, *Status and Prospects of Small Farmers in the South* (Atlanta: Southern Regional Council, Inc., 1976), 55; Harper and Hester, "Influence of Production Practices," 9.

32. Harper, "Marketing Georgia Broilers," 25; Hester and Harper, "The Function of Feed-Dealer Suppliers," 31; Gordon Sawyer, of Gainesville, Georgia, interview by author, July 15, 2003, tape recording in author's possession. A series of cases surrounding the contract from 1935 onward attest to northern investment in the poultry industry and attest to confusion over contracts. *Hall Brothers Hatchery, Inc. v. Hendrix* (1945); *Alpharaetta Feed and Poultry Co. v. Cocke*, 82 Ga. App. 718, 62 S.E. 2d 642 (1950); *Lynch v. Etheridge* (1945); *Jewell v. Martin* (1942); *Roper v. Holbrook* (1948); *Cloud v. Bagwell* (1946); *Oxford v. Jewell* (1960).

33. Testimony of Jesse D. Jewell, Hearings before the Subcommittee No. 6 of the Select Committee on Small Business, House of Representatives, 85th Cong., 1st Sess., 1957, Pt. 1, 216–41. Problems in the Poultry Industry, 1957; Arthur Flemming, interview by Lu Ann Jones, Apr. 21, 1987, transcript, p. 28, SAOHP; Richard K. Noles and Milton Y. Dendy, "Broiler Production in Georgia: Grower's Costs and Returns," University of Georgia College of Agriculture Experiment Stations, *Report* 34 (Dec. 1968): 3–30.

34. H.Y. Cook, "Annual Report of the Agricultural Extension Work, Hall County 1935," p. 16, M855, Roll 74, Georgia, 1909–44, Extension Service Annual Narrative and Statistical Reports, RG 33.6, NARA II; Blackstock interview, p. 11, Flemming interview, pp. 4, 8.

35. "An Interview with Jesse Jewell," *Broiler Industry,* Mar. 1959, 3; "The Story of Jesse D. Jewell," unpublished pamphlet dated 1965, Jesse D. Jewell Vertical File, The Georgia Mountain History Center, Gainesville, Ga.; Sanford Byers, interview by Lu Ann Jones Apr. 20, 1987, transcript, pp. 29, 30, SAOHP; Byers interview, p. 15.

36. Welborn interview, pp. 41–42; Byers interview, p. 37; Lu Ann Jones, *Mama Learned Us to Work: Farm Women in the New South* (Chapel Hill: University of North Carolina Press, 2002), 104.

37. J.H. Wood, "Poultry Possibilities of Georgia," unpublished paper dated 1927, Andrew Soule Papers, Box 26, Hargrett Rare Books and Manuscripts Collection, University of Georgia, Athens, Ga.

38. Byers interview, p. 13.

39. Sawyer, *The Agribusiness Poultry Industry,* 85–95; Testimony of Jesse D. Jewell, p. 217. On the evolution of standardized contracts, see Hester and Harper, "The Function of Feed-Dealer Suppliers," 19–20; and "Financing Production and Marketing of Broilers in the South: Part I: Dealer Phase," in *Southern Cooperative Series Bulletin* 38, Agricultural Experiment Stations of Alabama, Arkansas, Georgia, Louisiana, Mississippi, North Carolina, South Carolina, Tennessee, Texas, and Virginia, and the Agricultural Marketing Service, USDA (June 1954): 15.

40. Testimony of Jesse D. Jewell, p. 217; Flemming interview, p. 28; Noles and Dendy, "Broiler Production in Georgia"; Clay Fulcher, "Vertical Integration in the Poultry Industry: The Contractual Relationship," *Agricultural Law Update* (Jan. 1992): 4–6; E. Roy, *Contract Farming and Economic Integration* (Danville, Ill.: Interstate Printers & Publishers, Inc., 1972); J.M. Sprott and H. Jackson, "Contract Broiler Growers in Arkansas," in *Arkansas Farm Research* (Nov.–Dec. 1964): 11; Welborn interview, p. 40; Byers interview, p. 7.

41. Marshall and Thompson, "Status and Prospects of Small Farmers," 55; Sprott and Jackson, "Contract Broiler Growers in Arkansas," 11; Harper and Hester, "Influence of Production Practices," 15; Harper, "Marketing Georgia Broilers," 34; Fite, *Cotton Fields No More,* 201.

42. Welborn interview, pp. 42–43.

43. Gregory W. Blount, Douglas A. Henderson, and Debra Cline, "The New Nonpoint Source Battleground: Concentrated Animal Feeding Operations," *Albany Law Environmental Outlook Journal* 27 (Fall 2000).An early case dealing with environmental issues and the poultry industry is *Poultryland, Inc. v. Anderson, et al.* (1946). Residents near Jewell's poultry rendering plant petitioned for its closure.

44. This quotation is found in Sawyer, *The Agribusiness Poultry Industry.* He writes that it was from the *Eagle,* a Gainesville, Georgia, newspaper, on the eve of World War II. Sawyer, *The Agribusiness Poultry Industry,* 72; Range, *A Century of Georgia Agriculture,* 201; "Hall County Farm Statistics, 1900–1960," undated pamphlet from "Poultry Industry" vertical file, Hargrett Rare Books and Manuscripts, University of Georgia, Athens, Ga.; William Boyd and Michael Watts, "Agro-Industrial Just-in-Time. The Chicken Industry and Postwar American Capitalism,"

in *Globalising Food: Agrarian Questions and Global Restructuring,* ed. David Goodman and Michael J. Watts (New York: Routledge, 1997), 192–93.

45. Kirby, *Rural Worlds Lost.*

46. Boyd and Watts, "Agro-Industrial Just-in-Time," 193, 211, 214; Glenn E. Bugos, "Intellectual Property Protection in the American Chicken-Breeding Industry," *Business History Review* 66 (Spring 1992): 127–68; Eric Schlosser, *Fast Food Nation: The Dark Side of the All-American Meal* (New York: Houghton Mifflin Company, 2001), 141.

3

Rocking the Cradle: Downsizing the New England Family

Gloria L. Main

Sometime around the year 1800, if not before, couples throughout New England began talking to each other about the desirability of postponing children. Why they did so is something of a mystery, but the consequences of those conversations are unmistakable: The median size of completed families in the region halved for cohorts marrying between 1790 and 1840. The number of children per family fell in the rural interior as well as in crowded coastal communities. How couples in the period actually managed to control family size is also a mystery, because no magic pills or rubber condoms were then available. No one at the time even understood the physiology of human reproduction. People obtained their health information from gossip or folklore, and women shared recipes for herbal "remedies." The timing of ovulation was utterly unknown even to university trained doctors. Any rhythm method was necessarily based on false assumptions and any success with it based on luck. The only contraceptive barriers available in the early decades of the nineteenth century were clumsy sheaths made of animal organs used by city prostitutes and their customers. Their unsavory connotations aroused disgust and revulsion among the respectable few who knew about them, yet no acceptable alternatives existed.[1]

Ordinary families living in New England's countryside who avoided or terminated pregnancies did so without the aid of any new contraceptive technology or medical knowledge. Neither were they being encouraged in

From the *Journal of Interdisciplinary History*. Reprinted from *The Journal of Interdisciplinary History*, XXXVII (2000), 35–58, with the permission of the editors of *The Journal of Interdisciplinary History* and The MIT Press, Cambridge, Massachusetts.

their efforts by media campaigns or government-funded clinics, as more recently in Asia and elsewhere. Consequently, it was far more difficult to prevent babies in the New England of 1800 than it is today in Bangladesh.[2]

Given the technological obstacles to controlling fertility and the apparent unlikelihood of people deliberately foregoing sexual pleasure at a time when farming was still the dominant way of life, New England's claim to a precocious modernity invites scrutiny. Until recently, child/woman ratios calculated from federal census summaries have had to serve as proxies for actual birth rates in early America, because no states registered births or deaths before the middle of the nineteenth century, and only a few were doing so by 1900. Child/woman ratios, which are based on the relative sizes of key age groups as reported by census takers, are subject to such potentially confounding factors as age-differentiated migration patterns and changing mortality levels.

Hacker has recently argued that rising mortality in the nineteenth century reduced the numbers of young children appearing in the censuses relative to the numbers of women of child-bearing age. He views the declining ratios as a product not of women having fewer babies but of fewer babies surviving to be counted. By applying new estimates of child mortality to direct counts of women and children in samples from manuscript census schedules, he imputed missing children to census households and from them generated a new historical series of birth rates for the United States between 1830 and 1890. Hacker's revised rates show no sustained decline occurring before 1880, roughly the same time as it began in England and much of Western Europe.[3]

Hacker's argument pivots on the presumption of worsening mortality among children below the age of ten. In the absence of data based on direct reports of such deaths, he turned to a life table originally calculated in 1906 from vital data then available in several states. By fitting published estimates of white adult mortality in the nineteenth century to this life table, he estimated the proportions of white children who died. Direct counts of deaths by age and sex would obviously be preferable to such a roundabout procedure, just as our knowledge of the early history of fertility would be equally well served by counting the actual births in local records—a piecemeal approach at best, but the only alternative.

New England offers an exceptionally good place to begin, because its townships kept vital records, albeit of uneven quality. From these records and other local sources, literally hundreds of genealogists have generated family histories over the past 150 years. The best of them have been refereed by professionals and published by reputable presses. They offer major advantages for historians working in the pre-1850 era, because they document the links between specific parents and children and endeavor to supply birth, marriage, and death information about every family member. Nor do compilers of these genealogies rely solely on official vital statistics for their information. They also utilize a wide array of sources—such as wills, deeds, family Bibles, and gravestone markings, as well as the federal manuscript-census schedules for the years when they are available. Comprehensive compilations follow descendants in the male line wherever they went; some even track female lines, a far more difficult target. As a result, historians making use of such genealogies are not tied to a single locale, as in town studies, nor to a single source like the federal census. They can compare the life events of movers as well as of stayers in a variety of settings.[4]

New England is, admittedly, a distinctive region; it cannot serve as a surrogate for the country as a whole. But its inhabitants made up one-quarter of the nation's population in 1820, and their cousins and descendants settled across the entire northern tier of territories claimed by the United States—eventually reaching all the way to the Pacific. Knowing when and how New Englanders sought smaller family sizes will help to explain why they did so and provide insights into the phenomenon more generally.

Method

The present study uses a composite database of sample families culled from a broad spectrum of published genealogies. The sample includes only first marriages resulting in at least one child born in New England, beginning in 1620 through 1854. Although the sampling design deliberately omits childless couples and overstates births to some degree, it should not distort any trends, since this overstatement is likely to have been a consistent fraction of all first marriages. Applying state-based population weights to sample families according to where they lived when their first child was born permits a variety of demographic indices for New England as a whole from 1620 through 1864. Individual vital events that could not be precisely dated have been interpolated from other information. Families for whom information proved insufficient for such interpolation were not included in the sample.

Even the best modern genealogies are not without problems. Since male heads of large households generated longer paper trails, genealogies are inevitably biased toward large families with many male descendants. Likewise, founders with the largest families engendered the most numerous descendants, and their potential as an audience attracts the compilation and marketing of genealogical works. Easier to recognize are the errors and gaps in the underlying records that hinder the process of family reconstitution. Unfortunately, they multiplied in post-Revolutionary New England towns when previously credible recording systems began eroding due to high rates of mobility. New towns were slow to establish good recording systems and heavy out-migration from older towns led to the disappearance of many people. The effect of that slide on the quality of the genealogical data has been dampened by compilers' use of compensating sources, but the problem is sufficient to require efforts at measurement and correction.[5]

Note first that under-recording of births and deaths, especially of females, by town clerks in New England occurred from the outset. The ratio of sons to daughters recorded to sample couples was 112 before 1675, dropped to

103 between 1675 and 1775, and then rose again to 110. Reporting of deaths among male descendants in the genealogies was also better than that among females, averaging 55.5 percent of all recorded and interpolated male births in the sample. These rates did not worsen noticeably in the nineteenth century. The year of death could be discovered or inferred only for 43 percent of the entire sample of women. Coverage was poorest in the seventeenth century, gradually improving to 50 percent of those born between 1800 and 1840, before falling to 41 percent of those born after 1845. Information about the oldest females, especially widows, is the most scarce, as is evident in a comparison of the proportions of unknowns between the sexes when grouped by age. This invisibility of elderly women in the records imparts a strong downward bias to calculations of female life expectancy because their ages at death do not enter into calculations. Yet, genealogies often provide sufficient information, such as "died young," "served in wartime," or "had a marriage recorded," to estimate proportions of birth cohorts surviving to adulthood. This judgment is possible for four-fifths of sons and daughters in the sample born between 1750 and 1840, but, again, this information grows spottier for those born after 1840, when rates of survival can be determined for only 78 percent of males and 73 percent of females.[6]

Since rates of survivorship can be calculated for large majorities of the children in the genealogies, they offer valuable surrogates for estimates of life expectancy. Survivorship peaked for both sexes born between the years 1775 and 1824, inclusive, and began sliding thereafter. Judging by

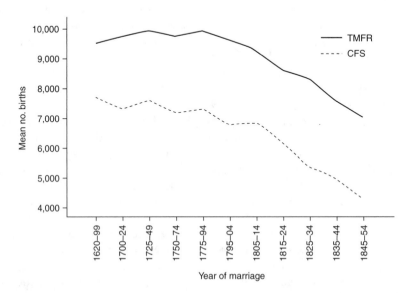

Figure 3.1 Total marital fertility rate and completed family size in New England, 1620–1845.

Source: Sample genealogies weighted by state, excluding cases in which the interval between the first and second births was longer than sixty months.

these data, the federal census of 1850 took place when life expectancy for children in New England was low, therefore reducing the number of children present to be counted by census takers. Hence, child/woman ratios calculated from the federal censuses significantly understate the birth rate between 1840 and 1850. Notwithstanding this serious problem in the 1850 census due to worsening mortality, prior federal censuses appear unaffected; movements in the child/woman ratios based on them probably replicate those in the birth rate itself.

Correcting for Biases

The argument for declining birth rates in New England, based on child/woman ratios, is supported by genealogical data, but the increasing severity of under-reporting requires attention. One way to test for, and correct, it is to track the length of intervals between first and second births in successive marriage cohorts, because couples presumably felt the least need to avoid pregnancy during this period. If that presumption is correct, any gap in the genealogies longer than four or five years could be camouflaging the birth of an unrecorded infant who died without leaving a trace. But longer intervals could also be due to such real causes as temporary infertility, longer absences by fathers, rising levels of miscarriages or abortions, or increasingly successful efforts at deliberate contraception.[7]

Of couples with two or more children in the marriage cohort of 1750–1774, 2.8 percent showed intervals of more than sixty months between the first two births. That percentage grew to 6 percent for the cohort of 1815–1824, 11.2 percent in 1835–1844, and 16.9 percent by 1845–1854. If this pattern is due solely to under-recording of early births, dubious cases must be excluded before calculating marital fertility levels. Figures 3.1 and 3.2 display three measures of marital fertility based on this narrowed sample, from the time of New England's founding through 1854. The total marital fertility rate, TMFR, measures reproduction among each marriage cohort of fecund women based on the childbearing history of every member. Completed family size, CFS, records the total number of births to couples who both survived to the wife's forty-fifth birthday. With both measures, the data summarized for each time period are *retrospective* in nature, and the cohorts stretch over decades, obscuring the timing of this major shift in human behavior. The third measure, KIDSBY30, provides a much more time-sensitive reading of the fertility decline, because the behavior under observation took place in a narrower frame of time and closer to the date of marriage for women from the same birth cohort. KIDSBY30 represents the number of births by age thirty to fecund women who married within a fixed and narrow age interval—in the present case, between the ages of twenty-one and twenty-three, bracketing the mean age at marriage that prevailed for most of the period under view. The data points are weighted by the relative size of the population in the colony/state where a couple's first child was born, making

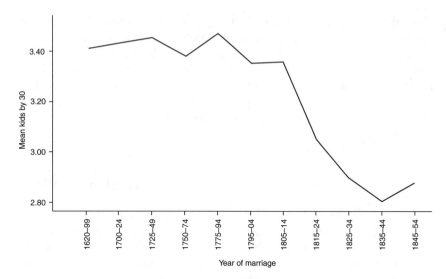

Figure 3.2   Number of births to mothers by age thirty and married between ages twenty-one and twenty-three in New England, 1620–1854.

Source: Sample genealogies weighted by state, excluding cases with intervals between first two births longer than sixty months.

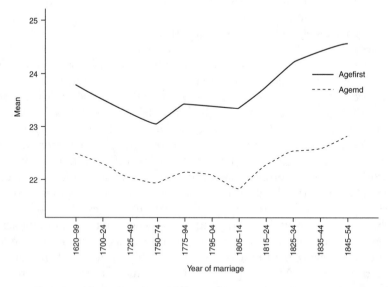

Figure 3.3   Wives' ages at marriage and at birth of first child in New England, 1620–1854.

Source: Sample genealogies weighted by state.

the cases from each state equivalent in weight to their proportion of the region's population in each period. As the figures suggest, fertility peaked in marriages formed between 1725 and 1749 and again between 1775 and 1794, declining thereafter. Altogether, TMFR fell from 10.4 children per married woman at its peak before 1750 to just 6.9 a century later, a drop of roughly one-third. Mean completed family size shows an even steeper decline, from 7.9 births to 4.3, and the median, not shown, halved in size, falling from 8 in the 1620–1794 period to 4 in the late 1830s. The number of children born to mothers by age thirty, of those marrying between twenty-one and twenty-three, fell by a fifth, from 3.45 to 2.80.[8]

Even after excluding cases with intervals between the first two births longer than sixty months, some couples in the sample were successfully avoiding pregnancies before the end of the eighteenth century, and many more were doing so from 1805 to 1814. The bias-adjusted measures of marital fertility in early New England show substantial declines long before 1850 and decades ahead of old England.

Clues about Motives

Why, and how, couples in New England started having fewer and fewer children are formidable questions, but the genealogies furnish some clues. A woman's age at first marriage was a powerful influence on how many children she would bear over the course of her childbearing years. Women in the sample married youngest in the early nineteenth century, as figure 3.3 depicts, and they began marrying at slightly older ages after the trough from 1805 to 1815. Thereafter, mean age at first marriage rose to nearly twenty-three, shortening the term of wives' connubial exposure by the equivalent of one pregnancy. Of greater significance, however, was the steep downturn in premarital pregnancy in the nineteenth century, not only because it lengthened the average interval of time between the wedding and the first child by more than half—visible in figure 3.4—but because it signaled a new willingness among young adults to control sexual impulses.[9]

As the figure suggests, premarital sex between engaged couples had become common practice in the eighteenth century, just as it did in England at the same time. This relaxation of sexual codes may have represented nothing more than a reversion to pre-Puritan ideas about the binding nature of marriage promises, or it may have been a response to loosening patriarchal controls. The important point is that the boom in early births came to an end in New England long before it did in England. This return to more stringent restraints on premarital sex in New England coincided with the onset of the sharp decline in the number of births to mothers by age thirty noted earlier. The lapse of time after the first birth before the next one also began climbing. Spacing between later children likewise grew as couples became more expert in managing. The interval before the last birth grew from 39.9 months between 1750 and 1774 to 50.6 months by the 1825–1834 period. By that same decade, women who married at ages twenty-one–twenty-three and who survived to age forty-five were ending childbearing a full three years sooner than they had in the years before 1750, at age thirty-seven rather than at slightly older than forty (see figure 3.5).[10]

This pattern of births exhibited by birth-controllers in New England is better described as "spacing" rather than "stopping" after a quick two or

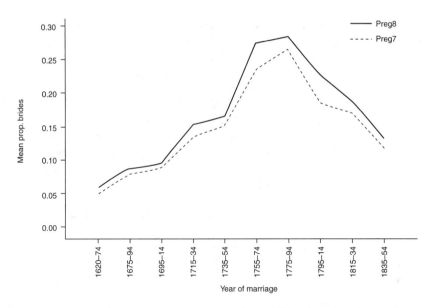

Figure 3.4   Premarital pregnancy rates in New England: children born 8 or 7.5 months after wedding.

Source: Vital records, town and family genealogies weighted by state.

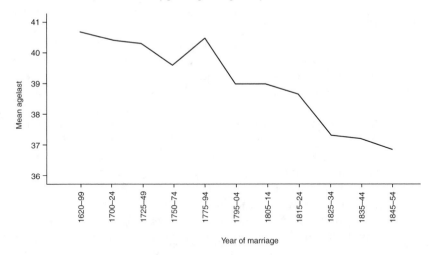

Figure 3.5   Mother's age at birth of last child in New England, 1620–1854: women who married between ages twenty-one and twenty-three and survived to forty-five.

Source: Sample genealogies weighted by state, excluding cases in which the interval between the first and second births was longer than sixty months.

three. The reasons for spacing rather than stopping become clear with the realization that control over reproduction was painfully achieved and not facilitated by any new contraceptive technology or scientific knowledge. According to Bogue, "Contraception is a goal-oriented, voluntary behavior, each episode of which is the result of conscious volition." Fertility decline, he argues, required "a distinctive behavior change" among an "increasing prevalence of couples." Not only did such couples have to beat against the tide of strong pronatal traditions in early New England, but, if the argument that follows is correct, they had to break the customary silence on personal matters between husband and wife in order to negotiate key changes in their sexual relations.[11]

According to the genealogical evidence, when couples began actively avoiding pregnancy, they did so early in their relationship. They were forced into new modes of expressing and gratifying sexual needs because existing contraceptive methods were too unreliable. The rubber necessary to make elastic condoms or syringes for cold vinegar–water douches did not yet exist. Only four methods of birth control were available: (1) More intensive and/or prolonged breastfeeding to extend postpartum amenorrhea, (2) increased resort to herbal or chemical abortifacients for unwanted pregnancies, (3) less frequent coitus, and (4) male withdrawal prior to orgasm during coitus. Wives did not need their husbands' support or consent to use the first and/or second techniques, whereas the third and fourth required the husband's active cooperation.[12]

Breastfeeding

Most women in early America nursed their infants as a matter of course, but breastfeeding is not without cost. It is disruptive to household routine and is time-consuming. How long mothers pursue it, and how intensively, determines how soon their ovaries resume ovulation. Modern studies indicate that breastfeeding can postpone the return of the menstrual cycle for as long as two years, but the actual delay for any particular mother depends on the strength and frequency with which her child suckles. Thus does the nursing relationship greatly influence how long a woman can avoid another pregnancy after she and her husband resume coital relations. The decision of when to wean a child probably depended on the state of its health and of the mother's health and whether suitable alternative foods for the baby, such as cow's milk, were seasonally available. Consequently, the duration of the intervals between pregnancies varied widely from woman to woman for reasons unrelated to any desire to avoid or terminate pregnancy.[13]

In a region where immigration was low, new ideas about baby care may have been slow to take hold. So long as women continued to practice their mothers' mode of nursing and weaning, the customary variation in birth intervals would center around a stable mean. The mean ceased to be stable after 1740, but there is no evidence that significant numbers of women in the late colonial period or in first half of the nineteenth century were adopting more intensive styles of breastfeeding or postponing weaning. Admittedly, finding such evidence would be difficult, but, in any event, breastfeeding's efficacy in postponing pregnancy was both limited and unsure, and its investment in a mother's time would have been sizable.

Abortion

Any decision to terminate a pregnancy would be the wife's to make, and it was not illegal if done early enough. The Massachusetts Supreme Court determined in 1812 that abortion early in pregnancy was beyond the scope of the law and not a crime. This decision remained the ruling precedent in the United States as a whole until the 1850s. Since a woman could not be adjudged to be pregnant with certainty until she felt the movement of the fetus, abortion was not "abortion" prior to that "quickening." Did married women freely resort to legal abortion? Klepp cites numerous references in letters written by women from the Philadelphia area during the Revolutionary and early national eras indicating knowledge of herbal remedies to "restore" menses. She argues that women were accustomed to controlling their fertility in this way and were the prime instigators of the fertility decline. Van de Walle, however, cautions that abortion did not lie behind every mention of herbs for menstrual regulation. Classical and medieval medical writers viewed menstruation as a wholesome purgation of bodily impurities and placed great importance on regular menstruation for women's health and to her ability to conceive. They often prescribed one or another of a large set of herbal emmenagogues to cause the uterus to shed its burden or to expel the placenta after birth. Van de Walle also notes that herbal abortifacients, though present throughout recorded history, were unreliable or ineffective, and dangerous to the mother. The extent to which women actually used them remains unclear.[14]

Whether married women in early New England commonly resorted to the use of abortifacients is likely to remain unsubstantiated for lack of objective sources. Nonetheless, since these herbs posed some danger to mothers, any increase in usage should have left traces in the mortality data. The proportion of women in sample families who died before age forty-five in New England actually fell between 1750 and 1825. Prior to 1750, 28 percent of mothers for whom the information is available (73 percent of all mothers in the sample) died before the age of forty-five, whereas from 1750 to 1824, only 17 percent died. Even in the higher mortality years from 1825 to 1854, just 22 percent failed to outlive their reproductive years. The reduction in childbearing after 1750 helped to lower the risk of dying in childbed, but the rise in the maternal survival rate between 1750 and 1824 easily exceeds any gain attributable solely to the decline in births during those years. Given this buoyant level of maternal well-being, self-induced abortion seems hardly to have been a primary means for controlling family size in New England, although it undoubtedly continued so for desperate women.[15]

Coital Infrequency

Longer intervals between lovemaking required greater self-control than married couples in New England had hitherto been accustomed to exercise. Some Pennsylvania Quakers in the eighteenth century may have adopted periodic abstinence for spiritual reasons, but marital abstinence was no virtue in conventional Protestant thought. As Morgan pointed out long ago, Puritans and their descendants most emphatically enjoyed sex. They would have been loathe to give it up. Yet something in their lives or circumstances began prompting young couples to manage their sex lives. In the nineteenth century, men who regarded themselves as progressive and enlightened came increasingly to accept a new, romanticized image of women as pureminded nurturers whose natural disinterest in sex could help their husbands discipline their own urges. According to David and Sanderson, however, women who acceded to this rarified version of their femininity could not significantly lower their chances of getting pregnant unless they and their husbands also employed a complementary contraceptive practice. David and Sanderson calculated the efficacy of alternative forms of contraception using data from a late-nineteenth-century California survey of "middle class" wives. They came to the surprising conclusion that reducing coital frequency from twelve times a month to four would, by itself, avoid only one pregnancy during the course of a woman's reproductive life! However, the addition of one other contraceptive practice caused the estimated completed family size to fall by at least one-half.[16]

Douching in an unheated bedroom with a cold vinegar rinse seems a particularly daunting method, especially in winter, and a sponge was far less effective in reaching the full extent of the birth canal than was the rubber syringe, which did not make its appearance until much later. Coitus interruptus, male withdrawal before orgasm, was the sole recourse. It was the probable method of choice in France. The Bible condemns the practice as unnatural, but it is simple in concept and requires no special equipment. To be effective, however, withdrawal requires good timing and special care by the husband to ejaculate well away from his wife. If husbands effectively and consistently combined this method with fewer episodes of lovemaking, they could substantially improve their wives' chances of avoiding pregnancy and, according to David and Sanderson, might reduce final family size by as much as two-thirds. Husbands had to be highly motivated to make infrequency and withdrawal work, and they ran a serious risk of frustrating themselves or their wives sexually.[17]

The success that couples in New England had in lowering their lifetime fertility is a measure of the strength of their motivation and the degree of their cooperation. Whereas a woman could decide on her own whether to try abortion, both partners had to work together to avoid pregnancy in the first place. Husbands had to overcome their fear of female sexuality and to respect their wives as stable, rational, and responsible individuals. The decision to restrict sex with their wives required self-control on their own part, but it also represented a vote of confidence in their wives' loyalty and self-discipline. Wives, too, had to refashion the feminine ideal for themselves. They had to cease regarding childbearing as a self-justifying end in itself and to embrace the new view of sexual reproduction as a process that could and *should* be under the control of wives and husbands.[18]

Planned and shared continence probably helped to make marriage a more equal partnership, and perhaps encouraged parents to invest more personal time with each young child. But why did they want fewer babies in the first place? The growth in life expectancy that took place between 1750 and 1825 gave parents more children to feed, clothe, house, and educate. But chance played such a large role in who and how many would survive that a modest improvement in average life expectancy at birth seems an unlikely inducement to give up the joy of spontaneous sex in order to prevent pregnancy, especially *early* in married life.

Motives for Restricting Family Size

The rewards of smaller families for women that loom largest to modern eyes are fewer encounters with the danger and pain of childbirth and more time free from pregnancy, diapers, and midnight feedings. Yet such prospects did not persuade couples in England to control their sexual relations; nor did they tempt New England families who were moving to newly opened territories in the late eighteenth and early nineteenth centuries. Unlike the comparatively crowded countries of the Old World, North America's high land-to-man ratio made farm ownership a viable prospect for many families, but usable undeveloped land was never free for the taking. Indians, the French, and the Spanish disputed access in the colonial period, and, after the imposition of certain treaties on Indian nations after the War of Independence, operating a farm remained a realizable dream only for those willing to move greater and greater distances from home. That dream was dying in the older settlements along the eastern coastline even before the colonial period ended.

Demographers making use of the federal censuses have long emphasized the early and persistently lower child/woman ratios in the more densely populated northeastern United States—the Mid-Atlantic states as well as New England—compared to the rest of the country. This marked disparity among the country's regions led scholars to hypothesize local land scarcity as the root cause of the fertility decline, but when tested at the local level, differential land prices do not predict birth rates.

Refinements of this thesis focused on inheritance practices and parental desires for old-age security. Most parents in the Northeast divided up the cash value of their estate equally among their children, giving land to sons, if possible, and personal estate to daughters. The more children that a couple had, the smaller were the individual portions. If family landholdings were no longer capable of subdivision among children without damage to their productivity, parents either directed their executor to sell the farm and divide the proceeds or else give the whole farm to one child, who would then pay the others their cash shares, usually by mortgaging the farm. Numerous siblings imposed a heavy burden on the primary heir, who often assumed care of the elderly parents as part of the bargain. If income from the farm did not cover all his costs, including mortgage payments, the heir had to sell out, evicting his aged parents in the process. Probate records in Massachusetts and Connecticut contain numerous examples of this dilemma beginning as early as the second decade of the eighteenth century. Presumably, couples in older settlements would have opted for fewer children when the good land was all taken up, whereas families moving to newly opened territory, where returns to labor were greater and the costs of portioning children lower, would have had more children.[19]

Theories about the consequences of land scarcity and old-age insecurity on family size are consistent with the downturn in fertility that took place first in the southern states of New England, where English settlements were oldest and densest. But are they both true and sufficient? Did young couples reach an economic tipping point at which they realized that large families simply cost too much? The kinds of data supplied by genealogies will not provide answers. Neither the occupations of male heads of households nor any other money-making activities by family members can be determined prior to the 1850 federal census. Not even family members' religious affiliations or voting habits are available to suggest nonmaterial motives for controlling births. Values were shifting in the eighteenth century, as the rising rates of premarital pregnancy suggest, and studies of an emerging consumer culture reveal changing lifestyles. Perhaps large families would have interfered with adults' enjoyment of such newly popular values as privacy, cleanliness, personal comfort, and social stimulation.

Probate inventories show that the material standard and style of living had been rising for half-a-century among people in middling circumstances. Household incomes had to have risen for them to afford the new consumer goods listed in these documents. Houses were larger and better constructed. People ate more nutritious diets, and they increasingly used pewter and ceramic ware. Farm women drank sweetened tea with their friends, and their husbands read newspapers in public houses over mugs of rum punch. Most children in Massachusetts and Connecticut attended public schools for at least a few months of the year, and the proportion of rural women of ordinary means able to write their own names had reached at least 50 percent by the era of the American Revolution.[20]

Economic Motives

The refinement of manners continued to spread deeper into the social strata in the new nation, and values continued to evolve in New England as religious revivals gained force. Standards for education rose and surely increased the expense of equipping children for independent adulthood at a time when household spending on consumption was rising. Did the cost of living increase so much that parents decided they could no longer afford more than four or five children? What was the value of child labor relative to the cost of child rearing, and how did it change as the economy developed from 1750 to 1850? These questions await research for definitive answers, but the context is hardly obscure, if a little puzzling.

The kind of mixed farming that characterized most of southern New England made heavy use of human labor only at haying and harvest time. When all of the undeveloped land was gone, older boys and young men sought other employment to supplement their pay as common laborers. Until the population reached a certain density, the lack of good means of transportation limited the market for local manufactures, discouraging successful artisans from expanding production and taking on apprentices. Consequently, the value of child labor in the rural interior of southern New England had probably sunk to its lowest point by the middle of the eighteenth century, but child labor was far cheaper in England at the time. There the birth rate was actually rising because couples were marrying earlier. England was far more densely populated. Land was so expensive, and wages so low, that ordinary people had no expectations of ever acquiring any. However, merchant-operated systems in the English countryside supplied tools and raw materials to rural families for manufacture at home, putting whole families to work. When England began industrializing, family size did not fall. Only *after* the country reached a mature stage of industrialization in the 1880s did birth rates begin their long-term sustained decline.[21]

Had the economy of southern New England failed to develop manufacturing occupations, average age at marriage would have risen, and far fewer young people would have been able to set up independent housekeeping. The birth rate would have fallen for these reasons alone, and sexual relations within marriage might not have altered. The putting-out system in textiles and shoemaking that began in 1780s Massachusetts marked a transition away from traditional ways of using family labor while greatly increasing paid employment in the countryside. The proliferation of carding machines and spinning mills sharply increased the demand for weavers' services, many of whom were women. The first spinning mill erected at Fall River in the early nineteenth century found the neighboring farm wives already fully employed as weavers for Providence mills. Hence, its owners opened a store in Hallowell, Maine (near modern Augusta), where it offered consumer goods to local women in exchange for weaving yarn supplied by the mill. Other forms of rural outwork eventually included the making of straw and palm leaf hats in the 1820s, but the craft that underwent the most complete transformation was shoemaking in eastern Massachusetts. Women became binders, and employers treated binders as independent workers. The practice gave rural women the opportunity for the first time to earn their own cash at home.[22]

As shops turned into small factories, the manufacturing processes subdivided in ways that opened up more employment for children and teenaged girls, relative to men and older boys. The same process did not cause the birth rate in England to fall. Have we a paradox? Young couples in southern New England were starving their sex lives in order to avoid conceiving a new baby despite the fact that the value of child labor was rising, at least until 1830. In old England, neither proto-industrialization, early factory jobs, nor Methodist religious revivals enticed couples into sacrificing their sexual enjoyment. Given that paid child labor was increasingly contributing to household incomes in both old and New England until 1830 or later, the fall in the latter's birth rate seems to have come *in spite* of expanding child employment, certainly not because of it.[23]

The solution to the paradox is undoubtedly more complicated than assessments of the availability of land, the value of child labor, or the opportunities for married women to earn cash at home can explain, but information from two state surveys taken just prior to 1820 facilitate further analysis. In Connecticut and New Hampshire, the census takers enumerated meetinghouses, schoolhouses, publichouses, stores, several kinds of mill, textile factories, tanneries, distilleries, printing establishments, banks, academies (high schools), and libraries by town. To test the effect that each of them had on marital fertility, a subset of couples in these states was created from those who married between 1810 and 1824. It includes only those in which the wives married between the ages of nineteen and twenty-three, lived to age thirty, and gave birth to a second child sixty months or less after their first. Setting these boundaries narrowed the already small sample size to exactly 100 cases, 54 from Connecticut and 46 from New Hampshire. In addition to the census counts, three more pieces of information were collected: coding of town population size in 1810 and 1820 for each couple; the numbers of cotton factories present in those towns, according to the 1832 Congressional manufacturing survey known as the McLane Report; and the proportion of the labor force employed in agriculture, commerce, and manufacturing in the county where each couple lived, as reported in the published summaries of the federal manufacturing census of 1820. These data make clear that the Connecticut and New Hampshire couples in this sample lived in sharply contrasting economic and demographic environments.[24]

The average population of sample towns in Connecticut was 3,247 compared to 1,622 for New Hampshire: The town population densities were 88.6 people per square mile and 56.8, respectively. The women in Connecticut married a little older, 21.3 versus 20.8, and died a little older, 70.1 versus 67.7. They also had 26 percent fewer children by age thirty, 2.94 compared to 3.70. As a result of their greater population density, Connecticut towns had more schools, commercial establishments, and the like, except saw mills, but the degree of difference was not uniform across the categories: No New Hampshire couple lived in a town with a distillery, whereas the towns in Connecticut averaged 1.57 distilleries apiece. Only four out of the forty-six New Hampshire couples lived in towns with printing establishments or banks, but disparities between the sample towns in these two states were greatest in their numbers of woolen factories, academies, and libraries. The Connecticut towns had twice as many cotton factories as those in New Hampshire before 1820. By the time of the survey for the McLane Report, five times as many of them were in Connecticut as in New Hampshire.[25]

The small number of couples in the subsample makes it difficult to determine which of the differences visible in the censuses related significantly to marital fertility as measured by the number of births by mother's age thirty. Pearson correlation coefficients proved significant only for town population size (and a few of the related co-variants, such as grist mills, tanneries, meetinghouses, and schoolhouses) but not for printers, banks, academies, libraries, nor textile-related manufacturers. Yet the number of births by mother's age thirty correlated positively with the proportion of the county's labor force employed in agriculture ($R = +.432$) and negatively with manufacturing ($R = -.420$) and commerce ($R = -.328$). In other words, the greater the nonagricultural sector of the county economy in the federal census of 1820, the lower was the number of babies born to young mothers.

Perhaps if the subset were much larger, more subtle connections might appear between the local economy and culture. However, an experiment that groups the census categories into three composite sets—producers, services, and amenities (the value of each being the arithmetic sum of its components)—might prove fruitful. School houses, pubs, stores, banks, and printers are denominated as services in the experiment; meetinghouses, academies, and libraries are amenities; and all others are producers. How well do any of these three composite sets predict marital fertility among couples in the subsample as measured by the number of births to mothers by age thirty? Pearson correlation coefficients and their degree of statistical significance are for amenities, $R = -.246$ (significance $= .014$); producers, $R = -.231$ (significance $=.021$); services, $R = -.132$ (significance $= .192$). Residents' fertility rates varied inversely with the number of each in their town, though services were not a significant factor. Note, however, that amenities were slightly more important to marital fertility than producers.

The results of this exercise with town data and sample families, limited as they are, support both kinds of explanations for the onset of the fertility transition in New England—the cultural as well as the land/inheritance/old-age-security model. There were more meetinghouses and libraries available in towns with low birth rates than population size or density, alone, would predict. Since women outnumbered men in church membership in early New England and were better educated and more politically aware than ever before, rising female status within the family may explain the greater willingness of men to cooperate in helping their wives avoid pregnancy.

Whatever the reasons for declining premarital pregnancy and fertility, young people in New England had a choice that their counterparts in old England did not: They could move far away from home, work hard, and build a farm, or they could stay, seize the new opportunities afforded by expanding markets, and, by controlling costs through sexual restraint, still hope to enjoy the high, and interesting, standard of living enjoyed by their elders. Both economic and cultural change began well before Independence; the pace was gradual but cumulative. By the time the great transportation and industrial revolutions were underway, the fertility transition in southern New England was already under full throttle, and the intimate lives of the people had already transformed. Who would have guessed that the need for sexual restraint would become patriarchy's gentle solvent?[26]

Notes

1. John C. Caldwell, "The Delayed Western Fertility Decline: An Examination of English- Speaking Countries," *Population and Development Review*, XXV (1999), 479–513; Janet Farrell Brodie, *Contraception and Abortion in Nineteenth-Century America* (Ithaca, 1994).
2. Susan E. Klepp, "Lost, Hidden, Obstructed, and Repressed: Contraceptive and Abortive Technology in the Early Delaware Valley," in Judith A. McGaw (ed.), *Early American Technology: Making and Doing Things from the Colonial Era to 1850* (Chapel Hill, 1994), 68–113.
3. See J. David Hacker, "Rethinking the Early Decline of Fertility in the United States: New Evidence from the Integrated Public Use Microdata Series," *Demography*, V (2004), 605–620; Maris Vinovskis, *Fertility in Massachusetts from the Revolution* (New York, 1981); Daniel Scott Smith, "Early Fertility Decline in America: A Problem in Family History," *Journal of Family History*, XII (1987), 73–84; Michael R. Haines and Hacker, "The Puzzle of the Antebellum Fertility Decline in the United States: New Evidence and Reconsideration," paper presented at the annual meeting of the Social Science History Association, Chicago, Ill., November 20, 2004. See discussion of the pertinent literature in Haines, "The White Population of the United States, 1790–1920," in *idem* and Richard H. Steckel (eds.), *A Population History of North America* (New York, 2000), 305–370; Herbert S. Klein, *A Population History of the United States* (New York, 2004), 77–82.
4. Jennifer Wahl, "New Results on the Decline in Household Fertility," in Stanley L. Engerman and Robert E. Gallman (eds.), *Long-Term Factors in American Economic Growth* (Chicago, 1986), 391–425; Lee L. Bean, Geraldine P. Mineau, and Douglas L. Anderton, *Fertility Change on the American Frontier: Adaptation and Innovation* (Berkeley, 1990). Mean completed family size and total fertility rates reported for New England by Wahl in table 8.7 on page 406 are much higher for the 1650–1749 period than those calculated from my sample of genealogies.
5. Compared to the IPUMS (http://en.wikipedia.org/wiki/IPUMS) New England sample from the federal census of 1850, the genealogies overstate the number of births by about 6 percent, even after adjusting for dead children missing from the census.
6. If a careful and conscientious compiler identified a child in an otherwise well-documented family but found no further information on that child, the child was coded as not surviving to adulthood. Age at death can be calculated or inferred for 82 percent of fathers and 69 percent of mothers. Coverage of women improved over time—60 percent in the seventeenth century, 65 percent in the first half of the eighteenth century, 71 percent in the second half, and 75 percent in the first half of the nineteenth century.
7. My thanks to David Hacker for suggesting a way to test under-recording of births by means of the length of the interval between the first two births. "Completed" families make up about two-thirds of the more than 10,000 first marriages of couples in the sample.
8. The total marital fertility rate (TMFR) is a composite figure that represents the total number of births that a woman of the place and time would have if she married at age fifteen, stayed married until age forty-five, and gave birth at the average rate of the women in each successive five-year age group. So long as a woman's age is known, her recorded fertility experience can be calculated even if she died or disappeared

from the records before she reached her forty-fifth birthday. The TMFR tends to overstate observed completed family size, but its great strength is that it is comparable across cohorts and makes use of *all* available information.

9. Of daughters who lived to age forty-five, the proportion never marrying rose from 4 percent before the American Revolution to 20 percent of those born after 1835.

10. Smith and Michael S. Hindus, "Premarital Pregnancy in America 1640–1971: An Overview and Interpretation," *Journal of Interdisciplinary History*, V (1975), 537–570.

11. Donald J. Bogue, "Normative and Psychic Costs of Contraception," in Rodolpho A. Bulatao and Ronald D. Lee (eds.), *Determinants of Fertility in Developing Countries. II. Fertility Regulation and Institutional Influences* (New York, 1983), 151, 153.

12. Comfortable and effective condoms made of latex did not appear until the 1930s. The introduction of the rubber-ball syringe, which allowed quick, effective douching through the powerful propulsion of the astringent, is difficult to date.

13. Ross W. Beales, Jr., "Nursing and Weaning in an Eighteenth-Century New England Household," in Peter Benes (ed.), *Families and Children* (Cambridge, Mass., 1987), 48–63. James W. Wood, *Dynamics of Human Reproduction: Biology, Biometry, Demography* (New York, 1994), 338–343, 368–370; Paula A. Treckel, "Breastfeeding and Maternal Sexuality in Colonial America," *Journal of Interdisciplinary History*, XX (1989), 25–51. Mary Beth Norton, *Liberty's Daughters: The Revolutionary Experience of American Women, 1750–1800* (Boston, 1980), 233–234, argues for many alterations in white women's lives in the post-Revolutionary era, among them cooperation between husband and wife in the prevention of pregnancy and a greater willingness among women to control fertility through extended breastfeeding.

14. James Mohr, *Abortion in America: The Origin and Evolution of National Policy* (New York, 1978). The anti-abortion movement, which began in the middle of the nineteenth century, was led by medical practitioners who claimed that one out of five pregnancies was intentionally terminated, a claim that Mohr and others have accepted at face value. Given the probability that doctors then did not know the normal rate of spontaneous abortion, they tended to identify every failed pregnancy as the result of deliberate action on the part of the mother. See the discussion of this issue in Paul A. David and Warren C. Sanderson, "Rudimentary Contraceptive Methods and the American Transition to Marital Fertility Control, 1855–1915," in Engerman and Gallman (eds.), *Long-Term Factors*, 331. Klepp, "Lost, Hidden, Obstructed, and Repressed," 68–90. Etienne van de Walle, "Flowers and Fruits: Two Thousand Years of Menstrual Regulation," *Journal of Interdisciplinary History*, XXVIII (1997), 183–203. Van de Walle seeks to rebut arguments by John M. Riddle, *Contraception and Abortion from the Ancient World to the Renaissance* (Cambridge, Mass., 1992), and Angus McLaren, *Reproductive Rituals: The Perception of Fertility in England from the Sixteenth to the Nineteenth Century* (London, 1984). See also van deWalle, "Towards a Demographic History of Abortion," *Population: An English Selection*, XI (1999), 115–131. Roger Thompson's examination of Middlesex County court records in seventeenth-century Massachusetts turned up only four instances of the use of savin or pennyroyal, all by unmarried women. The outcome is unknown in one case, but in the other three, "the women later gave birth" (*Sex in Middlesex: Popular Mores in a Massachusetts County, 1649–1699* [Amherst, 1986], 26). Cornelia Hughes Dayton relates the tragic story of a young unmarried woman who took an abortifacient at the urging of her lover and subsequently died ("Taking the Trade: Abortion and Gender Relations in an Eighteenth-Century New England Village," *William and Mary Quarterly*, XLVIII [1991], 19–49).

15. The greatest gains in proportions successfully reaching age forty-five between 1620 and 1749 and between 1750 and 1824 were those by mothers with five or fewer children.

16. Robert V. Wells, "Family Size and Fertility Control in Eighteenth-Century America: A Study of Quaker Families," *Population Studies*, XXV (1971), 73–82; Harry S. Stout, *The New England Soul: Preaching and Religious Culture in Colonial New England* (New York, 1986); Mark A. Noll, *America's God: From Jonathan Edwards to Abraham Lincoln* (New York, 2002); Edmund S. Morgan, "Puritans and Sex," *New England Quarterly*, XV (1942), 591–607; Nancy F. Cott, "Passionlessness: An Interpretation of Victorian Sexual Ideology, 1790–1850," *Signs*, IV (1978), 219–236; Carl N. Degler, "What Ought to Be and What Was: Women's Sexuality in the Nineteenth Century," *American Historical Review*, LXXIX (1974), 1467–1490; idem, *At Odds: Women and the Family in America from the Revolution to the Present* (New York, 1982). Jan Lewis and Kenneth Lockridge argue that upper-class Southern women manipulated their husbands into reducing coital frequency on the grounds that frequent pregnancy and childbirth endangered their health ("'Sally Has Been Sick': Pregnancy and Family Limitation among Virginia Gentry Women, 1780–1830," *Journal of Social History*, XXII [1988–1989], 5–19).

17. Jean-Louis Flandrin (trans. Richard Southern), *Families in Former Times: Kinship, Household and Sexuality* (New York, 1979), 219–225, believes that men practiced withdrawal at the behest of their wives who, until the eighteenth century, did not have sufficient status within the marriage to win such sympathy and consent. The Biblical reference to coitus interruptus is Genesis 38. David and Sanderson, "Rudimentary Contraceptive Methods," 356–359. The precise reduction achieved depends on assumptions about a wife's age at marriage, the probability of the method's failure and the couple's failure to use it, as well as coital frequency. Degler, "What Ought to Be and What Was," 1474.

18. Klepp, "Revolutionary Bodies: Women and the Fertility Transition in the Mid-Atlantic Region, 1760–1820," *Journal of American History*, LXXXV (1998), 910–945, examines women's changing ideas about nature and reproduction in the Philadelphia area and locates the origins of change in Revolutionary rhetoric. Cott, "Passionlessness," 219–236.

19. Morton O. Schapiro, "Land Availability and Fertility in the United States, 1760–1870," *Journal of American History*, XLII (1982), 577–600.

20. David H. Flaherty, *Privacy in Colonial New England* (Charlottesville, 1972); James Deetz, *In Small Things Forgotten: The Archaeology of Early American Life* (New York, 1996; orig. pub. 1977), 62–67; Michael P. Steinitz, "Landmark and Shelter: Domestic Architecture in the Cultural Landscape of the Central Uplands of Massachusetts in the Eighteenth Century," unpub. Ph.D. diss. (Clark University, 1988), 165–168; David W. Conroy, *In Public Houses: Drink and the Revolution of Authority in Colonial Massachusetts* (Chapel Hill, 1995), 189–240; Main, *Peoples of a Spacious Land: Families and Cultures in Colonial New England* (Cambridge, Mass., 2001), 215–222; idem, "An Inquiry into When and Why Women Learned to Write in Colonial New England," *Journal of Social History*, XXIV (1992), 579–589.

21. Lee A. Craig used a sample of rural households from the 1860 manuscript census to compare the relative contribution of children to farm output in the Northeast, the Midwest, and on the frontier (*To Sow One Acre More: Childbearing and Farm Productivity in the Antebellum North* [Baltimore, 1993]). Not surprisingly, children of either sex produced little before the age of twelve, and teenaged girls contributed far less than their male counterparts on northern farms.

22. Victor S. Clark, *History of Manufactures in the United States* (New York, 1949; orig. pub. 1929), I, 539; Mary H. Blewett, *Men, Women, and Work: Class,*

Gender, and Protest in the New England Shoe Industry (Urbana, 1988), 44–67. See also Blanche Hazard, *The Organization of the Boot and Shoe Industry in Massachusetts before 1875* (Cambridge, Mass., 1921).

23. Jan De Vries called this period the "Industrious Revolution," regarding it as a crucial transitional stage that supplied the infrastructure necessary for the development of full-blown industrial capitalism and helped to ease the break with tradition by encouraging all family members to work smarter in return for access to new consumer goods ("The Industrial Revolution and the Industrious Revolution," *Journal of Economic History,* LIV [1994], 249–270).

24. The child/woman ratios in these two states, calculated from their totals in federal censuses of 1800 through 1850 posted on the University of Virginia website, show a gradual convergence between the two states over the course of the half-century, from 1,512 for Connecticut and 1,848 for New Hampshire in 1800 to 928 for both states in 1850. A shift in the age categories used by the federal census after 1830 required an estimate of the numbers of females sixteen through nineteen and forty through forty-four in deriving these ratios.

25. John C. Pease and John M. Niles, *A Gazetteer of the States of Connecticut and Rhode-Island* (Hartford, 1819); John Farmer and Jacob B. Moore, *A Gazetteer of the State of New-Hampshire* (Concord, 1823); [Louis McLane, Secretary of the Treasury], *Documents Relative to the Manufactures in the United States* (New York, 1969; orig. pub. 1833), 2 v.

26. In their discussion of alternative schemes for explaining the fertility transition in the United States, Susan B. Carter, Roger L. Ransom, and Richard Sutch note that "Even in southern New England, which by all accounts was the locus of manufacturing and commercial development in the early decades of the century, it is difficult to relate the decline in rural fertility between 1810 and 1830 to the expansion of nonagricultural opportunities for young adults" ("Family Matters: The Life-Cycle Transition and the Antebellum American Fertility Decline," in Timothy W. Guinnane, William A. Sundstrom, and Warren Whatley [eds.], *History Matters: Essays on Economic Growth, Technology, and Demographic Change* [Stanford, 2004], 292). Their own life-cycle model for the fertility transition could apply to southern New England as early as 1750.

4

Exceptionalism and Globalism: Travel Writers and the Nineteenth-Century American West

David M. Wrobel

Since the publication of Edward Said's landmark study, *Orientalism* (1978), cultural historians have generally viewed travel writers within the theoretical contours of the postcolonial framework that Said helped construct.[1] Travel writers have been commonly characterized as the architects of imperial visions, the exoticizers, commodifiers, and objectifiers of colonized "others" who helped their readers in the imperial mother countries to understand, accept, and consume the exercise of empire. While travel writers could indeed be agents of empire, this scholarly approach has had the effect of flattening the discourse about empire in travel writing. In the postcolonialist treatment of travel writing, imperial advocates and critics, as well as those whose visions were marked by a great deal of ambiguity about imperial projects have been placed together, as if in harmony.

However, exploring the archive of nineteenth-century travelogues about the American West reveals more cacophony than harmony. Travel writers could levy influential criticism of the empires of rival nations as well as of their own nations' imperial projects.

The ubiquitous and enormously popular travelogue form often offered readers an important countercurrent to the common notion of the American West as an exceptional place, like nowhere else on earth. Many travelers placed the West into a broader, comparative global context, viewing it as one developing frontier among many, effectively putting the West into the world and thereby de-emphasizing its regional exceptionalism. These global visions can help us rethink our assumptions about western mythology and American exceptionalism, which has itself often rested on preconceptions

From *The Historian*. 68 (Fall 2006), 431–60. Published by Blackwell Publishing.

about the nature of the nation's western frontier experience. To understand how the West was envisioned by America and the world in the nineteenth century, the travel book may indeed be our best archive. This study draws on that archive to examine the relationship between American notions of national exceptionalism and the realities of American empire.

Exceptionalism and Empire

The tension between exceptionalism and empire stands today at the very heart of the American experience, as it has for more than two centuries. The idea of benign national distinctiveness, of republican purity and innocence, has continually collided with the notion of the United States as an empire, much like other empires that have risen and fallen in the course of human history.[2] From the earliest settlements in British North America, colonists viewed the western frontier within a wider context of global exploration, commerce, and imperial war. Empires traded, negotiated, and clashed on the frontier before colonial subjects considered the path of independence from the mother country. Prior to the Revolutionary War, the issue of westward movement into the great interior of the continent sparked tensions between those colonists who wanted the freedom to expand their geographic and economic horizons and an anxious empire that sought control over them and wished to reduce the potential for conflict with native peoples on the frontier.

A generation after the end of the Revolutionary War, the Louisiana Purchase of 1803 doubled the size of the emerging American nation. The following year, Meriwether Lewis and William Clark, authors of perhaps the most renowned of all western travel narratives, went off to explore the lands that the new republic had just purchased from France. The admission of Texas as a state in 1845 and the settlement of the Oregon boundary question with Britain in 1846 further expanded the young nation. The war with Mexico from 1846 to 1848 added more territory with the spoils of victory of the 1848 Treaty of Guadalupe Hidalgo (present-day Arizona, California, Nevada, New Mexico, Utah, and portions of Colorado and Texas—an area totaling 1,200,000 square miles), along with the postwar Gadsden Purchase from the recently defeated Mexican government in 1851 (the small piece of southwestern territory that Elliott West describes as "an after-dinner mint following the expansionist gorging"), further enlarged the borders of the West into the familiar shape we know today.[3] In the space of less than half a century, the new nation had tripled its size and its coastline. As Thomas Hietala notes, within the space of less than a decade during the administrations of John Tyler (1841–45) and James K. Polk (1845–49), the country acquired "nearly eight hundred million acres of land" and pressed for "commercial and territorial advantages beyond the continent in...Hawaii, China, Cuba, and Yucatán."[4]

American history textbooks generally apply the term imperialism to the end of the nineteenth century—the period of the Spanish-American War, the acquisition of the Philippines and other noncontiguous territories—the era immediately postdating the official closing of the frontier. But the imperialist label is generally not applied so readily to the earlier part of that century, the era of continental or frontier expansion. So long as the United States had a western frontier to move into, that process of expansion seemed ostensibly, and retrospectively, nonimperialistic. This perspective implies that America had its fleeting imperial moment a century ago. But the whole story of the nineteenth-century American West, of course, must include that of American foreign policy. The new territories entered the national body politic as full-fledged States, with all the rights and privileges of the existing States (a rather different practice from that of traditional empires with their tributary satellites). Their entry into the United States' orbit, nonetheless, cannot be accounted for by providence alone.[5] These developments mark the process of nineteenth-century American expansion as a story of empire building, one characterized by the contending voices of self-described imperialists and anti-imperialists. Yet the story of westward imperial expansion has often paraded, in our historical memory, in far less aggressive clothing—as the "Empire for Liberty" that Stephen A. Douglas championed in 1845, or an "Empire of Innocence," to use Patricia Nelson Limerick's irony-laden phrase of 1987.[6]

Evident for more than half a century, the global and comparative vision of western American history has gained momentum in recent years. Furthermore, the currently developing fields of Atlantic World and Pacific World history provide ample evidence of the heightened global emphasis among scholars of the United States today.[7] The portrayal of the nineteenth-century United States' territorial growth as one imperial-ist story among many in the period has been obscured in our historical field of vision by a far more popular and pleasing national narrative.[8] By moving into lands that it bordered, the United States' expansion into the West differed from the colonial ventures of the European powers by its contiguous nature, and advocates of the American empire certainly empha-sized that factor. Indeed, the pervasive hold of a manifest destiny on the American imagination has had such strength that we still have to remind ourselves that the story of America's westward expansion really did take place on a global stage. The notion of a nation growing into its foreordained boundaries has such power that we can forget the foreign policy context of nineteenth-century western history. The myth of a manifest destiny has endured so well because it provides such incredible comfort to the national psyche. Better for the national mental health to believe that the world's greatest democracy had grown naturally, providentially, into its God-given skin than to consider that it, like so many other nations, has a history of empire building. The West, so often declared as the most American part of America, has functioned as the primary stage for that imperial drama.

The story of national mission, God-given destiny, and American excep-tionalism has not unfolded as the result of any great conscious design, at least no more so than the nurturing of myths of national exceptionalism in other countries.[9] Nations gradually create identities because they need them, and the process is generally rather unsystematic.[10] The United States provides a good case in point. Shortly after the conclusion of the Revolutionary War, Benjamin Franklin noted that the western frontier, the part of the new nation farthest removed from the European-influenced and tainted East Coast, was the emerging heart of the nation.[11] In 1787, Thomas Jefferson wrote to James Madison: "Our governments will remain virtuous...as long as they are chiefly agricultural; and this will be as long as there shall be vacant lands in any part of America. When they [the people] get piled upon one another in large cities, as in Europe, they will become corrupt as in Europe, and go to eating one another."[12]

Thus, in a fascinating example of the inversion of the standard theory of center–periphery relations (an inversion that long predates postcolonial theory, which emphasizes the influence of the colonized on colonizers and of colonies on empires), the western periphery—the frontier—increasingly came to be seen as the center of Americanism as it shifted farther from the physical center of real national power and federal infrastructure—the eastern seaboard. Here, on the periphery, a distinctive Americanism would emerge, as Franklin, Jefferson, and other contemporaries suggested. This observation occurred more than a half century before newspaper editor John L. O'Sullivan popularized the term "Manifest Destiny" in 1845 in the contexts of the annexation of Texas and the Oregon boundary dispute, and more than a century before the historian Frederick Jackson Turner gave academic legitimacy to popular notions about the frontier's enormous significance.[13] While the particular concept of manifest destiny was clearly a creation of the moment by American expansionists seeking to justify an imperialistic course for their still quite new republic, the connection between the western frontier and the health of that republic had long been a staple in American thought.

Indeed, the development of a national consciousness of sorts in the nineteenth century depended partly on the notion that this new republic could somehow break the historical cycle of countries rising to greatness and then sinking into a state of decay. In this context, historian Dorothy Ross has explained, "the vast continent of virgin land that offered Americans an escape from republican decay assumed increasing, even mythic importance." The movement into the interior of the continent, into the heartland of the new country, could thus be viewed as a story of American escape from the world, of America discovering and expanding westward into itself. With its western safety valve, America could avoid the industrial violence, class division, and general social decay that had accompanied modernization in European countries; it could even escape the cycles of history and remain an Eden, suspended, as Ross notes, in "a position somewhere between the agrarian and commercial stages of development."[14] Having completed its ostensibly preordained continental expansion, America, with the closing of the frontier in the late nineteenth century, would have to make choices about imperial expansion, but not before then. But, of course, this new nation was not discovering itself or expanding into itself so much as constituting itself incrementally (in quite large chunks to be sure) on a world stage and displacing those residents who were already there—primarily Indians, Californios, Mexicans, and Tejanos.

The drama of national exceptionalism played out as the nineteenth century unfolded, and the prairies, plains, Rockies, and the Pacific Coast were acquired, explored, conquered, and settled. The numerous critics of the process of empire building, particularly in the 1840s, included intellectual luminaries such as Henry David Thoreau (whose famous "Essay on Civil Disobedience" directly commented on citizen rights in an age of empire) and an emerging young Whig politician, Abraham Lincoln (who worked hard to distance himself later in his career from his youthful anti-Mexican-American War stance). Furthermore, the Northeastern United States as a region generally opposed the mid-nineteenth century imperial turn.[15] Expansionists dismissed the reservations of their anti-imperialist and sectional adversaries and argued for a "republican empire," one involving the acquisition and exploitation of "land not people" ("the myth of an empty continent"), which thereby did not diminish the nation's exceptionalism but actually enhanced it.[16]

Yet this complex story of clashing imperialists and anti-imperialists has been largely subsumed in the national memory by an infinitely simpler tale (in keeping with the imperialist rationale of the 1840s) in which continental expansion has been rendered natural and only extracontinental expansion challenges the notion of national exceptionalism. More in the mainstream of national heritage construction were the young amateur and professional historians who told the story of the frontier/West in a stirring fashion, from Francis Parkman in *The Oregon Trail* (1849) to Theodore Roosevelt in *The Winning of the West* (3 vols., 1889–96), as well as Turner in his landmark essay "The Significance of the Frontier in American History" (1893) and in subsequent essays.[17] Writers, artists, performers, and later, moviemakers all contributed to a national consciousness of the frontier West as the heart and soul of America. That consciousness became the core of a benign story of national growth, a story removed from the global stages where the imperial pursuits of presumably base, unenlightened European nations played out.

The great drama of the West became just the first of many stories of national exceptionalism that have sprung up because the nation needed them, and they have proven hard to purge from the national consciousness for the very same reason. We should include among these stories that of the Progressive era as an age of purely altruistically motivated reform, the absolute antithesis of (and corrective to) the Gilded Age; the story of the 1920s as a happy, colorful, carefree interlude; the Great Depression as a triumph of American cooperation, compassion, and perseverance; World War II as "the Good War," with a wonderfully unified home front; and the Civil Rights Movement as a great redemptive moment, a triumph of integration marked by a healthy national recognition of the country's shortcomings in the arena of race. All of these memorable episodes were far messier, their contours less clearly, less dualistically defined, than the national collective memory has imagined. None of them quite qualify as the great morality plays and triumphs of America's better angels that the nation has remembered them to have been. Within the space of about thirty years, each of these purposeful interpretations of the past came under the questioning of professional historians; but like the story of the West and American exceptionalism, all continue largely intact in the broader public consciousness despite the weight of scholarly reservations.[18]

While the New Western History helped transform the history of the American West a generation ago, the contours of the story remained within an exceptionalist paradigm. Region sought to replace frontier as a theoretical framework (not that the frontier thesis served as a framework for many scholars by that time); conquest replaced settlement as the key descriptor for what happened in the West; and tragedy replaced triumph in the trope department. The contours of this rejuvenating wave of scholarship were far more nuanced than an enthused media, hungry for stories of gunfights at politically OK corrals, painted them. The story of the frontier/West, in the media representation, went from being an exceptionally noble one, a mark of national pride, to an exceptionally ignoble one, a tale of national embarrassment. Whether a uniquely benign story (an oversimplification of Turner's thesis) or a thoroughly malign one (a similarly facile interpretation of the New Western History), whether resting on a thematic foundation of frontier or region, the print media presented the West as a unique place, a place apart from the rest of the world, rather than a part of it.[19]

The accounts of foreigners have generally augmented the story of American exceptionalism. "What then is the American, this new man?" asked the French expatriate Hector St. John de Crèvecoeur in his *Letters from an American Farmer* in 1782. He declared that in the new continent, the European "leaves behind him all the ancient prejudices and manners...[and becomes] a free man acting upon new principles."[20] Alexis de Tocqueville, perhaps the most insightful of all foreign observers of American life, memorably emphasized the nation's uniqueness in his *Democracy in America* (vol. 1, 1835; vol. 2, 1840). The famed British observer Lord James Bryce's massive two-volume set of observations, *The American Commonwealth* (1893–95), generally remains in the memory of American Western historians for its comment about the West being the most American part of America. These observers have stood the test of time (all are still in print) not solely because they are wonderfully rich and observant works, full of insights and predictions that make us wonder, generations later, at the genius of their authors, but also because they tell a nation what it wants to hear: that it is different, special, unique, and exceptional.[21]

Yet this positioning of Tocqueville's *Democracy in America* as a foundational text in the annals of American exceptionalism tells only a part of the story. As Jennifer Pitts has demonstrated in her recent analysis and translation of Tocqueville's writings on empire and slavery, Tocqueville advocated

French empire building in Algeria. He visited Algiers in 1841 and 1846 and viewed the United States' efforts to address the "Indian problem" on its western frontier as a model for the French in dealing with the Algerian population.[22] This largely unknown side of Tocqueville's thinking leads to another understudied counternarrative to the story of American and Western American exceptionalism.

Numerous nineteenth-century foreign travelers to America, as well as American travelers, described western places and peoples in a broader global context. Exploring this interplay of global visions and exceptionalist dreams in American thought complicates our understanding of how the American West and the theme of national exceptionalism might have been perceived by the American public in the nineteenth century. For many of these travel writers, the West was clearly a part of the world, not apart from it. These global visions of the West were very much before American eyes, and they would surely have prompted that public to think about their nation comparatively, in relation to other expanding empires, rather than as a nation apart, a great benign exception or anomaly.

Such globally positioned accounts of American life, however, have not fully entered the national consciousness of the Western American past, partly because of the enormous power of the notions of manifest destiny and "westward expansion."[23] Restoring those comparative narratives or at least underscoring the space that they occupied in the national imagination when they first appeared will not change the well-established fact that in the memory wars these global visions lost out to exceptionalist dreams. However, resurrecting the globally contextualized West of the late nineteenth century—the West in the World, we might call it—does at least remind us that the American public and the world public, for that matter, was not fed a steady and unvarying diet of western exceptionalism. This complicates our understanding of the contours of the Western American past and its place in the national imagination.[24]

American Exceptionalism and The Traveler's Gaze

Close to 2,000 travel books were published in the United States between 1830 and 1900, and an even larger number of books were published in Europe in the same period.[25] Travel accounts, often serializations that later appeared as book-length travelogues, filled popular magazines and periodicals.[26] Travel writings were voluminous, ubiquitous, and vital to the public understanding or misunderstanding of place. Indeed, nineteenth-century travel books helped meet the public need for information about faraway places in what was still an age of discovery. American travel writer Paul Belloni Du Chaillu's *Explorations and Adventures in Equatorial Africa*, for example, sold nearly 300,000 copies in 1861, making it one of that year's best sellers;[27] and Mark Twain, to Americans in the late nineteenth century, "was first and foremost a travel writer" and "consistently, his travel books proved to be his best-sellers."[28] For the historian of the nineteenth-century West in American and European thought and culture, travel writings constitute a wonderfully rich storehouse of ethnographic observations and commentary on the conquest of the West.[29]

Travel writing, however, has to some degree slipped through the cracks of our historiographical consciousness in much the same way that the genre naturally slips through the cracks between literature and history. Travel writings are neither novels about nor historical surveys of places.[30] They generally are, as Barbara Brothers and Julia Gergits note, "hybrids— drawing in part from other genres such as autobiography, history, natural history, anthropology, sociology, archeology, or geography."[31] Until the last couple of decades, the travel-writing genre has not proven a fertile ground for literary scholars. As Brothers and Gergits suggest, while "Modernism dominated the academy...fiction, poetry, and drama" received the primary focus of critical attention, and more popular forms, such as travel writing, were generally forgotten or disparaged.[32]

Interestingly, however, as literary scholars largely ignored the travel book in the World War II and postwar years and as authors themselves declared it a dead form, American historical scholarship experienced a moment of intense engagement with the earlier perceptions of visitors, largely of British origin, to America.[33] The "hands-across-the-ocean" sentiment that World War II inspired in Britain and the United States initiated a heightened emphasis on what Americans could learn about their past from the keen observations of previous generations hailing from America's current primary wartime ally. Max Berger's *The British Traveller in America* appeared in 1943, at a time, the author noted, "when Americans are observing their English ally more closely and more critically than ever before..."[34]

A few years later in 1948, with Cold War tensions rising precipitously, Allen Nevins' *America Through British Eyes* was republished. The following year, Oscar Handlin's *This was America* appeared. Both are weighty tomes, each exceeding 500 pages and offering testimony to the nation's effort to "find itself" and define its national character in the postwar years.[35] In much the same vein, Robert Athearn's *Westward the Briton*, another analysis of the observations of nineteenth-century British visitors to the West, appeared in 1953. A few years later, in June 1957, the *Mississippi Valley Historical Review* published Thomas D. Clark's "The Great Visitation to American Democracy," delivered the previous month as the Presidential Address at the fiftieth annual meeting of that organization.[36]

Within this climate of Cold War anxiety in the 1940s and the 1950s, consensus history, intellectual and cultural history, and the related field of American Studies all appeared on the American scholarly scene as the nation sought better to understand itself. Works in these fields sought to chart the sources of the nation's distinctiveness, and they generally emphasized the positive nature of the American national character and its democratic institutions. In short, they shored up the foundations of American exceptionalism.[37]

As the nation searched for and proclaimed what Arthur Schlesinger, Jr. called "The Vital Center" (the hallowed middle ground of political democracy so distinguishable from totalitarian extremes of the right and left), scholars produced their studies of American exceptionalism. The various works of the 1940s and the 1950s on travel writings about America and the West augmented that scholarly search for an exceptional American history and national character.[38] In knowing how others had perceived America and American democracy, these historians presumably felt that they could more fully understand their nation's past and present through the eyes of others. Uncoincidentally, this period rediscovered Tocqueville's *Democracy in America*. Reprinted in numerous editions between 1945 and 1956, the book came to be considered as one of the core texts of American exceptionalism.[39] Not surprisingly, no concurrent American "rediscovery" occurred at this time of Tocqueville's writings on empire and slavery. Those texts have the effect of compromising the notions of a benign American exceptionalism by emphasizing the United States' harsh Indian policy as a model for French colonialism in North Africa and justifying the adoption of brutal means to secure France's imperial ends.[40]

We can certainly distinguish this generation of scholarship of the 1940s and the 1950s about foreign travelers to the United States by its generally positive tone. We can also distinguish it from the more recent trend, one influenced by the "formal end of European colonialism during the latter half of the twentieth century."[41] Since the publication of Said's *Orientalism*, scholars have become more disposed to emphasize the ominous side of travel writing, viewing it as a "colonial discourse" marked by "the rhetorical strategies of debasement [of other cultures]" and the maintenance of "cultural hegemony in the postcolonial world." The travel writers themselves are portrayed as white agents of empire.[42] Said, in *Culture and Imperialism* (1993), describes travel writing as a vital part of "the great cultural archive...where the intellectual and aesthetic investments in overseas dominion are made." "In your narratives, histories, travel tales, and explorations," he continues, "your consciousness was represented as the principal authority, an active point of energy that made sense not just of colonizing activities but of exotic geographies and peoples."[43] Said further explained that representational forms, including fiction, history, travel writing, and art, "depended on the powers of Europe to bring the non-European world into representations, the better to be able to see it, to master it, and, above all, to hold it."[44] Homi K. Bhabha makes the point even more directly in his *The Location of Culture* (1994), stating that "the objective of colonial discourse is to construe the colonized as a population of degenerate types on the basis of racial origin, in order to justify conquest and to establish systems of administration and instruction."[45] Bhabha goes on to argue that "the effect of colonial power" works against itself and ends up producing "hybridization rather than the noisy command of colonialist authority or the silent repression of native traditions."[46]

A landmark study in this more critical body of scholarship on travel writing is Mary Louise Pratt's 1992 book, *Imperial Eyes: Travel Writing and Transculturation*. Pratt positions her work as part of the academy's effort to "decolonize knowledge." She emphasizes the "contact zones," the "social spaces where disparate cultures meet, clash, and grapple with each other, often in highly asymmetrical relations of domination and subordination." Emblematic of that asymmetrical relationship, Pratt argues, are the "travel books by Europeans about non-European parts of the world," which created the "'domestic subjects' of Euroimperialism." Thus, Pratt asks "How has travel and exploration writing produced 'the rest of the world' for European readerships...?" She contends that the form, in conjunction with "enlightenment natural history," has produced a "Eurocentered form of global or...'planetary' consciousness." She explains that the travel writer embodies that privileged consciousness, viewing other cultures and landscapes as "the monarch of all I survey," the archetypal representative of empire.[47]

Clearly, in the postcolonial academic world, the visions of earlier generations of travelers have appeared increasingly less benign; indeed, increasingly sinister. Theirs is an imperial gaze. We see a shift, then, from the theme of American exceptionalism as confirmed through the eyes of white European visitors, to the imperial visions and racial predilections of white travelers, whether European or American, as they make others of the "traveled upon."[48] In both cases, however, the possibility of knowing one's own nation and culture better through travelers' eyes has motivated travel writers. But as scholarship on travel writing has shifted from the first stage to the second, the emphasis has increasingly illuminated the less laudatory aspects of western civilization. The transition has been, then, from the insightfulness of the travelers' vision to the harmfulness of the travelers' gaze—from an emphasis on the positive validation of American democracy that travelers offered to an emphasis on the cultural prejudices that they exhibited.[49]

However, as we approach the truly enormous archive of nineteenth-century visitors' accounts of America and the West that line both the dusty shelves of archives and the brighter shelves of contemporary bookstores, consider a theoretical framework that encompasses both of these extremes of benign exceptionalism and the imperial gaze. Such a framework must also include the more nuanced possible readings of travelers' visions of America and the American West that lie between those extremes. For example, scores of popular nineteenth-century travel writers offered critical accounts of the United States' conquest of its contiguous West and compared it to the colonial ventures of European powers on other continents. Recovering the work of two mid-nineteenth-century travelers, the American painter of Indians, George Catlin, who is well-remembered today, although not as a travel writer, and the German traveling and writing phenomenon, Friedrich Gerstäcker, who is hardly remembered at all today, can deepen our understanding of how Americans of that time might have envisioned the tension between empire and exceptionalism as well as the relationship between a globally contextual-ized American West and a quintessentially American frontier.

Comparative Visions of Colonialism

George Catlin traveled from the United States to England in 1839 to promote his famous Indian Gallery, which he opened to the public at London's Egyptian Hall in Piccadilly in 1840. The Gallery itself resulted from Catlin's earlier eight years of travel among the Indians in the United States and its territories.[50] The Egyptian Hall, which housed cultural arti-facts from Captain Cook's South Sea voyages, provided an appropriately global setting for Catlin's work. The public obviously did not mind the housing of South Sea Islands artifacts inside an Egyptian-inspired archi-tecture or the addition of paintings and people of the American West. The Hall functioned as a repository for the "exotic" from all over the world. The press described his public lectures there as a "journey into Indian country" for a public familiar with travel accounts of the American West.[51] Catlin discussed the manners, customs, and the fate of the North American Indians with his paintings as the props, and he often became highly critical of his nation's actions, proclaiming that "fire-water," "small-pox," and the "exterminating policy of the United States govern-ment..." doomed the Indians to extinction. Fortuitously for Catlin, as the crowds tired of his straight lectures by 1843, a group of nine Ojibways arrived from Canada. His gallery was soon filled not just with pictures but also with actual Indians, bringing dramatic life to his presentations. The Ojibways would leave Catlin to perform in another show, but a group of Iowas (men, women, a child, and an infant) soon arrived and Catlin touted them as "wilder," more "primitive," and more authentically Indian than the Ojibways.[52]

Catlin recorded these observations about his indigenous attractions in promotional broadsides for the shows. He also gathered them into a quite remarkable work of travel, the self-referentially titled *Catlin's Notes of Eight Years' Travels and Residence in Europe, With His North American Indian Collection* (1848). He later republished the work with a new title, *Adventures of the Ojibbeway and Ioway Indians, in England, France, and Belgium Being Notes of Eight Years Residence in Europe With the North American Indian Collection* (1852), which shifted the primary emphasis to the Indians.[53] He structured much of the book as a travel narrative about Europe through Native American eyes. Catlin recounted the observations of the Iowas as they traveled around London—to Lord's Cricket Ground, Vauxhall Gardens, and Windsor Castle where they met Queen Victoria and Prince Albert. The reader is taken vicariously on a journey with the Iowas as they respond to white people and white institutions. Catlin's enormous ego provides the true axis around which his Indian travelogue revolves. Still, the Iowas' travel experiences in the early 1840s, even refracted through Catlin's navel-gazing eyes, are revealing.[54]

During a journey to London's West End, the Iowas told Catlin that they "had passed two *Indians* in the street with brooms, sweeping away the mud; they saw them hold out their hands to people going by, as if they were begging for money..." Could they really be Indians begging? they asked Catlin. He explained that they were natives from the East Indies, Lascars, "left by some cruel fate, to earn their living in the streets of London, or to starve to death." The Iowas, Catlin noted, "seemed much affected by the degradation that these poor fellows were driven to, and resolved that they would carry some money with them when they went out, to throw to them."[55] Thus, the colonial subjects of one empire come face to face with those of another on the streets of the nineteenth century's world capital of empire, London.

Catlin traveled around England, Scotland, and Ireland with the Iowas, and then to Paris in 1845 where his Indian Gallery was displayed in the Louvre and King Louis Philippe and the French royal family visited.[56] He intended the show-casing of living Indians to underscore his central message: Indians were dying out. Then, tragically, some of the Iowas, including the infant boy, Corsair, and his mother, O-kee-wee-me, died of disease. The remaining Iowas returned to the United States. But Catlin's living tribute to a dying race continued. A group of Ojibway arrived in Paris and joined Catlin's show, and he shamelessly marketed them as superior Indians to the Iowas. Then, in 1846, eight of the Ojibways contracted smallpox, and two of them died. The survivors returned to the United States. The representatives of a dying race, working in a living history exhibit designed to highlight their fate, were dying. The deaths brought the show to an end; Catlin never exhibited Indians again.[57]

He wrote up the experience of his travels with the Indians in Europe into the travel book, *Catlin's Notes of Eight Years' Travels and Residence in Europe (and Adventures of the Ojibbeway and Ioway Indians)*, which he self-published and self-marketed in an effort to retrieve some of the losses from his European ventures; but the book failed to save the day for Catlin.[58] He then returned to a fascinating proposal he had first lectured on at the Royal Institution of London a decade earlier: a "Museum of Mankind." This ethnographic endeavor, Catlin explained, would "perpetuate the looks and manners and history of all the declining and vanishing races of man." He reminded his English audience that "Great Britain has more than thirty colonies in different quarters of the globe, in which the numbers of civilized men are increasing, and the native tribes are wasting away." Catlin then declared that "the march of civilization is everywhere, as it is in America, a war of extermination, and that of our own species." He even proposed that a ship would sail around the world exhibiting his museum of mankind.[59] Imagine the cruel irony of a ship sailing to the far-flung reaches of the globe where indigenous peoples were in decline, displaying the cultural remnants of those cultures.

As Catlin proposed his floating "Museum of Mankind," a German, Friedrich Gerstäcker, embarked on the second great journey of his life, traversing the world and comparing colonial systems and demographic catastrophes. Gerstäcker's remarkable account of his global travels, *Narrative of a Journey Round the World, Comprising a Winter Passage Across the Andes to Chili, With a Visit to the Gold Regions of California and Australia, the South Sea Islands, Java, &c*, was published in Germany, America, and England in 1853.[60]

Born in 1816 to a well-known opera singer and orphaned at age eight, Friedrich Gerstäcker read Daniel Defoe's *Robinson Crusoe* (1719) as a young boy and found inspiration for a life of travel and adventure. A cabin boy on his way to New York at the age of twenty-one, he worked at various jobs in the western territories in the late 1830s and the early 1840s and returned to Germany in 1843. In 1845, he published a novel, *Die Regulatoren in Arkansas*, based on his American experiences. The California Gold Rush brought him back to the United States but as part of a larger world tour lasting from 1849 to 1852, taking him across the Atlantic to South America and then to California, the Hawaiian and Society Islands, Australia, New Zealand, and Java before returning to Germany.[61] Gerstäcker joined 40,000 maritime gold rushers who traveled via Cape Horn or across the Isthmus of Panama in 1849. Another 42,000, Howard Lamar notes, went overland to California that year; their journeys occupy a more familiar place in the national memory. Six thousand more migrated to the California goldfields in 1849 from Mexico.[62] Gerstäcker traveled to South America again in 1860–61, to Egypt and Abyssinia in 1862, and to the United States again along with Mexico, the West Indies, Ecuador, and Venezuela in 1867–68. He died in 1872 after packing a great deal of traveling and writing into his fifty-six years of life.[63]

Gerstäcker knew America. By the time he left the country in 1843, he had traveled extensively (largely on foot, for over six years) and had become more familiar with the landscapes and the people of the Central and Western United States and its territories than all but a few Americans. Gerstäcker also knew the world, having walked, ridden, and sailed across a good part of it. And the world knew Gerstäcker too; he published a massive pile of works (approximately 150 books) of travel, adventure stories, and novels in the mid- to late nineteenth century. From the early 1850s until his death, Gerstäcker—a stranger to the modern literary and historical canons—was an enormously popular writer.[64] People would have read him without knowing it, as many of his stories were pirated and published as dime novels with no acknowledgment of the author. While Gerstäcker's colorful stories may have subliminally entered the national consciousness, his travel writings, also widely known then, have become virtually unknown today.[65] In these, he put the West into a world context; moreover, he put the world into the West, illuminating the amazing consequences of those multi-cultural meetings. In *Narrative of a Journey Round the World*, he provided a powerful reminder that California was a global stage and that the California Gold Rush was a world story.

In one of the many fascinating moments in this account of his 1849–52 journey, Gerstäcker related the story of an East Indian from Bombay who "came one day to Douglas's Flat, close to Murphy's digging (in the Southern goldfields), rushing into a tent, and summoning, in very broken English, the Americans to his help, saying that the Indians had attacked him, and robbed him of 1900 dollars worth of gold dust."

> The Americans at once snatched up their rifles to meet the Indians; the latter took to flight, and the others followed them into the mountains...In the meanwhile, some of the Americans may have recollected that they had proceeded a little too rashly in the affair, they, therefore, arrested the Mohammedan, whom...they began to suspect, and conducted him to Murphy's. Indians then came to our camp, and more and more evidence was brought forth that the East Indian had told a lie; and that he had not only not possessed 1900 dollars, but he had not even a cent. Indians and white men now guarded the Mohammedan; and a deputation went to the Indian village, there to inquire into the havock that had been done.

They learned that the Indians had invited the East Indian into their camp and that he had made inappropriate advances toward the women and been thrown out. The white deputation also found a California Indian dying from a bullet wound from the encounter with the American pursuers. The East Indian was subsequently held responsible for this death and "condemned to receive twenty-five lashes." Gerstäcker described the event:

> The following day (the 4th of July) was the anniversary of the declaration of independence of the United States, the greatest political festival of the North American, yet the sentence was nevertheless executed on that day. The first thirteen lashes were given by the American sheriff—the others by an Indian; and it was a strange but picturesque spectacle, on the fine sunny day, to see, under the waving American flag, the wretched isolated Mohammedan, who, conducted by a gang of white men and Indians to the cattle yard of the butcher, was there tied to a post and flogged, surrounded in a wide circle by Yankees, French, Germans, Spaniards, Mexicans, and men of other nations; and whilst the copper-coloured Indians, in their fanciful attire, climbed on the fence, and half-triumphantly and half-anxiously looked at the infliction of chastisement, the Mohammedan in vain invoked his Allah.[66]

Thus, a German traveler described the flogging of a man from Bombay, for the death of a California Indian, while white Americans, various Europeans, Mexicans, South Americans, and North American Indians observed—all in the American West, that most American part of America, and on Independence Day. Audiences in America and Europe could read the account in their separate editions of the book.

Gerstäcker's writing forced readers to consider the larger context of Indian–white relations in California, particularly the acute indigenous population decline that accompanied that contact. Gerstäcker wrote:

> The Indians of California no longer exist in reality, though a few scattered tribes may wander about yet in the distant hills, looking toward the setting sun, down upon a country which was once their own, and where the ashes of

their forefathers were given to the balmy breeze, or buried under the shady oaks of the plains.[67]

In recounting the story of the Bombay Indian, Gerstäcker did not prophesy and implicitly justify the inevitable destruction of California Indians as a primitive race (a nineteenth-century tendency that scholars have rightly criticized); rather, he explained that process by emphasizing the immorality and inhumanity of white colonists.[68] The Bombay Indian was held responsible for the death of the California Indian and punished. But white Americans (probably inspired more by the $1,900 than by any desire to assist the East Indian) did the actual killing, and other white Americans set fire to the Indians' village during the pursuit; they were not charged with any crime. Gerstäcker, who visited the Indian camp after the attack, described the wounded Indian—shot in the back: "death was written on his countenance." The story serves as a microcosm of the war of extermination that white settlers waged against California Indians. California's indigenous population of around 150,000 in 1848 had fallen to 30,000 twelve years later.[69] Disease accounts only for a portion of this loss. The numbers raise the issue of the applicability of the term genocide in America.[70] The topic of genocide, in turn, prompts the charting of moral equivalencies—the great counter to notions of benign American exceptionalism—thus rendering it perhaps as the most controversial topic for American historians.

Gerstäcker's account reminds us that such issues were very much in the American public eye a century and a half ago. He wrote that "the whites behaved worse than cannibals toward the poor, inoffensive creatures, whom they had robbed of nearly every means of existence and now sought to trample under foot." While the wife wailed over her dying husband, Gerstäcker admitted, "I ran down the hill as fast as I could, to be out of hearing of those dreadful sounds. I was ashamed of being a white man at that moment."[71] He presented his shame as a microcosm of the collective shame that he felt white people ought to have experienced for their inhumanity toward the California Indian.

A year later, in 1851, Gerstäcker traveled from California via the Hawaiian Islands to Australia where he again commented on race relations, reminding his readers: "the devil is never so black as he is painted." But the fate of Australia's aborigines seemed no brighter than that of California's Indians; they too, he declared, will be "swept from the face of the earth."[72] By this, Gerstäcker did not intend "ghosting the primitive"—positing indigenous extinction as a self-fulfilling prophecy—but to offer a counter explanation for processes that were occurring in Australia, California, Hawaii, and all around the globe. Worlds were being turned upside down by the discovery of gold, the introduction of European strains of disease, and the consequent decline in indigenous populations.[73] Gold and death went hand in hand. Entire races were declining so precipitously that they appeared headed for extinction, and Gerstäcker offered the genocidal acts of white people as a key cause.[74]

From Australia, Gerstäcker made one last stop on his global journey at the Dutch colony of Java where he offered a stinging indictment of Dutch colonialism, adopting an indigenous voice for the purpose:

> You shave my head in a severe winter, and then sell me a warm cap. Of course, the cap keeps my head warm, and I need it from time to time; but I do not see any reason why I ought to be obliged to you for it—the cap only keeps my head as warm as my hair would have done; but why did you not leave it to me?—only to sell me the cap.

Gerstäcker then provided his readers with a comparative analysis of European colonialisms in which the Dutch came off quite well:

> The Hollander leaves the native in his home, and to his gods, and does not trouble his soul as well as his body. Their households and their house-hold god are left to them; and they are not driven from the graves of their fathers by deeds and contracts, of which they understand nothing, and by persuasions and agreements closed with some chiefs, and enforced finally upon the whole nation, as English and Americans have done only too frequently.[75]

In May 1852, Gerstäcker arrived back in Germany after more than three years of travel. His *Narrative* appeared the next year with its comparisons of the Californian and Australian Gold Rushes, European and American colonialism, and the catastrophic demographic decline of indigenous peoples on different continents.[76] His coverage of Gold Rush California comprises one-fifth of the book, but illuminating parallels and departures between California and other places appeared throughout. America's West emerged as just one part of Gerstäcker's world, another developing frontier marked by violence against natives; it was not exceptional, not a world apart, but a West in the world.

A year later, in 1854, Catlin covered some of the same ground that Gerstäcker had traversed a few years earlier. Catlin, traveling in South America, hunted for gold in Brazil, explored the Amazon, crossed the Andes, and painted "vanishing" peoples.[77] The lives, works, and contradictions of these two chroniclers of the West in the world paralleled each other in interesting ways. Catlin died the same year as Gerstäcker, in 1872, although he had been born a generation earlier, in 1796. Gerstäcker's voluminous writings included many classic frontier tales, the kind of dime novel fare that nurtured the notions of American western distinctiveness. But Gerstäcker was an insightful travel writer as well as a dime novelist. Catlin has been raked over the coals by scholars frustrated at his mythologizing of the theme of the vanishing Indian. Indeed, Catlin's own father noted in 1838 that the value of his son's pictorial record of Indian peoples would increase as his subjects decreased in number.[78] Catlin, for his part, was a complex character who exploited Indians for financial gain and yet knew their cultures and loudly protested their mistreatment by the U.S. government. In the varied work and fascinating lives of just two individuals, we have a microcosm of the split or even multiple personalities housed within a national consciousness that could be globally envisioned yet still harbor exceptionalist dreams.

By recovering their work and the work of other travelers, we may better understand the global West of the nineteenth-century imagination as well as its exceptionalist counterpart, the American frontier. Their writings also suggest that the postcolonialist scholarly critique of the nineteenth-century traveler as an architect of empire could itself use some revision. Catlin and Gerstäcker number just two of the many travel writers of their time who illuminated the awful consequences of European and U.S. imperialism for indigenous peoples. Their concerns cannot be dismissed as mere "imperialist nostalgia"—a sense of purported longing for that which has been lost by those who have played a part in its destruction.[79] Indeed, they voiced their criticisms of colonial policy during a time when there was no shortage of enthusiastic imperialists who voiced no such concerns over the destructive consequences of empire building.

No record exists of these two men who both placed the fate of North American Indians into the global context of western civilization's expansion ever meeting, but they would surely have known each other's work. Certainly, George Catlin and Friedrich Gerstäcker were just two of the many writers who positioned the American West within a world context in the nineteenth century, before later generations of Americans chose to separate it from those global moorings and "nationalize" it. Their travel writings formed part of a large body of observations about America that probably served as a brake on the unqualified acceptance of the rhetoric of exceptionalism by the American public and may have even acted on the conscience of the nation.

There are lessons for the present in such a reexamination of nineteenth-century visitors' accounts. Clearly, we live in another age when the exceptionalist rhetoric of U.S. policy makers would be well-served by a healthy dose of global contextualization and comparative analysis. Indeed, the present administration struggles to maintain an exceptionalist framework for the Iraq War by emphasizing America's role in bringing freedom and democracy to the Iraqi people. It downplays the growing concern about rendition, torture, and Orwellian oversight that led the American and world publics to question that exceptionalism. The tension is becoming increasingly more taut and fraught. While that struggle between exceptionalism and imperialism is highlighted today in a wide array of electronic media outlets, the global travel writers in the nineteenth century were best positioned to remind the American public of that tension. The road maps of a globalized, comparative West that these writers provided are of renewed value now.

Notes

1. Edward Said, *Orientalism* (New York: Pantheon Books, 1978).
2. Thomas R. Hietala explores this tension in his chapter "American Exceptionalism, American Empire" in *Manifest Design: Anxious Aggrandizement in Late Jacksonian*

America (Ithaca, N.Y.: Cornell University Press, 1985), 173–214. Paul Kennedy positions the United States within this larger story of empires in *The Rise and Fall of the Great Powers: Economic Change and Military Conflict From 1500 to 2000* (New York: Random House, 1987).

3. Elliott West, "Thinking West," in *The Blackwell Companion to the American West*, ed. William Deverell (Malden, Mass., and Oxford: Blackwell, 2004), 25–50. For more on the travel narratives about Mexico during the Mexican–American War, see Howard R. Lamar, "Foreword," in *Down the Santa Fe Trail and Into Mexico: The Diary of Susan Shelby Magoffin, 1846–1847*, ed. Stella M. Drumm (Lincoln: University of Nebraska Press, 1982; orig. pub. with the Lamar "Foreword," New Haven, Conn.: Yale University Press, 1962, and first published by Yale in 1926), ix–xxxv.

4. Hietala, *Manifest Design*, 2.

5. Fred Anderson and Andrew Cayton, *The Dominion of War: Empire and Liberty in North America, 1500–2000* (New York: Viking, 2005), xv, emphasize how the realities of territorial acquisition undermine the rhetoric of exceptionalism.

6. On Stephen A. Douglas's use of the phrase, see John Mack Faragher and Robert Hine, *The American West: A New Interpretive History* (New Haven, Conn.: Yale University Press, 2000), 199. Patricia Nelson Limerick, "Empire of Innocence," in *The Legacy of Conquest: The Unbroken Past of the American West*, with a new Preface (New York: W. W. Norton, 2006; orig. pub. 1987).

7. Henry Nash Smith's *Virgin Land: The American West as Symbol and Myth* (1950) (emphasizes early Anglo exploration of the West as a search for trade routes to the Orient) and Walter Prescott Webb's *The Great Frontier* (Boston: Houghton Mifflin, 1952) are classic examples of the early global contextualization of Western American history. See also Howard Lamar's and Leonard Thompson's pioneering anthology, *The Frontier in History: North America and South Africa Compared* (New Haven, Conn.: Yale University Press, 1981); Walter Nugent's broad comparative piece, "Comparing Wests and Frontiers," in *The Oxford History of the American West*, eds. Clyde A. Milner II, Carol A. O'Connor, and Martha Sandweiss (New York: Oxford University Press, 1994), 803–33; Gunther Peck, *Reinventing Free Labor: Padrones and Immigrant Workers in the North American West, 1880–1930* (Cambridge: Cambridge University Press, 2000); and Patricia Nelson Limerick's presidential address to the Western History Association, "Going West and Ending Up Global," *Western Historical Quarterly* 32 (Spring 2001): 5–23. For an excellent example of the successful forays of a historian of the U.S. West into Pacific World history, see David Igler, "Diseased Goods: Global Exchanges in the Eastern Pacific Basin, 1770–1850," *American Historical Review* 109 (June 2004): 693–719. World historians have comfortably incorporated the story of U.S. expansion into the global contexts of their works. See, for example, J.M. Roberts, *The New Penguin History of the World* (New York and London: Penguin, 2004; orig. pub. 1976). Roberts writes: "there was much that was barely distinguishable from imperialism in the nineteenth-century territorial expansion of the United States, although Americans might not recognize it when it was packaged as a 'Manifest Destiny,'" 827–28.

8. The obvious imperial parallels include British colonization of India (under a policy of "Dual Control" from 1784, followed by the formal assumption of control in 1858), the French conquest of Algeria (1830–47), and the European nations' carving up of the African continent at the West African Conferences of Berlin (1884–85). Algeria's two most prominent leaders and resistors of French colonial authority, Abd-el-Kader and Ahmad Bey, surrendered to the French in 1847, the same year that American forces entered Mexico City.

9. For more on American exceptionalism, see Michael Kammen, "The Problem of American Exceptionalism: A Reconsideration," *American Quarterly* 45 (March 1993): 1–43; Ian Tyrrell, "American Exceptionalism in an Age of International History," *American Historical Review* 96 (October 1991): 1031–55; David Noble, *Death of a Nation: American Culture and the End of Exceptionalism* (Minneapolis: University of Minnesota Press, 2002); and Deborah L. Madsen, *American Exceptionalism* (Jackson: University Press of Mississippi, 1998).

10. Richard Slotkin, in *Regeneration Through Violence: The Mythology of the American Frontier, 1600–1800* (Middletown, Conn.: Wesleyan University Press, 1973); *The Fatal Environment: The Myth of the Frontier in the Age of Industrialization, 1800–1890* (New York: Atheneum, 1985); and *Gunfighter Nation: The Myth of the Frontier in Twentieth-Century America* (New York: Atheneum, 1992), contends that there was a more conscious construction of the national identity on a foundation of frontier mythology.

11. Benjamin Franklin, "The Internal State of America: Being a True Description of the Interest and Policy of that Vast Continent," in *The Writings of Benjamin Franklin*, ed. Albert K. Smythe, vol. 10 (New York: Macmillan, 1907), 117–18. See also James Paul Hutson, "Benjamin Franklin and the West," *Western Historical Quarterly* 4 (October 1973): 425–34.

12. For the Jefferson quotation, see Gilbert Chinard, *Thomas Jefferson: The Apostle of Americanism* (Boston: Little, Brown, 1929), 80–2; James C. Malin, *The Contriving Brain and the Skillful Hand in the United States* (Ann Arbor, Mich.: Edwards Brothers, 1955); and H.A. Washington, ed., *The Writings of Thomas Jefferson*, vol. 2 (Washington, D.C., 1854), 332.

13. John L. O'Sullivan's article "Annexation," addressing the opposition of European powers to the annexation of Texas, appeared in the *Democratic Review* 17 (July–August 1845): 5–10. His later, more famous expression of the concept of Manifest Destiny appeared as an editorial in the New York *Morning News*, December 27, 1845. For more on Manifest Destiny see Hietala, *Manifest Design*; David M. Pletcher, *The Diplomacy of Annexation: Texas, Oregon, and the Mexican War* (Columbia: University of Missouri Press, 1973); Robert W. Johannsen, "The Meaning of Manifest Destiny," in *Manifest Destiny and Empire: Antebellum American Expansionism*, eds. Sam W. Haynes and Christopher Morris (College Station: Texas A & M University Press, 1997), 7–20; and Julius Pratt, "The Ideology of American Expansion," in *Essays in Honor of William E. Dodd: By His Former Students at the University of Chicago*, ed. Avery Craven (Chicago: University of Chicago Press, 1935), 335–53. Pratt is also the author of two other useful articles, "The Origin of Manifest Destiny," *American Historical Review* 32 (July 1927): 795–98 and "John L. O'Sullivan and Manifest Destiny," *New York History* 14 (July 1933): 213–34. Frederick Jackson Turner, "The Significance of the Frontier in American History" (1893), in *The Frontier in American History* (New York: Henry Holt and Co., 1920), 1–38.

14. Dorothy Ross, "Historical Consciousness in Nineteenth-Century America," *American Historical Review* 89 (October 1984): 909–28.

15. For a good coverage of the American debate over the war with Mexico including Lincoln's "Spot Resolutions," see chapter ten "Conquest and Controversy, 1846–1850," in *Westward Expansion: A History of the American Frontier*, 6th ed., eds. Ray Allen Billington and Martin Ridge (an abridgement) (Albuquerque: University of New Mexico Press, 2001), 215–36, especially 220–21.

16. Hietala, *Manifest Design,* 173.

17. Francis Parkman, *The Oregon Trail: Sketches of Prairie and Rocky-Mountain Life* (Boston: Little, 1872; orig. pub. 1849); Theodore Roosevelt, *The Winning of the*

West, 4 vols. (New York and London: G. P. Putnam's Sons, 1889–1896). Turner's essays were collected in *The Frontier in American History*.

18. Among the more notable New Western History critics of Turner's frontier thesis are Limerick's "Introduction: Opening the Frontier and Closing Western History," in *The Legacy of Conquest*, and various essays by Limerick, Richard White, Donald Worster, and others in *Trails: Toward a New Western History*, eds. Patricia, Nelson Limerick, Clyde Milner, II, and Charles Rankin (Lawrence: University Press of Kansas, 1991).

19. The leading New Western historians, Limerick, White, and Worster, all viewed the West within a broader context of imperialism. The titles of Limerick's *The Legacy of Conquest* and Worster's *Rivers of Empire: Water, Aridity, and the Growth of American West* (New York: Oxford University Press, 1985) speak to a comparative global contextualization. Richard White's seminal textbook, *It's Your Misfortune and None of My Own: A New History of the American West* (Norman: University of Oklahoma Press, 1991), also parallels American empire building in the West with the efforts of other empires around the globe.

20. Hector St. John de Crèvecoeur, *Letters from an American Farmer* (New York: Fox, Duffield, 1904; orig. pub. 1782), 41, 43–44.

21. Alexis de Tocqueville, *Democracy in America*, Henry Reeve text as revised by Francis Bower, ed. Phillips Bradley, 2 vols. (New York: Macmillan, 1945); James Bryce, *The American Commonwealth*, 2 vols. (New York: Macmillan, 1893–95).

22. See Jennifer Pitts' "Introduction" in Alexis de Tocqueville, *Writings on Empire and Slavery*, trans. and ed. Jennifer Pitts (Baltimore, Md.: Johns Hopkins University Press, 2001), ix–xxxxviii, especially xxi. The pertinent Tocqueville writings in the volume are: "Essay on Algeria" (October 1841), 59–116, "First Report on Algeria" (1847), 129–73, and "Second Report on Algeria" (1847), 174–98.

23. I refer here to the broad concept of westward expansion and to Ray Allen Billington's textbook, *Westward Expansion: A History of the American Frontier* (New York: Macmillan and Co.), which first appeared in 1949 and has played an influential role in sustaining the notion that the story of the West is the story of white westward movement into the West.

24. An example of this placement of the West within the wider world in the genre of travel writing can be found in *The Western Journal, and Civilian*, published in St. Louis. In vol. 11 of this publication, subscribers could read about "Aubrey's Journey from California to New Mexico" (no. 1, October 1853, 84–96), a fast-paced, blood-filled, and highly questionable account of white endurance against Indian attacks and, just a few months later, could read Man Butler's "Exploration of the River Amazon: A Sketch from Lieutenant Herndon's Travels," a U.S.-government-sponsored expedition to the Amazon that began in May 1851 (no. 5, February 1854, 342–49).

25. Sarah Bird Wright, "Harriet Beecher Stowe (1811–1896)," *Dictionary of Literary Biography, vol. 189: American Travel Writers, 1850–1915*, eds. Donald Ross and James J. Schramer (Detroit, Mich.: Gale Research, 1998), 305–20, 307; hereafter referred to as *DLB*. Mary Suzanne Shriber notes that 1,765 books of travel were published in the United States between 1830 and 1900; see her *Writing Home: American Women Abroad, 1830–1920* (Charlottesville: University of Virginia Press, 1997), 2. Lynne Withey, in *Grand Tours and Cook's Tours: A History of Leisure Travel, 1750–1915* (New York: William Morrow and Co., 1997), 234, notes that at least 1,044 travel books about the Middle East were published in the nineteenth century. Max Berger in *The British Traveller in America, 1836–1860* (New York: Columbia University Press, 1943), 14, notes that 230 accounts by British travelers to America were published between 1836 and 1860.

26. Later in the century, in 1888, *National Geographic Magazine* first appeared to satiate the public's hunger for knowledge about far-flung places.

27. Mary K. Edmonds, "Paul Belloni Du Chaillu (1831?–1903)," in *DLB vol. 189*, 109–31.

28. Jeffrey Alan Melton, "Samuel Langhorne Clemens (Mark Twain), 1835–1910," *DLB vol. 189*, 65–78.

29. A good introduction to these archives can be found in the various essays *Travelers on the Western Frontier*, ed. John Francis McDermott (Urbana: University of Illinois Press, 1970). See also Ray Allen Billington, *Land of Savagery, Land of Promise: The European Image of the American Frontier in the Nineteenth Century* (New York: W. W. Norton, 1981); and, most recently, Roger L. Nichols, "Western Attractions: Europeans and America," *Pacific Historical Review* 74 (2005): 1–17.

30. James Schramer and Donald Ross in their "Introduction" to *DLB, vol. 183: American Travel Writers, 1776–1864* (Detroit, Mich.: Gale Research, 1997), xxv, explain that "the basic mimetic impulse in travel writing is sociological or anthropological rather than psychological—a major difference between travel literature and the novel." Generally classified today as nonfiction, the best travel writings are far more literary than the average book of essays in the nonfiction genre but are nonetheless very different from the novel and short story traditions.

31. Barbara Brothers and Julia M. Gergits, "Introduction," *DLB, vol. 204: British Travel Writers, 1940–1997* (Detroit, Mich.: Gale Research, 1999), xv–xxi, xviii.

32. Ibid.

33. I do not mean to suggest that this particular vein of historical scholarship first began to be mined in the World War II years. We can go back all the way to the Civil War and find Henry T. Tuckerman's *America and Her Commentators: With a Critical Sketch of Travel in the United States* (New York: Charles Scribner, 1864); this seems to be the earliest secondary work available on the topic of travel writers' perceptions of America. John Graham Brooks, *As Others See Us: A Study of Progress in the United States* (New York: The Macmillan Company, 1908) appeared during the Progressive era; and Allan Nevins's *American Social History as Recorded by British Travelers* (New York: Henry Holt and Company, 1923) was published another decade and a half later.

34. Berger, *The British Traveller in America*, 5.

35. Allen Nevins, *America Through British Eyes* (New York: Oxford University Press, 1948), originally published under the title *American Social History as Recorded by British Travelers*. Oscar Handlin, *This was America: True Accounts of People and Places, Manners and Customs, as Recorded by European Travelers to the Western Shore in the Eighteenth, Nineteenth, and Twentieth Centuries* (Cambridge, Mass.: Harvard University Press, 1949).

36. Robert G. Athearn, *Westward the Briton* (New York: Charles Scribner's Sons, 1953; reprint, Lincoln: University of Nebraska Press, 1962, 1969); Thomas D. Clark, "The Great Visitation to American Democracy," *Mississippi Valley Historical Review* 44 (June 1957): 3–28. That same year also saw the publication of Earl S. Pomeroy's *In Search of the Golden West: The Tourist in Western America* (New York: Knopf, 1957), which included a commentary on the observations of travel writers as well as of tourists.

37. This post–World War II search for an American character helps explain the appearance of various works that we tend to lump together as examples of the "myth and symbol school." Henry Nash Smith's classic *Virgin Land: The American West as Symbol and Myth* (Cambridge, Mass.: Harvard University Press, 1950) and John William Ward, *Andrew Jackson: Symbol for an Age* (New York: Oxford University Press, 1955) are particularly notable examples. In the field of

American intellectual history, Henry Steele Commager's *The American Mind: An Interpretation of American Thought and Culture Since the 1880s* (New Haven, Conn.: Yale University Press, 1950) stands as the most significant example of the postwar explorations of a distinctive Americanism. Likewise, another body of works that are generally defined as "consensus history" can be understood within the context of the post–World War II effort to define the national character and include: Richard Hofstadter, *The American Political Tradition and the Men Who Made It* (New York: Knopf, 1948); Daniel Boorstin, *The Genius of American Politics* (Chicago: University of Chicago Press, 1953); David M. Potter, *People of Plenty: Economic Abundance and the American Character* (Chicago: University of Chicago Press, 1954); and Louis Hartz, *The Liberal Tradition in America: An Interpretation of American Political Thought Since the Revolution* (New York: Harcourt Brace, 1955).

38. These works were not simply paeans to a benign national distinctiveness, to be sure (Smith's *Virgin Land*, e.g., offered a highly cautionary tale), but they are all marked by their efforts to chart the sources of the nation's distinctiveness and generally emphasize the benign nature of the national character and democratic institutions. Nevins' collection *America Through British Eyes* and Handlin's *This was America* both contained a number of very critical assessments of the American character and American institutions. Clark, to offer another example, concluded his Mississippi Valley Historical Association presidential address, "The Great Visitation," 27, with criticism of American materialism and of the nation's failure to live up to its vaunted purpose as outlined in the Declaration of Independence and the Bill of Rights. Yet, characteristic of the time when it appeared, Clark carefully added that even the most "malicious comments" of some foreign travelers "have never provoked a desire [among Americans] to deny free visitation to America and its institutions" (28).

39. The Henry Reeve text of Tocqueville's *Democracy in America* was published in New York by Alfred A. Knopf in 1945, 1953, 1954, and 1956. Oxford University Press also republished the Reeve text in 1947 and 1959.

40. Tocqueville, *Democracy in America,* xxi.

41. David Spurr, *The Rhetoric of Empire: Colonial Discourse in Journalism, Travel Writing, and Imperial Administration* (Durham, N.C.: Duke University Press, 1993), 1. Spurr's book begins with a chapter titled "Surveillance: Under Western Eyes," emphasizing the privileged nature of the writer's gaze that renders her/him as an objectifier but never as an object. Subsequent chapters on "Appropriation," "Aestheticization," "Classification," "Debasement," "Negation," "Affirmation," "Insubstantialization," "Naturalization," and "Eroticization," and a final chapter titled "Resistance" leave no doubt as to where the author stands vis-à-vis the nature, purpose, and consequences of the imperialist gaze. For more on this topic, see Steve Clark, ed., *Travel Writing and Empire: Postcolonial Theory in Transit* (London: Zed Books, 1999).

42. Ibid., 4.

43. Edward W. Said, *Culture and Imperialism* (New York: Vintage Books, 1994; orig. pub. New York: Alfred A. Knopf, 1993), xxi. David Cannadine offers a different perspective on the British empire and the ways in which it was perceived. He argues that "pace Edward Said and his 'Orientalist' followers, the British Empire was not exclusively (or even preponderantly) concerned with the creation of 'otherness' on the presumption that the imperial periphery was different from, and inferior to, the imperial metropolis: it was at least as much (perhaps more?) concerned with what has recently been called the 'construction of affinities' on the presumption that society on the periphery was the same as, or even on occasions superior to, society in the metropolis," *Ornamentalism: How the British Saw Their Empire* (New York: Oxford University Press, 2001), xix.

44. Ibid., 99.
45. Homi K. Bhabha, *The Location of Culture* (New York: Routledge, 1994), 70.
46. Ibid., 112.
47. Mary Louise Pratt, *Travel Writing and Transculturation* (London and New York: Routledge, 1992), 2, 4, 5, 201, 205–206. See also Inderpal Grewal, *Home and Harem: Nation, Gender, Empire, and the Cultures of Travel* (Durham, N.C.: Duke University Press, 1996).
48. For more information on the ways of viewing the "traveled upon," see Leah Dilworth, "Tourists and Indians in Fred Harvey's Southwest," Sylvia Rodriguez, "Tourism, Whiteness and the Vanishing Anglo," and David M. Wrobel, "Introduction: Tourists, Tourism, and the Toured Upon," in *Seeing and Being Seen: Tourism in the American West*, eds. David M. Wrobel and Patrick T. Long (Lawrence: University Press of Kansas, 2001), 1–34, 142–64, and 194–210, respectively.
49. There does seem to be a new generation of scholarship emerging, a kind of post postcolonialism that moves us beyond the easy assumptions concerning the imperialist gaze. An excellent example is Maya Jasanoff's *Edge of Empire: Lives, Culture, and Conquest in the East, 1750–1850* (New York: Alfred A. Knopf, 2005).
50. George Catlin, *Catalogue of Catlin's Indian Gallery of Portraits, Landscapes, Manners and Customs, Costumes, & c.... Collected During Seven Years' Travel Amongst Thirty-Eight Different Tribes, Speaking Different Languages* (New York: Piercy and Reed, 1837), and *Catlin's North American Indian Portfolio: Hunting Scenes and Amusements of the Rocky Mountains and Prairies of America/From Drawings and Notes of the Author, Made During Eight Years' Travel Amongst Forty-Eight of the Wildest and Most Remote Tribes of Savages in North America* (London: George Catlin, 1844; New York: James Ackerman, 1845).
51. See, e.g., the review of Catlin's exhibit from the *East India Chronicle*, reprinted in George Catlin, *Adventures of the Ojibbeway and Ioway Indians, in England, France, and Belgium; Being Notes of Eight Years Residence in Europe With the North American Indian Collection*, vol. 1, 3d ed. (London: George Catlin, 1852), 216. The book was originally published under the title *Catlin's Notes of Eight Years' Travels and Residence in Europe, With His North American Indian Collection. With Anecdotes and Incidents of the Travels and Adventures of Three Different Parties of American Indians Whom He Introduced to the Courts of England, France, and Belgium* (London: George Catlin, 1848).
52. The coverage here draws on Paul Reddin's excellent account, "Trembling Excitements and Fears: Catlin and the Show Abroad," in his *Wild West Shows* (Urbana and Chicago: University of Illinois Press, 1999), 27–52, quotations on 29–30.
53. A number of these broadsides are included in the George Catlin Collection, Frederick W. Beinecke Rare Book and Manuscript Library, Yale University.
54. Catlin was presenting an interesting, albeit not particularly new reversal of the standard travel narrative form in which white travelers comment on their experience among peoples of color. Voltaire and other French enlightenment thinkers had, nearly a century earlier, used the Indian travel narrative as a vehicle for illuminating the irrationality of Europeans.
55. Catlin, *Adventures of the Ojibbeway and Ioway Indians*, 1: 129–30.
56. King Louis Philippe abdicated the throne in 1848 and died in England in 1850. The French conquest of Algeria took place during his rule and that of his predecessor Charles X.
57. Catlin's wife, Clara, died in 1845 and his only son, Goergie, died the next year. Reddin's *Wild West Shows* covers these Catlin family deaths and the Indian deaths in excellent detail, 45–51.
58. Volume 1 is available as an electronic book and volume 2 is available as a paperback (Scituate, Mass.: Digital Scanning, Inc., 2001).

59. Ibid., 1: 61–62. Reddin provides coverage of the "Museum of Mankind" in *Wild West Shows*, 48.

60. Friedrich Gerstäcker may be best known to historians of the California Gold Rush as the author of a very handsome volume, *California Gold Mines* (Oakland, Calif.: Biobooks, 1946). The book serves as a good example of how the West has literally been taken out of the world in the public memory of the Gold Rush. *California Gold Mines* radically abridged *Narrative of a Journey Round the World*. Gerstäcker's *Narrative of a Journey Around the World*...also appeared the next year in an abridged British edition, *Gerstäcker's Travels: Rio de Janeiro, Buenos Ayres, Ride Through the Pampas, Winter Journey Across the Cordilleras, Chile, Valparaiso, California and the Gold Fields*, trans. Friedrich Gerstäcker (London: T. Nelson and Sons, 1854).

61. Jeffrey Sammons, "Friedrich Gerstäcker," in *DLB, vol. 129: Nineteenth-Century German Writers, 1841–1900*, eds. Siegfried Mews and James Hardin (Detroit, Mich.: Gale Research, 1993), 110–19, notes that this trip was financed in part by a small grant from Germany's provisional government and Gerstäcker later claimed to be the only person to have ever benefited from that government.

62. Howard R. Lamar in his "Foreword" to J.S. Holliday, *The World Rushed In: The California Gold Rush Experience* (Norman: University of Oklahoma Press, 2002, orig. pub. Simon and Schuster, 1981), xii, points to this global context. Holliday is certainly well aware of the world context surrounding the California Gold Rush but chooses to focus on the American overlanders. For more on maritime journeys to the goldfields, see Charles R. Schultz, *Forty-Niners "Round the Horn"* (Columbia: University of South Carolina Press, 1999).

63. Gerstäcker's life, marked by its alternating periods of writing and wanderlust, is strangely reminiscent of Theodore Roosevelt's, which is marked by its segmented periods of public service and adventuring. For excellent overviews of Gerstäcker's travels, see Sammons, *DLB, vol. 129*; his fuller coverage in *Ideology, Mimesis, Fantasy: Charles Seals.eld, Friedrich Gerstäcker, Karl May, and Other German Novelists of America* (Chapel Hill: The University of North Carolina Press, 1998), 113–200; and "Friedrich Gerstäcker: American Realities Through German Eyes," in his *Imagination and History: Selected Papers on Nineteenth-Century German Literature* (New York: Peter Lang, 1988), 249–63.

64. Erwin G. Gudde writes that Gerstäcker was "known throughout the Western world," in "Friedrich Gerstaecker: World Traveller and Author, 1816–1872," *Journal of the West* 7 (July 1968): 345–50.

65. These popular stories were fictions based on real familiarity with the settings—which places them well above the work of the average dime novelist.

66. Gerstäcker, *Gerstäcker's Travels*, 231–33. The story of the Bombay Indian is also told at somewhat greater length in the American edition of the book, *Narrative of a Journey Round the World, Comprising a Winter Passage Across the Andes to Chili, With a Visit to the Gold Regions of California and Australia, the South Sea Islands, Java, &c* (New York: Harper and Brothers, 1853), 214–17. The American edition, as the title suggests, includes coverage of the whole of Gerstäcker's trip.

67. Ibid., 214.

68. See, e.g., Richard Brantlinger, *Dark Vanishings: The Discourse on the Extinction of Primitive Peoples, 1800–1930* (Ithaca, N.Y.: Cornell University Press, 2003).

69. *The American West*, 249–50. Hine and Faragher.

70. Hine and Faragher in ibid., 249, refer to the campaign against the California Indians as the clearest case of genocide in the history of the American frontier. See also George Harwood Phillips, *Indians and Indian Agents: The Origins of the Reservation System in California, 1849–1852* (Norman: University of Oklahoma

Press, 1997), 167, and Benjamin Madley, "The Yuki of California and the Question of Genocide in America," unpublished paper.

71. Gerstäcker, *Narrative of a Journey Round the World*, 216.

72. Ibid., 395, 409, and 473.

73. In addition to the indigenous population decline that accompanied the gold rushes in both California and Australia, both places saw anti-Chinese rioting by white prospectors. Furthermore, in both the United States (with California leading the way) and Australia, restrictive immigration legislation in the late nineteenth century barred Asian immigrants. The White Australia policy of 1888 remained intact until the 1970s and in the United States, the Chinese Immigration Act of 1882 (renewed in 1892 and made permanent in 1924) was not overturned until the Hart–Cellar Immigration Act of 1964.

74. Brantlinger in *Dark Vanishings* offers a quite extensive treatment of the discourse on extinction and argues quite compellingly that the language of inevitable extinction, the "ghosting of the primitive," amounted to a kind of "self-fulfilling prophesy," thereby contributing to the broader acceptance of these "dark vanishings" in western culture. However, within the broad discourse on extinction there existed a very wide range of positions—from the forceful advocacy of extermination of indigenous people to the stinging critiques of governments that allowed genocidal acts to take place. Brantlinger lumps these highly divergent, indeed antithetical, positions together into a single category—"extinction discourse"—which fails to distinguish advocates from critics. For a fuller treatment of the topic as it relates to American Indians, see Brian Dippie, *The Vanishing American: White Attitudes and U.S. Indian Policy* (Lawrence: University Press of Kansas, 1991, 1982) and Billington, *Land of Savagery, Land of Promise*, 129–49.

75. Gerstäcker, *Narrative of a Journey Round the World*, 569–70.

76. The five parts of the book cover South America, California, the Hawaiian Islands, Australia, and Java.

77. See Eric Sterling, "George Catlin," in *DLB vol. 189*, 55–64.

78. See Dippie, *The Vanishing American*, 27.

79. Renato Rosaldo, "Imperialist Nostalgia," *Representations* 26 (1989): 107–22. The cynic might, of course, argue that Catlin, through his displaying of Indians and his pervasive evidence of their vanishing, was complicit in their destruction (though such arguments do rather undercut the role of Indian agency in these cultural displays). Nonetheless, Catlin's vociferous critique of his nation's Indian removal policy was clearly motivated more by anger over what was being done to Indians rather than by nostalgia for what was past.

5

Class War? Class Struggles during the American Revolution in Virginia

Michael A. McDonnell

After an extraordinary debate, even for an extraordinary time, legislators in the Virginia General Assembly in the fall of 1780 came up with a startling offer to needy whites in the state. For joining the Continental army, new recruits were promised not only a parcel of land large enough to enfranchise them but also an enslaved Virginian as an extra bounty. Yet this controversial offer was merely a compromise solution to conceal a more profound debate in the legislature that fall. Desperate for soldiers amid a series of British invasions, the Virginia legislature initially debated even more radical plans to redistribute property from the most wealthy in the state to the poorest in return for military service. Many legislators argued that the wealthiest slaveholders in particular, who generally had not fought in the war, ought to give up a larger share of their slaves to those who had.

Though many commentators, starting with James Madison, have remarked on the perverse logic of rewarding soldiers fighting for so-called liberty with enslaved Virginians, few have taken note of the full contours of the revealing debate that fall. In discussing this legislation, most delegates to the assembly seemed more concerned about class and labor issues and not quite so much about race and slavery as modern historians might expect. Legislators seemed to think that the only way to make military service attractive to potential recruits was to offer enslaved Virginians to nonslaveholding lower-class whites. Joseph Jones told Madison that the "Negro bounty cannot fail to procure Men for the War." On the other end of the social spectrum, Jones thought that though the "scheme bears

From the *William and Mary Quarterly* 63 (April, 2006) 305–44.

hard upon those wealthy in Negros," in the present political climate any opposition from wealthy slaveholders would come to naught. Jones told Madison: "You know a great part of our House are not of that Class or own so few of them as not to come within the Law shd. it pass." Indeed one representative from the western county of Botetourt, Thomas Madison, believed that the legislature introduced this scheme precisely because they wanted to make the wealthy pay their share of the war. Finally, the one major reason legislators did not do as James Madison and several others suggested and arm enslaved Virginians, Jones asserted, was because such a move would "draw off immediately such a number of the best labourers for the Culture of the Earth as to ruin individuals." What enslaved Virginians produced by their labor, Jones claimed, was "but barely sufficient to keep us joging along with the great expence of the war." Jones, though a supporter of eventual freedom for blacks, argued that it had to be done gradually so planters could find replacement laborers, "or we shall suffer exceedingly under the sudden revolution which perhaps arming them wod. produce."[1]

But if Jones worried about a revolution in labor practices, another wealthy Virginian, Theodorick Bland, was angry about a different kind of revolution he felt was brewing from below. Increasingly frustrated by Virginia's inability to defend itself in the face of repeated British invasions, Bland watched helplessly as his neighbors refused to turn out for military service and rioted against attempts to draft them into the army as his own enslaved population grew more restive. In addition to these challenges from below, Bland was also feeling the pinch of high progressive taxes laid by the legislature to pay for increasing bounties for soldiers. Bland worried that the elected legislators who supported middle-class demands for redistributive taxes—whether in slaves or any other kind of property—to pay higher bounties to lower-class soldiers were "enemies to America, or fools or knaves, or all three." He feared their actions might "bring on a revolution in this state," a consequence that he thought was actually the "wish of a majority of the assembly."[2]

What are historians to make of this revealing debate and recurring expressions of what seem to have been class divisions in a white society generally depicted as united in its opposition to Britain and in its shared social interests and coherent culture? Several interrelated issues seem to stand in the way of understanding this puzzle. Scholars have, perhaps understandably, focused a great deal of attention on race and slavery in Virginia. Most historians have, in a metaphorical sense, followed James Madison's cue and wondered about the contradictions inherent in a slaveholding society amid a war for supposed liberty. And in thinking about this paradox, historians are still under the influence of Edmund Morgan's powerful argument that the need for racial unity smoothed over class divisions in Virginia and created a shared commitment to racial slavery, which was the basis of a cohesive white culture in the eighteenth century. Moreover, whereas the imperatives of maintaining that system meant that elite literate Virginians were always reluctant to "air their dirty linen," as one scholar has put it,

Morgan's persuasive argument has also meant that historians have seldom looked for divisions among whites and have not been sure what to do with, or how much weight to give to, comments such as those of Theodorick Bland when they have found them. Scholars have been too quick to accept elites' self-reassuring rhetoric about the apparent unity and harmony of the state, especially during times of stress.[3]

In an important sense, then, Morgan's thesis has helped promote a powerful image that has obscured more than it was supposed to reveal: a general image of eighteenth-century Virginia as a slave society, one divided only by masters and slaves. There is, in this image, little room for serious economic inequalities, little room for those discontented others that have been found stirring up trouble elsewhere in the early modern world: the urban poor of London, Boston, or Philadelphia, for example, or the rural and recently dispossessed laborers and tenants of the Peak District, the newly opened mines of South Wales, or even the great manors of New York.[4] In Virginia the apparent absence or insignificance of such groups, combined with the shadow of slavery, has obscured any attempts to uncover nonracial divisions within the colony.

Despite popular images of Virginia as a slave society, divided between white planters and enslaved blacks, Virginia was a more complicated place.[5] Enslaved Virginians formed only the bottom of a hierarchical edifice that included male and female convicts and indentured servants, apprentices, free wage laborers and overseers, tenant farmers and nonslaveholding smallholders, slaveholding and nonslaveholding yeoman farmers and substantial slaveholding planters, and, finally, local and cosmopolitan elites who often held hundreds of Africans in bondage and owned thousands of acres of land throughout the colony. Moreover, even within some of these apparently monolithic social blocks, many, sometimes overlapping, layers of differences helped complicate social relations within and between different classes of Virginians. Ultimately, as any self-respecting gentleman, tenant farmer, or enslaved Virginian would know, this was a deeply divided and carefully defined hierarchical society in which social and economic inequalities were on conspicuous display.[6]

Scholarship has begun to delineate these divisions, yet it still seems difficult to talk about class in early modern Virginia. If a simplified black-and-white view of Virginia's social structure has often obscured the multilayered hierarchical complexity of the colony, a more general tendency to divide colonial society between dependents and independents has given rise to what seems to be one of the biggest challenges to a class analysis of the revolutionary era: the existence of a proportionally large group of landowning middling sorts. Most critics of the concept of class and its applicability to early American studies point to the size and growth of a group of people who were neither patricians nor plebeians, or among either the few or the many, but rather were independent farmers, merchants, and artisans.[7] Even if historians ignore the large number of landless whites in Virginia (to say nothing of enslaved Virginians), including servants, laborers, and tenants, they still have to acknowledge that a majority of white men in Virginia owned and farmed land; that is, they owned the means of production. But does that mean that Virginia landholders—the bulk of the people, the middling sort—somehow, as theorists, historians, and the public alike seem to assume, "lay outside the framework of class"?[8]

This large group of property holders seems to frustrate class analysis according to a long-standing theoretical and historiographical tradition, starting with Karl Marx and articulated most forcefully by E.P. Thompson, which has generally associated class with a particular kind of space (industrial, semi-industrial, waged work), period (late eighteenth and early nineteenth century), and political activism (horizontal consciousness and a self-aware articulation of alternative social and political visions, often at a national level). The history of class formation, too, centered on the working class and the rise of the proletariat: "the economic and political transformation during which artisans and small farmers lost control of their skills and land and were increasingly required to sell their labor for wages in the market." Given these associations, scholars should not be surprised if this kind of class was not present in other spaces, times, and forms. Eighteenth-century Virginia, for one, does not seem to fit this model of class, class consciousness, and class struggle. Where do landholding planters and farmers, great and small, fit?[9]

Yet if Thompson's earlier work seemed to create a barrier to thinking about class in other contexts, his later thoughts on the subject give historians the insights needed to demolish it. In a 1978 essay, for example, Thompson talked about class as a much more fluid historical category, one "derived from the observation of social process over time." And classes, at least before the nineteenth century, did not really exist outside the struggles that, in effect, helped define them. There are no simple equations, forms, or models, Thompson notes, because "class eventuates as men and women *live* their productive relations, and as they *experience* their determinate situations, within 'the *ensemble* of the social relations,' with their inherited culture and expectations, and as they handle these experiences in cultural ways."[10] Class, then, is a process, not a set of predetermined categories, and particular sorts of relations may or may not be based on people's relationships to the means of production, but they are at the very least based on material circumstances and economic inequalities and, as in the case of eighteenth-century Virginia, are interconnected with and shaped by other factors such as race and gender. Defined this way class can be used as a means to examine and interrogate relations between social groups, particularly where economic inequalities were marked.[11]

A more fluid definition of class and class struggles, then, frees historians to examine afresh the kinds of struggles and divisions that seemed to plague Virginia during the Revolutionary War. Indeed work that takes this broader view of class has already forced scholars to think anew. Woody Holton, among others, has persuasively argued that even the coming of the American Revolution was very much a product of class conflict, and in Virginia, no less. Yet class as a tool of historical analysis might be even more useful in studying the war itself, given the economic strains and demands it imposed on different social groups. Concerned elites began mobilizing for war in a manner that reflected a highly articulated class-based vision of society and their anxieties over the effects of possible war on the enslaved class (i.e., anxieties to secure their property). But a careful reading of mobilization in the state reveals that white Virginians constantly fought among themselves about who ought to serve and on what terms: conflicts that usually manifested themselves as riots against conscription, resistance to militia callouts, threats of civil disobedience, and even legislative turnover as enfranchised white Virginians took their grievances to the polls. In the end the demands made of various groups during the war forced people from different socioeconomic backgrounds to defend their interests individually, and then often collectively, sometimes coalescing as distinct classes to protect those interests and what they perceived, at times, as their rights. If these different groups were not conscious before the war of their collective interests as classes, in relation to one another, the revolutionary conflict certainly helped make those common interests much clearer.[12]

Ultimately, too, by looking at these contests, historians might better understand why Bland believed that Virginia was on the brink of real revolution. And scholars might also complicate and enrich Morgan's findings about the interrelationship between race, class, and slavery—because race and slavery played a part in the Revolutionary War, though not quite in the way scholars expected. Rebellious enslaved Virginians, for example, helped encourage the British to focus their attention on Virginia at various times throughout the war. Yet in the face of threats from within and without, whites did not unite and rally to the cause; instead, slavery helped to cripple mobilization and divide whites in diverse ways. Throughout the war lower- and middling-class white Virginians did not hesitate to organize collective and sometimes violent resistance to ruling-class measures. Slavery was therefore central to the Revolutionary War in Virginia, but in helping to divide whites, not unite them. Such divisions forced patriot leaders in the new state to finally think about some revolutionary proposals of their own.[13]

When patriot leaders in Virginia turned to the serious business of preparing for war in 1775, their initial proposals reflected a colonial military tradition based on an idea of a white society divided into three orders: gentlemen, the middling sort, and the lower sort.[14] To try to simultaneously rouse popular enthusiasm for the cause and provide for an effective defense, they designed a hierarchy of armed services: they created sixteen battalions of better trained and disciplined elite militia called the minutemen (designed to replace the "independant companies of gentlemen Volunteers"); they resurrected the regular militia (in which all free whites were expected to serve); and they established two regiments of regular troops who would serve as the Virginia contingent of the newly created Continental army. In creating a hierarchical military organization, patriot leaders in Virginia were gearing up for what was possibly the biggest confrontation they would ever face; they were also following a specific colonial tradition. Virginians had to worry about not only the might of the British army and navy but also the numerous threats from within. The most significant of these challenges came from their own slaves. Enslaved Virginians had panicked white Virginians on several occasions during previous wars. Blacks knew that war among whites presented opportunities for freedom. The imperial dispute only gave black Virginians further hope. Anxious patriot leaders knew that they were vulnerable should war come.[15]

Given the circumstances, most patriot leaders in Virginia wanted to send a clear and forceful message to enslaved Virginians contemplating insurrection or joining Governor Dunmore. They hoped that a semipermanent regular force combined with a reinvigorated militia and an elite group of minutemen would offer a sufficient internal as well as external line of defense. Just to be sure, though, delegates to the revolutionary convention also empowered commanding officers to appoint patrollers from among the militia as needed. Moreover, to try to smother the embers of black rebelliousness before they could ignite, the convention exempted all overseers of four tithables residing on a plantation from any militia service.[16]

In the initial flurry of enthusiasm for war, there should have been little difference between these services. But gentlemen themselves drew the first distinctions. George Mason, the chief architect of the military plan, gave strict instructions to his own son to join only the minuteman service. It was, he explained, "the true natural, and safest Defence of this, or any other free Country" and, as he told George Washington, would be composed of men "in whose Hands the Sword may be safely trusted." Another prominent patriot, George Gilmer, hoped the new minuteman plan would be "on such footing as essentially to draw in Gent'n of the first property in the Colony" and immediately signed up. In contrast, drawing on the rhetoric of anti-standing army ideology, Mason instructed a friend to tell his son that it was "very contrary to my Inclination" that he should enter into the regular service, and he was "by all Means against it." Mason wanted to encourage the success of the minuteman service, yet he also reflected the common belief and inherited Anglo-American tradition that only the dregs of society would serve in a professional army.[17]

Such attitudes did not bode well for the success of the new military arrangements. Initial mobilization for war exposed preexisting tensions and divisions among white Virginians. Many poorer or smallholding militia members particularly resented the exemptions allowed from the militia, for example. They believed the exemption of overseers shielded wealthier slave owners from military service at the expense of nonslaveholders. Several hundred militia, mainly from the southside, complained about the exemption in petitions sent to the same revolutionary convention that was to decide on independence. Because the law stipulated that a planter could exempt one overseer for every four enslaved Virginians, the petitioners believed that many wealthy planters had "become Overseers that Otherways would not, on purpose to Screen themselves from Fighting in defence of their Country as well as their own Property." Not only were most of them "Strong healthy able bodied Men" but also "many of them [were] possessed of Considerable Property in Lands and Slaves." Class differences were clearly at the forefront of such gendered complaints, and the petitioners did not hesitate to make these explicit. "Many of your Petitioners are poor men with Families that are Incapable of Supporting themselves without our Labour & assistance," they insisted. It was therefore "extreamly hard & no ways equatable or Just that we should be obliged to leave our Families in such a Situation that if ever we shou'd return again [we] Woud find our Wives & Children dispers'd up & down the Country abeging, or at home aStarving." Whereas the "Overseers are aliving in ease & Affluence," they complained, the petitioners forced to do military duty away from home would be "quite unable to help" their families procure "the Necessaries of life."[18]

Nor did white Virginians flock to the minuteman service. Enlistments were hampered by elites' own admission that gentlemen were not signing up in the numbers expected. Those who joined generally procured commissions as appointed officers in the minute service and were usually appointed by friends and family on presiding county committees. Smallholding farmers were loathe to spend more time than necessary in training and also were galled that appointed officers in the corps—usually gentlemen—were paid up to sixty times more than an enlisted man when they were training or on duty. Patriot leaders and officers had called for such a wide pay disparity to enforce discipline and subordination among the rank and file. But middling white Virginians, living amid a slave society, were hardly reconciled to the idea of subordination. Gilmer, in trying to rally his neighbors to join the minutemen, inadvertently pointed out the problem by using a metaphor that must have infuriated his neighbors. Since "time immemorial," he declared, "every head or chief has had marks of distinction and certain emoluments above those under him...The Custom is so prevalent with ourselves," he pointed out, "that every planter allows his Gang leader certain indulgences and emoluments above the rest of his slaves." In comparing the new military establishment with the institution of slavery in Virginia, Gilmer in one breath infuriated his neighbors and betrayed the anxieties that many prominent planters felt about the lack of control they had over their enslaved workers and their white inferiors.[19]

Incredibly, protests about the newly resurrected militia and faltering enlistments in the minuteman service came during the crisis that Virginia Governor Dunmore had unleashed with his well-known proclamation of November 1775, declaring all servants and enslaved people belonging to patriot masters free if they would join him in fighting their traitorous masters. Such problems showed that when racial solidarity was most essential, white Virginians had difficulty surmounting class differences. It might have seemed worse to patriot leaders that Dunmore's proclamation had given rise to reports throughout the colony detailing black and white cooperation in defiance of patriot authority. At Isaac Zane's Marlborough Iron Works in Frederick County, white convict servants and enslaved black workers banded together to escape to the British. In Fincastle County in the southwestern corner of Virginia, John Hiell tried to stir up cooperation between white servants and slaves after Dunmore's proclamation. Hiell told "a Servant man" that in about a month "he and all the negroes would get their Freedom." And on Virginia's Eastern Shore, patriot leaders worried that Dunmore's plans to unite "fishermen...all the lower Class of People," and a large enslaved population against the "Committee-Men and other principal People" had worked. They feared that without protection, they would be "exposed to the fury of the People."[20]

Despite such apparent threats from below, middle-class militia showed little inclination to lay aside their own interests for the sake of protecting gentlemen who seemed little inclined to protect themselves. Even something so basic as slave patrols raised class tensions in the early years of the war. In the April 1776 elections to vote for independence, Landon Carter was disgusted to hear that one man was elected after he had exclaimed "agst the Patrolling law, because a poor man was made to pay for keeping a rich mans Slaves in order." Middling and lower-class white Virginians resented the renewed power militia officers had to force them into serving as patrollers. Such reports fueled Carter's anxiety that the coming of independence would mean a heightening of class tensions. Others expressed similar fears in revealing language. One of Carter's neighbors, Walter Jones, described the electoral politics of late 1775 as a form of "plebeian Infamy." And an officer from Loudoun County, worried about a tenant uprising in that region that had been sparked by military mobilization in the early months of 1776, used the language of the English Revolution when he asked a colleague: "How goes on the spirit of Levelling? Is all quiet?" It was with some relief, then, that patriot leaders formed a new state government in the summer of 1776 and, shortly afterward, watched the dreaded Dunmore sail out of the Chesapeake toward New York.[21]

Resistance to these early mobilization efforts, and particularly the minuteman service—which actually suited Virginia's dispersed and vulnerable settlement patterns—forced patriot leaders to rely almost entirely on an enlarged regular force. By the end of 1776, they had completely scrapped the minuteman service and called for a much larger group of regular soldiers that would serve as a permanent wartime professional army for the protection of the state. To entice recruits they relied less and less on enthusiasm for the cause and more on offers and promises, often unfulfilled, of increasingly generous enlistment bounties and regular pay. Though it was not initially clear, the fledgling state had fallen back on a transatlantic tradition of targeting the unemployed, wage laborers, and the landless poor to fight the wars of the ruling government.

The full class-based contours of elites' military policy became clearer as the demand for soldiers increased. Though few explicitly stated it, most people believed that only the poor and the marginal would or should join the Continental army. New laws exposed and encouraged this general impression. Struggling to raise men for the new Continental regiments demanded by George Washington and Congress at the end of 1776, the new state government passed a law authorizing impressment of the increasing number of "rogues and vagabonds" that they believed besieged the state. The assembly gave justices of the peace and the governor wide powers to imprison and ultimately impress such people into the armed services. The representatives also defined vagabonds quite broadly as any able-bodied men who neglected or refused to pay their public county and parish levies and who had no visible estate. By accepting the very lowest classes, army recruiters also helped to reinforce a general impression that the Continental army was, like the British army, full of the dregs of society. In 1775 the convention had forbidden recruiters to enlist any servants at all, unless they were apprentices who had the written consent of their masters. Yet desperation drove recruiters to enlist anyone that seemed willing to serve. Indentured and convict servants took full advantage.[22]

So, too, did enslaved Virginians. The 1775 prohibition against enlisting servants also applied to them. At some point between late 1775 and early 1777, however, desperate recruiters began allowing at least free blacks into the Virginia line, leading many enslaved Virginians to present themselves to recruiters as freemen. Recruiting officers, desperate to fulfill their quotas of soldiers to gain commissions, were quick to turn a blind eye to such subterfuges and happily accepted black Virginians, free and unfree. The presence of the lowest classes of Virginians—servants and slaves—in the army only reinforced an impression that it was no place for respectable middling sorts, let alone gentlemen, unless in a position of authority.[23]

As General Washington's fortunes around New York went from bad to worse during the winter of 1776–77, he and Congress put considerable pressure on the states to coerce more citizens into the army. Attitudes about who should serve became more explicit as the demand for soldiers increased. Virginians at the continental level, at least, were clear about who ought to be targeted. Richard Henry Lee, a Virginia congressional delegate, told Thomas Jefferson that there were too many "lazy, worthless young Men" in the state who ought to be forced into service. Washington was more explicit about who ultimately ought to fill the ranks of the army, whatever method they chose to employ. The general felt that the army could only be filled with "the lower Class of People." Though he had hoped they could hold out sufficient inducements for the lower sort to enlist voluntarily, Washington believed that they could not now avoid the "necessity of compelling them to inlist."[24]

The Virginia General Assembly complied with the request, instituting a draft in the spring of 1777. But contrary to suggestions made by Washington and Congress to draft men indiscriminately and allow conscripts a chance to find substitutes, the assembly chose specifically to target the more vulnerable in society. Draftees would not be picked by open lottery but rather picked out by field officers and the four most senior magistrates of each county. If volunteers were not forthcoming, these officials were given the power to "fix upon and draught one man" who, in their opinion, could "be best spared, and will be most serviceable." The new recruits, or picked conscripts, were to serve for a full three years. As one recruiting officer put it later in the year, the draft was designed to force the "expendables" into service or, more explicitly, according to John Chilton, the "Lazy fellows who lurk about and are pests to Society."[25]

If patriot leaders and middling Virginians were content to shift the burden of fighting, the lower sort on whom that burden fell were quick to fight back. Would-be recruits forced patriots to raise bounty money, bargained with their neighbors for their services as substitutes in the militia, and resisted and evaded the draft when coerced into service. In some places they violently resisted any and all attempts to conscript soldiers. In other places, once drafted, they simply deserted and found refuge, usually with friends and family.[26]

Lower-class resistance was so vehement that by early 1778 Virginia legislators were forced to abandon the idea of raising men by a draft altogether and turn, instead, to high bounties and short terms of service. When the assembly made economic enticements the sole inducement to join the army in 1778 and 1779, the inflation of bounty rewards accelerated. By early 1779 Robert Honyman reported that recruiting officers were paying up to $450 more than the prescribed bounty of $300 to procure recruits. By the fall of 1779, the sums given to recruits for the army had reached critical proportions. Because of rising inflation, Edmund Pendleton thought that almost every man enlisted had cost, on average, about £5,000 each.[27]

More generally, a renewed demand for workers combined with the manpower needs of the military meant that wage earners commanded a new-found power over prospective employers. Those who labored for a living could also manipulate the recruiting laws to their own advantage. Potential recruits often found ways to capitalize on the desperation of patriot leaders to raise new troops. They took advantage of the already-generous enlistment schemes to give themselves maximum benefit and return on their risk. They took advantage of spiraling inflation, and they contributed to it. Recruits were also allowed to receive any payments that other men might give to serve in their stead. The evidence suggests that many did all they could to get as much money as possible for their desperately needed services. Even before recruiting began each year, bidding for potential soldiers helped drive up prices. Some recruiting officers had to resort to offering additional incentives to potential recruits, often out of their own pocket. One officer complained that such men had "spoilt the recruiting Service" by offering up to $50 per man. Yet officers were at the mercy of the men they were trying to recruit. Raleigh Colston, the captain of the sloop *Liberty*, learned this lesson when he tried to invoke patriotism as a good reason for his crew to take lower wages. The crew made it clear on what terms they would serve. The spokesman for the crew declared: "Country here or Country there, damn my Eyes and limbs but I'll serve them that give the best wages."[28]

Wealthier Virginians were particularly angry because they had to pay out so much, seemingly for so little. David Jameson complained that, though such exorbitant sums had been paid out to hire recruits, only a temporary and inadequate army had been raised. The bounty money recruits had received, Jameson asserted, was more than enough to secure their services for the duration of the war, instead of a mere eighteen months. He grumbled that it was really "enough for-life." Many gentlemen were furious that ordinary Virginians could and would protect their own interests. In a letter to George Washington in 1778, Pendleton complained about the demands of those he felt ought to bear the burden of military service. The "demon of avarice, and spirit of extortion," he exclaimed, "seem to have expelled the pure patriotism from the breasts of those who usually compose armies."[29]

The end result of lower-class resistance through the middle years of the war was that the war effort simply ground to a halt. Despite the pleas of continental officials, Virginia legislators failed to put teeth into their recruiting laws through the rest of 1778, 1779, and into 1780. By late May 1778, only 716 of the 8,000 men asked for the previous fall had been raised through the draft or through substitutions. Washington wrote in late May 1778 that out of the 1,500 recruits requested from the previous draft together with the 2,000 men the assembly ordered drafted in February 1778, they had only received 1,242 men. Washington lamented that this was "so horrible a deficiency." Of all the drafts and volunteers ordered raised, Patrick Henry thought that "not one half of the Number voted by the Assembly have got to Camp." One army chaplain wrote definitively, "Virginia makes the poorest figure of any State in the Recruiting way."[30]

As Virginians divided among themselves and hoped for peace, the British, believing themselves at a stalemate in the North, moved to bring the war to the South and open up a new front in the stagnating conflict. More thinly settled than the northern colonies, more vulnerable by sea, more dependent on foreign markets for imports and their exports, and arguably much more valuable to Britain than the northern colonies, the southern colonies loomed large in British thinking in late 1778 and early 1779. Moreover intelligence reports of loyalist support encouraged the British to think that they might make more progress in the southern states than they had in the northern ones. These reports, combined with the knowledge that enslaved Americans might augment British numbers, or at least keep a vulnerable people at home, encouraged the British to think they could more easily subdue the South than the North.[31] It was not until British strategy shifted southward that Virginia leaders again took the war seriously, though they only really did so after the state lost the remnants of its contingent of Continental army soldiers at the fall of Charleston in 1780. The assembly, under mounting pressure from Congress and officers such as George Washington, finally expanded their mobilization efforts. They did this by putting pressure on the middling classes: by requiring them for more extensive militia service and by reinstituting and expanding the draft, this time to include all men.

But middle-class militia members had their own agenda and, unlike their lower-class neighbors, they had the more direct political clout to force it on their elected officials in the assembly. They first demanded that calls on the militia be limited to short terms of service close to home. Most were adamant that they would not serve outside the state, particularly in what they believed to be the dangerous climate of the southern states. Yet middling militiamen were equally insistent that their taxpaying status should exempt them from fighting altogether and that the state ought to spend their tax money on raising a proper army and filling it with their lower-class neighbors. As one group of militia claimed as early as 1776, militia training was now unnecessary because Virginia had "an Army regularly trained," for which the militia were paying. Under these circumstances the militia ought to be called out only when needed to aid in defense against an invasion and ought not to be called "so frequently from their homes" unless absolutely "necessary." In arguing that the payment of taxes was sufficient sacrifice to secure protection, the militia from Chesterfield adopted a position similar to one taken by middle-class counterparts in England during the Seven Years' War.[32]

Such claims were put forth more insistently after it became clear that great sums of taxpayers' money had been spent trying to raise an army. Petitioners from Berkeley County, for example, were angry in 1780 that previous recruiting laws had increased their tax burden enormously without actually raising a more permanent army that would exempt most from frequent militia callouts and future drafts. They complained that for the money they had spent raising recruits they could have enlisted troops for the duration of the war. Distinguishing themselves from the kind of people most likely to join the army, the petitioners from Berkeley claimed that volunteers for the army were driven by profits, not patriotism. Such "Mersinary" soldiers used the laws to "make the best market of himself." Most potential recruits took note of the short enlistment periods and realized they could easily take advantage of the laws. The Berkeley militia pointed to a deepening divide between themselves and those whom they expected to do their fighting for them. They claimed that the laws gave such men the "power" and encouragement to "Fleece from the virtuous and good part of our Citizens Whatever their avaricious inclinations may prompt Them to exact."[33]

In making their case for a more permanent standing army, the militia from Berkeley succinctly articulated the views of many of their counterparts across the Atlantic. They pointed to the example of other nations, in fact "all nations and Countrys but ours," they claimed, who did not hesitate to take proper measures to keep "that Class of men, in the field as a standing army." Instead the upstanding middling-class militia members were "Haras'd" with callouts, taking them away from their families and estates. They contrasted their situation with "that Class of men" who had come to "depend upon the field [of battle] for his living." These men "will not work," according to the petitioners. Only by pushing them into a permanent army, they warned, could the government quell the "great uneasiness and disquiet in the Country" caused by militia callouts and high taxes.[34]

The petitioners from Berkeley made it clear that full citizens of the new Republic had the right not to do actual service in the cause of the state but to pay others to do that for them. Patriarchy was key. Once a standing army was raised, they claimed, "Then would your Loyal and faithfull Citizens enjoy that Domestic Tranquility which affords Contentment and Happiness even in the midst of Distressing war." In doing so they would be free to "struggle to maintain Their familys" and give "Support" to "the Glorious Cause in which they are engaged."[35]

Yet, in defending their rights, middling militia members lashed out at those above them as well as those below them. If they were going to be called on to pay more, or to serve more, they wanted that sacrifice to be measured proportionally. Earlier in the war, ordinary Virginians had succeeded in convincing the assembly to abolish regressive poll taxes and institute more progressive land and property taxes to pay for the war. Most Virginians also recognized that military service itself was a regressive form of taxation. Like the poll tax, it asked the same amount from everyone, regardless of wealth. But as middling militiamen were quick to point out, the laws favored the wealthy even more because they were often exempted from the militia or could and did buy themselves exemptions by procuring substitutes for the army. On top of all this inequality, as petitioners from Orange County pointed out, many older and wealthier men had been invalided from the militia payrolls. Because the laws put the obligation for military duty and contributions toward service wholly on the shoulders of remaining able-bodied militia, invalids and exempts could stand by and contribute nothing to the war effort beyond the taxes everyone was obliged to pay.

The cumulative effect of this system meant that by 1779 and 1780, many wealthier men were no longer compelled to contribute toward finding any recruits. The Orange County petitioners complained that many middling militiamen had gone to "much trouble" and contributed "large sums" of money above and beyond the state bounty of $300 to entice a recruit. They also stated the "poor Militia" members of the county were particularly "liberal in their contributions." The petitioners then contrasted their patriotic actions with wealthier men in the county who were not on the militia rolls and who seemed to be uninterested "by a desire of serving their Country." Referring to scripture the petitioners compared the efforts of the "poor Militia" men in the county with the wealthy: "it may be truly said they were like the widow in the parable who threw in all she possessed, when many that possess great estates...refused to contribute one farthing." As "injurious to the community" as this was, the petitioners felt it was also "highly unreasonable" because the wealthy were "so materially interested" in the outcome of the cause. Instead the poor, who had the least to lose, bore the biggest burden. They had to make the biggest sacrifices to try to raise men as some of the wealthiest men in the county stood by and watched them scramble for recruits and substitutes.[36]

Infuriated, the Orange County petitioners advanced a solution to this problem. They asserted that the "obligation is equal on all men, to defend their liberty and property," though they might not be able to do actual "bodily service." Accordingly, they insisted that any money raised for bounties ought to be collected from everyone, not just those in the militia, through a tax on all property in the county. Such a tax, they insisted, would then mean that all people owning property in the county would "pay their equal part of the monies actually advanced," and it would be far more in line with their belief in the "known course of Justice, propriety, and wisdom."[37]

Under a barrage of petitions, the Virginia General Assembly, when forced to reinstitute the draft in early 1780 under the pressure of the British invasion of the South, incorporated these new demands in their recruiting law. In the new law, bounty money raised by militia to hire soldiers would be paid in proportion to taxable property and would contribute toward the militia's next tax assessment. But the new law for recruiting Continental army troops stipulated that everyone with assessable wealth in the county—even those exempted from actual service—had to be included in a division and contribute toward raising bounty money and a soldier. Each division had to have roughly equal amounts of property. Thus any one division would not be composed of a disproportionate number of particularly poor or especially wealthy men.[38]

Most radically, each division was given the power to raise any amount of money—in addition to the state and continental bounties—to try to recruit soldiers to exempt themselves. The legislature did not cap the amount of money each group could raise as an added incentive to recruits. Any extra bounty money pledged to potential recruits would come out of the pockets of everyone in the division, not just the militia who were liable to be drafted. And the money would have to be paid by everyone in equal proportion to their wealth. Moreover the group as a whole was responsible for finding a recruit. The new law had shifted the burden of the draft from the individual to the community, and from people to property. Thus, in reintroducing the draft in Virginia, legislators had given all active militia members the power and means to buy themselves out of service with, in part, the wealth of the often inactive.[39]

The end result of the new law was that for the first time in the war, the loudest complaints about the new draft came from the wealthy. Many well-off Virginians, particularly those who were exempted from actually serving in the militia, were angry that their property was now at the disposal of poorer Virginians to hire recruits and escape the draft. One of the wealthiest men in the state, David Jameson, complained that the recruiting act would prove a "heavy tax" for people such as him. Few men, he believed, would take the risk of being drafted, so they would try to raise as much money within their division as they could. "Who will run the risk of being drafted," Jameson complained, "if he can by taxing his Neighbours procure a Man."[40]

Jameson was, at least in part, right. Many men with little or no taxable property ensured they did not fall prey to the draft. They pushed up the bounty money in a desperate bid to avoid a draft in their division. With the extra money raised in proportion to wealth, the bounty tax would fall heaviest on the wealthiest men. Robert Pleasants, an immensely wealthy Quaker from Henrico County, complained about the militia in his division who actually owned no property. He thought it was "highly unreasonable" that the men who were not liable to pay anything "should have it in their power, to hire a man on any terms they please at my expence, to screen themselves from a draft." Theodorick Bland Senior, another wealthy and prominent Virginian, also complained about the leveling effects of the new draft law. Bland owned property in at least two different counties and had thus been forced to pay out twice. Militia in his Amelia County division had demanded almost £525 from him alone, and his neighbors in his home county had run up a charge of £1,435. On top of this he had also paid £600 for his son's proportion toward a new recruit. With a total bill of more than £2,500, Bland was furious with the assembly's draft law. He expressed his disgust in clear class terms. The assembly had, he asserted, given too much power to the propertyless, or lower, classes. Legislators had effectively "put the power of taxation into the hands of the very lowest class of people," he claimed. Bland believed there would be only one result in such circumstances: such laws would "reduce the most opulent fortune to a level with that of the inferior class of people."[41]

Despite the popularity of the new recruiting law, the effects were obscured by a renewed British offensive in the South, this time targeted directly at Virginia. Beginning in October 1780, the British mounted a series of devastating raids in the state, which would eventually culminate in the rendezvous of Benedict Arnold and Charles Cornwallis, the near capture of Governor Thomas Jefferson, and the almost complete breakdown of mobilization in Virginia. Throughout the yearlong ordeal, slavery cast a long shadow on events, and the paralysis Virginia experienced helps reveal the extent to which slavery affected mobilization in Virginia and intersected with class and gender.

The British came to Virginia with an eye on the rich resources of the state, which included the thousands of enslaved Virginians who could either be turned into extra plunder or used to help bring the state's rebels to their knees. Many enslaved Virginians were eager to encourage the British. As in the past, when the British came calling, the lowest class of Virginians made the best of the opportunity. Though white Virginians complained that the British took enslaved Virginians as plunder, most knew that blacks sought their own freedom. Robert Honyman admitted in May that the British troops, officers and soldiers alike, had "enticed & flattered the Negroes, & prevailed on vast numbers to go along with them, but they did not compel any." Indeed, thought Honyman, enslaved Virginians "flocked to the Enemy from all quarters even from the remote parts."[42]

Though the actual number of enslaved Virginians who sought refuge with the British may have been exaggerated, wealthy Virginia slaveholders were mortified at the prospect of losing everything. Rumors and reports of great losses were rife. Honyman thought that some planters had lost "20, 30, 40, 50, 60 or 70 Negroes besides their stocks of cattle, sheep and horses." The damage the British had done and the losses inflicted on white Virginians in the Piedmont and tidewater sections of the James River, claimed Honyman, were "unspeakable." Along the Potomac and Rappahannock rivers, too, planters suffered from losses of slaves. When the British raided Mount Vernon, seventeen enslaved Virginians fled, including some of Washington's most trusted house servants and artisans. Further south John Banister lost eleven slaves in the first British raid on Petersburg; when the British suddenly returned in early May, the rest of his enslaved population vanished.[43]

Enslaved Virginians ran off in enough numbers that propertied Virginians put the protection of their valuables ahead of the common defense. Many planters began moving their stocks and enslaved population up the country and out of the way of the British. Many patriot leaders also took flight. Edmund Pendleton, Richard Henry Lee, and eventually George Mason were among the more prominent Virginians who abandoned their homes when the British were in the Piedmont. Even Thomas Nelson, who was at the head of the Virginia militia that had turned out, took time during Cornwallis's advance to return to his Hanover County plantation to pack up some of his property and his family and send them to safety. Some, like Pendleton, took as many enslaved Virginians as they could manage to convey.[44]

But many white, usually propertied, Virginians harbored a deep-seated fear that Virginia's enslaved population would not just take the opportunity to flee to the British. They had some firsthand evidence. For example Jack of Botetourt County, who had a previous history of rebellious behavior, tried to poison a Captain Madison and a Major Quirk when the British invaded the state. He then set about "enlisting several negroes to raise in arms and join Lord Cornwallis." Jack was to be their captain. After getting caught, Jack quickly escaped and helped free a number of deserters and Tories who were in chains with him, and he hid out for a number of weeks before being caught again. While in hiding Jack must have struck fear into whites in the area. One man said he was at large, "Sometimes going armed with a Gun and at other times with a Pistol" and "threatening Revenge upon those that apprehended him and those who were Witnesses against him." He was well known to neighbors as a "rebellious Servant and corrupter of other Servants."[45] With many wealthy Virginians on the run in an effort to save their property, many militia stayed at home during the British invasions. By 1781 most state officials were resigned that militia in the immediate vicinity of British forces simply would not turn out. When the British came calling in Hampton in Elizabeth City County in the fall of 1780, for example, militia officers told their men that "every man who had a Family" could retire and "do the best for them they could." The officers later told the assembly that they had been forced to put the "Personal welfare of their wives Children and themselves with their property" first and make terms with the British. After leading the militia in the lower counties during the British invasion in the fall of 1780, James Innes could only conclude that "no aid of militia could ever be drawn from the part of the Country immediately invaded." Whether trying to protect their property or protect their families from rebellious slaves, middling Virginians were adamant about guarding their patriarchy and independence.[46]

Virginia's lowest class, then, also helped cripple mobilization in the state by keeping white fears alive. Yet the influence of slavery on the course of the Revolutionary War did not end there. Though many historians have assumed that slavery helped unify white communities in times of trouble or stress, the ownership of enslaved Virginians caused deep divisions among whites in wartime. From the start of the war, for example, militia throughout Virginia were quick to point out that slaveholding exacerbated the inequities of military service in different respects. In addition to complaints about wealthy slaveholders making themselves overseers to avoid military service, militia from Chesterfield County also pointed out as early as 1776 that even when elites did their part, military service for nonslaveholders was a much greater burden than for those who owned enslaved Virginians. Absent slave owners still had workers in their fields. In contrast, Chesterfield petitioners claimed, militia service was particularly "burthensome" for the "poorer sort who have not a slave to labour for them." Such complaints grew more common as the demands of war put a greater strain on farmers' abilities to maintain their independence in the face of numerous and intrusive callouts. Even as the British were chasing legislators out of Charlottesville, militia members from counties farther west especially claimed that the planter-dominated legislature did not understand how difficult it was for farmers without slaves to leave their farms for any length of time. More than one hundred militia members from Pittsylvania County made their gendered worries explicit when they pledged their money, their service, and their supplies to the war effort, but only "in such a manner as would not totally ruin themselves, their Wives and Children." The present recruiting law, they claimed, would do just that, as many of the petitioners were "poor men without a single Slave, with a Wife and many small Children to maintain." Taking such men away from their families, the petitioners asserted, "would reduce them to the most indigent circumstances and hard grinding Want."[47]

Slaveholding, then, particularly toward the end of the war, increasingly became the touchstone for class divisions among white Virginians. Time and again, on different issues surrounding mobilization, militia from across the state, not just slave-poor regions, made claims based on slaveholding inequality. Sometimes their claims implicitly contrasted slaveholders with nonslaveholders. Militia from Botetourt County, for example, explained that yet another militia callout in the spring of 1781 would bring ruin to nonslaveholders especially: "The Season of the year is Such, that to Call on men, with Families, and who have no Other possible means to support themselves and Families but by their own Labour, no other alternative but inevitable Ruin, must be the Consequence, for before their Return the season for Sowing and planting will be over."[48]

At other times, however, militia were explicit about the inequalities in Virginia. In the spring of 1780, for example, Charlotte County militia members, in a petition to the legislature, rendered an explicit analysis of the problem of wartime mobilization by laying bare what they saw as the class-based injustice of military service. They told the assembly that "in the personal services expected from the Citizens of this Commonwealth, the poor among us who scarce obtain a precarious subsistence by the sweat of their brow, are call'd upon as often and bound to perform equal Military duty in defence of their little as the great & oppulent in defence of their abundance." Yet the petitioners were angry that many wealthy Virginians were able to avoid even an equal amount of service. The "great & oppulent," the petitioners asserted, "who contribute very little personal labour in support of their families, often find means to screen themselves altogether from those military services which the poor and indigent are on all occasions taken from their homes to perform in person." What was worse, they claimed, was that slaveholders benefited twice over; whereas nonslaveholding whites—the "poor and laborious," they claimed—risked their lives, their families, and their estates through their personal service in the militia, slaveholding planters exempted themselves from service and grew personally rich on the backs of their slaves' labor. They particularly resented that "the poor who bear the heat and burthen of Military duty" were taxed the same amount as owners of enslaved Virginians were for their laborers who worked, the petitioners claimed, "only to support the extravigance of a Voluptuous master."[49]

Given that slavery helped bring the British to Virginia in the first place, that slavery was at the center of divisions among whites, and that slavery helped cripple mobilization in diverse ways, patriot leaders in the state were presented with a revolutionary dilemma in the latter years of the war. Because fearful middling whites refused to serve in the armed forces and poorer farmers and laborers were resentful of slaveholders' wealth, patriot leaders were forced into thinking about some revolutionary proposals of their own.

In the fall of 1780, Joseph Jones revealed the outlines of the radical new plan to raise a more permanent army with which this article began. The plan showed not only how far the representatives were prepared to go to avoid a draft but also to what extent legislators had listened to class-based complaints that the wealthy in Virginia had not borne their fair share in paying for the war. And, in the end, even the compromise solution reflected a significant concession to poorer Virginians. New recruits who enlisted for the duration of the war—in effect to create the more permanent army George Washington had wanted from the start and that more middling Virginians had begun to demand as the war wore on—were promised a "healthy sound negro" from age ten to thirty or £60 in gold or silver (at the option of the soldier), plus three hundred acres of land to be received at the end of the war. Thus lower-class Virginians were finally able to extract a huge windfall in return for their services to the state. They would get enough land to vote and also receive money enough to establish themselves or an enslaved Virginian to make that land more productive. For their part anxious legislators may have hoped that in addition to raising a more permanent army they were also making a judicious move to create some kind of alliance between poor whites and wealthy slave owners.[50]

In the face of their desperate struggle with the British and their own population, however, some white patriots began exploring yet another, even more radical, alternative. James Madison, sitting as an observer in Congress, believed the idea of giving enslaved Virginians away as bounties was "inhuman and cruel." He thought it would be much better if patriot leaders in Virginia took the more obvious step and allowed the enslaved to serve in the army themselves. "Would it not be as well to liberate and make soldiers at once of the blacks themselves as to make them instruments for enlisting white Soldiers?" he asked Jones. Madison thought that such a move would "certainly be more consonant to the principles of liberty which ought never to be lost sight of in a contest for liberty."[51]

A few months later, a Major Alexander Dick agreed with Madison. Trying desperately to recruit men for one of the three regiments for the new state forces in the spring of 1781, Dick suggested that Virginia formalize an already informal practice of allowing enslaved Virginians to enlist in the army. Dick was having trouble recruiting a new state regiment and believed that there was "no probability of recruiting the Regiment" with white Virginians. In the circumstances Dick, echoing Madison's suggestion, argued that they should consider accepting "likely young negro fellow's" from planters who would then be given compensation. In turn the enslaved recruit would "be declared free upon inlisting for the War at the end of which, they shall be intitled to all the benefits of Conl. Soldiers." Dick believed that the plan would succeed because enslaved soldiers would make for good recruits and, apparently without a trace of irony, felt that the "the men will be equal to any."[52]

Perhaps because Dick had inadvertently pointed out the perils of such a plan, the legislature did not take up his suggestion. Yet Madison and Dick may not have been the only proponents of such a move, for Jones countered Madison's proposal with some seemingly well-rehearsed objections to arming enslaved Virginians. Significantly, Jones thought there were practical reasons for keeping slaves at home. He admitted that enslaved workers were vital to the independence of those who owned them, thus at least implicitly acknowledging the arguments of nonslaveholding militia. Though the freedom of enslaved Americans was an important object, Jones protested that it should be done gradually so the planters could find laborers to replace them, "or we shall suffer exceedingly under the sudden revolution which perhaps arming them wod. produce."[53]

But there were other objections, too. Perhaps white Virginians did not support the move in larger numbers because too many enslaved Virginians had, so far in the crisis, shown little inclination to support their patriot masters. Indeed Jones worried that arming enslaved Virginians might encourage the British to do likewise, as they had done before. No doubt with the nearly anarchic conditions of the fall of 1775 in mind, Jones thought that the British would be tempted once again to "fight us in our own way." They could probably count on full support from enslaved Virginians, unlike white patriots themselves. The consequences, Jones thought, would be disastrous. If the British armed the enslaved, "this wod. bring on the Southern States probably inevitable ruin."[54]

With such a scenario in mind, patriot leaders tried their luck with lower-class whites instead. Giving slaves as a bounty for soldiers was an ingenious response on the part of some elites to avert the kind of ruin Jones talked about and save the state. Yet the idea of taking those slaves from the wealthiest of planters in the state revealed the extent to which class conflicts, defined as conflicts that grew out of economic inequalities, had permeated the political culture of the new state. Taking enslaved Virginians from the wealthiest class was a response to middle-class complaints about having to shoulder too much of the burden of the war. Offering slaves to lower-class whites was a response, in turn, to rising demands from that class of people to be paid adequately for their service. That new recruits would be given not only an enslaved Virginian but also land and thus the vote meant that many elite whites were willing to make at least some sacrifices and concessions to their middling and lower-class neighbors. The heaviest price for this deal would be paid by enslaved Virginians as well as Native Americans, in whose hands the land promised to new recruits almost certainly lay. Class conflict in Virginia during the Revolutionary War ultimately resulted not in radical solutions such as freeing enslaved Virginians to fight for freedom but rather in more ingenious yet conservative solutions that continued the expropriation of the labor of slaves and the land of Native Americans.

As it turned out, the debate over the new legislation was overshadowed when the British launched another series of devastating raids on Virginia beginning in January 1781. And though historians remember 1781 for George Washington's victory over Charles Cornwallis at Yorktown, it was also the year in which tensions among white Virginians reached the boiling point and the full implications of the previously simmering class divisions became clear. Perhaps the most intriguing aspect of Virginia's mobilization throughout the war, but especially in 1781, is that, despite the immediate threat posed by the British and enslaved Virginians, white Virginians failed to act in concert. Instead they divided and argued among themselves. They passively resisted and verbally protested against militia service, and some went even further. As the British roamed freely across the state in May and June, many militia throughout Virginia actually rioted in protest against military service. Several hundred militia members gathered in places including Augusta, Accomack, Hampshire, and Northampton counties to force local authorities to stop recruiting. In many other places, threats of such collective action were enough to stop worried officials from acting.[55]

Though these riots and protests originated from diverse and sometimes particular causes, several began as a result of the smoldering resentment many poorer and economically vulnerable farmers felt toward wealthy slaveholding planters who had exempted themselves from military service or were quick to flee in the face of British raids. In one of the rare court martial records extant, such economically based grievances were laid bare. Amid a British raid up the Potomac in 1781, the militia of the Northern Neck were called out to defend the region. Instead several militia organized a barbecue in Richmond County to rally support among those who were fed up and unwilling to serve any longer. The barbecue ended in armed conflict against state authorities. The leaders made class-based appeals to their friends and neighbors. One man told authorities that the ringleaders of the conspiracy declared "the Rich wanted the Poor to fight for them, to defend there property, whilst they refused to fight for themselves."[56]

Behind this revealing bravado were men living on the edge. One alleged leader of the barbecue, Edward Wright—described as a "hard-working" but "illiterate" man by authorities—had served often in the patriot militia. Yet in 1781 he found himself unwell and struggling to make ends meet in the face of constant callouts and increasing taxes. He had told another man that he would happily turn out in a few weeks' time after he could lessen his stock to free up basic food stores for his family, and after he returned to full health. In dire circumstances Wright, like others, may also have been tipped over the edge by the numbers of gentlemen in Richmond County who had used their genteel connections to get themselves declared exempt from any militia duty at all on account of their age or health. In a desperate effort to protect his patriarchy, Wright was prepared to incite civil war amid one of the more dense populations of enslaved workers in Virginia. Racial solidarity was no protection against class divisions in Virginia's Revolutionary War.[57]

The Richmond County barbecue was only the tip of the insurrectionary iceberg in 1781. It was also typical of the rampant divisions among white Virginians that crippled mobilization in the state at another key moment in the war. Virginia may have had as many as fifty thousand militia in the state in 1781, but Governors Jefferson and Nelson were unable to concentrate such a force against Cornwallis. They were plagued by stubborn resistance to militia callouts, even to fight within the state, defending hearth and home. Lower-class and middling Virginians had simply had enough of the rich man's war. When Cornwallis made his fateful decision to move to Yorktown, General Washington made his move. Yet few of his fellow white Virginians were there at the final triumph of the Continental army. Even the best estimates of the number of militia at Yorktown show that perhaps no more than three thousand Virginia militiamen participated in some way, whereas seventy-eight hundred French troops and more than five thousand Continental army troops—mainly from states north of

Virginia—played the greatest role. Ironically, even tragically, there may have been more black Virginians with Cornwallis than white Virginians fighting with Washington.[58]

Close attention to mobilization, then, reveals that, contrary to elites' anxious rhetoric of unity, Virginia was racked by internal divisions, conflicts, and contests, often over the all-important question of who should serve. Acknowledging and identifying these wartime protests is difficult enough; explaining the roots of these divisions is even more problematic. But a careful reading of the protests reveals that these divisions were expressed in terms of the conflicting interests of different groups and the unjust or unequal effect of specific policies. Repeatedly, such divisions occurred along the lines of propertyholding and socioeconomic status. The war made tremendous economic demands on people; how one reacted to these demands was often a reflection of one's economic position.

Such divisions were not always expressed in a consistent and coherent language of class or class consciousness. But historians should not abandon the notion of class as a useful way of understanding the conflicts that clearly divided the state. The Revolution forced white men to recognize (if they had not already) that their apparently unified society was divided by deep-seated and conflicting socioeconomic interests. As they struggled to give expression to their differences, the men of the time spoke of rich and poor, of freedom and coercion, of manly independence and abjection, of the propertied and propertyless, and of the degrees of material wealth, usually in the form of acres of productive land and numbers of enslaved workers. To interpret what they were trying to say, historians need the vocabulary of class; yet, to understand class in revolutionary Virginia, scholars need to extend and complicate that vocabulary, attending to the locally and chronologically specific, and not simply look for the ghostly antecedents of a nineteenth-century model.

In this respect scholarship on independents and dependents helps modern historians appreciate that some of these struggles at least arose around deeply entrenched gendered notions of the household and household independence in particular. As Kathleen M. Brown has written, for wealthy planters in Virginia, independence and authority emanated from the home or plantation. Elite planters at least dreamed of "hegemonic authority over compliant wives, children, and slaves and of unquestioned political leadership over less privileged men." Though political leadership may not have been so important, the dependence of household members was crucial to the independence of, as Stephanie McCurry puts it, "masters of small worlds," too. Smallholding farmers—those whom McCurry has called "self-working farmers" with few or no slaves to work for them— especially worried about their mastery over the household independence as calls for their military service increased. They protested that their own labor was essential to their household economy. What they were most fearful of, they claimed, was that should they be compelled to serve in the military for longer terms, they might lose their independence by finding on their return that their wives and children were forced to go about, as they put it, "abeging" and "aSlaving." In an important sense, then, manliness was threatened, rather than affirmed, by extended periods of military service, particularly for those who owned insufficient dependents (enslaved Virginians) to maintain white household independence.[59]

These kinds of conflicts demonstrate, too, that slavery, race, and gender are important components of any explanation of wartime disunity in Virginia. Yet they also point to the fact that such explanations are insufficient without thinking about the ways in which class and perceptions of class intersected with race and gender and powerfully shaped what were or became class struggles during the revolutionary conflict. Elite Virginians, for example, acknowledged the importance of household independence and, early in the war, tried to target the lower sort for longer terms of military service, in part because they were not seen to be tied to a household. Elites believed the lower sort had no independence to preserve and no small world to master. But when the demands of the war forced the ruling class to expand their search for soldiers to more independent Virginians, smallholding farmers protested vigorously and sometimes violently. The more that self-working Virginians' ability to protect the household was eroded, the more violent their protests.[60]

Moreover, at various times during the war, many of these poorer and vulnerable yet aspiring middle-class farmers lashed out at their wealthier, slave-owning neighbors. At other times at least some of these same people focused their wrath on those below them, accusing lower-class propertyless whites of fleecing more virtuous citizens. But such class conflict also produced indirect as well as direct changes. The militia's assertion of their own rights, for example, reaffirmed a virulent form of patriarchy in their own households that in some ways transcended class. And enslaved Virginians' active resistance throughout the war brought about a backlash from whites that slowed progress toward emancipation. Indeed postwar proslavery petitions show that white militia not only used enslaved Virginians' resistance to justify continued bondage but also claimed that their own wartime sacrifices and military service, however limited they may have been, justified their claims to keeping a tenacious hold on their property. In doing so middling slaveholding militia, for the first time, used revolutionary principles and their revolutionary participation to legitimate the continued enslavement of black Virginians.[61]

The debate over slavery suggests that if class as a tool of analysis enriches modern historians' understanding of the Revolutionary War in Virginia—and, in particular, the desperate struggles that racked the state and undermined its ability to mobilize effectively—it also enriches scholars' understanding of the immediate consequences of such a massive failing. These conflicts, and the struggles of all to understand and express them, manifested themselves in a direct manner in Virginia's postwar politics, and the deep-seated anxieties of elites about the conduct of war and those troubled postwar politics also shaped the move toward the Constitution.

An examination of these events is beyond the scope of this article, but one or two examples are suggestive.

Throughout the war in Virginia, contemporaries had observed what to many seemed a disturbing phenomenon: high legislative turnover in the annual elections. At times such turnover was specifically attributed to discontent over military policies. Interest in elections in the spring of 1780 seemed to be higher than ever. Robert Honyman thought that voting Virginians were more unhappy than ever before and, accordingly, "choose those who make fair promises of altering things for the better." As a result Honyman believed that the quality of those chosen was diminished. "Many of those chosen," he reported, "are men of mean abilities & no rank." It was this same legislature that debated the plans to redistribute enslaved workers from rich Virginians to poorer ones. As Joseph Jones noted to James Madison, it was precisely because of the different composition of the legislature that such a proposal was even on the table, as it was also the same legislature that Theodorick Bland complained about so vehemently in January 1781.[62]

The high annual legislative turnover slowed in the postwar period, yet the more conflict-ridden politics did not. As Herbert Sloan and Peter Onuf have noted, the "most striking thing about Virginia politics in the postwar period" is that, despite a return to the same leadership of the prewar years, "the harmony so characteristic of the prewar years is completely absent." Postwar politics in the Old Dominion moved away from more consensual practices and marked the "beginnings of sustained conflict between legislative factions over public policy, and of issue-oriented appeals to constituents," usually over the same kind of vital economic issues that divided Virginians during the war: taxes, paper money, and debts. In short they were conflicts over who would pay for the war and how. Increasingly, in the postwar period more legislators were more willing to jeopardize provincial, and eventually national, harmony and consensus for the sake of the interests of their constituents. And learning more about the postwar political conflicts over paper money, debts, and taxes reveals that these, too, were often class conflicts that grew out of real economic inequalities.[63]

Recognizing and acknowledging the conflicts that divided Virginians during and immediately after the war, and the extent to which these conflicts severely crippled mobilization and later the repayments of wartime debts, might also help historians to finally bridge the gap between stories of what John Shy has characterized as the destructive American War of Independence and the so-called constructive political revolution that culminated in the creation of a federal Constitution. For, in the end, the divisive and crippling experience of the war helped produce a small group of committed nationalists who emerged from the patriot leadership. These men were generally those who had occupied important positions during the Revolution, but outside their own states. Significantly, this nationalist cadre included Continental army officers, such as George Washington, who were frustrated by the conflicts at the state level that undermined a successful war effort. Almost every general in the Continental army supported moves to strengthen the powers of the federal government. Precisely because so many people defended their class interests and refused to fight the war on terms proposed by elites, many elites themselves, in turn, began thinking about new ways of organizing society and politics to protect a notion of society that some, at least, believed was increasingly under threat. These new ideas became particularly evident in elites' responses to the massive tax resistance of the 1780s, in which thousands of farmers justified their refusal to pay taxes on the basis of their wartime military service and material sacrifices. Just as the anxiety of some elites found expression in a heightening of postwar political tensions among state legislators, it also pushed some to radically rethink the nature and structure of the fledgling union. The political settlement of 1787 thus reflected the class-based conflict that had been endemic throughout the war.[64]

At the very least, the divisive experience of the war and postwar period—the harsh realities of such a long and protracted war that clearly revealed divisions and internal conflict far more than consensus and shared values—goes far in explaining the change of mood "between the euphoria at Philadelphia in 1776," as Shy has written, "and the hard-headedness of many of the same men, when, eleven years later, in the same city, they hammered out a federal constitution." Class conflicts, then, helped produce a "new realism, almost a cynicism, about human nature that is one key to American political survival after 1783." Clearly, state and national leaders, the most self-conscious class of all, were affected not just by the arguments and debates of their colleagues in the legislative chambers but more fundamentally by the many voices and actions of those they lived with, listened to, and often struggled against. Further recovery of the complex nuances of those debates, dialogues, and struggles throughout this period would not only enrich but also irrevocably alter modern history's understanding of the founding period.[65]

Notes

Michael A. McDonnell is a lecturer at the University of Sydney, Australia. He owes many thanks to the diverse people who commented on earlier versions of this essay, including conference participants in three different countries, but particularly Terry Bouton, Seth Cotlar, Matthew Dennis, Dallett Hemphill, Katherine Hermes, Ron Hoffman, Woody Holton, Rhys Isaac, Marjoleine Kars, Allan Kulikoff, Simon Middleton, Marcus Rediker, David Rollison, Steve Sarson, Billy Smith, Robert Sweeny, Alan Taylor, Fredrika Teute, Frances Thomas, Peter Thompson, Peter Way, Andy Wood, and Al Young. More recently, new colleagues in the American History reading group in Sydney, and especially Frances Clarke, Clare Corbould, Stephen Robertson, Ian Tyrrell, and Shane White, have helped shape and sharpen this analysis, as have Australianists Kirsten McKenzie and Penny Russell, and students in his seminar class this past semester, titled "Class Struggles in the Atlantic World." He also wishes to thank Richard

Waterhouse and the School of Philosophical and Historical Inquiry and the University of Sydney for their generous support of his research.

1. Edmund Pendleton to James Madison, Jan. 1, 1781, Joseph Jones to Madison, Nov. 18, Dec. 2, Dec. 8, 1780, in William T. Hutchinson and William M. E. Rachal, eds., *The Papers of James Madison* (Chicago, 1962), 2: 268, 183, 219, 232–33; Thomas Madison to William Preston, Nov. 30, 1780, in Preston Papers, Virginia Historical Society, Richmond.

2. Theodorick Bland Sr. to Theodorick Bland Jr., Jan. 8, 1781, in Charles Campbell, ed., *The Bland Papers: Being a Selection from the Manuscripts of Colonel Theodorick Bland, Jr.* (Petersburg, Va., 1843), 2: 51. See also A. Drummond to John Coles, Mar. 13 [1781], in Carter–Smith Papers, Alderman Library, University of Virginia, Charlottesville.

3. Ironically, Edmund Morgan's analysis of seventeenth-century Virginia gave historians one of the most powerful and explicit class-based analyses of colonial society ever written (Morgan, *American Slavery, American Freedom: The Ordeal of Colonial Virginia* [New York, 1975]); see also T.H. Breen, "A Changing Labor Force and Race Relations in Virginia, 1660–1710," in *Puritans and Adventurers: Change and Persistence in Early America* (New York, 1993), 127–47. For gentlemen's reluctance to talk about problems, see Emory G. Evans, "Trouble in the Backcountry: Disaffection in Southwest Virginia during the American Revolution," in *An Uncivil War: The Southern Backcountry during the American Revolution*, eds. Ronald Hoffman, Thad W. Tate, and Peter J. Albert (Charlottesville, Va., 1985), 180 ("dirty linen"). When whites uncovered a conspiracy of enslaved Virginians who were plotting their escape in the event of open hostilities between the British and the Virginians on the eve of the Revolutionary War, James Madison thought it "prudent [that] such attempts should be concealed as well as suppressed [to] prevent the Infection" (Madison to William Bradford, Nov. 26, 1774, in Hutchinson and Rachal, *Papers of James Madison*, 1: 129–30).

4. See, for example, Gary B. Nash, *The Urban Crucible: Social Change, Political Consciousness, and the Origins of the American Revolution* (Cambridge, Mass., 1979); Edward Countryman, *A People in Revolution: The American Revolution and Political Society in New York, 1760–1790* (Baltimore, 1981); Billy G. Smith, *The "Lower Sort": Philadelphia's Laboring People, 1750–1800* (Ithaca, N.Y., 1990); Peter Linebaugh, *The London Hanged: Crime and Civil Society in the Eighteenth Century* (London, 1991); Andy Wood, *The Politics of Social Conflict: The Peak Country, 1520–1770* (Cambridge, 1999); Peter Linebaugh and Marcus Rediker, *The Many-Headed Hydra: Sailors, Slaves, Commoners, and the Hidden History of the Revolutionary Atlantic* (Boston, 2000); Thomas J. Humphrey, *Land and Liberty: Hudson Valley Riots in the Age of Revolution* (DeKalb, Ill., 2004). Important exceptions to the idea of an untroubled or undivided Virginia can be found in Rhys Isaac, *The Transformation of Virginia, 1740–1790* (Chapel Hill, N.C., 1982); Albert H. Tillson Jr., *Gentry and Common Folk: Political Culture on a Virginia Frontier, 1740–1789* (Lexington, Ky., 1991); Woody Holton, *Forced Founders: Indians, Debtors, Slaves, and the Making of the American Revolution* (Chapel Hill, N.C., 1999). In a similar vein, Stephanie McCurry writes about the powerful images that have obscured modern readers' view of lower- and middling-class farmers in antebellum South Carolina (McCurry, *Masters of Small Worlds: Yeoman Households, Gender Relations, and the Political Culture of the Antebellum South Carolina Low Country* [New York, 1995], esp. 37–45).

5. Even among African American communities, divisions were sometimes pronounced. See Ira Berlin, *Many Thousands Gone: The First Two Centuries of Slavery in North America* (Cambridge, Mass., 1998). The "Bulk of the People," as they were

sometimes called by literate elites, were not actually slave owners or, if they were, they owned one or two slaves at the most (George Mason to George Mason Jr., June 3, 1781, in Robert A. Rutland, ed., *The Papers of George Mason, 1725–1792* [Chapel Hill, N.C., 1970], 2: 693). In 1988 John E. Selby concluded that at war's end, "the typical white Virginia male was a small farmer...[who] had access to no more than a couple of hundred acres, at most a slave or two, and some cattle." Just under 50 percent of white males were small landowners, 10–20 percent were tenants (concentrated in the Northern Neck), and 20–30 percent were agricultural laborers or indentured servants. Of those who were farmers, even in slave-rich areas such as the tidewater and the heart of the Piedmont, as many as 30 percent of families worked their land without enslaved help. In some places this figure was much higher (Selby, *The Revolution in Virginia, 1775–1783* [Williamsburg, Va., 1988], 24). There was much regional variation. In Loudoun County, for example, situated in northwest Virginia but still to the east of the Blue Ridge Mountains, far fewer people owned slaves in 1784 and those that did usually owned only one or two slaves (Stanley B. Parsons et al., *United States Congressional Districts, 1788–1841* [Westport, Conn., 1978], 28–31; Loudoun County Tax Records, 1784, Library of Virginia, Richmond). A considerable part of the labor force in Loudoun was composed of wage laborers and white convict and indentured servants (analysis based on an examination of Cumberland and Loudoun counties, Personal Property Tax Records and Land Tax Records, 1782–1784, Library of Virginia). Richard S. Dunn concluded that "a majority of the whites stood outside of the slave system at the time of the Revolution" (Dunn, "Black Society in the Chesapeake, 1776–1810," in *Slavery and Freedom in the Age of the American Revolution*, eds. Ira Berlin and Ronald Hoffman [Charlottesville, Va., 1983], 67).

6. Isaac, *Transformation of Virginia*; Philip D. Morgan, *Slave Counterpoint: Black Culture in the Eighteenth-Century Chesapeake and Lowcountry* (Chapel Hill, N.C., 1998). See also Steven Sarson, "Landlessness and Tenancy in Early National Prince George's County, Maryland," *William and Mary Quarterly*, 3d ser., 57, no. 3 (July 2000): 585–94; Sarson, "Similarities and Continuities: Free Society in the Tobacco South before and after the American Revolution," in *Empire and Nation: The American Revolution in the Atlantic World*, eds. Eliga H. Gould and Peter S. Onuf (Baltimore, 2005). The literature on indentured and convict servitude is well known (though not often incorporated into the larger picture), but there is a dearth of work on the extent of tenancy in eighteenth-century Virginia. Close study is revealing: Loudoun County probably had one of the highest proportions of tenant farmers in Virginia. Overall perhaps as many as 466, or 38 percent, of the 1,225 landholders in the county were tenants. Many tenant farmers, too, were not slaveholders or owned only one or two slaves. Astonishingly, from 42 to 75 percent of white males in Loudoun may have been landless (Loudoun County Personal Property Tax Records and Land Tax Records, 1784, Library of Virginia; see also Willard F. Bliss, "The Rise of Tenancy in Virginia," *Virginia Magazine of History and Biography* 58, no. 4 [October 1950]: 429–30). For cosmopolitan versus local elites, see Darrett B. Rutman and Anita H. Rutman, *A Place in Time: Middlesex County, Virginia, 1650–1750* (New York, 1984), chap. 5. For divisions among yeomen and slaveholders, see McCurry, *Masters of Small Worlds*, esp. 47–55.

7. See esp. Jack P. Greene, *Pursuits of Happiness: The Social Development of Early Modern British Colonies and the Formation of American Culture* (Chapel Hill, N.C., 1988); Greene, "Convergence: Development of an American Society, 1720–1780," in *Diversity and Unity in Early North America*, ed. Philip D. Morgan (London, 1993), 43–72. Despite the now-vast literature on social conflict and the revolutionary period, very few scholars, with several notable exceptions, have openly talked about class conflict and the Revolution. As Allan Kulikoff has pointed out,

progressive scholars devised a kind of class interpretation of the Revolution, but they spoke primarily in terms of Madisonian interest groups rather than economic classes (Kulikoff, "The Death and Rebirth of Class Analysis in Early American History" [unpublished paper, 2001], 8). The progressives' general division of society into the haves and have nots, the few and the many, has left the door open for a great deal of criticism and has polarized the debate in a way that needlessly distracted and curtailed discussion. Neoprogressive scholars in the 1960s flirted with the idea of class conflict but, by and large, it submerged into a more general analysis of social conflict. The most obvious example is Richard B. Morris, "Class Struggle and the American Revolution," *WMQ* 19, no. 1 (January 1962): 3–29, which is actually a historiographical review. Steven Rosswurm's *Arms, Country and Class: The Philadelphia Militia and the "Lower Sort" during the American Revolution, 1775–1783* (New Brunswick, N.J., 1987), is probably one of the most explicit class analyses in the last twenty years. Apart from discussion of the middle classes, even scholars who are acutely aware of diverse layers of social conflict in early America refrain from using the phrase class conflict. Two exceptions appear in Alfred F. Young, ed., *Beyond the American Revolution: Explorations in the History of American Radicalism* (DeKalb, Ill., 1993): Gary J. Kornblith and John M. Murrin, "The Making and Unmaking of an American Ruling Class," 27–79; Allan Kulikoff, "The American Revolution, Capitalism, and the Formation of the Yeoman Classes," 80–119.

8. Allan Kulikoff, "Whither the Progress of Inequality," *WMQ* 57, no. 4 (October 2000): 832 (quotation). Significantly, historians of early America have long been comfortable with acknowledging elite perceptions of class and have spent a great deal of time of late demonstrating the various ways in which elites consciously strove to distance and distinguish themselves from other classes. Despite this literature, however, historians have much more trouble acknowledging lower- and middling-class consciousness. Surely, elites' constant striving to distance themselves from the rest of colonial society did not go unnoticed?

9. E.P. Thompson, *The Making of the English Working Class* (New York, 1963); Simon Middleton, "Rethinking Class in Early America: The Struggle for Rights and Privileges in Seventeenth-Century New York" (paper presented at the Seventh Annual Omohundro Institute of Early American History and Culture Conference, Glasgow, Scotland, July 12, 2001), 2, wherein Middleton argues that class is tied too forcefully and exclusively to the emergence of what he calls the "immiserating effects of early industrialization" in the nineteenth century and the emergence of a clear and coherent "working class." See also Simon Middleton and Billy G. Smith, introduction to unpublished paper.

10. E.P. Thompson, "Eighteenth-Century English Society: Class Struggle without Class?" *Social History* 3, no. 2 (May 1978): 147–50 (quotations, 147, 150). On the necessity for class struggles to predate class, Thompson writes: "Classes do not exist as separate entities, look around, find an enemy class, and then start to struggle. On the contrary, people find themselves in a society structured in determined ways (crucially, but not exclusively, in productive relations), they experience exploitation (or the need to maintain power over those whom they exploit), they identify points of antagonistic interest, they commence to struggle around these issues and in the process of struggling they discover themselves as classes, they come to know this discovery as class-consciousness. Class and class-consciousness are always the last, not the first, stage in the real historical process" (149).

11. Eschewing the "proletarianization paradigm," several new Anglo-American scholars, focusing particularly on the middling sort, have drawn on Marxist-feminist

theories of standpoint and, in Simon Middleton's words, begun to think about class "in terms of its effects—rather than as a condition embedded in social structures or as a self-consciousness arising (mystically) out of subjective experiences." Thus historians can begin to focus on the "endless variability in the conditions within which classes form and the volatility of interests and struggles that develop with classes" (Middleton, "Rethinking Class in Early America," 3 [quotation]. See also Wood, *Politics of Social Conflict*, chap. 1; Peter Way, "Rebellion of the Regulars: Working Soldiers and the Mutiny of 1763–1764," *WMQ* 57, no. 4 [October 2000]: 765; C. Dallett Hemphill, "Manners and Class in the Revolutionary Era: A Transatlantic Comparison," *WMQ* 63, no. 2 [April 2006]: 345–72). Allan Kulikoff echoes this idea of class as a social relationship rather than a structure or location and also argues that human agency is central to class as men and women "not only respond to structural constraints on their lives, but make decisions that profoundly shape the formation of classes and the relationship between them" (Kulikoff, "Death and Rebirth of Class Analysis," 7). Thus, even leaving aside the rather astonishing levels of obvious inequalities that a growing number of scholars have been uncovering in early America, from the urban cities of the middle and northern colonies, to the fields of the Chesapeake, and extending beyond—even among the Creek Indians in the western parts of the lower South—it seems clear that the middle classes, however dominant they were in revolutionary America, not only did not exist outside the framework of class but also could be class conscious (see, for example, Nash, *Urban Crucible*; Carla Gardina Pestana and Sharon V. Salinger, eds., *Inequality in Early America* [Hanover, N.H., 1999]; Sarson, *WMQ* 57: 569–98; Claudio Saunt, "Taking Account of Property: Stratification among the Creek Indians in the Early Nineteenth Century," *WMQ* 57, no. 4 [October 2000]: 733–60).

12. Holton, *Forced Founders*. See also the large corpus of work of Rhys Isaac, who made historians rethink many commonly held assumptions about Virginia society and the Revolution, esp. Isaac, *Transformation of Virginia*. See also Kulikoff, "Death and Rebirth of Class Analysis," 32. My debt to Allan Kulikoff, in particular, for his theoretical work and long-term perspective is great. In addition to the other works cited in this article, see also Kulikoff, *The Agrarian Origins of American Capitalism* (Charlottesville, Va., 1992), esp. chaps. 1–2; Kulikoff, "Was the American Revolution a Bourgeois Revolution?" in *The Transforming Hand of Revolution: Reconsidering the American Revolution as a Social Movement*, ed. Ronald Hoffman and Peter J. Albert (Charlottesville, Va., 1996), 58–89; Kulikoff, "Revolutionary Violence and the Origins of American Democracy," *Journal of the Historical Society* 2, no. 2 (April 2002): 229–60.

13. To appreciate these challenges, historians must first acknowledge elite denials of divisions for what they were—a self-reassuring rhetoric designed to try to isolate the disaffected and promote unity in an otherwise disunited society—and begin to pay much more attention to the grievances of those who protested against elite attempts to mobilize for war. When they discussed it, most gentlemen dismissed protests as self-interested and unpatriotic, merely the actions of a small but vocal group of the disaffected, or a few disgruntled Tories who could and should be ignored. A more subtle reading of the conflicts that racked Virginia reveals, however, that if many of the men labeled as Tories were not prepared to fight for the patriots, neither were they prepared to die for the British. In times of war, as scholars have learned again only too recently, the first casualty is usually a fair and adequate airing and representation of dissenting opinions and views. For a look at the language of loyalty, see Michael A. McDonnell, "A World Turned 'Topsy Turvy': Robert Munford, *The Patriots*, and the Crisis of the Revolution

in Virginia," *WMQ* 61, no. 2 (April 2004): 235–70. For a look at the extent of so-called loyalism in Virginia, see esp. Adele Hast, *Loyalism in Revolutionary Virginia: The Norfolk Area and the Eastern Shore* (Ann Arbor, Mich., 1982); Evans, "Trouble in the Backcountry."

14. Elites and others in Virginia did not always use a specific language of class. But as Keith Wrightson, David Cannadine, and others have shown, the early modern era was a period of transition in the kinds of language used by contemporaries to describe their views of society. At least three kinds of descriptions were in use and would gradually merge into a "discourse of class" by the mid- to the end of the eighteenth century. These characterizations included an idea of society as finely graded hierarchies or ranks (that had evolved from the medieval notion of the three estates) comprised of "sorts of people": usually the "better sort" versus the "meaner sort" or "poorer sort" and, at least since the mid-seventeenth century, the "middling sort." Such language choices overlapped in their use were "conceptually muddled, but...admirably flexible," and each was used to characterize social relations and inequalities even as a more specific class discourse was emerging in the eighteenth century (see esp. Wrightson, "Class," in *The British Atlantic World, 1500–1800,* ed. David Armitage and Michael J. Braddick [Basingstoke, Eng., 2002], 133–38 [quotations, 134–36]; see also Cannadine, *The Rise and Fall of Class in Britain* [New York, 1999], esp. chap. 1).

15. Fairfax County Militia Association [Sept. 21, 1774], in Rutland, *Papers of George Mason,* 1: 211 ("gentlemen Voluntiers"). See esp. William Lee to R.C. Nicholas, Mar. 6, 1775, in Worthington Chauncey Ford, ed., *Letters of William Lee, 1766–1783* (Brooklyn, N.Y., 1891), 1: 144; James Madison to William Bradford, Nov. 26, 1774, in Hutchinson and Rachal, *Papers of James Madison,* 1: 129–30; Gerald W. Mullin, *Flight and Rebellion: Slave Resistance in Eighteenth-Century Virginia* (New York, 1972); Peter H. Wood, "The Changing Population of the Colonial South: An Overview by Race and Region, 1685–1790," in *Powhatan's Mantle: Indians in the Colonial Southeast,* eds. Wood, Gregory A. Waselkov, and M. Thomas Hatley (Lincoln, Neb., 1989), 38; Sylvia R. Frey, *Water from the Rock: Black Resistance in a Revolutionary Age* (Princeton, N.J., 1991); James Titus, *The Old Dominion at War: Society, Politics, and Warfare in Late Colonial Virginia* (Columbia, S.C., 1991), 75–76; Wood, "'Liberty is Sweet': African-American Freedom Struggles in the Years before White Independence," in Young, *Beyond the American Revolution,* 154, 160; Holton, Forced Founders, 141, 248.

16. Robert L. Scribner and Brent Tarter, eds., *Revolutionary Virginia: The Road to Independence* (Charlottesville, Va., 1977), 3: 406, 463, 466, 471, 476; William Waller Hening, ed., *The Statutes at Large: Being a Collection of all the Laws of Virginia...* (1821; repr., Charlottesville, Va., 1969), 9: 27–35.

17. George Mason to Martin Cockburn, Aug. 5, 1775, in Rutland, *Papers of George Mason,* 1: 245–46 (quotations, 245); Mason to George Washington, Oct. 14, 1775, ibid., 1: 255–56; George Gilmer to Charles Carter, July 15, 1775, in R.A. Brock, ed., *Miscellaneous Papers, 1672–1865...in the Collections of the Virginia Historical Society...* (Richmond, Va., 1887), 91; Gilmer, Commonplace Book entry (summer 1775), ibid., 90. See also Gilmer to Thomas Jefferson [July 26 or 27, 1775], in Julian P. Boyd, ed., *The Papers of Thomas Jefferson* (Princeton, N.J., 1950), 1: 238. For studies of this martial tradition, see Morgan, *American Slavery, American Freedom,* 340; E. Wayne Carp, "Early American Military History: A Review of Recent Work," *VMHB* 94, no. 3 (July 1986): 272; Don Higginbotham, "The Military Institutions of Colonial America: The Rhetoric and the Reality," in *War and Society in Revolutionary America: The Wider Dimensions of Conflict* (Columbia, S.C., 1988), 19; Titus, *The Old Dominion at War,* 4, 59, 80, 98–99.

18. "Petition of Amelia County Militiamen" [May 23, 1776], in Scribner and Tarter, *Revolutionary Virginia*, 7: 236–39; Proceedings of the Fifth Virginia Convention, June 4, 1776, ibid., 7: 349; "Petition of Inhabitants of Lunenburg County" [Apr. 26, 1776], ibid., 6: 474–77 ("Overseers that Otherways," 475). See also Mecklenburg County Petition, May 13, 1776, ibid., 7: 114–15; see also Proceedings of the Fifth Virginia Convention, May 10, 1776, ibid., 7: 87, for a similar petition from Chesterfield County (the actual petition has never been found); Hening, *Statutes at Large*, 9: 89, 28, 31. Allan Kulikoff discusses the struggle over exemptions of overseers and its significance in Kulikoff, "American Revolution, Capitalism, and Formation of the Yeoman Classes," 80–119.

19. Charles Lee and George Washington later noted that a wide pay gap was essential to military discipline and subordination in the ranks. If an officer was in no way distinguished, Washington argued, his men would "consider, and treat him as an equal; and...regard him no more than a broomstick" (Washington to the President of Congress, Sept. 24, 1776, in John C. Fitzpatrick, ed., *The Writings of George Washington from the Original Manuscript Sources, 1745–1799* [Washington, D.C., 1932], 6: 108–9 (quotation, 110); Lee to Benjamin Rush, Oct. 10 [1775], in *The Lee Papers, Vol. 1: 1754–1776*, in *Collections of the New-York Historical Society for the Year 1871* [New York, 1871], 212; General Orders, Apr. 3, 1776, in "Orderly Book of the Company of Captain George Stubblefield, Fifth Virginia Regiment, from March 3, 1776, to July 10, 1776, Inclusive," in Brock, *Miscellaneous Papers, 1672–1865*, 159; "Address of George Gilmer to the Inhabitants of Albemarle," ibid., 126, 128). For a full account of the minuteman failure, see Michael A. McDonnell, "Popular Mobilization and Political Culture in Revolutionary Virginia: The Failure of the Minutemen and the Revolution from Below," *Journal of American History* 85, no. 3 (December 1998): 946–81.

20. "Dunmore, Proclamation, Nov. 7, 1775," in Scribner and Tarter, *Revolutionary Virginia*, 4: 334–35; "To the Public," "Thirty Dollars Reward," [Williamsburg] *Virginia Gazette* (Dixon and Hunter), June 15, Nov. 22, 1776. See also "Norfolk, September 20," notice for Plim, *Va. Gaz.* (Dixon and Hunter), Sept. 23, 1775; Thomas Parramore and John Bowdoin Jr. to the Committee of Safety, Apr. 23, 1776, in Scribner and Tarter, *Revolutionary Virginia*, 6: 449; Fincastle County Committee Proceedings, Jan. 10, 1776, ibid., 5: 376, 382 n. 28; Memorial of John Hiell, May 11, Nov. 23, 1785, in Audit Office 13/31, Public Records Office, London. White Virginians were besieged on all sides by reports of cooperation between rebellious slaves and disgruntled whites. Reports emanating from Maryland were particularly worrying. See, in particular, Ronald Hoffman, *A Spirit of Dissension: Economics, Politics, and the Revolution in Maryland* (Baltimore, 1973), 147–48; Committee of Northampton County to the President of the Continental Congress, Nov. 25, 1775, in Scribner and Tarter, *Revolutionary Virginia*, 4: 468–69. See also Accomack County Committee to the Delegates of the Proceedings of the Fourth Virginia Convention, Nov. 30, 1775, ibid., 4: 498; John Collett to Lord Dunmore, Dec. 20, 1775, ibid., 5: 198, 204 n. 3; Patrick Henry to Edmund Pendleton, Dec. 23, 1775, ibid., 5: 227; Petition of Inhabitants of Norfolk and Princess Anne Counties [Jan. 8, 1776], ibid., 5: 362–63; Proceedings of the Fourth Virginia Convention, Jan. 13, 1776, ibid., 5: 396–97.

21. Walter Jones to Landon Carter, Oct. 14, 1775, in Sabine Hall Collection, University of Virginia. For an account of the circumstances surrounding this episode, see Michael A. McDonnell, *The Politics of War: Race, Class, and Conflict in Revolutionary Virginia*, chap. 5, forthcoming. James Hendricks to Leven Powell [June] 5, 1776, in Robert C. Powell, ed., *A Biographical Sketch of Col. Leven Powell* (Alexandria, Va., 1877), 85. For a full account of the Loudoun County uprising, see Woody Holton and Michael A. McDonnell, "Patriot vs. Patriot: Social Conflict in Virginia

and the Origins of the American Revolution," *Journal of American Studies* 34, no. 2 (August 2000): 231–56. Landon Carter to George Washington, May 9, 1776, in W.W. Abbot and Dorothy Twohig, eds., *The Papers of George Washington, Revolutionary War Series* (Charlottesville, Va., 1991), 4: 236–37, 240, 240 n. 5. For the coming of independence and the reestablishment of government as a relief to patriot leaders, see Holton, *Forced Founders*; McDonnell, *Politics of War*, esp. chap. 7. Scholars have been influenced by an older, more patriotic scholarship, reinforced by Charles Royster's powerful image of the *rage militaire* that gripped the colonies in 1775–76, in Royster, *A Revolutionary People at War: The Continental Army and American Character, 1775–1783* (Chapel Hill, N.C., 1979), and backed up by detailed New England studies such as Robert A. Gross, *The Minutemen and Their World* (New York, 1976). The extent of the *rage militaire* in places such as Virginia remains suspect. See McDonnell, *Journal of American History* 85: 946–81.

22. By mid-1777 George Washington believed that the Virginia line of the Continental army was full of convict servants purchased from their masters by recruiting officers. "Convict Servants," he explained to Congress, "compose no small proportion of the Men from the Upper and more interior Part of that State" (Washington to the President of Congress, May 13, 1777, in Fitzpatrick, *Writings of George Washington*, 8: 56; Nicholas Cresswell, *The Journal of Nicholas Cresswell* [London, 1925], 176, 180, 186–87 [Dec. 14, 1776, Jan. 7, Mar. 3, Mar. 10, 1777]). The assembly formalized the practice of enlisting servants in May 1777 when it allowed recruiting officers to enlist servants and apprentices, apparently without their masters' consent (see Hening, *Statutes at Large*, 9: 12, 216–17, 275–76).

23. Hening, *Statutes at Large*, 9: 280. By May 1777 enough enslaved Virginians had run away and joined the army to alarm the assembly. Legislators complained that "several negro slaves" had deserted their masters and enlisted, and they tried to close the loophole by declaring the practice of enrolling black or mulatto Virginians unlawful unless they produced a certificate affirming their free status from a local justice of the peace. In doing so they gave official sanction to the practice of enrolling free blacks into the army, a practice not adopted in Maryland until 1780 and not adopted at all south of Virginia. They also opened the door for enslaved Virginians to gain their freedom from their masters by offering to serve as substitutes for them if they were drafted (see Benjamin Quarles, *The Negro in the American Revolution* [Chapel Hill, N.C., 1961], 56–57).

24. Richard Henry Lee to Thomas Jefferson, Apr. 29, 1777, in Boyd, *Papers of Thomas Jefferson*, 2: 13–14; George Washington to Patrick Henry, May 17, 1777, in Fitzpatrick, *Writings of George Washington*, 8: 77–78.

25. Hening, *Statutes at Large*, 9: 275–80; Diary of Robert Honyman, Jan. 2, 1776–Mar. 11, 1782 (see esp. Aug. 29, 1777), Alderman Library, University of Virginia (on microfilm); Edmund Pendleton to William Woodford, June 28, 1777, in David John Mays, ed., *The Letters and Papers of Edmund Pendleton, 1734–1803* (Charlottesville, Va., 1967), 1: 215; John Chilton to his brother [Charles Chilton?], Aug. 11, 1777, in Keith Family of Woodburn, Fauquier Co., Papers, Virginia Historical Society. The field officers and justices were also responsible for pooling their own money and raising a man themselves. Ironically, advertisements for deserters may have also contributed to faltering voluntary enlistments in the army, since they were very similar in tone to advertisements for runaway servants and slaves and painted a graphic picture of the motley crew who were compelled and coerced into the army.

26. For details of lower-class resistance in 1777 and 1778, see McDonnell, *Politics of War*, chaps. 8–9. See also McDonnell, "Fit for Common Service? Class, Race and

Recruitment in Revolutionary Virginia," in *Revolutionary War and Society*, ed. John P. Resch and Walter Sargent (DeKalb, Ill., 2006).

27. Diary of Robert Honyman, Mar. 12, 1779, Alderman Library, University of Virginia; Arthur Campbell to Patrick Henry, Mar. 15, 1779, in Wm. P. Palmer, ed., *Calendar of Virginia State Papers and other Manuscripts, 1652–1781, Preserved in the Capitol at Richmond* (Richmond, Va., 1875) 1: 317; Edmund Pendleton to James Madison, Sept. 25, 1779, in Mays, *Letters and Papers of Edmund Pendleton*, 1: 308–9.

28. Col. Digges to Theodorick Bland, Sept. 16, 1777, in Campbell, *Bland Papers*, 1: 69; Granville Smith to Leven Powell, Aug. 28, 1777, in "The Leven Powell Correspondence, 1775–1787," *John P. Branch Historical Papers of Randolph-Macon College* 2 (June 1902): 125; Raleigh Colston to William Aylett, Oct. 24, 1777, in Selby, *Revolution in Virginia*, 172. The aggrieved captain thought the crew were "a sett of unfeeling animals." As the Virginia legislature continued to print money to pay the large bounties it promised and other wartime costs, prices for goods and also for military labor rose quickly. As early as January 1777, Robert Honyman reported that "every thing rises exceedingly in price, owing to the immense quantity of paper money, & likewise to the precariousness of its credit" (Diary of Robert Honyman, Jan. 16, 1777, Alderman Library, University of Virginia. See also Apr. 10, 1777). In 1778 Lund Washington also noted that it was difficult to find seamen to outfit a privateer in his possession because they were in such high demand. He was furious that he had to negotiate so much with a local carpenter (ibid., June 6, 1778; L. Washington to George Washington, Mar. 18, Apr. 1, 1778, Library of Virginia, see also Sept. 2, 1778; H. R. McIlwaine, ed., *Legislative Journals of the Council of Colonial Virginia* [Richmond, Va., 1918], 2: 99, 112–13 [Mar. 7, Mar. 30, 1778]). On labor shortages in the mid-Atlantic region during the war, see esp. Michael V. Kennedy, "The Home Front during the War for Independence: The Effect of Labor Shortages on Commercial Production in the Mid-Atlantic," in *A Companion to the American Revolution*, ed. Jack P. Greene and J. R. Pole (Malden, Mass., 2000), 332–41.

29. David Jameson to James Madison, Sept. 20, 1780, in Hutchinson and Rachal, *Papers of James Madison*, 2: 94; Edmund Pendleton to Madison, Sept. 25, 1780, Pendleton to George Washington, Dec. 22, 1778, in Mays, *Letters and Papers of Edmund Pendleton*, 1: 309, 276–77. For "demon of avarice," see Pendleton to Washington, May 21, 1778, in John Robert Sellers, "The Virginia Continental Line, 1775–1780" (Ph.D. diss., Tulane University, 1968), 289. See also Diary of Robert Honyman, June 6, 1778, Feb. 15, 1779, Alderman Library, University of Virginia.

30. George Washington to Richard Henry Lee, May 25, 1778, in Fitzpatrick, *Writings of George Washington*, 11: 452. See also ibid., 11: 438 n. 43; Patrick Henry to Henry Laurens, June 18, 1778, in Hutchinson and Rachal, *Papers of James Madison*, 1: 245; David Griffith to Leven Powell, June 3, 1778, in Powell, *Biographical Sketch of Col. Leven Powell*, 79; Lee to Thomas Jefferson, May 2, May 3, 1778, in Boyd, *Papers of Thomas Jefferson*, 2: 176–77. See also Baylor Hill to Theodorick Bland, May 5, 1778, in Bland Family Papers, Virginia Historical Society. The draft also short-circuited the volunteer scheme. In particular the high prices paid by many counties and individuals to induce men to serve in their stead or as part of the county quota drove up bounties generally. Potential recruits simply refused to volunteer for the armed forces when they could sell their services to their neighbors for much higher prices. Robert Honyman noted in mid-March 1778 that recruiting for the volunteer scheme "scarce advances at all." There were "none at all offering for that service" (Diary of Robert Honyman, Mar. 15, 1778, Alderman Library, University of Virginia).

31. Don Higginbotham, *The War of American Independence: Military Attitudes, Policies, and Practice, 1763–1789* (New York, 1971), 352–54.

32. Proceedings of the Fifth Virginia Convention, May 7, 1776, in Scribner and Tarter, *Revolutionary Virginia*, 7: 47; Hening, *Statutes at Large*, 9: 140; Eliga H. Gould, "To Strengthen the King's Hands: Dynastic Legitimacy, Militia Reform, and Ideas of National Unity in England, 1745–1760," *Historical Journal* 34, no. 2 (June 1991): 329–48; Gould, *The Persistence of Empire: British Political Culture in the Age of the American Revolution* (Chapel Hill, N.C., 2000), esp. 72–105.

33. Berkeley County Petition [Nov. 18, 1780], Virginia Legislative Petitions, Library of Virginia.

34. Ibid.

35. Ibid.

36. Orange County Petition [May 13, 1779], ibid. Poorer militia were materially interested in procuring recruits under this voluntary system of raising soldiers because it meant they would also be relieved of future, and perhaps more coercive, calls on them to fill the army. If the assembly instituted another draft, individuals might have to raise far more money to avoid service.

37. Ibid. See also Culpeper County Petition [May 18, 1779], ibid.

38. Hening, *Statutes at Large*, 10: 257–62.

39. Ibid. The legislature also targeted pacifists, including Quakers and Mennonites, who were now expected to carry the full costs of finding substitutes.

40. David Jameson to James Madison, Aug. 13, 1780, in Hutchinson and Rachal, *Papers of James Madison*, 2: 58.

41. Robert Pleasants thought that when his neighbors believed themselves safe from a draft, they "don't...feel for others." He had heard that one of the men in his division had announced he would give £50,000 for a recruit "rather than submit to a draft" (Pleasants to Col. Turner Southall, Sept. 3, 1780, in Robert Pleasants of Curles, Henrico County, Letterbook, Library of Virginia). Theodorick Bland Sr. to Theodorick Bland Jr., Oct. 21, 1780, in Campbell, *Bland Papers*, 2: 37–38.

42. Extract of Court Records, Prince William County [June 7, 1781], Virginia Legislative Petitions, Library of Virginia; Diary of Robert Honyman, May 11, June 1, June 5, July 22, 1781, Alderman Library, University of Virginia. See also *Journal of the House of Delegates of Virginia* (Charlottesville, Va., 1781), 14; H.J. Eckenrode, *The Revolution in Virginia* (1916; repr., Hamden, Conn., 1964), 259; Edmund Pendleton to James Madison, May 7, 1781, in Mays, *Letters and Papers of Edmund Pendleton*, 1: 354; Selby, *Revolution in Virginia*, 274; Frey, *Water from the Rock*, 156–57.

43. Diary of Robert Honyman, May 11, May 27, 1781, Alderman Library, University of Virginia; John Banister to Theodorick Bland, May 16, 1781, in Campbell, *Bland Papers*, 2: 68–70; Richard Henry Lee to William Lee, July 15, 1781, in James Curtis Ballagh, ed., *The Letters of Richard Henry Lee* (1914; repr., New York, 1970), 2: 242; R.H. Lee to [George Washington], Sept. 17, 1781, ibid., 2: 256; Selby, *Revolution in Virginia*, 275; Frey, *Water from the Rock*, 159, 167; Berlin, *Many Thousands Gone*, 259. Cassandra Pybus does a good job separating rhetoric from reality regarding the number of enslaved Virginians who fled to the British in Pybus, "Jefferson's Faulty Math: The Question of Slave Defections in the American Revolution," *WMQ* 62, no. 2 (April 2005): 243–64. The exaggerated accounts given by contemporaries, however, raise intriguing questions about the perceptions and magnified fears of planters during the crisis.

44. Diary of Robert Honyman, May 27, May 30, 1781, Alderman Library, University of Virginia; Richard Henry Lee to Arthur Lee, June 4, 1781, in Ballagh, Letters of Richard Henry Lee, 2: 230; Edmund Pendleton to James Madison, July 6, July 23, 1781, in Mays, *Letters and Papers of Edmund Pendleton*, 1: 365, 367;

George Mason to Pearson Chapman, May 31, 1781, in Rutland, *Papers of George Mason*, 2: 688; Emory G. Evans, *Thomas Nelson and the Revolution in Virginia* (Williamsburg, Va., 1978), 100–101; Selby, *Revolution in Virginia*, 271–72; Frey, *Water from the Rock*, 166.

45. Contrary to usual practice, locals demanded that the court execute Jack and make him "an example of Justice and not of Mercy" (Palmer, *Calendar of Virginia State Papers*, 1: 477–78; Patrick Lockhart to Governor Nelson, Nov. 16, 1781, ibid., 2: 604–5).

46. Elizabeth City County Petition [Mar. 8, 1781], Virginia Legislative Petitions, Library of Virginia; James Innes to Thomas Jefferson, Oct. [21?], 1780, in Boyd, *Papers of Thomas Jefferson*, 4: 55. The problem seems to have been widespread. See, for example, the General Assembly of North Carolina to Jefferson, Feb. 14, 1781, ibid., 4: 610–11. Even officers were not above abandoning their duties. In Westmoreland County in 1781, William Holland, a militia captain, refused to turn out when called to guard against British plundering up the Potomac. Holland told his neighbors that he would not turn out to act as a guard because "the people in Boston, New York & Phil: that stayed by their property rescued it, & those that flew into the Country & took up arms lost it totally." Holland "swore by God if the enemy came upon the spott, he would not take up arms in defence of his country, but would stay by his property & would make the best terms he could" (Affidavits of Saunders, Harper, and Washington, June 25, 1781, and Beesly Edgar Joel to the Governor, July 1, 1781, in Palmer, *Calendar of Virginia State Papers*, 2: 183, 916). There is remarkably little direct evidence that white lower and middling Virginians lived in fear of rebellious slaves. Only after the Revolution did Edmund Randolph recall that the poor militia turnout in the face of the British raids in 1781 was due to enslaved Virginians. He wrote that the "helpless wives and children were at the mercy not only of the males among the slaves but of the very women, who could handle deadly weapons; and these could not have been left in safety in the absence of all authority of the masters and of union among neighbors" (Randolph, *History of Virginia*, ed. Arthur H. Shaffer [Charlottesville, Va., 1970], 285).

47. Proceedings of the Fifth Virginia Convention, May 7, 1776, in Scribner and Tarter, *Revolutionary Virginia*, 7: 47; Hening, *Statutes at Large*, 9: 140; Gould, *Persistence of Empire*, esp. 72–105; Gould, *Historical Journal* 34: 329–48. For "most indigent circumstances," see Pittsylvania County Petition [June 19, 1781], Virginia Legislative Petitions, Library of Virginia. See also Amherst County Petitions [May 29, 1781], ibid.

48. George Skillern to Jefferson, Apr. 14, 1781, in Boyd, *Papers of Thomas Jefferson*, 5: 449–50.

49. Charlotte County Petition [May 26, 1780], Virginia Legislative Petitions, Library of Virginia.

50. See Joseph Jones to James Madison, Nov. 18, 1780, in Hutchinson and Rachal, *Papers of James Madison*, 2: 182–83; undated bill, Legislative Department, Rough Bills, Library of Virginia (brought to my attention by Brent Tarter at the Library of Virginia). Hening, *Statutes at Large*, 10: 326–37.

51. James Madison to Joseph Jones, Nov. 28, 1780, Jones to Madison, Dec. 8, 1780, in Hutchinson and Rachal, *Papers of James Madison*, 2: 209, 233. The editors note that Madison intended this part of his letter for publication. Maryland leaders authorized the enlistment of enslaved men into the army in their legislative session in the fall of 1780. The following year, however, they stopped short of raising an entire regiment of enslaved Marylanders (ibid., 2: 210 n. 1; Quarles, *Negro in the American Revolution*, 56–57).

52. Alexander Dick to the Speaker of the House, May 11, 1781, box 2, Executive Communications, Library of Virginia.

53. Edmund Pendleton to James Madison, Jan. 1, 1781, Joseph Jones to Madison, Dec. 8, 1780, in Hutchinson and Rachal, *Papers of James Madison*, 2: 268, 232–33.

54. Joseph Jones to James Madison, Dec. 8, 1780, in Hutchinson and Rachal, *Papers of James Madison*, 2: 232–33.

55. For a full account of the riots and protests of 1781, see McDonnell, *Politics of War*, chap. 13.

56. Testimony of Vincent Redman and others, "Proceedings of a General Court Martial," June 18, 1781, in Executive Papers, Library of Virginia.

57. Testimony of William Bernard and others, "Proceedings of a General Court Martial," June 19, 1781, ibid. For a full account of the insurrections and problems of mobilization in 1781, see McDonnell, *Politics of War*, chap. 12.

58. Robert Honyman, who raced to Yorktown to see the showdown between George Washington and Charles Cornwallis, was disappointed with the small number of Virginia troops he found there. He believed that there were "but few" in the camp before York and no more than about fifteen hundred of the estimated fifteen thousand troops he saw there were militia members. Most, he reckoned, were French troops (Diary of Robert Honyman, Sept. 3, Sept. 5, Sept. 15, Oct. 7, Oct. 15, 1781, Alderman Library, University of Virginia). William Davies made the estimate of the total number of militia members available based on returns available to him at the war office in July 1781. He included all militiamen east of the Allegheny Mountains (see Davies to David Jameson, July 14, 1781, in Palmer, *Calendar of Virginia State Papers*, 2: 219). For militia members not staying the course, see Evans, *Thomas Nelson*, 117–18; Davies to Thomas Nelson, Sept. 15, Oct. 10, 1781, in War Office Orders [Letters], Aug. 15–Nov. 1, 1781, Library of Virginia; Nelson to Davies, Sept. 19, 1781, in H.R. McIlwaine, ed., *Official Letters of the Governors of the State of Virginia* (Richmond, Va., 1929), 3: 59; James Clay to Nelson, Sept. 13, 1781, in Executive Papers, Library of Virginia. For the number of enslaved Virginians with Cornwallis and the British, see Pybus, *WMQ* 62: 256–57.

59. Kathleen M. Brown, *Good Wives, Nasty Wenches, and Anxious Patriarchs: Gender, Race, and Power in Colonial Virginia* (Chapel Hill, N.C., 1996), 321. Brown noted that Virginia gentlemen secured their power through five sources: land ownership, control over sexual access to women, rights to the labor of slaves and servants, formal access to political life, and the ability to create and manipulate symbols signifying these other sources of power (323–27, 347). For enslaved Virginians and early royal efforts to subdue the patriots, see Holton, *Forced Founders*, esp. chap. 5; McCurry, *Masters of Small Worlds*, 50.

60. For the importance and centrality of patriarchy and the household economy, see esp. McCurry, *Masters of Small Worlds*, as well as Alice Kessler-Harris, "Treating the Male as 'Other': Redefining the Parameters of Labor History," *Labor History* 34, nos. 2–3 (Spring–Summer 1993): 202. Patriarchy is key. Elites' acknowledgment of patriarchy's being almost as important as property in creating, and co-opting, a citizenry of virtuous republicans can be seen in George Mason's constitutional proposal to enfranchise fathers with three children to support (see Rutland, *Papers of George Mason*, 1: 303).

61. Some middle-class demands were transatlantic in scope. As Peter Way has shown, the British army was very much a protocapitalist organization (Way, *WMQ* 57). And, as Eliga Gould has discovered in Britain, middle-class taxpayers there demanded the right to be armchair citizens and exempted themselves from military service (Gould, *Persistence of Empire*). As Allan Kulikoff notes, farmers and artisans not only struggled with great planters and land speculators for control over their land and property but also supplied essential support for slavery and the regulation of laborers and servants. Drawing on Eric Olin Wright's work, Kulikoff notes that

the middle classes "can be dominant and subordinate, exploited and exploiting. To maintain their grip on property, they make complex interclass alliances, tying themselves to rulers or—less often—to classes beneath them" (Kulikoff, *WMQ* 57: 832). For postwar, proslavery petitions, see Fredrika Teute Schmidt and Barbara Ripel Wilhelm, "Early Proslavery Petitions in Virginia," *WMQ* 30, no. 1 (January 1973): 133–46.

62. Diary of Robert Honyman, Dec. 20, 1779, Apr. 15, 1780, Alderman Library, University of Virginia (see also July 4, 1780). Edmund Pendleton to James Madison, Jan. 1, 1781, Joseph Jones to Madison, Nov. 18, Dec. 2, Dec. 8, 1780, in Hutchinson and Rachal, *Papers of James Madison*, 2: 268, 183, 219, 232–33; Thomas Madison to William Preston, Nov. 30, 1780, in Preston Papers, Virginia Historical Society. Robert Honyman and Theodorick Bland were not the only ones who complained about elections and the composition of the House in 1780. Almost as soon as the assembly convened, George Mason began a movement to bring in a new law for regulating elections. Mason agreed with Honyman about the quality of the members of the assembly: recent assemblies had been filled with "ignorant or obscure" men "so unequal to the Office." But Mason thought the problem was that many representatives had lately "been the Choice of a Handful, a Neighborhood, or a Junto" and as such were only the "nominal" rather than "the real Representatives of the People." Ignorant and obscure men, Mason continued, could have a "considerable Influence within a narrow Circle; but it will seldom extend thro' a County." But because Mason believed that so few voters attended elections, he thought that "a factious bawling Fellow, who will make a Noise four or five miles round him," could "prevail upon his party to attend" and "carry an Election against a Man of ten times his Weight & Influence in the County." Men of greater stature and more "Modesty & Merit," in his eyes, thus not only were discouraged from offering themselves as candidates but also could not compete if they did ("Remarks on the Proposed Bill for Regulating the Elections of the Members of the General Assembly" [ca. June 1, 1780], in Rutland, *Papers of George Mason*, 2: 629–32 [quotations, 630]).

63. See Herbert Sloan and Peter Onuf, "Politics, Culture, and the Revolution in Virginia: A Review of Recent Work," *VMHB* 91, no. 3 (July 1983): 280, 279. See also Norman K. Risjord, *Chesapeake Politics, 1781–1800* (New York, 1978), and more generally, the revealing findings of Woody Holton, "'Divide et Impera': *Federalist 10* in a Wider Sphere," *WMQ* 62, no. 2 (April 2005): 175–212, and esp. Holton, "'From the Labours of Others': The War Bonds Controversy and the Origins of the Constitution in New England," *WMQ* 61, no. 2 (April 2004): 271–316.

64. The link between army officers and Federalists is an old one, but the reasons for this connection have been less well explored. See Stanley Elkins and Eric McKitrick, *The Founding Fathers: Young Men of the Revolution* (Washington, D.C., 1962), but for a more recent take on this idea, see Don Higginbotham, "War and State Formation in Revolutionary America," in Gould and Onuf, *Empire and Nation*.

65. For John Shy's comments, see Shy, "American Society and Its War for Independence," in *A People Numerous and Armed: Reflections on the Military Struggle for American Independence* (New York, 1976), 119, 131–32. For an extended rumination on this theme, see Michael A. McDonnell, "National Identity and the American War for Independence Reconsidered," *Australasian Journal of American Studies 20*, no. 1 (July 2001): 3–17. That article owes a great deal to the suggestive insights of John Murrin, "Roof without Walls: The Dilemma of American National Identity," in *Beyond Confederation: Origins of the Constitution and American National Identity*, eds. Richard Beeman, Stephen Botein, and Edward C. Carter (Chapel Hill, N.C., 1987). For two other suggestive outcomes of tying the war years together with the postwar years, see Saul Cornell's nuanced and

class-based evaluation of anti-federalism, in Cornell, *The Other Founders: Anti-Federalism and the Dissenting Tradition in America, 1788–1828* (Chapel Hill, N.C., 1999); and Terry Bouton's superb piece, Bouton, "A Road Closed: Rural Insurgency in Post-Independence Pennsylvania," *Journal of American History* 87, no. 3 (December 2000): 855–87.

6

"I Have…a Lot of Work To Do": Cotton Mill Work and Women's Culture in Matoaca, Virginia, 1888–95

Beth English

"They say the mill will stop some in the summer and if it does I will come," wrote Anthelia Holt, a textile mill operative from Matoaca, Chesterfield County, to her friend Lottie Clark in March 1892. "But it is so hard to get out if it is running that I can never promise you faithful."[1] Much to Anthelia's disappointment, the mill did not stop production as she had hoped, and she was unable to make her visit that spring to Lottie, who lived in the nearby community of Namozine, Amelia County. The demands of industrial employment circumscribed the life of Anthelia Holt despite her "strong notion for leaving."[2] Born in 1861, Anthelia Holt (1861–1950) was the eldest of ten children born to Alpheus Jenkin Holt (1836–1898) and Mary Ann Blankenship Holt (1838–1907).[3] Anthelia ultimately became a weaver at the Matoaca Manufacturing Company (MMC) and, thereby, a member of the first generation of the New South's industrial workforce. Her world, however, was also firmly grounded in the traditions of an agricultural community and her family's rural roots. The letters she wrote to Lottie from her family's home in the Matoaca mill village offer unique insight into the ways in which Anthelia and other female employees at the MMC engaged, as women and as workers, with each other, their families, and the larger community. The regimens of factory work, family duties, and networks of mutual aid and assistance largely defined the lives of Matoaca's mill women. Yet, they blended these realities and responsibilities with outings in the

From *Virginia Magazine of History & Biography*. Originally published in volume 114, number 3 (2006) of *The Virginia Magazine of History and Biography*, the quarterly journal of the Virginia Historical Society.

country, church services, and rituals of courtship and marriage to create a white, working-women's culture in late-nineteenth-century Matoaca.

Although the workforce of the post–Civil War southern textile industry was overlooked for many years by historians specializing in the South, by the early 1990s, studies on this group had become, in the words of one scholar, "something of a cottage industry."[4] Beginning in the 1970s, historians influenced by the analytical approaches of E.P. Thompson and Herbert Gutman began using new written and oral sources to fashion a more inclusive account of the American textile industry.[5] This new social history shifted the focus away from corporations and those who managed them to the textile industry's millhands. Such groundbreaking works as the collaborative *Like a Family* analyzed the process of industrialization in the New South through the experiences of the textile workers themselves. Historians began concentrating not just on the workplace but also on how individuals acted within a context of industrial employment to create distinct attitudes and cultures that transcended the boundaries of work and extended into their homes and communities.[6]

Building on these earlier works, textile industry scholars have recently gone on to delve deeper into such issues as the nature of workers' power within the system of southern mill village paternalism, the ways in which various intersections of race and gender have shaped working-class politics on local and state levels, and the question of why the textile industry and the South as a whole have historically been the least unionized manufacturing sector and region in the United States.[7] By concentrating on individuals and their experiences, attitudes, and actions within various contexts, these studies have allowed a deeper understanding and appreciation of those who labored in the nation's textile mills. However, as noted by historian Dolores Janiewski, "It is particularly difficult to recapture the texture of family life. Domestic routines were little recorded in the documents of the time, and women did not often discuss daily events in formal interviews."[8]

The Holt–Clark letters help to do just that. Purchased by the College of William and Mary during the 1940s as part of a general statewide solicitation of family papers relevant to local Virginia history, the collection provides an immediacy of experience and offers a rare look into the day-to-day life of a late-nineteenth-century white female textile operative.[9] The correspondence illuminates intimate aspects of Anthelia Holt's life. It also lends insight into the experiences of other women living and working in Matoaca. Such records of the lives of female mill workers are exceedingly rare. As such, Anthelia's letters to Lottie contribute in a distinctive way to a greater understanding of the ways in which mill work, household tasks, and women's relationships with one another came together and produced a female culture in Matoaca and in other mill towns across the South.

Throughout the antebellum South, industrialization occurred largely to the extent that it served the interests of the region's slave-based agricultural economy. Railroads, iron works, and cotton, grist, and saw mills served as offshoots of the southern plantation. Most investments in antebellum southern industry were directly related to fluctuations in cash-crop prices. When cash-crop prices were high, land and slaves were primary outlets for surplus capital. But there were also southerners who invested capital in industrial concerns, so that by the 1820s and 1830s manufacturing facilities were established in southern cities and, like the Matoaca Manufacturing Company, were scattered throughout the countryside. The development of southern industries remained limited through the Civil War, but the small antebellum factories that survived into the postwar years, and those built as part of a broad "cotton mill campaign" through the turn of the century, provided livelihoods for increasing numbers of southerners.[10]

First chartered in 1836 as a cotton and paper mill, during the final two decades of the nineteenth century the MMC was a small textile manufactory producing coarse cotton goods and employing about 200 workers. In 1880, of the 593 individuals living in Maroaca, 23 percent of the women and 9 percent of the men worked full-time at the mill. Of those women who earned wages outside their homes, mill operatives were a clear majority, constituting more than 90 percent of all paid female workers. Although the number of Matoaca women working outside their homes dropped significantly by 1900 to just over 8 percent of the 1,569 residents then living there, more than 85 percent of these still worked at the Matoaca Manufacturing Company.[11] At that date, the majority of MMC employees rented company houses in what was dubbed "the village," but throughout the duration of her 1888–1895 correspondences with Lottie Clark, Anthelia Holt lived near the Matoaca mill on what is now Stuart Street with her family in a house owned by her father.[12]

Transformations that occurred in southern agriculture after the Civil War played an integral part in the late-nineteenth-century development of the South's textile industry and in bringing people like Anthelia Holt to work for wages in a cotton mill. The war brought about a fundamental alteration in the operations of small, white-owned farms throughout the region. During the antebellum and war periods, Piedmont farmers focused much of their energies on subsistence-based, diversified agricultural pursuits. Farming families remained largely self-sufficient by raising a wide array of grains, fruits, vegetables, and livestock and engaging in local networks of barter and exchange for goods or services to meet basic household needs. Shortly after the end of the war, however, many small farmers found themselves plunged into debt and progressively drawn into the cultivation of cash crops like cotton and tobacco as they sought credit from local merchants in their attempts to rebuild farms and replenish herds of livestock lost during wartime.[13]

The growth of the post–Civil War southern textile industry was, in large part, tied to these white southerners who saw in mill work an opportunity for steady employment and economic stability. Many farming families found that their children's labor, particularly that of their daughters, was worth more in a local textile mill than it was on the land. As one strategy for familial survival and as an insulation from debt, poverty, tenancy, and destitution in the emergent postbellum economy, members of these families worked in the mills with the intention of earning wages that might keep a farm viable or support a household with "public" work when the land no longer could.[14]

Employment at the Matoaca mill, as in textile mills throughout the South, was race-specific. Antebellum southern mill owners had overwhelmingly used white labor in their mills because it was cheaper to employ than buying a slave workforce. This racial hiring preference remained after the war as transformations in the economy of the countryside created a large pool of cheap white labor. In a number of mills, African-American men held jobs in the "yard," loading and unloading wagons and trains as well as breaking apart bales of cotton, while black women sometimes found jobs as cleaners and custodians. Although mill owners could have employed black operatives at an even lower cost than whites, the majority of southern industrialists, nonetheless, rarely deviated from the regional norm dictating that only white labor would be employed in manufacturing positions in the South's cotton mills. Indeed, part and parcel of the growth of the southern textile industry after the Civil War was the creation and maintenance of a social proscription that made mill work an employment option for whites only. Mill owners tapped into many poor whites' racial fears that the abolition of slavery meant direct competition with free blacks for jobs in agriculture and industry, potentially leading to a disruption of traditional patterns of white supremacy. Manufacturers and industrial boosters alike argued that textile mill work was a way for dispossessed white farmers to reintegrate themselves into the regional economy, facilitate their escape from "degrading" competition with black farm labor, and ensure that southern industry could grow while consolidating white hegemony. All of the production employees of the Matoaca Manufacturing Company through the 1880s and 1890s were white.[15]

The MMC was just one of several enterprises undergirding the mixed industrial and agricultural post–Civil War economy of Chesterfield County. Scattered throughout the county were sites of extensive timbering as well as industrial enterprises, including textile mills in Matoaca, Ettrick, and on Swift Creek, two brickyards at Robious Station, extensive coal-mining operations in Midlothian and Clover Hill, a tannery in Hallsboro, a cannery in Drewry's Bluff, and iron works and cotton and woolen mills in Manchester. The Richmond and Danville, Richmond and Petersburg, and the Farmville and Powhatan railroads linked these towns and the surrounding countryside to the county's major trade and shipping outlets in Petersburg and Richmond. Small farmers throughout the county continued to practice a type of diversified agriculture that had been typical of their antebellum yeoman predecessors. "Nowhere has nature been more lavish in dispensing her bounties in providing for such a diversity of crops...," one observer noted. "Passing along the roads of the county, we see one farmer making a specialty of dark shipping tobacco; another, fancy bright leaf; and another corn, wheat, rye, oats, peanuts, cotton, or vegetables for home and foreign consumption....The uplands are particularly adapted to the growth of apples, peaches, grapes, strawberries, & c."[16]

By combining the produce of gardens and orchards, meat from hogs, and cash earned by selling cotton, corn, oats, or tobacco, some of these farming families remained self-sustaining throughout the last decades of the nineteenth century. Although removed from their rural roots, mill families regularly cultivated gardens, tended fruit trees, and kept chickens, pigs, and perhaps a cow, all on small plots of land. The Holt family was no exception. During the spring planting and autumn harvesting seasons, Anthelia filled her letters to Lottie with news of weather conditions, rains that made the family's garden "look right pretty" but interfered with her father's plans to sow oats, a desire for Lottie to help her "drink cider [and] eat apples and peaches," and the slaughter of her father's pigs, providing the Holt family with "plenty of meat."[17] These efforts, though, were secondary in importance to the family's work-related income. Through the 1880s the Holt' household economy depended on the wages that Anthelia; her father Alpheus, a Civil War veteran; and her brother William earned at Matoaca's textile mill. As such, the Holt household was one of many in that community and the wider New South making the transition from farm to factory.[18]

This shift was felt in the regimented schedule of life at the mill. Employees at the Matoaca Manufacturing Company consistently worked ten- to twelve-hour days, six days a week. Fatigue weighed heavily on Anthelia, to the point that she was "so tired" she "could not sleep" at night.[19] In late autumn, in preparation for the yearly Christmas rush, thirteen- or fourteen-hour shifts were not uncommon. Such circumstances often made factory work a heavy burden to bear. Agonizing that she was at the mill "untill after seven oclock every night and until four oclock every Saturday," Anthelia beseeched Lottie to "know that I am in the penitentiary now for we won't see anything out doors only on Sunday."[20]

White women and men both worked at the MMC, but the division of labor in the mill was largely gender-specific. Such sex-typing of jobs in mills often physically separated men from women. Most men held positions as managers, loom-fixers, clerks, and packers. Women, overwhelmingly, worked as spinners, carders, and like Anthelia Holt, as weavers.[21] The female workers at the Matoaca mill, like their counterparts throughout the region, created gendered bonds of commonality in the workplace by sharing daily work routines. These connections regularly reinforced relationships outside the mill as well.[22]

Anthelia Holt and her co-workers were accustomed to hard work in their homes and on their family farms, but these women found factory employment tiring, tedious, and physically taxing in new and challenging ways. What did not change throughout these years of transition, however, was the unpaid and undervalued work that women provided through the day-to-day organization of and responsibility for the care of homes and children.[23] Although fewer than 20 percent of the women employed at the

Matoaca mill between 1880 and 1900 were married, most of the female operatives faced a form of the double day: work outside the home while still remaining responsible for traditional "female" tasks.[24] Through their employment at the MMC, many of Matoaca's workers became part of a growing southern white female wage-earning class, but husbands, fathers, brothers, and the women themselves expected a continuation of the gendered roles that defined men as providers and women as caretakers and nurturers. As such, the latter not only toiled at their spindles and looms an average of seventy hours a week but also held full-time jobs outside the mill, raising children, washing laundry, and preparing meals. The difficulties of managing both public and private work were myriad. "I wish you would come down and help me...I have...a lot of work to do," Anthelia wrote to Lottie, "and dont have any time" except "at night."[25] A domestic ideal of women as homemakers and men as breadwinners certainly influenced but often did not reflect the realities of Matoaca's textile mill women.

Anthelia Holt was neither a wife nor a mother during her employment at the Matoaca Manufacturing Company, but domestic tasks still filled many of her hours outside the mill. Daughters of farming and mill families alike performed household chores from a young age, simultaneously helping their mothers while learning to replicate tried and true cleaning, cooking, and child-rearing skills.[26] "You must excuse the mistakes," Anthelia scrawled to Lottie during a night spent watching her younger siblings, "for the children make so much noise that I hardly know what I am doing."[27] For Anthelia, these evenings were just a taste of what lay ahead when she would, presumably, marry and become mistress of her own household. Until then however, she only felt the full brunt of the double day when her mother was ill or visiting relatives. When Anthelia's mother, father, and sister Velvie, went on a short out-of-town trip in 1891, Anthelia noted that she had to "keep house while they are gone," recalling later that she "had to get up at four oclock every morning" to prepare "corn and butter beans for breakfast" before leaving for a full day of work at the mill. When Anthelia's shift ended, her workday was only half finished. She returned home in the evening to prepare supper and "ironed all the clothes" before retiring to bed.[28] Clearly understanding the responsibilities, hardships, and expectations that came along with the joys of love, companionship, and children, Anthelia admitted that even though "the marriage fever has broke out...and is spreading very fast...I think getting married is serious business."[29]

Shared work experiences, both at home and in the mill, ultimately produced networks that became an integral part of the culture of Matoaca's mill women. Defined as "a set of habits, values, practices, institutions, [and] way of seeing the world," working women's culture in general, and specifically in Matoaca as revealed by Anthelia in her letters to Lottie, formed out of intersections of workplace experiences, family responsibilities, and community networks.[30] Indeed, networks of female friends, co-workers, and kin proved a gender-specific means of sustenance and support for these women as they actively participated in the creation of collective strategies to cope with the daily restrictions that industrial work imposed upon them. They built their networks on notions of neighborliness, obligation, cooperation, and mutual exchange, preserving values found throughout the rural South but reshaped to serve the specific needs of women and families involved in a transition from farm to factory. Because they worked long hours at the mill, women needed assistance to carry out their responsibilities for the nurturing and care of family, friends, kin, and community. Being able to rely on others to help nurse the sick or tend their homes buffered the difficulties faced daily by Matoaca's female operatives. They provided mill workers like Anthelia Holt a safety net for themselves, their households, and their loved ones. The networks became an essential part of life for these women, and by extension, their families and the entire community.[31]

Relationships outside the Matoaca mill often originated in and had a special purposefulness inside the factory itself. Knowing that surplus labor was abundant and that their posts could be filled easily and permanently by someone else, Matoaca mill women were particularly careful about leaving their jobs, even for short periods, because of illness, family obligations, or vacations. Akin to their counterparts throughout the New South, Anthelia and her co-workers regularly watched each other's looms so that they could take periodic breaks from their physically taxing work. They used workplace networks to find temporary replacements who could tend their machines for a few hours, days, or even weeks. The operatives, in turn, acted as conduits through which their replacement women, usually friends or kin from the wider community, might secure long-term employment at the mill. Anthelia Holt knew firsthand the difficulties and personal discomfort that could result when she could not make such arrangements. "I cannot say that I am well," Anthelia told Lottie during the summer of 1889, but because no women were free to watch her looms, she was "up and at work" despite having "fallen away so you would hardly know me."[32] Yet, when Anthelia wanted to take a short vacation from work during 1893, she was able to make arrangements for a woman seeking a full-time position there to take over her looms temporarily. Because she "succeeded in getting someone," Anthelia relished that she could take her "rest" without fear of losing her job while, at the same time, providing a set of looms on which the woman could train so that she could go to work for good upon Anthelia's return.[33]

Such networks of reciprocity permeated the wider Matoaca community. Women often spent their scarce free hours caring for the ill and infirm. Anthelia sometimes used "nearly all" her hours after work "going to see the sick."[34] They cared for each other during periods of illness, shared one another's sadness, and offered sympathy and support. The women of Matoaca gave what little time and energy they had left after a long day at the mill to family members and friends, often at the expense of rest and other small enjoyments. Anthelia did not get any "April fools" in 1890 because she tended to a cousin who "was very low," lamenting to Lottie that "I thought he would die in spite of all we could do... Willie was so bad off that I did not leave his bed five minutes at a time."[35] The networks also extended from one's family members to include unrelated women, particularly female neighbors and co-workers. Sitting up all night with a sick friend in September of 1889 made Anthelia "so sleepy" that she could "hardly see now to write."[36] Likewise, when a young friend of Anthelia's became ill, she was "over there all the time" that she "was from work" and noted when the friend died four days later that "we had a lot of fun together and I certainly will miss her." Residents of the mill community became part of Anthelia Holt's extended family. She was one of many women who risked her own health and well-being to nurse friends and co-workers through bouts of pneumonia, typhoid fever, and "congestion on the brain."[37] These acts strengthened and were integral facets of the culture of Matoaca's white female mill operatives.

The networks Matoaca women used as they cared for the physically sick helped them through the times of psychological distress that accompanied death as well. On a regular basis, these women soothed the emotional wounds of family members and co-workers who faced the deaths of loved ones from disease and accidents. Anthelia comforted and shared the grief of a friend whose beau had passed away, never feeling "as sorry for any boddy" in her life, believing that "if anybody were to come and tell me my fellow was dead... I should choke to death."[38] In turn, Anthelia knew that in her time of need she could rely on these same friends and co-workers for succor. When her oldest brother, William, died in a railroad accident in 1890, Anthelia reached out, in writing, to Lottie Clark. "He did not live but one hour after he was hurt he was mashed through his body and had one leg nearly cut off," she grieved, "I loved him so good and now I can never see him any more."[39] Subsequent letters from Lottie gave her great comfort, and visits from friends and co-workers lifted her spirits as they lent her their support.

The female networks within the Matoaca mill community also created opportunities for women to share good times while helping each other with tedious tasks and arduous chores. Work-sharings, events during which members of the community gathered to help an individual or family complete difficult or time-consuming tasks, had a long tradition in rural communities. While men built barns, shucked a harvest of corn, or cleared new ground for planting, women worked in groups to quilt, can and preserve fruits, and make wine and apple cider. The successful completion of the day's tasks often ended with a community party. For the female textile operatives of Matoaca, work-sharings survived the transition from country to town and continued to be an integral part of their collective culture throughout the postbellum period. Such cooperative efforts not only got work done but also united Matoaca's individual members in a spirit of reciprocity. When the women of the Holt family held a quilting in November of 1891, they "had a large crowd plenty of music and singing."[40] The woman or family who hosted a work-sharing reaped the profit of the day's toil and willingly repaid in kind. Anthelia worked all day helping a co-worker at an 1893 "sugar stew" and "had a splendid time."[41] The sharings reminded those who participated that neighborliness and mutuality were not simply duties owed. They were values to celebrate and pass on to future generations. The events gave women a chance to visit, gossip, and refresh their ties to one another away from the mill. Work-sharings were a poignant example of how the bonds of mutuality that existed between the women of Matoaca could successfully join work and play, business and pleasure, practical needs and fun.[42]

In addition, weddings were occasions, much like work-sharings, at which Matoaca's female operatives supported one another. The sometimes simple, but often elaborate, ceremonies joining men and women in marriage, reinforced the bonds that united the entire community. The assistance female friends and co-workers lent both before and during a wedding, however, accentuated the gender-specific relationships that these women had with one another. Anthelia commonly spent the night before fellow operatives' nuptials with the bride-to-be, helping her prepare for the following day's events. On one occasion, "the groom come Sunday morning at six o'clock," hurrying Anthelia "to death" before she could "get the bride ready."[43] Sustaining one another during celebrations as they did in moments of sorrow, Matoaca's mill women "stood up" for one another during the actual wedding service. Two friends of Anthelia's "were married at church" and "looked very nices." She remarked that "they had twenty waiters ten boys and ten girls." The boys wore "black suits white ties white gloves...the girls all wore white dresses and white flowers."[44]

Matoaca's female networks also played an important role in defining acceptable and unacceptable behavior by community members. The institution of marriage and the wedding services themselves were joyous but also serious. Anthelia criticized the participants of one 1893 wedding when the revelry went too far. "They were not married until eleven o'clock and most of the crowd was drunk," she wrote, and much to her dismay, "the bride groom was so drunk that he could hardly stand up."[45] Participating in a wedding while drunk caused gossip and scandal within Anthelia's circle of female friends. Transgressions of customary manners also provoked hit condemnation. She wrote in disgust to Lottie about the remarriage of a widower, whose wife Anthelia had tended while she lay dying a month earlier. "We are going to have a marriage here next week," Anthelia reported to Lottie, "a Miss Candle and Mr. Bridgewater his wife was burried just five weeks ago I never heard of such a thing befor I hardly know what to think of it."[46] In Anthelia's eyes, Bridgewater and Candle did not conform to normal standards of decorum and respect for the dead, opening themselves and their relationship to censure from the community. The culture that bonded Matoaca's mill women into networks of reciprocity and mutual assistance also functioned as a moral compass for the wider community, celebrating acceptable behavior but reproaching errant conduct.

The wedding of two mill employees was one of the most important and popular occasions for men and women to gather, dance, and socialize. In a typical Matoaca wedding, the couple was "married at church and the church was crowded...then the crowd went to the house...[and] they danced and played."[47] Although Matoaca's mill women created and relied daily upon the networks that evolved in a gendered society and workplace, mixed-sex socialization was a central element of this female culture as well. At wedding celebrations friends and family encouraged young, single women like Anthelia to "have a good time and make a mash and get married soon."[48] Sometimes, however, such advice backfired. She "did not have much of a time" at a wedding she attended in February of 1889, ruining one of the few leisure activities she attended that month. Anthelia complained that "a fellow went with me that I did not like and I was relly mad all the time."[49] But, as in all other aspects of life, work at the mill often impeded operatives from engaging in such events. In one extreme instance when responsibilities at the mill interfered, the wedding of two employees "did not come off" because "the poor bride worked all day." When Anthelia discovered that the groom also worked through his wedding day, she admitted she "never heard of any thing to beat that."[50] The women employed at Matoaca's mill, nevertheless, effectively maneuvered around the restrictions and regularities of factory employment and their duties to families and friends to make time for fun.

Leisure time was a scarce commodity for Matoaca's female mill workers. Long hours at the factory coupled with domestic and community responsibilities left little time to rest, relax, or recreate. Anthelia found the limitations that work imposed on her life difficult to accept at times. Though she wrote to Lottie that "I am very glad you are going to school," she added, "I wish that I could go."[51] Not wanting to "loose the time from work" was also a typical reason to miss a social event, forgo a vacation, or cut short a day of jollity. Anthelia once went to a fair in Richmond during which she saw "large cows and hogs and sheep," visited "exhibits from the different counties...all very good and very nicly arraigned," and saw a "splendid" tight rope performance in which "one man rode on a bycle backwards and forwards up on the rope and two more men were in a swinger fastened on the rope." She wrote to Lottie that "I wish you could have seen them" and that she had only stayed one day because she "could not get off" from work.[52] Despite the demands of the workplace, when the mill closed Saturday evenings, Sundays, and for Christmas and Easter, Anthelia and her friends from the mill led surprisingly active social lives.

Unscheduled mill stoppages, frequently the result of the cheap but unreliable use of the Appomattox River as a source of power, also provided a respite for the operatives. When "high water washed everything to pieces at the mill," in 1889, the Matoaca Manufacturing Company "stopped five weeks."[53] Heavy summer rains or cold snaps when "everything at the mill froze up" caused suspensions of production that turned into unofficial holidays for Matoaca's mill workers.[54] One such stoppage gave Anthelia a chance to "see a game of base ball" with some of her friends and left them hoping that the mill would remain closed long enough so they could "go up the river and have a fish fry."[55]

During these free hours, days, or weeks, outings to the country proved to be some of the most cherished times in the lives of Matoaca's female millhands. These excursions provided a chance to be away from the stifling mill and to enjoy the outdoors, something largely lost to workers in the farm-to-factory transition. Anthelia gushed about a weekend trip on which she "went fishing...and had lots of fun" and another where she could admire the wonders of springtime. "The partridges were hallering bob white," she informed Lottie, "and the whipowills were trying themselves."[56] Days in the country were also chances for the female operatives to socialize with men of the same age, something that was, for the most part, absent at work. The fish fry Anthelia planned to attend during the summer of 1893 mill stoppage included "seven boys and seven girls."[57] And, to Anthelia's delight in the winter of 1889, she "had such a nice time...up in the country" where she "made several mashes" when "two young men from Petersburg came up and a young man from the country came down" for a picnic.[58] These brief escapes to the country played an important role for Matoaca's female mill-hands. They provided an opportunity to socialize with each other and with men, and in a rural setting that harkened back to their country roots.

Religious services and church-sponsored activities, similarly, provided a social outlet for the mill workers of Matoaca. As was typical of black and white southerners alike, and among those living in both farm and factory communities throughout the region, Anthelia and her co-workers blended religiosity and recreation. Anthelia attended church services several times on Sundays and habitually held prayer meetings in her home. Guest preachers, speaking on Sundays and weekday evenings, drew huge crowds from Matoaca and surrounding towns. "The hall is crowded every night" to hear two Scottish preachers, Lottie learned in 1895, "people begin to go about five oclock and we have to hurry up when we get home [from the mill] to get any seat."[59] Revivals and protracted meetings that often lasted weeks at a time were occasions when one could visit with neighbors and co-workers and were events that elicited religious devotion and community fellowship. One "gracious revival" made Anthelia "determined to love and serve my heavenly Father better in the future." Noting that the church "was revived generally," Anthelia expressed joy that "two of my sisters were con-verted...and a lot of my friends...40 of them were baptised."[60] For young, single women like Anthelia though, these religious events did more than just strengthen the bonds that Matoaca's mill workers had with their God, their families, and their community. They also fostered social interaction and even courtship.[61]

Church-sponsored socials were gatherings at which Anthelia and her young, single co-workers could meet prospective beaus. At such events, the mill women usually designed activities to introduce the men and women in attendance to one another. At one "feast," Anthelia and her friends made ties that "went like hotcakes" when put up for sale to the young men. Each tie gave the man who purchased it the pleasure of spending the day with the woman in the crowd wearing an apron that matched his tie. Anthelia's match treated her to ice cream.[62] In the same fashion, the mill women "had a box Partie...for the benifit of the church" in 1894. Anthelia recounted for Lottie, "the girls all carried a box filled with some thing nice to eat and put them up and sold them to the young men at the highest bid," who, she continued, "then had to eat what was in the box with the girl it belonged to."[63] The female millhands also used these socials to make known their committed relationships to the entire community. In doing so, however, they also opened themselves and their "fellows" to public scrutiny. Anthelia met and approved of the man courting a friend and co-worker, remarking that "his head is red as fire and he is real good looking."[64] But Anthelia reproached her sister Addie and her intended for "looking like two dead frogs in the sunshine."[65]

Courting in Matoaca regularly occurred in the context of a religious or church-sponsored activity. Sunday church services and home prayer meetings were situations during which family members or the entire community could act as a couple's chaperone. For Anthelia Holt and most other unmarried female mill workers, a trip to church would not be complete unless a male suitor went along. Anthelia had "a grand time" during the mill closure for Easter in 1889, making "several mashes." When five men wanted to escort her to the Easter evening service, she solved the problem by letting "the first one who asked me go and two of the others walked in front and the other two behind...you may know we had lots of fun." When they reached the church, Anthelia was not surprised that "very girl in the crowd had a beau."[66] Likewise, "when a lot of men" called on Anthelia at her family's home one evening in October 1891, the men "proposed having a prayer meeting," telling Anthelia if she "would lead it they would do the praying."[67] Reflecting the significance Anthelia and her community placed upon both religion and romance that might lead a young couple to marriage, a type of church-sponsored, community dating ultimately evolved as a courtship ritual within Matoaca's female mill culture.[68]

In the end, Matoaca's mill women embraced these public courting rituals while simultaneously reserving for themselves a degree of autonomy.[69] As was typical throughout the South during the nineteenth century, Matoaca's residents placed great significance upon the importance of marriage and family. Yet, even though courting usually took place under the watchful eyes of parents, co-workers, and church members, choosing to marry one's suitor was a decision that, while influenced by societal norms and expectations, was ultimately a choice for the individual to make. Matoaca's female millhands exerted a great deal of agency in the judgment of when, to whom, and even if they would marry. "[T]here was two widdowers here yesterday," Anthelia explained to Lottie, "one took dinner here and had a fine horse and buggy...I went driving with two of them." But, she added, "I would not give the snap of my finger for all the men I saw yesterday."[70]

She vowed never to marry "but just have a good time with all the boys the rest of my life," rejecting a marriage proposal in 1893 because she "loved somebody else" and would "never marry any body while a certain fellow lives."[71] One Matoaca couple went so far as to leave the town completely, "run away and went to No[rth] C[arolina]," when the young woman's father "objected to her getting married."[72] Responsibilities and duties as women and mill workers often shaped the decisions made and activities participated in by Matoaca's mill women, but they exerted an element of control over their interpersonal relationships that was often absent from other aspects of their lives.

At the end of Anthelia Holt's 1888–1895 correspondence with Lottie Clark, she was thirty-four years old, still single, and working as a weaver at the Matoaca Manufacturing Company. Following the death of her father Alpheus three years later, she and her siblings provided the primary means of financial support for the Holt family. Anthelia and her twenty-three-year-old sister Allie both worked at the MMC, while her brothers Thomas, age twenty, and seventeen-year-old James also worked for wages, as a farm laborer and a cotton packer, respectively. Anthelia was single and continued to work at the Matoaca mill until she was forty years old, an age by which the vast majority of Matoaca's mill women had married, when she herself became the wife of Marshall Robinett, a widower with three children. Anthelia moved with her new husband and children to Norfolk. She lived there until her death in 1950.[73]

Anthelia, as a member of the workforce at the Matoaca Manufacturing Company for more than twenty years of her life, shared in a culture forged with other women employed at the mill from their common experiences. This culture was a touchstone of strength, sociability, and sustenance. Rooted in shared values of mutual aid and community fellowship, but shaped within an industrial reality, such a dynamic was repeated by women in textile mill towns throughout the late-nineteenth- and early-twentieth-century South. As numerous historians of the region have documented, these ties among communities of women were a major source of the solidarity that underlay much of the sustained wave of labor militancy in the southern textile industry in the 1920s and 1930s in which women were actively engaged.[74] Even for those women, like Anthelia, who had long since left the industry, the culture in which they not only participated but also were active agents in shaping, had defined, cushioned, and often given meaning to the reality of their lives as both women and cotton mill operatives.

Notes

1. Anthelia Holt (hereafter cited as AH) to Lottie Clark (hereafter cited as LC), Mar. 21, 1892, Lottie V. Clark Collection, Earl Gregg Swem Library, Manuscripts and Rare Books Department, College of William and Mary, Williamsburg (hereafter cited as Clark Collection). Unless noted otherwise, the spelling and punctuation have been retained from the original correspondences. Matoaca is located in Chesterfield

County, about four miles west of Petersburg and approximately thirty miles south of Richmond. Namozine is located about fifteen miles west of Matoaca in neighboring Amelia County.

2. Ibid.
3. Anthelia's siblings were William Benjamin (1865–1890), Joseph Arthur (1869–1952), Addie (1872–1948), Allie Dallas (1875–1965), Thomas (1878–1964), James Owen (1881–1964), and Belvedore "Velvie" (1884–1900). Two children born in the 1860s died during their first years (Larry Franklin Holt, "Anthelia Holt Robinett of Matoaca, Virginia"); U.S. Census Bureau, Tenth Census, 1880, Chesterfield County; U.S. Census Bureau, Twelfth Census, 1900, Chesterfield County. The 1890 U.S. Census has not been included in this analysis because a Washington, D.C., fire in the 1920s destroyed all the 1890 records for Chesterfield County.
4. Jacquelyn Dowd Hall, quoted in Robert H. Zieger, "Southern Textiles: Toward a New Historiographic Synthesis (Introduction)," in Gary M. Fink and Merl E. Reed, eds., *Race, Class, and Community in Southern Labor History* (Tuscaloosa, Ala., 1994), p. 4.
5. See E.P. Thompson, *The Making of the English Working Class* (New York, 1966); and Herbert Gutman, "Work, Culture, and Society in Industrializing America, 1815–1919," *American Historical Review* 78 (1973): 531–88.
6. Jacquelyn Dowd Hall et al., *Like a Family: The Making of a Southern Cotton Mill World* (1987; Chapel Hill, 2000). Other examples include Melton Alonza McLaurin, *Paternalism and Protest: Southern Cotton Mill Workers and Organized Labor, 1875–1905* (Westport, Conn., 1971); David Carlton, *Mill and Town in South Carolina, 1880–1920* (Baton Rouge, 1982); Cathy McHugh, *Mill Family: The Labor System in the Southern Cotton Textile Industry, 1880–1915* (New York, 1988); Ronald Eller, *Miners, Millhands, and Mountaineers: Industrialization of the Appalachian South, 1880–1930* (Knoxville, 1982); Dolores Janiewski, *Sisterhood Denied: Race, Gender, and Class in a New South Community* (Philadelphia, 1985); Jacquelyn Dowd Hall, "Disorderly Women: Gender and Labor Militancy in the Appalachian South," *Journal of American History* 73 (1986): 354–82; Victoria Byerly, *Hard Times Cotton Mill Girls: Personal Stories of Womanhood and Poverty in the New South* (Ithaca, N.Y., 1986); I.A. Newby, *Plain Folk in the New South: Social Change and Cultural Persistence, 1880–1915* (Baton Rouge, 1989); and Wayne Flynt, *Poor But Proud: Alabama's Poor Whites* (Tuscaloosa, Ala., 1989). Although they focus on factories in New England, there are a number of additional works that are instructive about the creation of workplace cultures within the nineteenth- and early twentieth-century U.S. textile industry. See especially Thomas Dublin, *Women at Work: The Transformation of Work and Community in Lowell Massachusetts, 1826–1860* (New York, 1979); Tamara K. Hareven, *Amoskeag: Life and Work in an American Factory–City* (New York, 1978); Tamara K. Hareven, *Family Time and Industrial Time: The Relationship Between the Family and Work in a New England Industrial Community* (New York, 1982); John Cumbler, *Working-Class Community in Industrial America: Work, Leisure, and Struggle in Two Industrial Cities, 1880–1930* (Westport, Conn., 1979); and Mary Blewett. *The Last Generation: Work and Life in the Textile Mills of Lowell Massachusetts, 1910–1960* (Amherst, Mass., 1990).
7. See, e.g., Douglas Flamming, *Creating the Modern South: Millhands and Managers in Dalton, Georgia, 1884–1984* (Chapel Hill, 1992); Bryant Simon, *A Fabric of Defeat: The Politics of South Carolina Millhands, 1910–1948* (Chapel Hill, 1998); Bryant Simon, "Rethinking Why There Are So Few Unions in the South," *Georgia Historical Quarterly* 81 (1997): 465–84; and Cletus Daniel, *Culture of Misfortune: An Interpretive History of Textile Unionism in the United States* (Ithaca, N.Y., 2001).
8. Janiewski, *Sisterhood Denied*, p. 6.

9   Information about the acquisition of the Holt-Clark correspondence obtained by the author during a discussion with Dr. John D. Haskell, Jr., associate dean and director of manuscripts and rare books, Earl Gregg Swem Library, College of William and Mary, 10, 2005.

10 Eric Foner, *Reconstruction: America's Unfinished Journey, 1863–77* (New York, 1988), pp. 210–15; Patrick Heardan, *Independence and Empire: The New South's Cotton Mill Campaign, 1865–1901* (DeKalb, Ill., 1982), pp. 7–13; Benjamin Ford, "A Profitable and Creditable Establishment: Industrial Textile Manufacturing and Capitalist Relations of Production in the Antebellum Central Virginia Piedmont" (Ph.D. diss., University of Virginia, 1998); Randall Miller, *The Cotton Mill Movement in Antebellum Alabama* (New York, 1978), pp. 2–4, 9–24, 106–7; Jonathan Wiener, *Social Origins of the New South: Alabama, 1860–1885* (Baton Rouge, 1978), pp. 138–45; Edward Ayers, *The Promise of the New South: Life After Reconstruction* (New York, 1992), p. 111.

11. Tenth Census, Chesterfield County; Twelfth Census, Chesterfield County.

12. Anthelia's brother, James Owen Holt renovated the home during the early twentieth century to include a second story (Holt, "Anthelia Holt Robinett of Matoaca, Virginia," n.p.).

13. Foner, *Reconstruction*, pp. 393–408; Gavin Wright, *Old South, New South: Revolutions in the Southern Economy Since the Civil War* (New York, 1986), pp. 19–35, 99–111; C. Vann Woodward, *Origins of the New South, 1877–1913* (1951; Baton Rouge, 1993), pp. 179–86; Hall et al., *Like a Family*, pp. 3–6; Ayers, *Promise of the New South*, pp. 13–15, 198–205; Flamming, *Creating the Modern South*, pp. 19–22; Carlton, *Mill and Town in South Carolina*, pp. 13–19; Steven Hahn, *The Roots of Southern Populism: Yeoman Farmers and the Transformation of the Georgia Upcountry, 1850–90* (New York, 1983), pp. 4–9; Gilbert Fite, *Cotton Fields No More: Southern Agriculture, 1865–1980* (Lexington, Ky., 1984), pp. 18–22.

14. Wright, *Old South, New South*, pp. 129–30; Hall et al., *Like a Family*, pp. 10–18, 31–40; Foner, *Reconstruction*, p. 536; Ayers, *Promise of the New South*, pp. 113–14; Flamming, *Creating the Modern South*, pp. 25–26, 30–35; Janiewski, *Sisterhood Denied*, pp. 55–66; Newby, *Plain Folk in the New South*, pp. 23–61, 83–86; McLaurin, *Paternalism and Protest*, pp. 17–18; McHugh, *Mill Family*, pp. 7–8.

15. Tom Terrill, "Eager Hands: Labor for Southern Textiles, 1850–1860," *Journal of Economic History* 36 (1976): 84–90; Allen Heath Stokes, Jr., "Black and White Labor in the Development of the Southern Textile Industry, 1880–1920" (Ph.D. diss., University of South Carolina, 1977), pp. 1–12, 98–120, 163–96; Hall et al., *Like a Family*, pp. 66–67; Woodward, *Origins of the New South*, pp. 205–22; Flamming, *Creating the Modern South*, pp. 56–57; Newby, *Plain Folk in the New South*, pp. 463–90; Broadus Mitchell, *The Rise of Cotton Mills in the South* (Baltimore, 1921), pp. 127–32; Wright, *Old South, New South*, p. 13; Mary Oates, *The Role of the Cotton Textile Industry in the Economic Development of the American Southeast: 1900–1940* (New York, 1975), pp. 118–23; Tenth Census, Chesterfield County; Twelfth Census, Chesterfield County.

16. William Washington Baker, *Chesterfield County Virginia: A Handbook, Giving a Description of Topography, Climate, Productions, Minerals, Fruite, Educational Facilities, Manufacturing Advantages, and Inducements the County Offers the Industrious and Intelligent Farmer* (Manchester, Va., 1894), pp. 3–18, 14–15 (quotation); Francis Earle Lutz, *Chesterfield: An Old Virginia County* (Richmond, 1954), pp. 192–95, 283–84.

17. AH to LC, Apr. 29, 1891 and Oct. 8, 1894; May 20, 1891; Aug. 11, 1891; Nov. 28, 1891 and Nov. 25, 1894, Clark Collection.

18. Holt, "Anthelia Holt"; Tenth Census, Chesterfield County.

19. AH to LC, June 23, 1891, Clark Collection.

20. Ibid., Sept. 31, 1889.

21. Tenth Census, Chesterfield County; Twelfth Census, Chesterfield County.

22. Hall et al., *Like a Family*, pp. 3–14, 65–77; Gary R. Freeze, "Poor Girls Who Might Otherwise Be Wretched: The Origins of Paternalism in North Carolina's Mills, 1836–1880," in Jeffrey Leiter, Michael Schulman, and Rhonda Zingraff, eds., *Hanging By a Thread: Social Change in Southern Textiles* (Ithaca, N.Y., 1991), pp. 21–32; Gay L. Gullickson, "Technology, Gender and Rural Culture: Normandy and the Piedmont," in Leiter, Schulman, and Zigraff, eds., *Hanging By a Thread*, pp. 34–44, 53; Alice Kessler-Harris, *Out to Work: A History of Wage Earning Women in the United States* (New York, 1982), pp. 114–15; Julie Matthaei, *An Economic History of Women in America: Women's Work, the Sexual Division of Labor, and the Development of Capitalism* (New York, 1982), p. 214.

23. The emerging cash economy and the shift toward market-oriented agriculture throughout the New South altered patterns of household production and consumption. Women increasingly purchased goods, like soap and clothes, that they had traditionally made themselves. Growing access to and reliance upon mass-produced consumer goods and the cash needed to buy such items pushed many women and children into the ranks of wage-earners (Hall et al., *Like a Family*, pp. 13–18; Newby, *Plain Folk in the New South*, pp. 58–59; Flamming, *Creating the Modern South*, pp. 25–26).

24. Tenth Census, Chesterfield County; Twelfth Census, Chesterfield County.

25. AH to LC, July 5, 1891, Clark Collection.

26. Hall et al., *Like a Family*, pp. 44–113, 154–62; Janiewski, *Sisterhood Denied*, pp. 31–35, 128; McLaurin, *Paternalism and Protest*, pp. 24–30; Gullickson, "Technology, Gender, and Rural Culture," pp. 33–57; Ayers, *Promise of the New South*, p. 188; Flamming, *Creating the Modern South*, p. 25; Douglas Flamming, "'Give Her Some Out of That': Cotton Mill Girls, Family Wages, and the Question of Female Independence in the New South," in Glenn T. Eskew, ed., *Labor in the Modern South* (Athens, Ga., 2001), p. 61; Hareven, *Family Time*, pp. 1–4, 69–84.

27. AH to LC, Jan. 2, 1889, Clark Collection.

28. Ibid., Oct. 4 and Nov. 1, 1891.

29. Ibid., Apr. 11, 1892.

30. Ava Baron, "Gender and Labor History: Learning from the Past, Looking to the Future," in Ava Baron, ed., *Work Engendered: Toward a New History of American Labor* (Ithaca, N.Y., 1991), p. 11. On women's culture in other late-nineteenth- and early-twentieth-century workplace settings, see: Susan Porter Benson, *Counter Cultures: Saleswomen, Managers, and Customers in American Department Stores, 1890–1940* (Urbana, Ill., 1986); Tean W. Hunter, "'Work that Body': African-American Women, Work, and Leisure in Atlanta and the New South," in Eric Arnesen, Julie Greene, and Bruce Laurie, eds., *Labor Histories: Class, Politics, and the Working Class Experience* (Urbana, Ill., 1998); Patricia Cooper, *Once a Cigar Maker: Men, Women, and Work Culture in American Cigar Factories, 1900–1919* (Urbana, Ill., 1987); Margery W. Davies, *Women's Place is at the Typewriter: Office Work and Office Workers, 1870–1930* (Philadelphia, 1982); Barbara Melosh, *The Physician's Hand: Work Culture and Conflict in American Nursing* (Philadelphia, 1982); Kathy Peiss, *Cheap Amusements: Working Women and Leisure in Turn-of-the-Century New York* (Philadelphia, 1986); and Martha Vicinus, *Independent Women: Work and Community for Single Women, 1850–1920* (Chicago, 1985).

31. Famming, *Creating the Modern South*, pp. 60–61; Janiewski, *Sisterhood Denied*, pp. 28–51; Hall et al., *Like a Family*, pp. 3–4, 13–16.

32. AH to LC, July 17, 1889, Clark Collection.

33. Ibid., Mar. 28, 1893.
34. Ibid., Oct. 4, 1892.
35. Ibid., Apr. 11, 1890.
36. Ibid., Sept. 13, 1889.
37. Ibid., June 23, 1892.
38. Ibid., Dec. 25, 1892.
39. Ibid., July 18, 1890.
40. Ibid., Nov. 28, 1891.
41. Ibid., Jan. 20, 1893.
42. Eller, *Miners, Millhands, and Mountaineers*, pp. 34–35; Hall et al., *Like a Family*, pp. 13–14, 20–22; Ted Ownby, *Subduing Satan: Religion, Recreation, and Manhood in the Rural South, 1865–1920* (Chapel Hill, 1990), p. 91.
43. AH to LC, Sept. 31, 1889, Clark Collection.
44. Ibid., Dec. 25, 1892. In *Plain Folk in the New South*, I.A. Newby argued that "Marriage…involved a display of emotions that made the folk uncomfortable; moreover, most folk disliked being the center of attention. They therefore wanted to downplay the ceremony." As seen in this 1892 letter and others in the Clark Collection, however, a number of Anthelia Holt's descriptions of weddings that took place in Matoaca contradict Newby's assertion (see Newby, *Plain Folk in the New South*, p. 291).
45. AH to LC, Mar. 20, 1893, Clark Collection.
46. Ibid., June 23, 1891.
47. Ibid., Dec. 25, 1892.
48. Ibid., 11 Apr. 1892.
49 Ibid., Feb. 15, 1889.
50. Ibid., Feb. 14, 1892.
51. Ibid., Feb. 28, 1890.
52. Ibid., Nov. 1, 1891.
53. Ibid., July 17, 1889.
54. Ibid., Feb. 12, 1895.
55. Ibid., Aug. 21, 1893. On mill stoppages as a time for recreational activities, see also Hall et al., *Like a Family*, pp. 20–22, 47–48, 86–90.
56. AH to LC, Apr. 11, 1890 and June 7, 1892, Clark Collection.
57. Ibid., Aug. 21, 1893.
58. Ibid., Feb. 15, 1889.
59. Ibid., Mar. 26, 1895 (phrase added for clarification).
60. Ibid., May 25, 1890.
61. For additional information on religion and church-sponsored activities, see Ayers, *Promise of the New South*, pp. 160–86; Fite, *Cotton Fields No More*, pp. 44–45; and Newby, *Plain Folk in the New South*, pp. 389–417.
62. AH to LC, July 18, 1888, Clark Collection.
63. Ibid., Mar. 28, 1894.
64. Ibid., Apr. 29, 1893.
65. Ibid., Dec. 25, 1892.
66. Ibid., Apr. 26, 1889.
67. Ibid., Oct. 4, 1891.
68. On the importance of the church in southern courting rituals, see Hall et al., *Like a Family*, pp. 141–42; and Ownby, *Subduing Satan*, pp. 138–39.
69. Douglas Flamming investigated the impact that the ability to earn cash wages had on the autonomy of single female mill workers within their families and the wider community. See Flamming, "'Give Her Some Out of That.'"
70. AH to LC, July 5, 1891, Clark Collection.
71. Ibid., Oct. 4, 1892 and Dec. 1, 1893.

72. Ibid., Apr. 26, 1889 (phrase added for clarification).

73. Twelfth Census, Chesterfield County; Holt, "Anthelia Holt."

74. See, e.g., Hall, "Disorderly Women," pp. 354–82; and Hall et al., *Like a Family*, esp. pp. 226–31, 328–50. Thomas Dublin also saw a similar phenomenon underlying labor protests in Lowell, Massachusetts, textile mills during the early nineteenth century. See Dublin, *Women at Work*, esp. pp. 86–131.

7

"It is His First Offense. We Might As Well Let Him Go": Homicide and Criminal Justice in Chicago, 1875–1920

Jeffrey S. Adler

Chicago's Pleasant Place erupted in violence on April 23, 1907, when John Nesczuk began work on a fence along the property line behind his house. Nesczuk's neighbor, John Wijas, complained that the fence intruded into his garden. "What are you doing that for? You are spoiling my garden," Wijas roared from his window. "Come down here and we'll show you," Nesczuk answered.[1] Rather than accepting the challenge, Wijas—or perhaps another inhabitant of his home—hurled a brick out the window, hitting Nesczuk, breaking the fence builder's arm, and temporarily halting construction on the "spice fence."[2] Five days later Nesczuk's sons and two friends resumed work on the fence, and the violence flared anew. When Wijas, a forty-eight-year-old factory foreman, ventured near the disputed turf, the elder Nesczuk screeched "now we've got him. Kill him."[3] Nesczuk's son Joseph attacked Wijas with a hammer, striking him on the head and "crushing in his skull."[4] As soon as Wijas crumbled to the ground, Nesczuk's other son, Lawrence, and their friends pounced on the factory foremen, bludgeoning him with the boards they had gathered for the fence. John Wijas remained hospitalized for two months before his condition improved enough for him to return home. During this period he engaged an attorney, who sought a warrant for the arrest of the Nesczuks. A local judge, however, refused to issue the warrant. On July 21 Wijas succumbed to his injuries, and the police arrested the Nesczuk brothers, charging them with homicide.[5] A grand jury indicted only one of the brothers, the hammer-wielding Joseph. In the fall of 1907, a criminal court jury found the killer "not guilty" and released him, concluding that Joseph Nesczuk had been provoked into smashing Wijas's skull.[6] According to the Cook County criminal justice system, the Nesczuk brothers had acted lawfully when they beat to death John Wijas in his Pleasant Place garden.

The acquittal of Joseph Nesczuk generated scant attention, for this was not an unusual homicide case. Seemingly trivial disputes often fueled lethal violence in the city, and Cook County juries routinely exonerated and acquitted killers. Between 1875 and 1920 fewer than one Chicago killer in four was convicted.[7] True to its reputation, Chicago was a tough town.

The low conviction rate notwithstanding, this was an era of rapid criminal justice reform and legal modernization in the city. Chicago officials created the nation's first juvenile justice system during the final decade of the nineteenth century, and early in the twentieth century they forged specialized courts to adjudicate domestic disputes and morals cases.[8] Similar innovation and specialization transformed local policing during this era, as municipal officials formed a homicide squad, an "Italian [crime] squad," and other units designed to focus the investigative expertise of law enforcers.[9] Reflecting the "sociological jurisprudence" of the period, Chicago judges and prosecutors were also quick to invite social scientists and other experts into their courtrooms, and psychologists, "alienists," and physicians often testified in homicide cases. Likewise, the police and state's attorneys embraced the latest investigative techniques. Chicago law enforcers pioneered the use of the Bertillon criminal identification system in 1888 and finger printing in 1904.[10] A decade later Chicagoans established a "Psychopathic Laboratory," where defendants were observed, evaluated, poked, and prodded.[11] Legal reformers also demanded more professional training and operating procedures for local law enforcers.[12]

Yet, for all of these innovations and improvements, Chicago killers were rarely punished. Furthermore, despite the increasing momentum and the achievements of Progressive legal and institutional reform, the conviction rate in local homicide cases fell between the 1890s and 1920. A Chicago killer was nearly four times more likely to be convicted in 1895 than his counterpart a quarter century later. Lamenting the trend, a state's attorney in 1903 speculated that lethal violence had become so commonplace in the city that "murders are coming to be regarded with little more importance than fist fights. The jury," Charles S. Deneen added, "is inclined to say when a man is tried for murder: 'It is his first offense. We might as well let him go.'"[13] Even as twentieth-century practices and institutions blossomed, Chicagoans seemed to cling to nineteenth-century notions of justice.

*   *   *

Chicago's criminal justice system was swift and sure. Cases moved through the legal system at breakneck speed, often progressing from the coroner's inquest, which typically occurred the day after the homicide, to completed trial in a matter of weeks or, at most, months.[14] Between July 25 and

November 23, 1907, for example, Joseph Nesczuk was arrested, appeared before a coroner's inquest jury, a grand jury, and a criminal court jury, and was acquitted. The local criminal justice system was as sure as it was swift, seldom convicting killers. Between 1875 and 1920, 7 percent of murderers immediately committed suicide, and almost one-third of killers evaded arrest. Municipal law enforcers made arrests in 61 percent of Chicago homicide cases. Among those arrested for homicide during this period, 42 percent were exonerated by coroner's juries or by grand juries, and the remaining 58 percent went to trial in the Cook County Criminal Court. Thirty-six percent of arrested killers were convicted. Thus, of the total pool of Chicago killers between 1875 and 1920, including those who escaped arrest, 37 percent faced a criminal trial, and 24 percent were convicted. Six percent of convicted killers—and 1.2 percent of all killers in Chicago between 1875 and 1920—were executed. Local law enforcers enjoyed their greatest success in 1885, convicting 48 percent of Chicago killers, and in 1876, 1877, 1879, and 1920, the police and the state's attorneys suffered through particularly bad years, securing convictions in fewer than 13 percent of the city's homicide cases.[15]

Chicagoans were acutely aware of the shortcomings in their criminal justice system. As a nationally recognized "laboratory" for social reform and the home of the University of Chicago (and its teams of sociologists, economists, social workers, and policy analysts), the city endured repeated investigations of its legal institutions. The findings were consistent, well-publicized, and embarrassing: "Murderers Go Free," the *Chicago Inter Ocean* concluded after one such assessment.[16] Police chief Leroy Steward reported to municipal officials in September of 1910 that law enforcers had secured convictions for 19 percent of the city's homicides during the previous four years.[17] Three years later, the *Chicago Tribune*, drawing on another four-year slice of crime statistics, echoed this view. "Murders Spread as Police Fail," the newspaper's headline announced. "The chances of a person charged with murder escaping punishment in Chicago are better than four to one in his favor, after the information has been presented to the grand jury."[18] Casting the net more broadly, the *Report of the City Council Committee on Crime*, chaired by the University of Chicago political scientist and reformer Charles E. Merriam, calculated in 1915 that "on felony charges, there is only one chance in five of a man ever getting to the Criminal Court for trial, and only one chance in thirty of going to the penitentiary or reformatory."[19]

To the horror of municipal officials, reformers, and other citizens, Chicago's conviction rate fell during the early twentieth century, even as the city's homicide rate soared. The conviction rate in homicide cases fluctuated wildly from the mid-1870s through the mid-1890s, after which it plummeted (see figure 7.1). Between the late 1890s and 1920, Chicago's homicide rate rose by 104 percent, while its conviction rate in homicide cases fell by 63 percent.[20]

Such a record of sustained failure reflected the efforts of law enforcers at every level of Chicago's criminal justice system. "In the protection of its

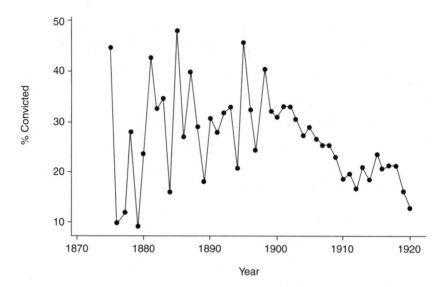

Figure 7.1 Proportion of Chicago homicides in which a defendant was convicted, 1875–1920.

citizens through the swift, sure and severe punishment of their assailants," Dr. W.T. Belfield told a group of physicians and lawyers in 1907, "Chicago compares with London, Berlin or Vienna as does an ox team with an express train for travel."[21] Contemporary observers, however, found particular fault with Chicago's police force. A detective hired by the influential City Club to investigate the local police offered a scathing assessment. "The condition is 'rotten,'" Louis Grossman reported in 1904. "The police of Chicago are piano movers, bums, cripples, janitors, ward heelers—anything but policemen."[22] Blending ridicule with sarcasm, the muckraking journalist Lincoln Steffens expressed concern for the safety of the police. Chicago's police department, he explained, was "so insufficient (and inefficient) that it cannot protect itself."[23] Another investigation of local law enforcers, this one conducted by New York policemen, warned Chicagoans that they had "practically no protection."[24] Nor was the situation improving, according to local reformers. A study of Chicago law enforcement during the 1920s concluded that "numerically, our police force may have kept pace with crime, but in matters of efficiency and intelligent methods of crime detection we seem to have learned little and done less."[25] Underfunded, understaffed, poorly trained, mired in corruption, and shackled to political institutions, Chicago policemen contributed significantly to the bumbling and toothless character of the local criminal justice system.

Yet, for all of their well-documented problems, local policemen made arrests in an increasing proportion of Chicago homicide cases (see figure 7.2). During the late 1870s and the 1880s, the city's law enforcers apprehended suspects in 44 percent of homicide cases. Between 1890

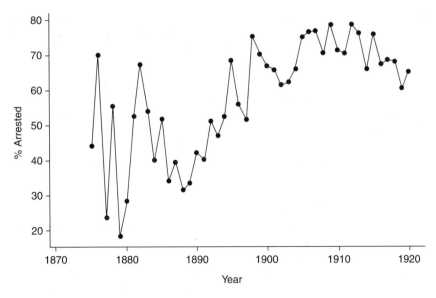

Figure 7.2 Proportion of Chicago homicides in which the police made an arrest, 1875–1920.

and 1910, the figure jumped to 66 percent, and during the 1910s the police secured arrests in almost 70 percent of local homicide cases. Their investigative skills may not have kept pace with their arrest rates, and therefore the increasing proportion of arrests did not necessarily indicate more effective police work. Nonetheless, the trend suggests that the police alone were not responsible for Chicago's low conviction rate in homicide cases.

At least according to contemporary legal reformers, coroners and state's attorneys also contributed to the ineptitude of the city's criminal justice system. Coroners remained elected officials in Illinois during this era. They typically lacked medical or scientific training and were bound up with the rough-and-tumble world of local politics. Peter M. Hoffman, a store clerk-turned-politician, served as the Cook County coroner from 1904 until 1922. Though he faced many charges of corruption and would be convicted for contempt of court during the mid-1920s, when he served as the county sheriff, Hoffman prosecuted particular kinds of homicide cases aggressively, staking his political fortunes on crusades to protect the innocent. He also established the county's "chemical laboratory," appointed experienced chemists and pathologists to help investigate potential homicides, and spearheaded the expansion of homicide charges to include automobile accidents in which the reckless behavior of the driver caused the fatality.[26] Hoffman even stacked inquest juries with the "right" men to increase the likelihood that particular suspects would be charged with homicide, selecting ministers, high-school principals, or others he believed would be unsympathetic to suspected killers.[27] But if Hoffman and his colleagues pursued many cases zealously, the inquest process remained haphazard. The jurors in coroners' inquests, for example, were often "political hangers-ons" and "Fridays"—individuals who served repeatedly in order to collect the one-dollar-per-hearing stipend paid to jurors.[28]

Also elected officials, state's attorneys remained tethered to partisan politics, pursued cases selectively, and proved, at best, inefficient. Furthermore, the assistant state's attorneys who handled homicide cases tended to be young and inexperienced.[29] According to John Healy, who had served as the Cook County State's Attorney from 1904 until 1907, "the prosecution of felony cases in preliminary hearing in the municipal court of Chicago is mainly in the hands of *incompetent and indifferent assistant state's attorneys* [italics in original], who know nothing about the facts in the cases and are not prepared to and do not render efficient service."[30]

Although coroners and state's attorneys played important roles in the turn-of-the-century criminal justice system, jurors determined the fate of most suspects in homicide cases—at the coroner's inquest, at the grand jury hearing, and at the criminal court trial. And Cook County jurors were quick to exonerate, "no bill" (i.e., not return a bill of indictment at the grand jury proceeding), and acquit killers, even those found glowering over their victims, gun—or hammer—in hand. In 1827 the Illinois legislature added a statutory provision to state's criminal code making jurors the "judges of the law and the fact."[31] The legislature repeatedly re-affirmed the provision, and the state's Supreme Court upheld it until 1931.[32] Illinois's highest court held that jurors "are not bound by the law, as given to them by the court, but can assume the responsibility of deciding, each juror for himself, what the law is…according to their [sic] own notions of the law."[33] In effect, the Illinois criminal code sanctioned jury nullification, permitting jurors to define for themselves complex legal terms, such as self-defense, provocation, criminal intent, and culpable negligence. Armed with the authority to determine both matters of law and matters of fact in criminal cases, Cook County jurors consistently favored defendants. Even as residents clamored for greater protection from murderers, Chicago jurors exonerated and acquitted, concluding that killers had acted lawfully when they employed lethal violence to resolve petty disputes. In short, more than the "piano movers" and "bums" who patrolled local streets, more than the crassly political coroners who oversaw inquests, and more than the "incompetent and indifferent" prosecutors who presented cases to grand juries and who conducted trials, Chicago jurors freed homicide suspects.

Local jurors often concluded that killers had acted in self-defense, embracing an expansive, malleable definition of the phrase and then stretching it even further to meet ideals of popular justice. If jurors judged a fight to have been "fair," regardless of the level of brutality or who initiated the conflict, they typically found in favor of the defendant. Thus, prosecutors usually failed in homicide cases arising from drunken brawls, only one-fourth of which yielded convictions, even though these killings most often occurred in full view of witnesses and the suspects were easily identified and quickly apprehended.

Some commentators speculated that class and ethnic biases fueled exonerations and acquittals, with jurors caring little about the sorts of residents involved in most deadly affrays. In many instances, the stodgy *Chicago Tribune* speculated, jurors believed "the victim to have deserved his fate."[34] According to a local crime-beat reporter, jurors often concluded that "both parties belong to the lowest of the low and the loss of life would not have been any detriment to other people."[35] Legal reformers more frequently focused on the "weak sentimentality" of jurors. "Our hereditary sympathies are for the under-dog, for the man who is down and out, and the criminal is too frequently pictured as being only the victim of hard luck or a bad environment, fighting for his life or freedom against the powerfully organized, impersonal forces of the commonwealth."[36]

More visceral, more basic, and more gendered notions of fairness and justice, however, produced predictable jury decisions in barroom fights, street brawls, and other scuffles in which both the killer and his victim were active, willing participants. Men, jurors reasoned, must be permitted to stand their ground; Chicagoans typically rejected the view that they should back down from conflict or retreat from an aggressor, the niceties of the law and the instructions of judges notwithstanding.[37] If all Chicago men, because they were men, were entitled to resist challenges, yield no ground, brook no disrespect, and stand up to threats, virtually any violent behavior in a rough-hewn saloon or working-class neighborhood could be viewed as an act of self-defense.

Cook County jurors also freed men who killed in defense of manly honor. Chicagoans, like other Americans during this era, frequently invoked a plastic concept known as the "unwritten law." In its purest form, the unwritten law permitted—indeed required—a man to kill the scoundrel who "attacked" or "dishonored" his wife, daughter, or sister.[38] On October 16, 1913, for example, William Keith learned that his wife had been "intimate" with Walter Paul. Keith tracked Paul to a local saloon and shot the home wrecker in the chest. A butcher by trade, Keith immediately summoned the police and explained that he was "justified in killing Paul...and under the 'unwritten law' his [Paul's] life should be forfeit."[39] Although Mrs. Keith, who had also been intimate with at least eight other men during her marriage, had made her husband promise not to kill Paul, she conceded to the police that she knew that he could not keep his pledge. "He wouldn't have been a man if he had [refrained from killing Paul]," she told local law enforcers. A Cook County jury concurred and acquitted William Keith.[40]

Likewise, Greek immigrant Achilles Pantarakas, upon discovering that his friend George Barbaresos had "made love to my wife," determined that killing him "was a justifiable execution of the unwritten law."[41] Pantarakas explained that "I took my ax in my hand and with the ax split his skull. He deserved death. In my country death alone answers for his crime."[42] Not content with killing the thirty-year-old Barbaresos, Pantarakas hacked off his friend's head, arms, and legs. "If they hang me the American law is queer," Pantarakas told the police. "In Greece we protect our women and no one shall have my wife."[43] Chicago jurors found the argument compelling and acquitted Pantarakas. In many similar homicides, defendants also invoked the unwritten law and were exonerated or acquitted.[44]

Other Chicagoans insisted that the unwritten law "justified" the killing of anyone who disrupted their homes. On August 17, 1918, Italian immigrants Joseph Tamprullo and Earlerogo Piro declared "it is not wrong to kill a man who speaks ill of one's wife," and they shot and stabbed Piro's cousin, Pasquale, for "traducing" their wives. Although the killers proclaimed "we do not repent," a Cook County jury acquitted them.[45] While not specifically invoking the unwritten law, Joseph Manne relied on a similar explanation and justification for his violence. On April 7, 1920, a coroner's inquest jury exonerated Manne for the beating death of Travers Walsh, a twenty-nine-year-old soda clerk. Walsh and two friends, all of whom were "intoxicated on Jamaica ginger," loitered on a downtown street corner, flitting with women and occasionally insulting those who rebuffed or ignored them. Enraged that his wife had been subjected to such behavior, Joseph Manne attacked Walsh and beat him to death. Accurately gauging public opinion and then pandering to it, Coroner Peter M. Hoffman decried the "menace" posed by "habitual flirts" and announced that the case determined that "a killing is justified for an alleged flirtation or insult to another man's wife."[46]

Again and again, local judges and prosecutors instructed jurors "not to consider the 'unwritten law' and to rely only upon the facts."[47] During one trial, the Cook County state's attorney issued a public statement on the topic, warning that his office "does not recognize the unwritten law" and reminding the defendant that "his lawyers would have to present some facts."[48] Jurors disagreed and consistently endorsed, and in some cases applauded, the use of aggressive self-help to resolve affairs of honor.[49]

Chicago women embraced their own version of the unwritten law during the early twentieth century. According to defendants and their attorneys, a "'new' unwritten law" gave a woman the "right" to kill any man who betrayed or abused her, even if she used the violence in a pre-emptive way.[50] Grace Doyle termed her use of deadly force against her abusive husband, Timothy, "self defense in advance" and explained that the shooting was a "morally justifiable killing."[51] Relying on such arguments, more than 90 percent of white husband killers were exonerated or acquitted, prompting the assistant state's attorney in one trial to warn that "if this jury sets the precedent that any woman who is attacked or is beaten by her husband can shoot him, there won't be many husbands left in Chicago six months from now."[52] Even while exasperated judges and other legal observers dismissed the new unwritten law as "a mock sense of chivalry" or "mere sentimentality," Cook County jurors freed the killers.[53]

Simply put, Chicagoans believed that some behavior was so despicable that lethal violence represented a reasonable or at a least justifiable response. Pauline Plotka's killing of her former lover, on February 15, 1918, focused public scrutiny on this notion—and commanded national attention.

A twenty-five-year-old dress designer, Plotka had been sexually involved with Anton Jindra, a twenty-five-year-old physician. Plotka charged that the young doctor had "wronged" her and then had reneged on his promise to marry her.[54] "He brought me to shame and then spurned me."[55] At the coroner's inquest, she revealed that "three different times be performed operations [i.e., abortions] on me."[56] When Jindra jilted Plotka, she secured a gun, proceeded to the Cook County Hospital where he worked, sneaked into the interns' quarters, and fired three bullets into the doctor's body. On his deathbed, Jindra denied that he had dishonored Plotka. "She shot me [because] she wanted me to marry her," he stated moments before dying.[57] Plotka immediately announced that she would defend herself "on the ground of [sic] unwritten law," and, after deliberating for ten minutes, the jury at the coroner's inquest exonerated her, returning a verdict of "justifiable homicide."[58] "The evidence showed that Anton Jindra's treatment of her [Plotka] was most tantalizing, annoying, and brutal," the jury wrote, "and because of this we believe the said Pauline Plotka should be given the benefit of the doubt."[59] National observers lampooned the verdict and, with it, Chicago's criminal justice system. The *New York Times* averred that "the law, as so interpreted, is that it is a capital crime to be 'tantalizing, annoying and brutal' toward a woman, and that the penalty of death may legally be inflicted on the spot by the person aggrieved."[60] In an unusual legal maneuver, State's Attorney Maclay Hoyne rejected the inquest jury's verdict and brought the case to a grand jury and to a criminal court jury. On June 27, 1918, the criminal court jury accepted Plotka's explanation, affirmed the authority of the unwritten law, and freed the young dress designer.[61] Like William Keith and Achilles Pantarakas, Pauline Plotka had every right to seek personal vengeance, while the state of Illinois had no right to prevent a resident from defending his or her honor, according to local jurors.

In homicide cases that did not revolve around issues of honor, local jurors typically focused on the intent of the killer. According to Illinois law, questions of intent distinguished manslaughter from murder. But local jurors, as "judges of the law," often interpreted the state's law of homicide more loosely and determined that killers who lacked the intent to kill should be exonerated or acquitted.

Though hundreds of killers between 1875 and 1920 were freed as a consequence of this interpretation of the law of homicide, few cases illustrated jurors' "notions of the law" as clearly as William E. Doherty's trial. After a long evening of Christmas revelry in a Thirty-Fifth Street saloon in 1904, Doherty and his friends began "arguing over the respective marksmanship of the soldiers in the Russian-Japanese war." Happily besotted, Doherty asked his drinking buddies "you fellows ever hear of William Tell? Well, I'll show you how he did the trick. I'm the greatest shot ever."[62] Just then, Elmer Hunt, the saloon's nineteen-year-old African-American porter, began his shift. "Here, Elmer, stand back there and hold a spittoon on your head," the brash marksman commanded. "Without much persuasion," according to a crime-beat reporter, "Hunt was induced to stand with the cuspidor on his head."[63] Doherty lifted his revolver, but paused, and instructed Hunt to move backward. "Why, I can drive nails at this distance," Doherty crowed.[64] When Hunt had reached the far wall of the saloon, Doherty aimed, fired, and missed, causing his friends to erupt in laughter. Anxious and embarrassed, Doherty quickly raised his weapon and squeezed off another round. The bullet hit Elmer Hunt "squarely between the eyes."[65]

The coroner's jury ruled Hunt's death an unfortunate accident and exonerated Doherty. No doubt, both the race of the victim and the intent of the shooter influenced the verdict. But this decision was more than even Peter M. Hoffman could abide, and the Coroner set aside the verdict, re-arrested the would-be William Tell, and sent the case forward to the state's attorney's office. A criminal court jury, however, concurred with the coroner's jury and acquitted William E. Doherty.[66]

Similarly, a Cook County jury acquitted Thomas Chat, a bartender, for the 1911 shooting death of Michael Heinen. A seventeen-year-old teamster, Heinen "scratched matches on top of the bar," even after Chat had asked him to stop. When Heinen kicked Chat's dog, the bartender had had enough. He grabbed his revolver and shot the "boisterous" patron in the head, killing him. "Heinen wouldn't behave," Chat explained, "and I fired several shots at the ceiling to frighten him. It was an accident."[67] Sympathizing with the bartender, understanding his frustration, and accepting the argument that a bullet fired into the ceiling had struck Heinen in the head, the jury ordered Chat to be released.

When local law enforcers attempted to expand the scope of the law and criminalize reckless behavior that caused deaths, jurors would have none of it, rejecting the effort and relying on their own interpretations of state law. Hoffman championed the use of homicide law to punish drunken and negligent drivers who killed pedestrians, though local jurors eschewed Hoffman's legal theory and exonerated 80 percent of the defendants during the coroner's inquest. Of the remaining 20 percent, who were tried in criminal courts, nearly 70 percent were acquitted, even when vehicle operators were intoxicated or drove on sidewalks. Law enforcers secured convictions on 6 percent of the automobile drivers charged with homicide between 1905 and 1920. Likewise, the early-twentieth-century crusade by coroners and prosecutors to treat botched abortions resulting in deaths as homicides passed legal muster but failed to persuade Cook County jurors, who exonerated or acquitted 89 percent of the defendants brought before them.[68] Despite the campaigns of Progressive legal and social reformers, Chicago jurors believed that citizens assumed certain risks when they worked in saloons, walked on sidewalks, or visited midwives, and killers should not be held legally responsible for accidental or unintentional deaths.[69]

*   *   *

If jurors exonerated or acquitted killers such as Joseph Nesczuk, Joseph Manne, and William E. Doherty, who was convicted of homicide in turn-of-the-century Chicago? What elements or behaviors made Chicagoans, in the eyes of their peers, culpable for killing? Nearly one killer in four, after all, was convicted between 1875 and 1920.

In most respects, convicted killers differed little from those who were exonerated and acquitted. The backgrounds of Chicagoans who were punished for committing homicide, for example, were virtually identical to those who were arrested and charged but not convicted. Eighty-three percent of those convicted, 81 percent of those exonerated, and 80 percent of those acquitted held unskilled or semiskilled positions. Similarly, the mean age of those convicted was thirty-one, while the mean age of those acquitted in homicide cases was thirty. The crucial difference between the groups was typically bound up in the nature of the crime. Residents charged with particular kinds of homicides tended to be convicted.

Chicago jurors reserved guilty verdicts for cowardly killers or for cold-blooded killers. Four kinds of homicide cases fell into these categories and disproportionately produced convictions. Local jurors convicted wife killers at the highest rate of any group of homicide defendants. Between 1875 and 1920, nearly 40 percent of Chicago wife killers immediately committed suicide. An additional 12 percent of these men evaded arrest. Thus, slightly more than half of wife killers, one way or another, were not brought before local juries. But Chicago jurors convicted 73 percent of the murderous husbands who were arrested. Especially during the late nine-teenth century, wife killers often defended their violence, insisting either that the murders had been accidental or that their drunken or disrespectful wives had needed to be "disciplined." For example, Thomas Walsh, upon finding his wife drunk on February 18, 1883, took a strap to her. "I did not mean to kill her," Walsh explained, "but thought when she got sober in the morning the beating would have a good effect."[70] Local jurors, however, convicted the twenty-eight-year-old teamster, and a judge sentenced him to thirty-five years at Joliet Penitentiary.[71]

Jurors typically rejected honor-based justifications for uxoricide, for not even evidence of their wives' infidelity protected Chicago men from convic-tion. "Wayward" Ella Kurtz, for instance, died at the hands of her husband on March 24, 1894.[72] Ella had left her spouse and moved to a hotel, where she had "entertained other men," according to Frank Kurtz. When con-fronted, she told her husband that this was "none of [his] business," and the angry, cuckold shot his wife four times.[73] Despite Ella's purported infidel-ity, a Cook County jury convicted Frank Kurtz, and a judge sentenced him to a life term at Joliet Penitentiary.[74] In short, murderous husbands unsuc-cessfully employed defense strategies that nearly always succeeded in other contexts. Between 1890 and 1910, Chicago's uxoricide rate surged, and local jurors, all of whom were men, proved unforgiving toward wife killers and convicted 80 percent of the husbands who were arrested.

A cluster of overlapping factors contributed to this high conviction rate, transforming otherwise incompetent cops, indifferent prosecutors, and inattentive, gullible jurors into hard-edged, unyielding defenders of social order and moral propriety. First, the identity of the killers was seldom in doubt. Wife killers typically planned their violence. They often announced their intentions to friends and frequently contemplated or even attempted suicide and composed letters to relatives explaining their acts.[75] Similarly, they rarely tried to escape. Those who did not attempt suicide usually waited for law enforcers to arrive, either because they were despondent or because they were certain that their spouses had needed to be beaten and hence believed the violence was entirely appropriate. Likewise, while wife killing occurred in private, the violence unfolded in ways well known to relatives and neighbors. In many instances, a history of domestic violence preceded the final, fatal act of patriarchal authority. More often, particularly after the 1890s, the murders took place as the women tried to dissolve marriages, usually by separating from their husbands. The killer frequently begged his wife to return, and relatives, neighbors, and other witnesses often heard the husband scream, as William Arf did on October 7, 1908, "you won't [return home], won't you? Then I'll kill you" an instant before the lethal shot was fired.[76] But this explanation fails to account for the high rate of conviction, since most Chicago killers during this period remained at the scene of the crime until the police arrived. In other kinds of cases, juries typically freed killers on the grounds of justifiable homicide or self-defense—rather than because of questions regarding the identity of the assailant.

More important, wife killing violated popular notions of fairness. Uxoricides were not honorable, fair fights between equals. Instead, bigger, stronger men, most often using firearms, slaughtered smaller, weaker women. Nor were the victims perceived to have been willing participants in the one-sided battles. In contrast to using a hammer to crush the skull of an unarmed man or shooting a porter with a spittoon on his head during a drinking binge, wife killing was, in the eyes of turn-of-the-century Chicagoans, "cowardly" and unfair.[77] While respectable men could ignore barroom brawls, deadly neighborhood affrays, or even a bit of wife beating, wife killing was another matter altogether.

Class identity infused this perspective. Despite the use of "Fridays," jurors in homicide cases tended to belong to the city's middle class. According to a 1920s study, "tradesmen" comprised the largest single occupational category of jurors in Cook County felony trials, though white-collar workers dominated the jury pools, with salesmen, clerks, superintendents/managers, accountants, and retailers comprising the next largest categories. For every laborer or "railroad man" serving on a jury, there were ten salesmen, eight clerks, and four accountants.[78] These jurors celebrated the rugged masculinity that spawned loose definitions of self-defense (even as their own lives became more regimented and sedentary), and they were relatively unbothered when local toughs mauled one another. But middle-class jurors stridently embraced older notions of chivalry and masculine respectability.[79] Since wife killers tended to be clustered in the upper tier of the city's working class, convicting and punishing murderous husbands fortified the boundary between rough and respectable, tamping down the ill-behaved ruffians who tried to rise above their station.[80] At the same time, punishing these wife killers re-established men, especially respectable men, as the protectors of women, even if the protection proved to be posthumous. In short, in the eyes of turn-of-the-century Chicago jurors, wife killing was an unmanly, cowardly act, and wife killers deserved to be punished. Although murderous husbands made up 7 percent of all Chicago killers, they comprised more than 14 percent of those executed between 1875 and 1920.

Cook County jurors also convicted murderous robbers at a very high rate. Prosecutors won convictions in 64 percent of the robbery–homicide cases for which the police made an arrest. No group of Chicago killers elicited greater fear and anxiety. If a sense of justice and chivalry undergirded convictions in uxoricide trials, feelings of terror and vulnerability fueled convictions in robbery–homicide cases. Chicago experienced a surge in robbery and robbery–homicide during the early twentieth century, and respectable Chicagoans panicked.[81] Although the identity of robber–murderers was often in doubt, jurors not only convicted nearly two-thirds of those arrested, but law enforcers executed these killers at an extraordinarily high rate. More than one-eighth of the men arrested for robbery–homicide were executed, seven times the overall rate. Put differently, robber–murderers made up 7.5 percent of Chicago killers from 1875 to 1920 and comprised 43.5 percent of those executed for murder.

During trials and again during pardon and commutation hearings, prosecutors described robber–murderers as "cold-blooded" killers.[82] They were predators who preyed on the respectable and the innocent. Crime-beat writers, as well as prosecutors, focused on the social distance that separated robbers from their victims. "Fish-blooded" criminals targeted residents with money or goods—successful, hard-working Chicagoans, like the jurors themselves.[83] In one trial, which ended with a conviction and an execution, an assistant state's attorney asked the jurors "if you think society should be allowed to protect itself against these birds of prey who slink out into the night with guns in their pockets and potential murder in their hearts."[84]

Like wife killers, murderous robbers were considered unmanly. They skulked in the night and ambushed citizens of means and substance, transforming strong, solid men into helpless, terrified, feminized victims. If Chicagoans could abide honor-based violence, if they maintained a curious reverence for fair fights, and if they even believed that residents assumed certain risks when they ventured in public, local jurors expressed only loathing for killers who struck without giving their victims a fighting chance, particularly when the attackers belonged to the working class and the victims belonged to the middle class. Robbery–homicide, according to one prosecutor, was "cowardly, deliberate, wanton murder."[85]

African Americans comprised the third group of Chicagoans disproportionately convicted in homicide cases. In the age of lynching and Jim Crow, the city's African-American population skyrocketed, rising from 4,784 in 1875 to 109,458 in 1920. During the late 1910s alone, Chicago received more than fifty thousand African-American migrants, most of whom were from the Deep South and were young.[86] As white Chicagoans, natives as well as immigrants, competed with the newcomers for work and for housing, racial conflict exploded, sparking many violent exchanges and culminating in the Race Riot of 1919, which resulted in thirty-eight deaths and more than five hundred injuries. Again and again, gangs of whites, often masquerading as "athletic clubs," attacked African-American Chicagoans during the early twentieth century. Local law enforcers often watched passively as the violence erupted and then arrested every African American in the vicinity of the battle. As a consequence, the arrest rate in homicide cases with African-American suspects was nearly 40 percent higher than the corresponding figures for white suspects.[87] Despite the policy of indiscriminately arresting and charging African-American residents (or, perhaps, as a result of the beliefs that motivated such a law enforcement strategy), African Americans were convicted at more than double the rate of white Chicagoans; 45 percent of cases with African-American suspects produced a conviction, compared with 21 percent of cases with white suspects. In homicides where the police made an arrest, 60 percent of African-American defendants were convicted; nearly double proportion of convictions in cases with white defendants.

Not surprisingly, the imbalance became still more pronounced when the violence crossed racial lines. As both African-American residents and Progressive reformers recognized, white Chicagoans could attack and kill the newcomers with virtual impunity.[88] African-American defendants charged with killing white residents, however, encountered a very different criminal justice system. "Negroes suffer gross injustice in the handling of criminal affairs," the Chicago Commission on Race Relations reported in 1922.[89] In cases where the police made an arrest, prosecutors won convictions in 62 percent of black-on-white homicides but only 14 percent of white-on-black homicides. Likewise, while no white Chicagoan was executed for murdering an African-American resident during this era, more than 9 percent of African-American defendants charged with murdering white Chicagoans were executed.[90] When homicide suspects were African American, systemic racism outweighed middle-class indifference toward the violent tendencies of the poor, for justice proved to be relative and situational in turn-of-the-century Chicago.

Finally, local jurors did not abide or excuse cop killing. Despite their dissatisfaction with the police, and despite their inclination to exonerate and acquit, Cook County jurors stood squarely with the city's law enforcers. When policemen used deadly force, even when they shot children who were innocent bystanders, jurors supported the police, exonerating or acquitting nearly every cop who killed while on the job.[91] When local ruffians killed local law enforcers, two-thirds of arrested suspects were convicted and 14 percent were executed.

Wife killers, robbers, African Americans, and cop killers represented the proverbial exceptions that proved the rule, demonstrating that the criminal justice system could dispense punishment. Excluding homicide–suicides, Chicago law enforcers secured convictions in 43 percent of these cases—and in 62 percent of those in which they made an arrest. By comparison, between 1875 and 1920 the police and prosecutors won convictions in only 17 percent of all other homicides—and in 27 percent of all other cases in which they arrested a suspect.

*   *   *

Was Chicago unique? Although the explanations for patterns of exoneration and acquittal might have been different elsewhere, jurors in other settings during the nineteenth and early twentieth centuries were also reluctant to convict homicide defendants.[92] In nineteenth-century New York City, where homicide rates were lower than in Chicago, the lion's share of homicide cases ended without convictions.[93] Late-nineteenth-century New Orleans jurors convicted homicide suspects at similarly low rates, as did jurors in the American southwest, though both areas endured much higher rates of violence than New York or Chicago and had less well-developed legal institutions.[94] Likewise, in late-nineteenth-century England, Scotland, Ireland, and Wales, where levels of violence were far lower than in the United States, juries typically convicted only a minority of homicide defendants.[95] Thus, in areas with high rates of violence, as well as in areas with low levels of violence, nineteenth- and early-twentieth-century jurors consistently favored defendants in homicide cases, just as they did in places with strong, mature legal institutions and in places with weaker or younger criminal justice systems.[96] Legal institutions and pressures for civility and emotional restraint appear to have exerted only a modest influence on conviction rates.[97] Because Illinois state law forged a kind of democratic jurisprudence and gave jurors unusually free rein to reach verdicts based on their own ideals of fairness and culpability, Cook County courts were probably distinctive in degree more than in kind.

Legal and institutional reforms, in short, did not immediately alter core notions of justice, manliness, or chivalry. Rather, the machinery of Chicago's criminal justice system changed more rapidly than the sensibilities of local jurors. At least in homicide cases, older attitudes toward fairness, honor, culpability, risk, and popular justice survived well into the twentieth century, even as Progressive reformers and policy makers introduced greater efficiency and professionalism into the criminal justice system and as they extended the reach of the state in order to protect residents from the dangers around them. In fact, the combination of resilient notions of justice and institutional reform produced a falling conviction rate in Chicago homicide cases. Responding both to the city's rising homicide rate and to innovative legal and institutional impulses, law enforcers brought more cases to local juries, investigating deaths and prosecuting cases that would have been overlooked in earlier eras, such as infanticides and abortion-related deaths. But local jurors, emboldened by an anomalous provision in the state's criminal code, relied on popular definitions of self-defense, provocation, and negligence to counter these efforts, and they exonerated or acquitted the defendants. Hence, the increasing caseload along with unchanging—or slowly changing—standards of culpability produced falling conviction rates.

Despite the efforts of Progressive reformers, Chicago jurors, perhaps like their counterparts elsewhere, demonstrated little inclination to permit the legal system to mediate social relations. Instead, their verdicts in homicide cases, at every level of the criminal justice system, indicated that they believed that men must be allowed to be men, that the law should not interfere in affairs of honor, and that residents assumed risks when they engaged in particular kinds of behavior. At least in Progressive-era Chicago, a blend of gender-, race-, and class-based notions of justice trumped the rule of law, generating low homicide conviction rates during a period of soaring violence. Thus, Chicagoans simultaneously railed about their feckless law enforcers, complained about local violence, and pronounced that Joseph Nesczuk had acted within his rights when he bashed in John Wijas's skull with a hammer on Pleasant Place during the spring of 1907.

Notes

1. *Chicago Tribune,* July 22, 1907.
2. *Chicago Record-Herald,* April 29, 1907.
3. *Chicago Tribune,* July 22. 1907.
4. Ibid.
5. Ibid.
6. Chicago Police Department, "Homicides and Important Events, 1870–1920," Illinois State Archives, Springfield, IL.
7. This figure—and other quantitative evidence in this essay, unless otherwise noted—was calculated using the Chicago Police Department's homicide files, recorded in "Homicides and Important Events, 1870–1920." In these ledger books, the police recorded every homicide occurring in the city and updated the entries as cases worked their way through the legal system. Health Department, coroner's, and newspaper tallies of homicide were consistent with the totals in these police files. I created a data set of 5,645 cases, and, using standard record-linkage techniques, cross-checked, corroborated, and completed each entry by consulting court records, prison records, health department records, and newspaper accounts of individual homicide cases. In calculating conviction rates, I excluded cases in which the killer committed suicide prior to arrest. In addition, I tested my calculations against various newspaper and government investigations of the city's criminal justice system. My case-level data set yielded nearly identical figures to the aggregate-level sources.
8. See David S. Tanenhaus, *Juvenile Justice in the Making* (New York, 2004); Victoria Getis, *The Juvenile Court and the Progressives* (Urbana, 2000); Michael Willrich, *City of Courts* (New York, 2003).
9. For the "Italian squad," see *Chicago Evening Post,* March 15, 1911.
10. Richard C. Lindberg, *To Serve and Collect* (Carbondale, 1991), 24; Simon A. Cole, *Suspect Identities* (Cambridge, MA, 2001), 152, 177–81.
11. See Willrich, *City of Courts,* 241–77.

12. See *Report of the City Council Committee on Crime of the City of Chicago* (Chicago, 1915); John H. Wigmore, editor, *The Illinois Crime Survey* (Chicago, 1929); Mark H. Haller, "Historical Roots of Police Behavior: Chicago, 1890–1925," *Law and Society Review* 10 (Winter 1976): 309.

13. *Chicago Record-Herald,* February 21, 1903.

14. William N. Gemmill, "Crime and Its Punishment in Chicago," *Journal of the American Institute of Criminal Law and Criminology* 1 (July 1910): 39.

15. These calculations exclude killers who committed homicide–suicide.

16. *Chicago Inter Ocean,* September 28, 1910.

17. *Chicago Inter Ocean,* September 28, 1910; *Chicago Tribune,* September 28, 1910.

18. *Chicago Tribune,* January 1, 1913. This figure was based entirely on murder cases. Analyzing data on murders committed in 1919, Edward W. Sims, the president of the Chicago Crime Commission, concluded that the conviction rate was even lower. See Sims, "Fighting Crime in Chicago: The Crime Commission," *Journal of the American Institute of Criminal Law and Criminology* 11 (May 1920): 24.

19. *Report of the City Council Committee on Crime of the City of Chicago,* 192.

20. These figures are based on the crude homicide rates—i.e., both the homicide rate figure and the conviction rate figure are calculated on the basis of all recorded homicides in the city, including infanticide cases, abortion-related homicides, and automobile fatalities defined as homicides. To control for annual fluctuations, the rates for the late 1890s are based on five-year averages. Also see Edith Abbott, "Recent Statistics Relating to Crime in Chicago," *Journal of Criminal Law, Criminology, and Police Science* 13 (November 1922): 337–39; Arthur V. Lashly, "Homicide (in Cook County)," in *The Illinois Crime Survey,* 637.

21. "Race Suicide for Social Parasites," *Journal of the American Medical Association* 50 (January 4, 1908): 55.

22. *Chicago Tribune,* March 2, 1904.

23. Lincoln Steffens, "Half Free and Fighting On," *McClure's Magazine* 21 (October 1903): 563.

24. George Kibbe Turner, "The City of Chicago: A Study of the Great Immoralities," *McClure's Magazine* 28 (April 1907): 589. For a similar assessment, see Henry Barrett Chamberlin, "The Chicago Crime Commission—How the Business Men of Chicago are Fighting Crime," *Journal of the American Institute of Criminal Law and Criminology* 11 (November 1920): 391.

25. John J. Healy, "The Prosecutor (in Chicago) in Felony Cases," in *The Illinois Crime Survey,* 289.

26. Ludvig Hektoen, "The Coroner (in Cook County)," in The *Illinois Crime Survey,* 377; Jeffrey S. Adler, "'Halting the Slaughter of the Innocents': The Civilizing Process and the Surge in Violence in Turn-of-the-Century Chicago," *Social Science History* 25 (Spring 2001): 36–38.

27. See *Chicago Evening Post,* August 24, 1912; *Chicago Evening Post,* July 17, 1914; *Chicago Tribune,* December 6, 1918; *Chicago Tribune,* April 8, 1920.

28. Lashly, "Homicide (in Cook County)," 596–98. Also see David S. Tanenhaus and Steven A. Drizin, "'Owing to the Extreme Youth of the Accused': The Changing Legal Response to Juvenile Homicide," *Journal of Criminal Law and Criminology* 92 (Spring/Summer 2002): 651–52. Hoffman defended his use of "Fridays," arguing that he chose worthy, solid men who were honest but down on their luck. "I'm proud of helping those old fellows," he explained in 1918, and "I wish I could help more of them." See *Chicago Tribune,* December 6, 1918.

29. Healy, "The Prosecutor (in Chicago) in Felony Cases," 306; Gustave F. Fischer, "The Juries, in Felony Cases, in Cook County," in *The Illinois Crime Survey,* 226.

30. Healy, "The Prosecutor (in Chicago) in Felony Cases," 329.

31. *Schnier v. Illinois* 23 Ill. 17, 19 (Illinois, 1859); *Fisher v. Illinois* 23 Ill. 218, 227, 231 (Illinois, 1859); *Illinois v. Bruner* 343 Ill. 146, 148, 163, 171 (Illinois, 1931); Healy, "The Prosecutor (in Chicago) in Felony Cases," 285; Fischer, "The Juries, in Felony Cases, in Cook County," 226–28.

32. *Illinois v. Bruner* 343 Ill. 146, 148, 163; Ossian Cameron, *Illinois Criminal Law and Practice* (Chicago, 1898), 394–95; R. Waite Joslyn, *Criminal Law and Statutory Penalties of Illinois,* 2nd edition (Chicago, 1920), 181.

33. *Fisher v. Illinois* 23 Ill. 218, 231.

34. *Chicago Tribune,* July 10, 1882.

35. *Chicago Times,* May 19, 1880.

36. Raymond B. Fosdick, *American Police Systems* (New York, 1920), 43–44. Also see *Chicago Tribune,* February 21, 1912.

37. For discussions of this issue, see Instructions to the Jury, *People v. Patrick Furling,* February, 1899, term, Criminal Court of Cook County, Archives of the Criminal Court, Chicago, IL. Also see Richard Maxwell Brown, *No Duty to Retreat* (New York, 1991).

38. See Robert M. Ireland, "The Libertine Must Die: Sexual Dishonor and the Unwritten Law in the Nineteenth-Century United States," *Journal of Social History* 23 (Fall 1989): 27–44; Hendrik Hartog, *Man & Wife in America* (Cambridge, MA, 2000), 219–37.

39. *Chicago Evening Post,* October 16, 1913.

40. Ibid.; *Chicago Tribune,* October 17, 1913; *Chicago Tribune,* October 18, 1913.

41. *Chicago Inter Ocean,* March 30, 1911.

42. *Chicago Tribune,* March 29, 1911.

43. *Chicago Inter Ocean,* March 30, 1911.

44. For other examples, see *Chicago Tribune,* August 16, 1913; *Chicago Daily News,* July 18, 1917; *Chicago Tribune,* June 30. 1917.

45. *Chicago Tribune,* August 19, 1918.

46. *Chicago Tribune,* April 8, 1920. For an account of a similar case, with the same outcome, see *Chicago Inter Ocean,* September 6, 1912.

47. *Chicago Tribune,* June 30, 1917.

48. *Chicago Tribune,* August 16, 1913.

49. See ibid.

50. *Chicago Record-Herald,* March 21, 1905; *Chicago Inter Ocean,* July 22, 1912; *Chicago Tribune,* April 26, 1919.

51. *Chicago Record,* July 3, 1899.

52. *Chicago Inter Ocean,* January 10, 1906. For a fuller discussion, see Jeffrey S. Adler, "'I Loved Joe, But I Had to Shoot Him': Homicide by Women in Turn-of-the-Century Chicago," *Journal of Criminal Law and Criminology* 92 (Spring/ Summer 2002): 882–88.

53. *Chicago Evening Post,* March 16, 1914; *Chicago Tribune,* August 22, 1920. Also see Frederick L. Hoffman, *The Homicide Problem* (Newark, 1925), 38.

54. *Chicago Daily News,* February 16, 1918.

55. *Chicago Tribune,* February 17, 1918.

56. *Chicago Tribune,* February 22, 1918.

57. *Chicago Daily News,* February 16, 1918.

58. *Chicago Tribune,* February 17, 1918; *Chicago Tribune,* February 22, 1918.

59. *Chicago Tribune,* February 22, 1918.

60. *New York Times,* February 16, 1918; Fosdick, *American Police Systems,* 45.

61. *Chicago Tribune,* June 28, 1918.

62. *Chicago Record-Herald,* December 27, 1904.

63. Ibid.

64. Ibid.

65. Ibid.; *Chicago Inter Ocean*, December 27, 1904; *Chicago Tribune*, December 27, 1904.

66. Chicago Police Department, "Homicides and Important Events, 1870–1920."

67. *Chicago Inter Ocean*, February 11, 1911; *Chicago Tribune*, February 11, 1911.

68. Put differently, the men who served on Cook County juries rejected Hoffman's (and leading physicians') attempts to prosecute and punish those performing abortions—even those who killed their patients. See Leslie J. Reagan, "'About to Meet Her Maker': Women, Doctors, Dying Declarations, and the State's Investigation of Abortion, Chicago, 1867–1940," *Journal of American History* 77 (March 1991): 1248.

69. Adler, "Halting the Slaughter of the Innocents," 29–52.

70. *Chicago Times*, February 20, 1883.

71. Joliet Convict Registers, Illinois State Archives, Springfield, IL.

72. *Chicago Tribune*, March 25, 1894.

73. Ibid.; *Chicago Record,* March 26, 1894.

74. Joliet Convict Registers. For a case with a similar outcome, see *Chicago Tribune,* August 18, 1896.

75. See *Chicago Evening Post,* March 26, 1901; *Chicago Tribune,* July 30, 1906. Also see Jeffrey S. Adler, *First in Violence, Deepest in Dirt* (Cambridge, MA, 2006), 45–84.

76. *Chicago Tribune,* October 8, 1908. For other examples, see Benedict J. Short [Assistant State's Attorney] to the Illinois State Board of Pardons, October 2, 1908, petition for commutation of the sentence to imprisonment for life of Andrew Williams, Executive Clemency Files, Illinois State Archives, Springfield, IL; *Chicago Times-Herald,* February 5, 1899.

77. *Chicago Times-Herald*, May 13, 1896.

78. Fischer, "The Juries, in Felony Cases, in Cook County," 231–32.

79. See Gail Bederman, *Manliness and Civilization* (Chicago, 1995), 5–20.

80. The mean age of wife killers was thirty-eight, and, by comparison with all Chicago killers between 1875 and 1920, they were older and more clustered in skilled occupations.

81. Abbott, "Recent Statistics Relating to Crime in Chicago," 332.

82. Illinois Board of Pardons to Governor Richard Yates, April 20, 1904, in Petition File of Harvey Van Dine for Commutation of Death Sentence, Illinois Board of Pardons, Executive Clemency Files, Illinois State Archives; *Chicago Daily News,* October 14, 1916.

83. Turner, "The City of Chicago," 590.

84. "Demands Noose for Earl Dear," Unidentified newspaper clipping contained in the Application of Earl Dear for Commutation of Sentence, Executive Clemency Files of Governor Frank O. Lowden, Illinois State Archives.

85. Testimony of James C. O'Brien, Assistant State's Attorney, to the Illinois Board of Pardons and Parole, June 19, 1919, Application of Earl Dear for Commutation of Sentence.

86. James R. Grossman, *Land of Hope* (Chicago, 1989).

87. Eric H. Monkkonen found a similar pattern in his study of homicide in New York City. See Monkkonen, *Murder in New York City* (Berkeley, 2001), 148.

88. Chicago Commission on Race Relations, *The Negro in Chicago: A Study of Race Relations and a Race Riot* (Chicago, 1922), 332, 352–53; *Chicago Defender,* March 18, 1911.

89. Chicago Commission on Race Relations, *The Negro in Chicago,* 622. Also see Elizabeth Dale, *The Rule of Justice* (Columbus, 2001).

90. In intra-racial homicides involving African Americans, 2 percent were executed.

91. *Chicago Tribune*, June 20, 1893; Abbott, "Recent Statistics Relating to Crime in Chicago," 356–57.

92. It is difficult to calculate comparable conviction rates because of differences in extant sources and research methods. Depending on whether scholars rely on police records, coroner's records, indictment reports, criminal court records, newspaper accounts, or some combination of these sources, the denominators in calculating the rates differ.

93. In his study of homicide in nineteenth-century New York City, Eric H. Monkkonen found similar conviction rates. See Monkkonen, "The State From the Bottom Up: Of Homicides and Courts," *Law and Society Review* 24 (April 1990), 529; Monkkonen, *Murder in New York City,* 167. Also see William Francis Kuntz, II. *Criminal Sentencing in Three Nineteenth-Century Cities* (New York, 1988), 264–65; Lawrence M. Friedman, *Crime and Punishment in American History* (New York, 1993), 457–58.

94. See, for example Dennis C. Rousey, "Cops and Guns: Police Use of Deadly Force in Nineteenth-Century New Orleans," *American Journal of Legal History* 28 (January 1984), 64; Clare V. McKanna, Jr., *Homicide, Race, and Justice in the American West, 1880–1920* (Tucson, 1997), 62, 96, 150.

95. See Carolyn A. Conley, The *Unwritten Law* (New York, 1991), 51; Conley, *Melancholy Accidents* (Lanhan, MD, 1999), 92; Conley, *Certain Other Countries: Homicide, Gender and National Identity in Late Victorian England, Ireland, Scotland and Wales* (forthcoming; Columbus, 2007); V.A.C. Gatrell, "The Decline of Theft and Violence in Victorian and Edwardian England," in *Crime and the Law,* edited by V.A.C. Gatrell, Bruce Lenman, and Geoffrey Parker (London, 1980), 287.

96. According to Roger Lane's study, Philadelphia prosecutors secured convictions at a somewhat higher rate than their counterparts in New York, Chicago, and New Orleans. See Lane, *Violent Death in the City* (Cambridge, MA, 1979), 68–69.

97. A number of leading historians of violence have drawn from Norbert Elias's theory of a "civilizing process" and argued that cultural and institutional pressures gradually discouraged impulsive, volatile behavior and thus reduced levels of violence. Such a process, however, does not appear to have redefined the sensibilities of jurors, for convictions rates were low in both high-violence and low-violence settings during the nineteenth and early twentieth centuries. See Norbert Elias, *The Civilizing Process: The History of Manners* (1939; reprint edition. New York, 1978); Elias, *The Civilizing Process: Power and Civility* (1939; reprint edition. New York, 1982). For thoughtful applications of Elias's theory, see Eric A. Johnson and Eric H. Monkkonen, editors, *The Civilization of Crime* (Urbana, 1996).

8

Educating the Eye: Body Mechanics and Streamlining in the United States, 1925–1950

Carma R. Gorman

During the second quarter of the twentieth century, many writers on industrial design noted that, prior to about 1925, attractive appearance was not designers' or consumers' priority, at least not in the product categories that a *Fortune* magazine writer defined in 1934 as the "formerly artless industries": aluminum manufactures, baby carriages, sleds, railroad cars, cash registers, clocks, electrical appliances, food packaging, automobiles, eyeglasses, pens, refrigerators, scales, sewing machines, stoves, and washing machines.[1] Consultant industrial designer Harold Van Doren, writing in 1940, stated that in contrast to the fields of ceramics, glassware, textiles, silverware, jewelry, wallpaper, and furniture, in which products "are sold, and always have been sold, largely on appearance," "in the manufacture of engineered products like typewriters, utility and price were the prime concerns of manufacturer and purchaser alike until a few years ago."[2] Similarly, Van Doren's contemporary Raymond Loewy, writing in 1951, noted that in the nineteenth and early twentieth centuries, American consumers had been satisfied with "engineered as you go" mechanical products that were characterized by a "haphazard, disorderly look" (see, e.g., figure 8.1a).[3]

Both period commentators and historians have agreed that *after* 1925, however, consumers began to demand beauty even in those products for which there had been, as Van Doren put it, a "lack of an educated demand for attractive appearance in years past."[4] In an era when refrigerators or washing machines in a given price range could be expected to work and to wear

From *American Quarterly*. Gorman, Carma R. "Educating the Eye: Body Mechanics and Streamlining in the United States, 1925–1950." *American Quarterly* 58:3 (2006), 839–868. © The American Studies Association. Reprinted with permission of The Johns Hopkins University Press. Note: four of the original illustrations have been omitted from this printing about equally well, newly professionalized American industrial designers acknowledged that they were "designing for the eye"—trying to lure consumers with products that were distinguishable from one another stylistically more than technologically.[5] Particularly during the Depression, it was widely acknowledged that "the sales curve would not respond to the old forms of pressure...[and] the product had to be made to sell itself" through attractive appearance.[6] The clean-lined style that consultant industrial designers developed to meet consumers' demands for beauty in the formerly artless industries went by the name "streamlining" (e.g., figure 8.1b).[7] The origins of the term *streamlining* lie in hydro- and aerodynamics, but most industrial designers—even proponents of scientific streamlining such as Norman Bel Geddes—admitted that in the 1930s, streamlining was primarily an aesthetic device rather than an aerodynamic one, and further claimed that their aesthetic was derived primarily from the form of the human body.[8]

Period observers and historians have both offered many different explanations for how and why this post-1925 shift in tastes and demands occurred, and for the rise of the popularity of streamlining.[9] Many of the well-known explanations are "supply-side" ones, in which particular designers or exhibitions or manufacturers or merchandisers are understood to be the drivers of stylistic change. Consumers, in this paradigm—when they are understood

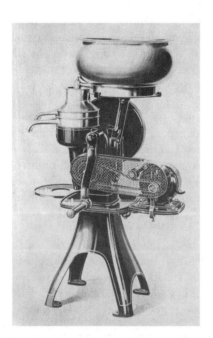
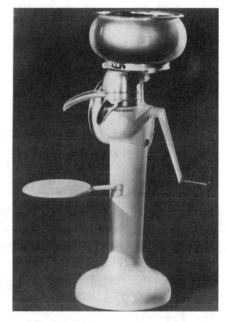

Figure 8.1 a, b Raymond Loewy, McCormick–Deering cream separator, before (a) and after (b) Loewy's redesign (1945), from Raymond Loewy, *Industrial Design* (Woodstock, NY: Overlook Press, 1988), 121. TM/©2007 Raymond Loewy by CMG Worldwide, Inc. www.RaymondLoewy.com.

to affect the design of products at all—do so by adopting new styles after seeing them in exhibitions, magazines, movies, and department stores. Designers then are presumed to cater to consumer tastes by making more products that look like the ones that have already sold well. The problem with this model is that it assumes two things: first, that consumers develop taste preferences primarily through informal means (such as skimming a magazine) rather than through formal ones (such as undergoing a required course of study at school), and second, that consumers develop ideas about and tastes for consumer goods only by looking at *other* consumer goods. Both assumptions are unwarranted. Between 1925 and 1950, there were at least two important formal mechanisms for the teaching and acquisition of taste that had implications for the appearance of the artless industries: "related art" and "body mechanics" training. These forms of education, which flourished in elementary, high school, and college classrooms, have clear implications for the history of taste in this period, yet have not been taken into account by scholars of design. Neither related art nor body mechanics training focused specifically on the aesthetics of the formerly artless industries, but both emphasized the personal and social importance of good form, and taught students how to recognize it and analyze it in the decorative arts and in the human body, respectively. Textbooks and works of pedagogy from these disciplines are resources that scholars have not previously related to the history of design and consumption, but an examination of these forms of literature makes it clear that they can provide insight into the shifts in consumer tastes and product styles that occurred after 1925.[10]

This essay thus addresses two different kinds of *technology*: tangible artifacts and abstract systems. First, I attempt to provide a new explanation for how certain technological artifacts—in this case, streamlined machines of the 1930s and 1940s, and human bodies that were subjected to the discipline of "body mechanics" during that same period—came to look the way they did. "Technology" in this sense of the word, then, refers specifically to machines, as well as to organisms—human bodies—that period writers construed as mechanical systems. The second kind of technology that this essay addresses, however, is not a tangible artifact, such as a washing machine or a perfectly poised body, but rather a system of practices and intellectual and visual tools that is, to borrow from Herbert Simon's famous definition of design, "aimed at changing existing situations into preferred ones."[11] The subdiscipline of physical education called "body mechanics," together with its attendant standards, charts, photographs, statistics, games, and so on (each tools/artifacts in their own right), constituted a technology of bodily—and ultimately, its proponents hoped, social and economic—improvement. This technological *system*—though seemingly unrelated to the technological *artifacts* that are also the subject of this essay—did, I argue, have an important impact on the appearance and reception of streamlined goods in the 1930s and 1940s.

By focusing on the ways of seeing and thinking that were promoted by body mechanics instruction, I contend that streamlining, the style that designers created for use in the formerly artless industries in response to consumers' new demand for beauty, owed at least part of its commercial success to an audience of well-educated, middle- and upper-middle-class consumers who had been primed by their schooling to expect bodies and products to conform to similar standards of beauty and efficiency.[12] For as art historian Michael Baxandall has argued, the visual skills that a society values highly tend to be the ones promoted in its system of formal education, and such consciously learned ways of seeing (which are teachable because they rely on a technology of "rules and categories, a terminology and stated standards") often shape "[the] categories with which [an individual] classifies his visual stimuli, the knowledge he will use to supplement what his immediate vision gives him, and the attitude he will adopt to the kind of artificial objects seen."[13] Studying the ways of looking that are promoted by formal education, Baxandall suggests, is one way to better understand the tastes of viewers (or consumers), because "much of what we call taste" lies in "the conformity between discriminations demanded by a painting [or other designed object] and skills of discrimination possessed by the beholder."[14]

Training in visual discernment via body mechanics instruction ultimately encouraged participants not only to understand the body as a mechanism, but also to judge mechanisms (such as formerly artless products) as beautiful to the degree that they looked like bodies. In distinction, then, to the many scholarly arguments that explore the ways in which the machine served as a model for the human body and its behavior in the 1920s through 1940s, I argue that the human body also became a model for the appearance of machines and other formerly artless products due to the rhetoric of, and emphasis on visual discernment in, the body mechanics instruction that was so heavily promoted in U.S. schools and other organizations in the 1920s, 1930s, and 1940s.[15] Further, I suggest that paying attention to the body mechanics literature explains more directly than many previous theories do why technological products that looked like human bodies (i.e., streamlined formerly artless goods) would have resonated with consumers: they had been taught, through body mechanics instruction, to understand both bodies and formerly artless goods as "mechanical," and as products of similar Taylorist technologies of improvement.

Body Mechanics: Origins and Aims

As dancing and etiquette manuals from past centuries attest, posture has been a preoccupation—and has been justified as a field of study in various ways—for much of Western history. Until the mid- to late 1920s, most writers on human carriage tended to use the word *posture* to describe their field. For example, Jessie Bancroft, founder of the American Posture League and author of an important 1913 book called *The Posture of School Children*, used the word *posture* almost exclusively.[16] However, when posture became a subject of "serious" scientific study in the 1910s and 1920s to physicians such as Joel Goldthwait, Robert Tait McKenzie, Armin Klein, Robert Osgood, Eliza Mosher, and George Fisher, the nomenclature of the field changed.[17] In the 1920s "body mechanics" became the theorists' favored term, because it was understood to be "more inclusive and descriptive" than the term *posture*.[18] Body mechanics referred not only to stance, but also to "the mechanical correlation of the various systems of the body with special reference to the skeletal, muscular, and visceral systems and their neurological associations."[19] Posture, a word derived by way of the French *positure* from the Latin *ponere*, "to place," probably sounded too static, given that body mechanics dealt with the body in motion as well as at rest. It also connoted "posing" and "posturing," which implied artificial, deceitful, and ultimately damaging uses of the body, as opposed to the "natural" and therapeutic ones physicians wished to cultivate. "Mechanics," in contrast, was a useful word not only because it referred to the field of mathematics concerned with motion and equilibrium, but also because it connoted machines and technology, since the word was derived from the Greek root *mechane*, meaning machine or contrivance. Indeed, many body mechanics theorists made explicit comparisons between bodies and machine systems; for example, the authors of a government report noted that "one of the most complicated and yet mechanically efficient products of the age is the automobile. It is incomparably less complicated and less efficient than the human body, yet the driving public are frequently made aware of the fact that slight disturbances of alignment in an automobile's working parts and slight dysfunctions of its electrical organs, may interfere with its function and cause it to develop chronic diseases."[20] The physicians' use of the term "body mechanics," then, suggested a certain willingness to conflate the categories of the biological and the mechanical/technological.

The physicians promoting body mechanics—whose credentials distinguished them from the many other individuals and groups interested in posture during this period (such as Joseph Pilates, F. Matthias Alexander, and chiropractors)—successfully justified the scientific study of body mechanics by arguing that modern, sedentary life was wreaking havoc on the physiques and health of Americans, especially children, to the detriment of personal and social efficiency.[21] Statistics derived from the military draft during the Great War, from examinations made of matriculating students to Ivy League and Seven Sisters schools, and from the so-called Chelsea Survey funded by the Children's Bureau of the Department of Labor in 1923–24 suggested that approximately 75–80 percent of young Americans exhibited poor body mechanics.[22] These findings were troubling, the physicians argued, because proper body mechanics was linked to good digestion and elimination, healthy weight gain in children, increased alertness, emotional well-being, decreased absences from school, efficient combustion by the lungs, and decreased menstrual and gynecological problems, among a host of other benefits. In clinical studies, physicians noted that what were otherwise unexplainable improvements in chronic health conditions seemed to coincide with corrections in posture. Studies showed that groups of students that had received posture training, for example, had lower rates of absences from school than did control groups.[23]

Absence of disease was not the only reason that physicians and other writers promoted good body mechanics, however. As Jessie Bancroft made clear in her 1913 book—and through her inclusion of scientific management experts Frank and Lillian Gilbreth on the board of the American Posture League—a desire for increased bodily and mental efficiency (in the scientific management sense of the term) was another of the reasons for the renewed interest in and respectability of the field of body mechanics in the 1910s, 1920s, and 1930s. Bancroft, who clearly was enamored of Frederick Winslow Taylor's techniques for achieving industrial efficiency and often made reference to efficiency as a primary benefit of body mechanics instruction, contended that "fatigue comes less readily in correct posture, and the energy spent through unconscious muscular action in maintaining a bad position is available in good posture, for other uses. In good posture, also, better circulation, respiration, and digestion keep the stores of energy and sense of well-being at a higher level, and the efficiency and even the spirits of the individual are thereby placed on a loftier plane."[24] Similarly, Marguerite Sanderson of the Boston School of Physical Education claimed in 1922 that for men, "the strong, erect figure is desired not only for military fitness, but is [also] being demanded more and more in industry."[25] Even character and moral qualities were understood to be linked to good form; Henry Eastman Bennett, author of *School Posture and Seating* (1928), went so far as to argue that "the highest human traits and the finest moral perfections are inseparably associated in our thinking with erectness of carriage and posture. Our very language testifies that our concepts of moral qualities are derived from physical bearing: witness such terms as 'uprightness,' 'poise,' 'well-balanced,' 'level-headed,' 'backbone,' 'chesty,' and a host of others. We inevitably judge character from postural evidences. We ascribe poise, dignity, confidence, courage, self-reliance, self-respect, leadership, aggressiveness, and dependability to those whose posture expresses such traits."[26]

As Anson Rabinbach has shown in the case of Germany, and as Carolyn Thomas de la Peña has discussed in the case of the United States, even before the publication of Taylor's book *The Principles of Scientific Management* in 1911, late-nineteenth- and early-twentieth-century physical educators and physicians were busily preoccupied with developing technologies for minimizing fatigue and maximizing physical and mental energy.[27] But Taylorism proved a particularly useful and persuasive technology for conceptualizing and maximizing bodily efficiency. Both theorists and educators argued, for example, that the purpose of body mechanics training was "to develop the highest physical efficiency for the largest number of people" and "to prepare the body for the greatest usefulness in the world"—phrasings that seem directly inspired by Taylor's ideas, but that also echo the sentiments of eugenicists of the period.[28] However, although some of the people who promoted body mechanics in the 1920s and 1930s were probably also sympathetic to eugenics, most seemed dedicated to the proposition that the majority of postural defects was caused by environmental rather than hereditary factors.[29] The rhetoric of body mechanics suggested that everyone—except possibly "idiots and mental defectives," as Bancroft bluntly termed them—could achieve good (or at least improved) body alignment and thus better health and greater personal efficiency, if only they were willing to work hard enough at it.[30] Willpower, physical training, and visual discernment, rather than good genes, were touted as the sole endowments that most people needed to achieve a more beautiful, efficient body. As Bennett claimed, "postural habits are controllable" and are "as definitely subject to educational direction as are habits of language, of thought, of manners, of conduct, or other objectives in teaching."[31] It was through this faith in the efficacy of education and in the malleability of human bodies and minds that body mechanics promoters most differed from eugenicists. The point of body mechanics, as of Taylorism and other similar technologies, was that it could be systematized and replicated, taught and learned.

The Reach of Body Mechanics Instruction

Although much of the theory of body mechanics was established by physicians in the 1900s and 1910s, the push to have body mechanics taught in schools gained real momentum in the 1920s and the early 1930s. The federal government, for example, published pamphlets through the Government Printing Office in the late 1920s on body mechanics theory and pedagogy, and under President Herbert Hoover sponsored the 1932 White House Conference on Child Health and Protection.[32] At this conference, four (male) physicians and one (female) physical education professor constituted the Subcommittee on Orthopedics and Body Mechanics (hereafter "the Subcommittee"), which was part of the conference's Committee on Medical Care for Children.[33] Not surprisingly—given the importance they attributed to good posture—the Subcommittee members recommended in their final report (hereafter "the Report") "that steps be taken to make it not only possible but compulsory for all the children of the United States to receive instruction in good body mechanics."[34] They particularly stressed that "body mechanics should be made the basic principle of all physical education," and that all games and sports should be used to develop good posture.[35]

Although it is difficult to assess precisely the reach of body mechanics education across the nation, a number of kinds of evidence point to its ubiquity by the 1930s. First is the number of states that mandated physical education. In 1900, only four states had laws mandating physical education in public schools, but by 1930, thirty-nine states had passed such laws, and twenty-two states had state directors of physical education.[36] Granted, training in physical education could, in the 1930s, comprise anything from military drill to gymnastics to calisthenics to dance to competitive sports to body mechanics, but even before the Subcommittee published its recommendations in

1932, California, Delaware, and Utah boasted physical education programs in which "training in posture and body mechanics is given as an integral part of the health and physical education program in all the preparatory schools of the state."[37] Similarly, at the time the Subcommittee wrote the Report, in thirteen other states, "there is some recognition of the importance of body mechanics, but no coordinated state program," and in "many localities where health education is provided in the public schools, the subject of body mechanics is considered and given a place of varying importance on the program" (the Subcommittee members singled out Los Angeles and Boston public schools for their particularly impressive programs).[38] Physical education teachers were also being schooled in body mechanics at this time; in response to a Subcommittee questionnaire sent to 223 schools of physical education, 82 percent of those schools that replied (the response rate was 76 percent) answered "yes" to the question "Does your school give any specific formal instruction in the theory and practical application of Body Mechanics or posture...in its relation to the health of the individual and distinguished from 'Calisthenics' or corrective work for poor muscular development?"[39] Presumably the number of states and local programs offering such instruction both to schoolchildren and to physical educators increased after the publication of the Subcommittee's report, and flourished in tandem with the growth of physical education programs generally. Second, although body mechanics/posture training is usually mentioned in passing, if at all, in most histories of physical education, the prominence of American Posture League (APL) incorporators and board members in shaping physical education theory and pedagogy in the public schools, in the military, and in civilian organizations such as the Boy Scouts suggests that body mechanics training had a wide reach in American society.[40]

The Pedagogical Literature on Body Mechanics

Although the 1932 White House Conference Report spelled out very clearly the nature of the posture problem, it was neither a motivational tool nor a practical guidebook for the teaching of good body mechanics. Before the 1932 conference, there were only a few texts available that focused on the pedagogy rather than the theory of body mechanics. One of these was Bancroft's 1913 book *The Posture of School Children, With Its Home Hygiene and New Efficiency Methods for School Training*. The content of Bancroft's book was split about equally between theory and pedagogy, but—as its subtitle made clear—her notion of pedagogy primarily involved applying the principles of Taylorism to classroom management and record-keeping, and secondarily explaining physical exercises that teachers could prescribe to their students. Her method was similar to that of "social efficiency" educators such as John Franklin Bobbitt and W.W. Charters, who modeled their curricula and their language on Taylor's theories of industrial production (they referred to school superintendents as "educational engineers" and—as Bancroft did—to school buildings as "plants").[41]

Bancroft dedicated only a couple of pages to other methods of teaching, such as drawing, studying pictures, and so on.[42]

However, a somewhat kinder and gentler approach to body mechanics education was promoted by Leah Thomas in the following decade. Thomas, a professor of physical education and the sole woman (and nonphysician) on the Subcommittee, was probably appointed to the group because the second edition of her book *Body Mechanics and Health* (1929) was essentially the first published text that served both as an overview of the theory of body mechanics *and* as a thorough resource for its teaching.[43] Thomas's book not only contained suggestions for exercises, but also included games, rhymes, songs, and pictures that she believed were motivational. Thomas's book set the tone for subsequent works of body mechanics pedagogy, and later writers emulated and expanded upon it.

One of these authors was Ivalclare Sprow Howland, an associate professor at Battle Creek College in Michigan, author of the 1936 book *The Teaching of Body Mechanics in Elementary and Secondary Schools*.[44] Reacting to the relative dearth of pedagogical literature on posture, Howland wrote her book specifically in response to the 1932 White House Conference report (4). The scope and length of her book, its engaging approach, its eminently respectable and scientific underpinnings (namely, the Report), and its balancing of the social efficiency agenda with Deweyism, made it a particularly useful resource for teachers, who generally reviewed it favorably.[45] Thomas and Howland, then, more than any previous authors, promoted "fun" approaches to learning good body mechanics, including plays, games, pictures, and discussions, as well as or in lieu of corrective exercises.

Bancroft's, Thomas's, and Howland's books were some of the first widely published, comprehensive books on body mechanics written expressly for teachers, and upon their publication probably had a fairly wide impact on the way body mechanics (and physical education generally) was taught in classrooms across the nation. Because physical education was a school subject in which textbooks were usually not used, these works of pedagogy are some of the best remaining indicators of what posture instruction in schools of the 1920s and 1930s was like. Not only were these books widely distributed (most major university libraries still own copies today), but their impact is also evident in the subsequent pedagogical literature on body mechanics.[46] The authors' methods thus merit careful examination.

Educating the Eye: A Technology for Biomechanical Improvement

Although one might expect a physical education instructor to stress foremost the importance of physical training to the development of good posture, as indeed Bancroft and a number of other writers did, Thomas and Howland instead proceeded on the assumption that physical exercises alone were not a conducive means of developing good body mechanics in students. Although Howland noted that "to express himself by 'doing and experiencing' is truly educational and inspirational" for the student of body mechanics, and although she did prescribe many games and physical activities for her students, at heart her method was visual. "Body Mechanics," she argued, "can best be taught by educating the 'eye'" (37). Howland and her colleagues thus employed a many-pronged strategy for developing their students' "artistic and esthetic sense" through "recognizing and practicing good body alignment and posture" (112). Their method was thus a logical extension of the physicians' assumption that the quality of the body's "mechanical correlations" was visible in its contours.

Primary among the educators' techniques was teaching students to recognize the difference between good and poor body mechanics, which they did through reference to government-published standards that were available in six varieties: thin, intermediate, and stocky for both boys and girls (figure 8.2).[47] In all of the standards, the "grade A" body was compactly disposed around a central vertical axis that ran from approximately the ear to the arch of the feet, displaying only restrained convex curves at the shoulder blades, buttocks, and chest/stomach. In contrast, the bodies with poor posture were characterized by greater deviance from the vertical axis via "exaggerated" curves in the spine, as well as inward slumping of the chest and an outthrust, lowered chin. Part of the body mechanics educators' strategy, then, lay in teaching students to be connoisseurs of curves, and to distinguish between "normal" curvature and "exaggerated" curvature. It is easy to see how this kind of aesthetic education could play a role in shaping consumers' expectations for beauty in the formerly artless industries, since in effect, the skills that Howland and her colleagues asked students to apply to the human body were similar to those one would use to "appreciate" and criticize a designed object or a work of art, especially a streamlined one.

Much of the body mechanics educators' method depended on having students analyze their own profiles and compare them to the posture standards. "'To see ourselves as others see us,'" Howland wrote, "is profoundly important in taking personal inventory of one's bodily attitudes" (23). Physicians and early body mechanics educators like Bancroft had devised a number of ways of gauging the quality of body mechanics (and by implication, of bodily health and efficiency) from the contours of the body seen in profile—the view in which "others see us," but which we cannot ourselves see directly. Bancroft promoted the use of what she called the "vertical line test," which involved holding a window pole next to the body to help gauge "the whole figure at a glance."[48] But ideally, according to Howland, teachers would have had equipment available with which to take silhouettograph photos, which yielded permanent, accurate profile images that students could use to compare their own posture to that of the standards.[49] For those schools that could not afford the equipment required to make these indexical records, however, body mechanics assessments had to take other forms. "Posture stamps" developed by American Posture League member

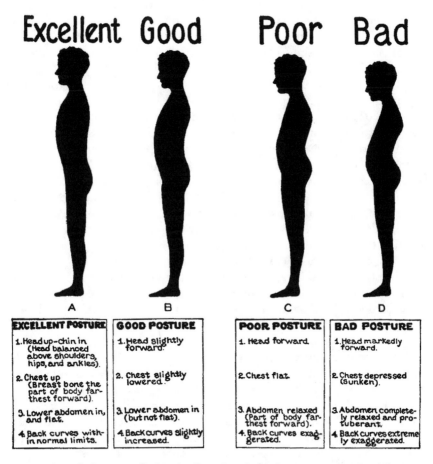

POSTURE STANDARDS

Intermediate-Type Boys

Excellent Good   Poor   Bad

A   B   C   D

EXCELLENT POSTURE	GOOD POSTURE	POOR POSTURE	BAD POSTURE
1. Head up–chin in (Head balanced above shoulders, hips, and ankles).	1. Head slightly forward.	1. Head forward.	1. Head markedly forward.
2. Chest up (Breast bone the part of body farthest forward).	2. Chest slightly lowered.	2. Chest flat.	2. Chest depressed (sunken).
3. Lower abdomen in, and flat.	3. Lower abdomen in (but not flat).	3. Abdomen relaxed (Part of body farthest forward).	3. Abdomen completely relaxed and protuberant.
4. Back curves within normal limits.	4. Back curves slightly increased.	4. Back curves exaggerated.	4. Back curves extremely exaggerated.

Children's Bureau, United States Department of Labor, Washington, D.C., 1926.

Figure 8.2 "Intermediate-type boys," from Armin Klein, M.D., "Posture Clinics: Organization and Exercises," U. S. Department of Labor/Children's Bureau Publication No. 164 (Washington: Government Printing Office, 1926), 12. TM.

Lillian Drew and available to educators from the Robey French Company, Boston, could be used to cheaply rubber stamp index cards with diagrams and checklists useful in student posture inspections.[50] The teacher judged the posture of partially disrobed students for common flaws (weak arches, hyperflexed knees, round upper back, low chest, protruding abdomen, etc.), and made marks on the cards indicating the severity of each imperfection. Follow-up inspections, recorded on the same card in different colors of ink, charted students' progress visually and verbally.

Howland urged students to take advantage of other chances for self-assessment, too; she encouraged self-study in the mirror at home, and also sideways glances in store windows, which she claimed were particularly useful because they showed the disposition of the body in motion (the significance of her recommendation that students view an image of their bodies as reflected in a pane of glass that also displayed consumer goods will become apparent shortly). She also recommended having the instructor "mirror" or mimic students' posture as they marched in single file past her, no doubt to the great amusement of all. She noted that, not surprisingly, "a second march by the mirror may reveal a change in the 'every-day tallness' of the students" (112). The public nature of this last kind of assessment was apparently part of what was believed to make it successful. The "mirror" exercise, which was performed publicly and which had the potential to be embarrassing if one's posture were poor, was only one example of Howland's use of the airing of imperfections as an inducement to faster learning (a technique she may have adapted from Bancroft, who believed that peer pressure was an excellent motivating tool).[51]

If helping students to see themselves as others did was one of the body mechanics educators' most important strategies for educating the eye, having students learn to critique the body mechanics of other people was nearly as important. One of the ways in which Howland gauged students' progress was through their development of critical faculties: "Do they report recognizing poor body mechanics in others?" (14). To that end, she devised games and competitions in which students, rather than teachers, were the judges of bearing, and in which they were required to use their skills of visual discernment on their peers. She suggested that "one group for a month at a time may serve as cleanliness inspectors for their classrooms....One method is to have the children sit in their seats while the inspectors pass down the aisles; another method is to have the children pass in file by the inspectors. Charts and records may be kept for individuals or by groups" (57). Howland further suggested that the groups take on different names, such as the "Spicks" and the "Spans," and that the competition in inspection be arranged between the said groups, or between boys and girls, or between different classes (57). The winners, she suggested, should be treated by the other half of the class to simple awards such as bookmarks, tags, or arm bands. She also suggested a similar peer-monitoring activity for a schoolwide Good Body Mechanics and Posture Week: "Posture cops—selected to tag all good postures each day" (59).

These kinds of games—especially the ones that emphasized the keeping of "charts and records"—again seem clearly derived from Taylorist forms of education like Bancroft's. It is also hard not to be reminded of Michel Foucault's discussion of surveillance and discipline when reading about these "games"; they were clearly intended to develop a culture of surveillance in order to enforce properly disciplined carriage.[52] Indeed, Bancroft noted (with, one feels, a certain degree of glee at the success of her motivational techniques) that "the boys in one class waylaid a classmate after school and pommeled him because his poor posture kept the class from one hundred per cent."[53] Both official and unsanctioned monitoring activities like these communicated to students not only that they were being constantly watched and judged based on their form, but also that they should in turn feel free—even obligated—to judge the health, efficiency, and character of others based on their form.

Fortunately for their students, though, Thomas and Howland did suggest many less-public techniques for cultivating visual discernment. Once students had learned how their own bodies looked and were able to track their improvement (through the use of Taylorist technologies such as silhouettographs, cards, mirrors, charts, competitions, etc.), they were encouraged to compare their own bodies not only to the posture standards but also to other exemplary bodies. These other bodies could include those of athletes, actresses, and physical education teachers, all of whom were presumed not only to have excellent posture, but also to be people whom students were anxious to emulate.[54] Or these exemplary bodies could come from the fine arts: "Let the children choose a statue or picture in the school or city park as an example of good posture," Howland advised (113), claiming that "the selection of famous paintings and sculpture that serve as examples of good body mechanics is very stimulating and inspiring" (50). Bancroft argued that "with pictures of Washington and Lincoln before them, of kings and queens, of pioneers and heroes, who figure in history and literature, it should not be hard to inspire any child with a desire for the best carriage he can cultivate."[55] Thomas provided a list of paintings—"Beatrice d'Este, Elizabeth, Countess of Derby, Queen Mary, The Blue Boy"—that she considered to be "examples of excellent posture," and also illustrated a John Faed painting of George Washington and an Augustus Saint-Gaudens sculpture of Abraham Lincoln in her book. Howland provided a long list of "suitable pictures" that she believed demonstrated good body mechanics, although she did not illustrate any of the items. It included the following works of art and architecture, which she stated could be acquired from art extension societies or art publishing houses (50):

George Washington by Stuart
Song of the Lark by Breton
Sistine Madonna by Raphael
Signing of the Declaration of Independence by Trumbull
Pilgrims Going to Church by Boughton

Sir Galahad by Watts
Spirit of 1776 by Willard
Washington Crossing the Delaware by Leutze
Windmills of Holland by Hencke
Pueblo Indian by Amick
Blue Boy by Gainsborough
Bridge of Avignon by Garrison
Milan Cathedral, Italy
Rheims Cathedral, France
Roman Forum
Roman Coliseum
Appeal to the Great Spirit by Dallin

As Howland made clear through this list of recommended images, yet another kind of visual comparison that she encouraged her students to make was between bodies and buildings. Though the point of comparing one human form to another (whether actual or painted/sculpted) is fairly clear, the usefulness of comparing the body to the architectural monuments toward the end of Howland's list is more difficult to discern. What was there about Milan cathedral, for example, that could inspire good posture? Were students really expected to make a connection between vertical spires of stone and upright spines of bone? Although in the West there is a long history of comparing the human body to a column and the body of Christ to the plans of churches, neither of these comparisons has typically been drawn in the interest of fostering good posture, nor is either comparison a good parallel for what Howland did. But apparently students were expected to make the connection without difficulty, for Howland made such architectural comparisons frequently. She suggested the phrase "Economic Architecture" as a body mechanics poster slogan (39); she captioned her book's frontispiece—which may have depicted her daughter Gloria—as "Dynamic Architecture"; she suggested that students "tag trees and buildings demonstrating poise and beauty in perfect alignment" (62); she recommended that senior high students discuss the sentence "each one of us is the architect of his own body" (160); and she assigned first-through fourth-graders to "discuss the posture of buildings....Illustrate with pictures....Contrast strong, well-balanced structures with those about to fall over" (113). These comparisons all point to her belief in a widely shared understanding of the usefulness of buildings—whether classical temples or skyscrapers—as models for human bearing on both formal and metaphorical levels. The implication is that both buildings and bodies are "designed" objects and can be evaluated similarly, in that they are technological artifacts that in turn are used as tools for other purposes.

However, real bodies, painted and sculpted bodies, and buildings were not the only designed objects to which Thomas and Howland and their colleagues urged students to compare their own bodies. Although many of the games that Thomas recommended compared the human form to animals (camels, rabbits, giraffes, horses, etc.) and to plants (poplars, apples, hollyhocks), some of her exercises compared the human body to machines and other "formerly artless" consumer products. Her "Story Play" called "Change! Change! Change!" directed students to "[sit] at desks with one hand on chest; pretend chest is an elevator; raise and lower chest; sometimes stop halfway to allow passengers to step out; other times it is express to top floor" (123). A game called "Lights on, Lights off" compared children to lightbulbs.

> Two members of the class with habitual good posture are chosen to be the men who want to buy electric light bulbs. The rest of the class are the bulbs. They are in the shop; that is, they are lined up along the walls of the room. If they are very straight against the wall, they are good bulbs. The men choose or "buy" alternately, and as each is bought it finds its socket, which is a chair, or a place on the floor, if the game is played in the gymnasium. One "man" says, "Lights on." All stand. The teacher is "tester." She names any one who is in poor posture. That one is a poor bulb, and must go back to the shop for repairs. The other "man" says, "Lights off," and all sit. The teacher again names any who are in poor posture. These go for repairs. She then names those that are "mended," and they return to their places. At the end of five minutes, or any time agreed upon, the side having the greatest number of lights in place is declared the winner.[56]

Howland made many similar body/machine comparisons in her book. For example, echoing the Report, she claimed that "the body is like the machine; its working parts must be accurately adjusted to one another and, if any one part is out of position, the machine does not work perfectly" (114). Further, in dedicating her book "to my little daughter Gloria[,] and to all children[,] in the hope that their bodies may become dynamic mechanisms of beauty and symmetry, capable of supreme service for lives of happiness and worth," Howland used a machine metaphor that seemed not only to emphasize the use a well-tuned body could give its owner, but also to emphasize the ways in which that individual body could serve industry, "the race," and so on (iii). And echoing some of Thomas's games, an exercise Howland recommended for fifth- and sixth-graders was to "discuss the beauty and efficiency of inanimate machines such as automobiles, machines in factories, the corn popping machine, the doughnut fryer, etc." (115).

The point of Thomas's and Howland's many body/machine comparisons seems to have been twofold: that "good" bodies and machines should be efficient at operation/production, and that they should be characterized—like the posture standards—by a taut disposition of forms around a central axis and an absence of "exaggerated" curves or bulges. These authors' intriguing comparison of bodies to formerly artless products such as lightbulbs, doughnut fryers, and corn poppers casts an interesting light on Howland's aforementioned recommendation to students to view their bodies in the reflections of store windows—where their images presumably would have been juxtaposed, ghostlike, with exactly these kinds of products. Also, comparisons of human bodies to productive technologies such as elevators, lightbulbs, and factory machines—artifacts designed to manipulate conditions and/or do work—makes it clear that body mechanics educators conceived of the human body not only as designed, but also as mechanical, even technological. Although many historians have argued that the point of machine/body comparisons in this period was that the machine served as a model for the modern body, a notion that the body mechanics literature supports, these comparisons could cut both ways: that is, even when the comparisons were meant to serve as lessons for how to manage and form the body, they also suggested that perhaps bodies could serve as models for machines and products.[57]

Designers on Streamlining and the Body

Indeed, many consultant industrial designers of this period made exactly the same point about streamlined products: that their form was derived from the appearance of the ideal human body. Renowned designer Raymond Loewy's before-and-after pictures of McCormick–Deering cream separators (figures. 8.1a and b) show particularly effectively the ways in which streamlining "humanized" the form of products by making their skins or contours tauter, more compact, and more axial. Loewy not only implicitly compared the form of the female body to different forms of architecture and design in his well-known 1930 "evolution charts" of design (figures 8.3 and 8.4), but also made such comparisons explicit using photographs. In his autobiography *Never Leave Well Enough Alone* (1951), he compared an automobile chassis to a human skeleton (a female one, in this case; her bracelets, rings, and high heels are visible on the X-ray), as well as comparing good and poor automobile design to what he considered to be beautiful and ugly female forms. Loewy described the poor auto design as "bulbous, fat, and without character: what we call the 'jelly mold school of design,'" a phrasing that closely echoes the body mechanics educators' assessments of the physical and moral qualities of bodies that displayed poor posture.[58] On the other hand, Loewy's chosen model for good design, the sculpted female figure, could easily have been a poster girl in Thomas's or Howland's body mechanics classes. Her tautly contoured, not-too curvy body was very similar to the bodies illustrated in the posture standards, and to other sculptures shown as examples in body mechanics books. Loewy concluded that good automobile body design "obeys the same aesthetic canons of slenderness and economy of means as the human figure," and claimed that "even when you look at these illustrations upside down or sidewise, the results are equally pleasing or repellent," suggesting that the ideal human body could be used as a model for objects of all orientations and sizes.[59]

Loewy's use of the human body as a source for his streamline aesthetic was shared by many other consultant industrial designers. Adrienne Berney has noted that "industrial designers as well as advertising companies recognized the parallel aesthetics between automobiles and women's bodies," and quotes Paul Frankl as saying that continuity of line "was characteristic of the modern style as we find in the stream-line body of a car or in the long

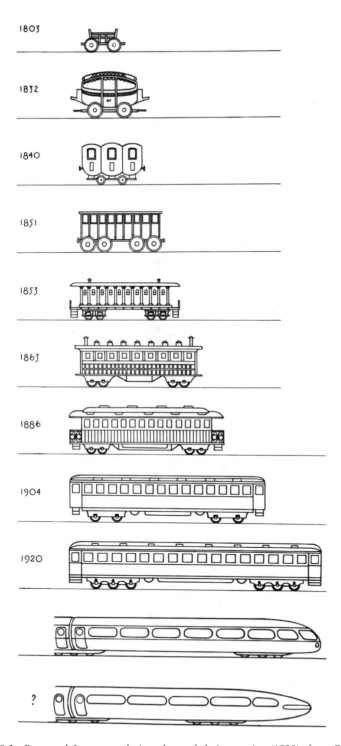

Figure 8.3 Raymond Loewy, evolution chart of design: trains (1930), from Raymond
Loewy, *Industrial Design* (Woodstock, NY: Overlook Press, 1988), 74. Reproduced with
permission of Laurence Loewy. TM/©2007 Raymond Loewy by CMG Worldwide, Inc.
www.RaymondLoewy.com.

Figure 8.4 Raymond Loewy, evolution chart of design: women's bathing suits (1930), from Raymond Loewy, *Industrial Design* (Woodstock, NY: Overlook Press, 1988), 76. Reproduced with permission of Laurence Loewy. TM/©2007 Raymond Loewy by CMG Worldwide, Inc. www.RaymondLoewy.com.

unbroken lines in fashions."[60] Similarly, Walter Dorwin Teague claimed that "the human body [was] the source of balance and symmetry in design," and that "the healthy, vigorous human body in action is the most productive field of study we can find."[61] J. Gordon Lippincott claimed that "much of our appreciation of the abstract is based on our inherent sensitivity to the nude form. The flowing rhythmic lines of nature have been man's natural environment, and therefore it is not surprising that he applies this feeling to his expressions in abstract creation."[62] Industrial designer Egmont Arens, who assuredly knew the technical meaning of the term streamlining, nonetheless often used it as a synonym for "sleek" or "beautiful." In a 1934 telegram to President Franklin D. Roosevelt, for example, he described a slide lecture he had given in which he showed images of "streamlined Trees, Flowers, Whales, Diving Girls, Refrigerators, Houses, Gadgets, [and] Women[']s Fashions."[63] What he meant by streamlined trees and flowers is debatable, but by streamlined women's fashions and diving girls he no doubt referred to the restrained, taut curves that are seen in Loewy's sculpture. Claude Bragdon, whose Theosophist architectural theories were known to many industrial designers (most notably to Teague), stated that "a study of the human figure with a view to analyzing the sources of its beauty cannot fail to be profitable. Pursued intelligently, such a study will stimulate the mind to a perception of those simple yet subtle laws according to which nature everywhere works, and it will educate the eye in the finest known school of proportion, training it to distinguish minute differences, in the same way that the hearing of good music cultivates the ear."[64] Bragdon's assertion, in particular, echoes very closely the rhetoric of body mechanics writers, even down to the phrase "educating the eye," which he also envisioned doing through study of the human body. It seems, then, that designers were well aware that their audience expected bodies and machines to conform to similar standards of beauty and efficiency.

Conclusion

The shift in consumer tastes and demands in the late 1920s that so many period commentators noted but could not fully explain—and the rise of streamlining seemingly in response to it—was likely related to the aesthetic training that many young people received between the 1920s and the 1940s in body mechanics coursework. Although the visual training that the discipline of body mechanics provided young women and men is of course not the only factor in the rise of consumers' "object consciousness," certainly the effect of body mechanics training should not be ignored as a potentially significant factor in consumers' increased demand for "good form" in the formerly artless industries, and for the particular configuration of good form—streamlining—that became popular during that era.[65] Most students who attended elementary school, high school, and/or college between the 1920s and 1940s would have been required to develop, at least to some extent, an "educated eye": a vocabulary for describing form, an "artistic and esthetic sense" (as Howland put it), and a mind-set that encouraged them to see parallels between bodies and designed goods, especially between bodies and machines (37, 115). This significant segment of the population constituted a group of people who shared specialized visual and cognitive habits and vocabulary. These consumers' skills at assessing the form of bodies were available to be used even for the analysis of those categories of goods whose value had formerly been judged almost exclusively by their function: the formerly artless industries.

Not coincidentally, streamlining, the style that designers applied to the formerly artless industries after 1925, was by all accounts most popular with a white upper-middle-class audience (the same demographic group that would have received the greatest number of years of posture training in high school and/or college).[66] It was admirably suited to the visual proclivities of consumers of the 1930s and 1940s who had undergone body mechanics training. The taut "skins" and restrained curves of post-1925 streamlined formerly artless products lent themselves to precisely the same kind of analysis that body mechanics educators urged when they asked students to compare their own posture to lightbulbs, buildings, cars, doughnut fryers, and corn poppers, and indeed, designers claimed that their products were modeled on the body. Given that young Americans were taught to interpret an erect, compact, subtly curved body as being possessed of positive physical and even moral qualities, and that they were repeatedly asked to compare bodies to certain kinds of products, it is entirely likely that they transferred standards of and ideas about bodily good form to the assessment of objects, and came to expect machines and other artless products not only to reveal their efficiency and "character" through their contours, but also to conform to human standards of beauty.

The body mechanics literature—like other forms of educational literature that promote the teaching of visual discernment—is thus useful to American studies scholars in a number of ways. First, it provides insights into early-twentieth-century conceptions of the relationship between bodies and machines that examination of either the bodies or the machines alone would not. Second, it provides a means of theorizing stylistic change as consumer- rather than designer-driven. And third, it helps us understand why early-twentieth-century consumers might have been drawn, very specifically, to purchase mechanical products that looked like human bodies: they had been taught, through body mechanics instruction, to understand both bodies and formerly artless goods as "designed," as mechanical in nature, and as products of Taylorist-inspired technological systems.

Notes

Many people have helped me with the research, writing, and images for various versions of this essay over the years, and I am grateful to them all. However, I would particularly like to thank Cortney Boyd, Carolyn Thomas de la Peña, Paul Groth, Phil Howze, Kathleen James-Chakraborty, Ken Friedman, Jiawei Gong, Laurence Loewy,

Margaretta Lovell, Stacey Lynn, Sharon Marcus, Eric Peterson, Marita Sturken, Siva Vaidhyanathan, the members of the Berkeley Americanists' Group, the School of Art and Design at Southern Illinois University Carbondale, and an anonymous reviewer for *American Quarterly* for their kind assistance.

1. "Both Fish and Fowl," *Fortune*, February 9, 1934, 98.
2. Harold Van Doren, *Industrial Design: A Practical Guide* (New York: McGraw-Hill, 1940), 4–5.
3. Raymond Loewy, *Never Leave Well Enough Alone* (New York: Simon & Schuster, 1951), 11.
4. Van Doren, *Industrial Design*, 43.
5. "Designing for the Eye" is the title of an article by Franklin E. Brill, *Product Engineering* 4.1 (January 1933): 16–17.
6. "Both Fish and Fowl," 40.
7. By "streamlining," I do not mean the teardrop-shaped, aerodynamics-inspired transportation designs by Norman Bel Geddes and Buckminster Fuller, but rather, the more restrained and commercially successful kind of streamlining that was applied to "formerly artless" products of the period.
8. Norman Bel Geddes, "Streamlining," *Atlantic Monthly*, November 1934, 553, 556–58. The derivation of streamlining from the form of the human body is discussed later in this essay.
9. For period observers' explanations, see, e.g., Christine Frederick, *Selling Mrs. Consumer* (New York: The Business Bourse, 1929), 355–57; Van Doren, *Industrial Design*, 43; and Earnest Elmo Calkins, in the introduction to *Consumer Engineering: A New Technique for Prosperity*, by Roy Sheldon and Egmont Arens (New York: Harper, 1932), 4–6. For historians' explanations, see, e.g., Jane N. Law, "Designing the Dream," in *Streamlining America: A Henry Ford Museum Exhibit*, ed. Fannia Weingartner (Dearborn, Mich.: Henry Ford Museum and Greenfield Village, 1986); Dianne H. Pilgrim, "Design for the Machine," in *The Machine Age in America, 1918–1941*, ed. Richard Guy Wilson, Dianne H. Pilgrim, and Dickran Tashjian (New York: Brooklyn Museum in association with Abrams, 1986); Karen Davies, *At Home in Manhattan: Modern Decorative Arts, 1925 to the Depression* (New Haven, Conn.: Yale University Art Gallery, 1983); Donald J. Bush, *The Streamlined Decade* (New York: George Braziller, 1975); Christina Cogdell, "The Futurama Recontextualized: Norman Bel Geddes's Eugenic 'World of Tomorrow,'" *American Quarterly* 52.2 (June 2000): 193–245; Cogdell, *Eugenic Design: Streamlining America in the 1930s* (Philadelphia: University of Pennsylvania Press, 2004); Ellen Lupton and J. Abbott Miller, *The Bathroom, the Kitchen, and the Aesthetics of Waste: A Process of Elimination* (New York: Kiosk, 1992); Adrienne Berney, "Streamlining Breasts: The Exaltation of Form and Disguise of Function in 1930s' Ideals," *Journal of Design History* 14.4 (2001); Jeffrey Meikle, *Twentieth-Century Limited: Industrial Design in America, 1925–1939* (Philadelphia: Temple University Press, 1979); and Neil Harris, "The Drama of Consumer Desire," in *Cultural Excursions: Marketing Appetites and Cultural Tastes in Modern America* (Chicago: University of Chicago Press, 1990).
10. For a discussion of related art pedagogy and its relation to consumer tastes and design, see Carma R. Gorman, "'An Educated Demand': The Implications of *Art in Every Day Life* for American Industrial Design, 1925–1950," *Design Issues* 16.3 (Autumn 2000): 45–66.
11. Herbert Simon, *The Sciences of the Artificial*, 3rd ed. (Cambridge, Mass.: MIT Press, 1998), 112.
12. For varying scholarly assessments of the commercial success of streamlining, see Regina Lee Blaszczyk, *Imagining Consumers: Design and Innovation from*

Wedgwood to Corning (Baltimore: Johns Hopkins University Press, 2000); Shelly Nickles, "Preserving Women: Refrigerator Design as Social Process in the 1930s," *Technology and Culture* 43.4 (October 2002): 693–727; and Herbert J. Gans, "Design and the Consumer: A View of the Sociology and Culture of 'Good Design,'" in *Design Since 1945*, by Kathryn B. Hiesinger, George H. Marcus, and Max Bill (Philadelphia: Philadelphia Museum of Art, 1983).

13. Michael Baxandall, *Painting and Experience in Fifteenth-Century Italy: A Primer in the Social History of Pictorial Style* (New York: Oxford University Press, 1972), 37, 40.

14. Ibid., 34.

15. Useful discussions of 1920s–1930s body/machine comparisons can be found in Joel Dinerstein, *Swinging the Machine: Modernity, Technology, and African American Culture Between the World Wars* (Amherst: University of Massachusetts Press, 2003); Mark Seltzer, *Bodies and Machines* (New York: Routledge, 1992); Terry Smith, *Making the Modern: Industry, Art, and Design in America* (Chicago: University of Chicago Press, 1993); Cecelia Tichi, *Shifting Gears: Technology, Literature, Culture in Modernist America* (Chapel Hill: University of North Carolina Press, 1987); Martha Banta, *Taylored Lives: Narrative Productions in the Age of Taylor, Veblen, and Ford* (Chicago: University of Chicago Press, 1993); and Carolyn Thomas de la Peña, *The Body Electric: How Strange Machines Built the Modern American* (New York: New York University Press, 2003), esp. 16–17, 22–25, 42, and 98.

16. Jessie H. Bancroft, *The Posture of School Children, With Its Home Hygiene and New Efficiency Methods for School Training* (New York: Macmillan, 1913). See also Henry Ling Taylor, M.D., "The American Posture League: Its History, Work and Future," *Modern Medicine* (December 1920): 777–79; and George J. Fisher, M.D., "The American Posture League," *Journal of Health and Physical Education* 6 (October 1935): 16–17.

17. Drs. Lloyd Brown and Roger Lee initiated the use of the term "body mechanics" in their assessment of the Harvard freshman class in 1916. George T. Stafford, *Preventive and Corrective Physical Education* (New York: A. S. Barnes and Company, 1928), 59.

18. *Body Mechanics: Education and Practice. Report of the Subcommittee on Orthopedics and Body Mechanics of the White House Conference on Child Health and Protection* (New York: Century Company, 1932), 5.

19. Ibid., 3. Armin Klein and Leah C. Thomas's report on the Chelsea Survey, *Posture and Physical Fitness*, Children's Bureau Publication No. 205 (Washington, D.C.: Government Printing Office, 1931), is reprinted as Appendix I of *Body Mechanics: Education and Practice*.

20. *Body Mechanics: Education and Practice*, 21–22.

21. The aspects of modern civilization that the body mechanics theorists understood to inhibit children's natural development included cramped city dwellings, polluted air, adulterated food, child labor, ill-fitting clothing and shoes, and enforced inactivity in schools—the last made even worse by chairs that "violate[d] the fundamentals of posture hygiene" by being the wrong size and shape for most children. Henry Eastman Bennett, *School Posture and Seating: A Manual for Teachers, Physical Directors and School Officials* (Boston: Ginn and Company, 1928), iii.

22. *Body Mechanics: Education and Practice*, 19–20. Members of the survey team studied the posture of 1,708 children of five to eighteen years of age in the city of Chelsea, Massachusetts, in 1923–24.

23. Ibid., 23–26.

24. Bancroft, *Posture of School Children*, 108.

25. Marguerite Sanderson of the Boston School of Physical Education, in the introduction to *Body Mechanics and Health*, by Leah C. Thomas and Joel E. Goldthwait (Boston: Houghton Mifflin, 1922), 7.

26. Bennett, *School Posture and Seating*, 53–54.

27. Anson Rabinbach, *The Human Motor: Energy, Fatigue, and the Origins of Modernity* (Basic Books, 1990); Thomas de la Peña, *Body Electric*.

28. Thomas and Goldthwait, *Body Mechanics and Health*, 26; Goldthwait, in the introduction to Leah C. Thomas, *Body Mechanics and Health*, rev. ed. (Boston: Houghton Mifflin, 1929), 5.

29. An example of a body mechanics writer who would surely have been familiar with eugenic theory (though who seems not to have adopted it, at least not wholesale) is Ivalclare Sprow Howland; she was employed at (the second) Battle Creek College, which had been founded by J. H. Kellogg, a promoter of eugenics who hosted the First National Conference on Race Betterment (1914) and the Third National Conference on Race Betterment (1928) in Battle Creek. For a discussion of these conferences, see Robert Rydell, *World of Fairs: The Century-of-Progress Expositions* (Chicago: University of Chicago Press, 1993), 40–41. W. H. Sheldon and E. A. Hooton, who conducted posture studies at Ivy League universities in the middle of the century, were more obviously interested in eugenics. See Ron Rosenbaum, "The Great Ivy League Nude Posture Photo Scandal," *New York Times Magazine*, January 15, 1995, 26ff. In contrast, examples of body mechanics writers who clearly stated the importance of environmental rather than hereditary factors on body mechanics are Josephine Rathbone, *Corrective Physical Education* (Philadelphia: W. B. Saunders, 1934), 88; and Mabel Lee and Miriam Wagner, *The Fundamentals of Body Mechanics and Conditioning: An Illustrated Teaching Manual* (Philadelphia: W. B. Saunders, 1949), 156.

30. Bancroft, *Posture of School Children*, 5.

31. Bennett, *School Seating and Posture*, 4.

32. Two notable government publications of this period were Armin Klein, M.D., "Posture Clinics: Organization and Exercises," U.S. Department of Labor/ Children's Bureau Publication No. 164 (Washington, D.C.: Government Printing Office, 1926), and Armin Klein and Leah C. Thomas, "Posture Exercises: A Handbook for Schools and for Teachers of Physical Education," U.S. Department of Labor/Children's Bureau Publication No. 165 (Washington, D.C.: Government Printing Office, 1926).

33. *Body Mechanics: Education and Practice*, ii, xi. The members of the Subcommittee on Orthopedics and Body Mechanics were Robert B. Osgood, M.D., Professor of Orthopedic Surgery at Harvard University (chair); Lloyd T. Brown, M.D., Instructor in Orthopedic Surgery at Harvard; John B. Carnett, M.D., Vice Dean and Professor of Surgery at the Graduate School of Medicine, University of Pennsylvania; Armin Klein, M.D., Assistant Professor of Orthopedic Surgery at Tufts College Medical School; and Leah C. Thomas, Assistant Professor in the Department of Hygiene and Physical Education, Smith College.

34. *Body Mechanics: Education and Practice*, 41.

35. Ibid., 42.

36. Mabel Lee, *History of Physical Education and Sports in the U.S.A.* (New York: Wiley, 1983), 166.

37. *Body Mechanics: Education and Practice*, 28.

38. Ibid.

39. Ibid., 33–34.

40. A particularly striking example of the lack of attention to the history of body mechanics in the physical education literature occurs in Lee's *History of Physical*

Education and Sports. Lee, who had herself previously coauthored *Fundamentals of Body Mechanics and Conditioning*, made almost no mention of posture or body mechanics in her history. For a list of incorporators and directors of the American Posture League, see George J. Fisher, "The American Posture League," *Journal of Health and Physical Education* 6 (October 1935): 16–17. Prominent members and leaders/directors of the APL included Robert Tait McKenzie, M.D.; George J. Fisher, M.D.; Thomas A. Storey, Ph.D., M.D.; and Frank and Lillian Gilbreth. Biographies of McKenzie, Fisher, and Storey can be found in Lee, *History of Physical Education and Sports*; Paula D. Welch, *History of American Physical Education and Sport*, 2nd ed. (Springfield, Ill.: Charles C. Thomas, 1996); and C.W. Hackensmith, *History of Physical Education* (New York: Harper & Row, 1966).

41. Herbert M. Kliebard, *Forging the American Curriculum: Essays in Curriculum History and Theory* (New York: Routledge, 1992), chap. 7.

42. Bancroft, *Posture of School Children*, 247–50.

43. The first edition of Thomas's book, coauthored with Joel Goldthwait (Boston: Houghton Mifflin, 1922), included little of the pedagogical material that characterized the second edition.

44. Ivalclare Sprow Howland, *The Teaching of Body Mechanics in Elementary and Secondary Schools* (New York: A. S. Barnes, 1936). When Howland's authorship is made clear by the context, subsequent references to pages in her book will be made in parentheses in the body of the text. On the second Battle Creek College, see James C. Whorton, *Crusaders for Fitness: The History of American Health Reformers* (Princeton, N.J.: Princeton University Press, 1982).

45. On social efficiency education, see Herbert M. Kliebard, *The Struggle for the American Curriculum*, 98, 119, 121. For reviews of Howland's book, see, e.g., Mary Fread, review of *The Teaching of Body Mechanics* by Ivalclare Sprow Howland, *Teachers College Journal* 7.6 (June 1936): 136. Even a detractor such as Jay B. Nash, in his review of Howland's book in *The Elementary School Journal* 37 (June 1937): 792–94, praised her inclusion of the posture play "The Slump Family."

46. See, e.g., Margaret H. Strong, "Hutchinson Students Become Posture Conscious," *Minnesota Journal of Education* 20.9 (May 1940): 360–61; Lee, *Fundamentals of Body Mechanics and Conditioning*; Ellen Davis Kelly, *Teaching Posture and Body Mechanics* (New York: A. S. Barnes, 1949).

47. A weight- and sex-neutral standard was available from Harvard University; Howland illustrated it, rather than the six government standards, in her book.

48. Bancroft, *Posture of School Children*, 9.

49. "To furnish the child with a silhouettograph picture of his habitual poor postural position and another of an improved or corrected position," Howland claimed, "serves as a worthy incentive for practice in body mechanical improvement" (23).

50. The use of these cards is discussed in Howland, 16–17.

51. See Bancroft, *Posture of School Children*, 187–88.

52. Michel Foucault, *Discipline and Punish: The Birth of the Prison*, trans. Alan Sheridan (New York: Vintage Books, 1995).

53. Bancroft, *Posture of School Children*, 208.

54. Howland argued that photographs of athletes in action could "teach many lessons that words cannot accomplish" (50). And Janet Lane, author of a popular (rather than pedagogical) text on posture, said of actresses that "time after time, they prove our points about the beauty and reliability of a well-adjusted physical machine." Janet Lane, *Your Carriage, Madam! A Guide to Good Posture*, 2nd ed. (New York: John Wiley and Sons, 1947), 135.

55. Bancroft, *Posture of School Children*, 250.

56. Thomas, *Body Mechanics and Health*, 120–21.

57. See note 15 for references to this literature.

58. Loewy, *Never Leave Well Enough Alone*, 213.

59. Ibid., 312ff.

60. Berney, "Streamlining Breasts," 336. Berney also suggests that "breast ideals helped to shape design styles for machinery" (340n7).

61. Walter Dorwin Teague, *Design This Day* (1940; repr., New York: Harcourt, Brace, 1949), 174.

62. J. Gordon Lippincott, *Design for Business* (Chicago: Paul Theobald, 1947), 94.

63. Arens, draft of a telegram to President Franklin D. Roosevelt, November 14, 1934, cited in Meikle, *Twentieth-Century Limited*, 164. According to Meikle, secretary M.H. McIntyre acknowledged receipt in a letter to Arens of November 15, 1934.

64. Claude Bragdon, *The Beautiful Necessity: Seven Essays on Theosophy and Architecture* (Rochester, N.Y.: Manas Press, 1910), 50.

65. The term "object consciousness" is from Harris, "Drama of Consumer Desire," 175.

66. See note 12.

9

The Grape Vine Telegraph:
Rumors and Confederate Persistence

Jason Phillips

In July 1864 the news was too good to be true. General Ulysses S. Grant, the "butcher" whose war of attrition had already cost thousands of lives, was dead. A Texas cavalryman serving in Louisiana shared the report with his father. The soldier heard it from a friend who claimed that a captain saw an official dispatch from General Robert E. Lee reporting that "Grant made desperate assaults upon Richmond and was defeated...and tis said led the last one himself and was killed." The Texan thought the story had merit because it "accords with the report of a woman from Vicksburg that the flag was at half mast on account of the death of Grant." Even better, the story was "corroborated" by a lieutenant colonel who left Richmond shortly before the attacks. According to the Texan, the colonel reported that "Grant's army was completely routed and that ours was in pursuit." The cavalryman thought, "This is glorious news," but he admitted that "it seems too good to believe."[1]

Grant's death was reported again later that month. This time he was watching Union shells explode over Petersburg when a shot from a rebel cannon tore his arm off. Rumors spread that he bled to death on the surgeon's table later that day, July 17, 1864. Virginia artilleryman James W. Albright joked, "Grant is *still* dead; but, comes to life occasionally." Despite the wisecrack, Albright was unsure of the truth. For days he could neither confirm nor disprove the report; its elusiveness and optimism teased the artilleryman. He started to view other information as clues about Grant's fate. When the Federal bombardment slackened, Albright thought it could mean the enemy had a new commander.[2]

From the *Journal of Southern History*. *Journal of Southern History*, LXXII, No. 4 (November 2006), 753–88.

Accounts of Grant's death mingled with other positive news for rebels in the heady month of July 1864. As an isolated non-event, the rumor had little impact on Confederate soldiers. But the false report contributed to a heap of misinformation that collectively affected Confederate perceptions of the war. In Georgia Confederate general John B. Hood replaced General Joseph E. Johnston as commander of the Army of Tennessee. Within days of his promotion, the aggressive Hood attacked General William Tecumseh Sherman's army outside the gates of Atlanta. Telegrams declared a stunning victory for the rebellion.[3] Meanwhile in Maryland, General Jubal A. Early was leading a daring raid on Washington, D.C. A year after Gettysburg and Vicksburg, it seemed the pendulum of war was swinging in the Confederates' favor. As an Alabama infantryman put it, "we are about to turn the joke on the Yankees instead of them getting our Capitol we are about to get theirs."[4] Diehard rebels gathered rumors, telegraph dispatches, and newspaper reports. They spun fantastic speculations. While guarding Richmond, a Georgia captain predicted that Grant's death and Early's success would "cause the forces menacing this place & Petersburg to be withdrawn." He sent his wife a newspaper detailing Early's victories.[5] Days later a North Carolina lieutenant wrote home that the enemy was retreating from Richmond. "Everything is bright & brightening for us," he exclaimed.[6]

As Confederate fortunes declined in 1864 and 1865, remarkably positive rumors swirled through rebel armies, spreading false hopes and postponing reality. As one rebel explained, reports were "transmitted to us by the 'grape vine telegraph,' a machine that can be worked by any one," and "the most ridiculous rumor will be operated as a fact after going a few yards."[7] Anyone could spread potent rumors that promised to unveil conditions obscured by distance, military secrecy, and general uncertainty. By spreading rumors any lowly private or bewildered corporal could express his beliefs and affect his surroundings. In other words, rumors offered soldiers an empowering channel, or grapevine, of expression. Such actions may seem inconsequential within the universe of war, but rumors' impact on armies and society was anything but trivial. Whether true or false, news traveled far and fast because thousands corresponded with loved ones. Confederate authorities lacked censors and modern propaganda agencies, and a highly partisan media whirled at top speed. As rumors gained momentum, they profoundly influenced southerners' perceptions of the war and its outcome.

Though rumors peppered Civil War diaries, correspondence, telegrams, and newspapers, few historians have examined wartime gossip closely. Their neglect is understandable. Historical hindsight discounts false rumors. Scholars who read Confederate diaries from July 1864 know that Grant lived to be president, Early's raid failed, Sherman outgeneraled Hood, and the Army of the Potomac did not leave Richmond until it chased Lee to Appomattox in April 1865. Almost by reflex, historians consign inaccuracies to the detritus of time. Conversely, true rumors do not seem like gossip at all; in retrospect they become news. There is another problem. Rumors, by their very nature, complicate (and often elude) historians' search for causation. Tracing the roots and effects of current rumors is difficult enough; uncovering the origins and impact of 140-year-old rumors is far more complex. Some Civil War scholars have mentioned rumors, but perhaps for these reasons, none have focused on the slippery subject. What, for example, do the persistent rumors of Grant's death mean? What can they tell us about the Confederates who spread them and about the universe of war where pieces of gossip flashed and faded like shooting stars?[8]

Studying rebel rumors enhances current scholarship that reconsiders Confederate persistence and its links to postwar defiance. Over the past ten years, historians have challenged older notions that a hollow, bombastic Confederacy, wracked with internal divisions, deteriorated rapidly from 1863 to 1865. If the rebellion were as rotten as some historians insist, one might expect that troops would have spread dreadful rumors when class divisions, military defeats, financial woes, and the disintegration of slavery sapped Confederate will. Perhaps dissatisfied and daunted rebels fed their fears by spreading wild talk of slave insurrections, enemy atrocities, starving families, economic disasters, class warfare, and Federal subjugation. A close examination of hundreds of rebel soldiers' writings in this period proves the opposite was true. During the nadir of Confederate morale, diehards intoxicated each other with gossip of improbable victories, northern catastrophes, and foreign intervention. To be sure, discontent pervaded the Confederacy during its final years. The "quiet rebellion" that Paul D. Escott uncovered existed, but it was quiet in ways he perhaps did not realize. During the war's final period, the loudest gossips in the Confederate army were not disgruntled yeomen on the verge of deserting but diehards searching for good news. The rumors these men spread offer historians an invaluable glimpse into the mentalities of diehard rebels and provide scholars with tangible evidence of Confederate nationalism late in the war.[9]

Rescuing rumors from historical obscurity means going forward without the aid of much scholarship. The most relevant study of wartime rumor, *The Psychology of Rumor*, was published in 1947 by two Harvard psychologists, Gordon W. Allport and Leo Postman. During World War II American social scientists examined rumors to combat mass anxiety and promote national solidarity. They understood that rumors not only imparted news about a particular event but also revealed the hopes and fears of the society that spread them. Sociologists who collected American rumors during the summer of 1942 reached an important conclusion: fears and hatred, more than hopes and wishes, sparked popular imagination and produced rumors. After categorizing gossip, the scholars discovered that only 2 percent of the rumors reflected people's wishes. Conversely, 25 percent expressed widespread fears such as biological warfare and secret enemy plans. Finally, 66 percent criticized and undermined the war effort; this category included racist rumors and suspicions about government activity and corporate involvement in the war. Americans were frustrated during this dark hour of the war, and rumors exacerbated their low morale. Even after important turning points favored the Allies, "wish rumors, with their characteristically optimistic coloring, were relatively few until the collapse of Germany was imminent." Thus, upbeat rebel gossip during the Civil War not only counters the grand narrative of Confederate decline, desertion, and disaffection but also contrasts sharply with American rumors during World War II. This essay is the first attempt to explain the phenomenon and its significance.[10]

The rumor of Grant's death reveals the tone and transmission of Confederate gossip. Soldiers often reduced military campaigns to personal contests between opposing generals. This habit of reduction, so common in discourse, is evident in diaries and letters: "Grant had left our front"; "General Lee did not fall back"; "as soon as Grant commenced to move Lee commenced also"; "Grant is building a railroad...Lee will not allow it."[11] Rumors reinforced this simplification. A North Carolinian spread the rumor that Grant sent word to Lee that he expected to dine in Richmond on June 18, and "Lee sent him word that he might would sup in h_ll." A parallel rumor simultaneously whirled through the Army of Tennessee. There, Sherman informed Johnston that he would celebrate the Fourth of July in Atlanta.[12] This habit of personalization made the death of Grant more than the demise of a hated adversary. If the Virginia theater was an elaborate contest between Grant and Lee and the former was dead, the Confederates would win the campaign. Diehards speculated that Grant's replacement would retreat to Washington and regroup as so many of Lee's opponents had done in the past. In July 1864 such gossip promised a beautiful release from a tense stalemate of trench warfare under the summer sun. No wonder the rumor spread like wildfire through Lee's trenches.

Confederates also transmitted the rumor of Grant's death because it offered them vengeance. Quests for retribution motivated many rebels through the war's final period. James M. McPherson has argued that revenge "became almost an obsession with some Confederates."[13] The shelling of Petersburg particularly galled Lee's men because they lacked the strength to silence the barrage and had to suffer watching it. Seeing Union shells fly over their lines and pummel the helpless town behind them, rebels cursed the enemy for preferring to fire on civilians. A Virginia soldier wrote his brother after a day of "terrible cannonading" that "the Yankee batteries...are plenty close to tear the town to pieces." Tents and pineboard shelters dotted the ground around the First Corps Headquarters—citizens were clinging to the army for protection. An officer noted that "many of these people [are] of some means and all [are] of great respectability," meaning they were white southerners and infinitely finer than the scum who fired on their homes. He remarked that "about the time they thought the people were going to church, [the Federals] commenced a tremendous cannonade, as if with the hope of killing women and children en route to church."

Visiting the city on a twenty-four-hour pass, an artilleryman witnessed the terrible effectiveness of incendiary shells as fires consumed four neighborhoods. "As the smoke of these fires rose in the air they presented an excellent mark for the enemy, and they were not slow to avail themselves of it."[14] Confederates who blamed Grant for this atrocious mode of fighting delighted in spreading the rumor that he died because of his barbarity. A rebel shell struck Grant while he was entertaining himself watching the effect of Federal artillery on the helpless town. A Confederate sergeant admitted that "it is a good story & looks like retribution—hope it is true." Men who were powerless to stop the bombardment of Petersburg found revenge in such stories.[15]

Finally, the rumor of Grant's death supports an insight that Allport and Postman had nearly sixty years ago: rumors have multiple layers of meaning. At first glance, rumors aspire to nothing higher than news—they acquire significance by promising timely, critical information during uncertain moments. "Yet on second look," Allport and Postman explain, "the type of discourse represented in . . . rumors often has a hidden mode of signification" that judges rather than informs. In short, the rumor of Grant's death is more than bogus news; it is a story. As the critic Walter Benjamin spells out, "The value of information does not survive the moment in which it was new. . . . A story is different. It does not expend itself. It preserves and concentrates its strength and is capable of releasing it even after a long time."[16] Stories stand alone and often contain morals. In this one, the general meets a fitting end because of his atrocious tactics. The rumor becomes a parable for chivalrous warfare.

As an Alabama infantryman observed, when Confederates refuted one rumor, "Phoenix-like another takes its place."[17] Hood's thrashing of Sherman, for instance, supplanted stories of Grant's death and fascinated Confederates some more. If hope sprang eternal for some rebels, wish rumors helped to replenish the wellspring. But we cannot assume that positive gossip only affected those inclined to believe it. All soldiers pieced together the war's momentum as best they could from scraps of information they found in telegrams, official reports, letters from home, newspapers, and political speeches: rumors infiltrated all these sources. Similar to Edward L. Ayers's research on the Shenandoah Valley, studying rumors "offers a history of the Civil War told from the viewpoints of everyday people who could glimpse only parts of the drama they were living. . . . It emphasizes the flux of emotion and belief, the intertwining of reason and feeling, the constant revision of history as people lived within history."[18] A wide range of rumors spanning military campaigns, northern morale, and foreign affairs encouraged predictions and brightened Confederates' perceptions of the distant war, an enormous conflict that moved by countless, remote developments. No matter how bad things looked on their own front, rebels always found wish rumors that heralded Confederate victories in far-off places.

Though persistent hope was at the heart of wish rumors, Confederate gossip in 1864–1865 also reveals the rising desperation of rebel morale. At first glance, rumors of military events, the Union home front, and European intervention spread concurrently. All three topics were popular among rumormongers from January 1864 through April 1865. But a close inspection of Confederate gossip reveals a broad pattern. Over time Confederates looked for victory from sources that were farther from their reach. Before the fall of Atlanta, false reports of military victories seemed credible and thus spread from Virginia to Texas. Military gossip crescendoed in the summer of 1864, when rebels inflicted ghastly casualties on Federal armies. After Atlanta fell in September, rumors of battlefield triumphs dwindled. Confederates who remained committed to independence looked to other sources for optimism. During the summer and fall of 1864, the presidential campaign captivated many rebel gossips. This period witnessed a profusion of news about northern secession, treason, and mutiny. While military victory seemed less likely over time, Confederates still clung to northern unrest as a way to independence until Lincoln's reelection. After they were assured of four more years of Lincoln, diehard rebels increasingly talked about foreign intervention. By 1865, when military triumph and Union internal revolt seemed improbable if not impossible, Confederates focused on the last potential source of victory, Europe. As the final embers of rebellion died out, faint and pitiful talk of world wars and international aid sparked and faded.[19]

In the spring of 1864, as the armies resumed active campaigning, rumors of southern military success multiplied. Confederates looked to General Robert E. Lee for hope and victory. Gary W. Gallagher has claimed that rebels' trust in Lee and his ranks was "the single greatest factor engendering Confederate hope after the midpoint of the war." This faith in Lee is evident in rumors that exaggerated the general's achievements across the South.[20] When the Virginia campaign erupted in early May, pronouncements of Confederate victories at the Wilderness and Spotsylvania raced across the region. In Kinston, North Carolina, a Texas infantryman noted in his diary, "it is rumored this morning [May 17] that Lee is whiping the Yankees vary bad at Richmond." Three days later a cavalryman reported the same news from his post in Texas: "Good news from Virginia, Lee has whiped the Yankees again." Within days more complete accounts reached the western troops. In Lewisville, Arkansas, cavalryman Edwin H. Fay exalted, "we have been hearing rumors of a great deal of good news here lately." According to Fay, General Edmund Kirby Smith received "official information" that Lee's army "killed, wounded, and captured 40,000 of the enemy, [and] 100 pieces of Artillery" at the cost of ten thousand casualties. The actual numbers for the first four weeks of the Virginia campaign were about forty-four thousand Federal casualties and twenty-five thousand Confederate losses. Fay concluded that "Grant's & Meade's armies are completely discomfited and demoralized" and hoped that "the infamous wretches may be compelled by their sad experience to make proposals for peace."[21]

Pronouncements of Confederate victories in Virginia increased in June and July, despite the fact that Grant's enormous army was pinning Lee's defenders within earshot of the Confederacy's capital. In Louisiana Henry G. Orr relayed to his father the news that "success was still crowning our arms on every hand" and Lee's troops were "jubilant." According to Orr, there was "no fear for the safety of Richmond." In Georgia Henry Orr's brother James reported similar "cheering news from Virginia" to their mother. A Texas cavalryman concurred, "Grant had been repulsed with terrible loss." Whether it was accurate or not, news of heavy Federal casualties and confirmations of Richmond's safety buoyed rebels' faith in Lee and his ultimate triumph in Virginia.[22] From a distance, it looked like the Confederacy was winning the war in the East.

Rosy reports from the western theater also teased rebels all summer long. For many Confederates, what seemed to be "the great battle of the campaign" erupted at Kennesaw Mountain on June 27. There General Sherman funneled men into a devastating field of fire, losing three thousand before he quit. General Johnston suffered only six hundred casualties. When the victors described the battle to people at home, they greatly overestimated Federal losses. Common soldiers' myopic perspective of battle partly explains these distortions, but inaccuracy also plagued the scouting reports, newspaper accounts, and official estimates that soldiers relied on. The day before the battle, Confederates read newspapers that assessed Sherman's casualties for the campaign at thirty thousand men (the actual number was closer to seventeen thousand). A scout told John Rankin that Sherman's army was "one mass of stragglers." Rankin spread the rumor that Sherman was waiting for forty thousand reinforcements to replace his losses in the campaign. After Kennesaw Mountain, Private John W. Cotton claimed "from there own accounts we have killed and wounded betwixt 50 and 75 thousand of there men" since April. Even General Johnston shared this appraisal. He guessed that Confederate casualties (excluding the cavalry) numbered almost ten thousand and presumed the enemy losses were "six times as great." Unlike early estimates for the eastern campaign, numbers for the western theater strayed far from the truth. Johnston had lost about fourteen thousand men while inflicting only seventeen thousand losses on the enemy. Nonetheless, Tennessean James Madison Brannock told his wife that "Johnston is drawing [Sherman] farther & farther, & when the proper time arrives will no doubt *crush his army completely*."[23]

After receiving these exaggerations, distant rebels celebrated Johnston's victory as a decisive one. Some of the blame for rosy interpretations must be placed at the feet of optimists who sought good news. A soldier in Virginia strained to consider Kennesaw Mountain "the next thing to a decisive victory." He predicted that Sherman would be forced back to Kentucky "if he does not surrender his whole army" first. In Petersburg an artilleryman admitted that he and his comrades were "looking daily for news that

Johnston has defeated Sherman." He speculated that a decisive victory in Georgia would mean that "we will undoubtedly receive sufficient reinforcements...to assume the offensive and then, alas poor Grant! Farewell, a long farewell, to all thy glory."[24] Both of these men illustrate a habit that was common in the ranks; they anticipated good news from other theaters and magnified the significance of anything that sounded like a victory.

Similar reports emanated from Georgia in July when General John B. Hood assumed command from Johnston and on July 20 attacked Sherman's columns. Local and distant opinions of these battles differed remarkably. Up close (and in hindsight) the battle was a disastrous failure and the rebels' costliest engagement of the campaign to date. Two days later, Hood struck again, deploying General William J. Hardee's corps at Jonesboro. This time the Confederates suffered half as many casualties as they had lost in ten weeks under Johnston. Unsatisfied, Hood charged again on July 28 and bloodied his ranks for no strategic gain. In eight days the young commander cost his army fifteen thousand casualties while inflicting only six thousand on Sherman's troops. Hood's soldiers pined for the return of Johnston, a general who had always been careful to avoid high casualties.[25]

Distant Confederates, however, celebrated Hood's assaults as great victories. Southern newspapers printed extras to cover the event. One Richmond paper claimed, "Atlanta is now felt to be safe, and Georgia will soon be free from the foe," and another celebrated, "Everything seems to have changed in that state from the deepest despondency." A War Department clerk exalted, "Sherman's army is *doomed*." Henry Calvin Conner spoke for many comrades when he expressed a hope that "Hood will be able to exterminate Sherman before he quits him and recover the whole of northern Georgia from his poluting tred." A Virginia artilleryman hoped that the "glorious news from Atlanta" would result in Confederate armies invading, and perhaps occupying, Tennessee and Kentucky. As if parting clouds had let the sunlight through, Hood's supposed victories brightened the military landscape. Alabama captain Elias Davis told his wife to expect peace soon.[26]

After Hood's futile assaults, both sides settled down to a siege in which neither army gained an advantage for a month, but rumors of victories at Atlanta enchanted far-off rebels throughout August. In Virginia, Captain W.R. Redding passed on the rumor that "Sherman has been routed from Atlanta." He was "proud to hear of Sherman's defeat" and hoped that Hood's army would "press him into Ohio before they stop." In Arkansas, Sergeant Edwin Fay reported, "there is a rumor too via Camden that Hood has defeated Sherman & is at present driving him back towards Chattanooga. If true this is glorious." It was not true. These rumors of victory when no battle had been fought further misled troops who were already disoriented by rosy reports of actual engagements.[27]

When most of Sherman's army left its trenches on August 25–26, Hood and his men assumed the enemy was finally retreating. Rebels rejoiced and claimed victory for four days while Sherman's columns slid south to cut

Hood's last supply line. On August 30 the rebel commander discovered his adversary's intentions and sent two corps to intercept the Federals. It was too late. The Union army crushed these troops and launched a powerful counterattack. Facing annihilation or surrender if they remained in town, Confederates evacuated the city to save the remains of their army. On September 1 Atlanta, a symbol of Confederate tenacity second only to Richmond, belonged to the enemy.[28]

When Atlanta fell, distant Confederates received the news slowly and doubted its validity. Having hoped for military triumph all summer, many rebels could not believe the bad news. In Winchester, Virginia, on September 6, artilleryman Creed Thomas Davis read a Richmond paper that announced "big fights in the neighborhood of Atlanta Ga on the 1st & 3rd" but did not report Hood's evacuation. When Davis and his unit learned the news days later, it was the "topic of conversation" throughout the camp. Davis admitted, "The boys do not reconcile themselves to it so readily." After months of positive rumors, rebels found it difficult, emotionally and cognitively, to accept that Atlanta was gone. Word reached the Trans-Mississippi Department much later. Separated from the rest of the nation by Union control of the Mississippi, troops in the western Confederacy were often most susceptible to false reports. On September 12 William W. Heartsill noted in his diary, "we have rumors this evening that Atlanta has fallen, don't believe a word of it." From his camp in Texas, Heartsill did not concede the loss of Atlanta until mid-October![29]

After reports confirmed Sherman's victory, something remarkable happened: rumors spread that Hood had recaptured the city. A North Carolinian in Lee's trenches first heard of Atlanta's fall on September 3. Two days later "a rumor was afloat that Atlanta had been retaken with thirty thousand prisoners and with a loss to us of ten thousand men." John Cotton's cavalry unit was in East Tennessee when he heard that Hood recaptured the city in late September. In Virginia Sergeant James Albright heard that Hood reacquired Atlanta in early October. Albright considered the news proof that "there is nothing to be discouraged at—all goes well as could be expected."[30] Rather than accept the consequences of losing the city, Confederates spread misinformation that upheld their views of the military situation.

Even after these rumors of Hood retaking the city proved false, some rebels still sought any sign that Atlanta would be redeemed. John Walters thought General P.G.T. Beauregard's appointment as commander of the Department of the Southwest and General Nathan Bedford Forrest's success behind Sherman's lines meant the Union would have trouble holding the town. Army surgeon Spencer Glasgow Welch was "anxious to hear something from General Hood, for if he can whip Sherman at Atlanta the situation may be entirely changed." He still believed "if Sherman is forced away from Atlanta and we can hold Richmond this winter...we shall have peace" with independence. Rebels stubbornly refused to accept the significance of Hood's defeat. In the Petersburg trenches Major Thomas

Claybrook Elder conceded that Atlanta's fall "cast a shade of gloom over all" and reported that "the Yankees are greatly rejoicing over the event and predict a speedy end of the rebellion in Georgia." But Elder thought the event was "mere stuff" that would "have its effect in putting off the day of peace" but would not endanger Confederate victory. Likewise, a Texas cavalryman in Arkansas feared that the loss of Atlanta would "prolong the war for some time yet" but not alter its result. He wrote home that the same newspaper that reported Atlanta's fall also claimed that Forrest recaptured Nashville. When they admitted that Atlanta was gone, some Confederates even questioned the city's strategic value and tried to convince themselves that the place was expendable.[31]

Rebel reactions to Atlanta's fall, the greatest Confederate military set-back of 1864, illustrate how positive rumors that preceded and followed bad news could soften the blow of a major defeat. The first word from other battlefields and campaigns was often optimistic and exaggerated: Hood battered Sherman outside Atlanta; Lee smashed Grant in the Wilderness. Soldiers who anticipated good news sometimes accepted these reports as facts. Then troops received a more accurate account that tempered or refuted early declarations of triumph. These sober reports came from officers' dispatches, letters from relatives who had fought in the battles, or even northern papers. Finally, a second round of wish rumors often followed the bad news. Gossip that Hood had retaken Atlanta offset gloomy facts and sustained soldiers' hopes. When combined, these waves of positive rumors and bad news obscured the war's course and clouded the finality and significance of dire events.

This bewildering interplay between fact and fiction, distant events and innermost hopes, illustrates the "deep contingency" that marked a soldier's life. On one hand, events big and small, real and unreal, shaped how participants viewed the contest. On the other, people's hopes and beliefs gave magnitude and meaning to the plethora of war news. Together, events and individuals spun dense webs of experience more complex than any grand narrative can portray. A soldier's place and behavior within this muddle affected his perceptions and motives. This insight enhances current scholarship on Civil War soldiers. Over the past ten years, historians have explained Confederate troop determination late in the war by pointing to ideology, camaraderie, masculinity, vengeance, faith in General Lee, and the generational values of the last slave owners. All these elements contributed to rebel persistence, but none of these factors offered what rumors appeared to provide—tangible evidence that made continued resistance seem reasonable. Without concrete reasons for their hopefulness, diehards seem fanatical, delusional, or stupid. For this reason, many scholars agree with Reid Mitchell's dismissal of diehard behavior as "insane Confederate optimism." Diehards may have been more devoted to the cause than other southerners, but they were also rational beings who, with the help of rumors and other evidence, perceived a war that was going better than the Yankees (and historians) claimed it was.[32]

Rumors about distant battles made up only a fraction of the gossip that swirled through rebel ranks. As the panorama of war stretched to the northern home front and Europe, so did the topics of hearsay. Rumors of military success resonated with accounts of northern disaffection and foreign aid for the rebellion. Like their Revolutionary ancestors, Confederates knew they did not need to conquer the enemy to win independence; they merely had to outlast them. If the rebellion continued indefinitely, at some point the United States would consider the price of reunion too costly and quit. Confederates thought the war could be won in countless ways: a decisive victory, a series of stalemates, foreign intervention, a collapse on Wall Street, secession of the West, and a northern peace movement were all popular anticipated means to achieve independence. The most likely possibility in 1864 centered on the presidential election. If Union armies failed in the spring and summer, war-weary northerners might elect a peace candidate and let the Confederacy go. With this in mind, rebels eager for peace and independence scanned northern newspapers for war weariness, interrogated Union deserters and prisoners, and collected rumors that substantiated imminent Confederate triumph.

Hopes that a peace movement would cripple their foes encouraged many Confederates to exaggerate northern internal strife and spread bizarre rumors on the subject. Northern despondency was real in 1864, but Confederates anticipated northern disintegration, secession, and treason. Army surgeon Junius N. Bragg passed on the story that "Wisconsin Troops will return home as soon as the spring opens, for the purpose of carrying on a partisan war in their own state." The report bolstered Bragg's "abiding faith in our ultimate success." Infantryman Paul Higginbotham centered his expectations on Ohio. He wrote his brother that "some fellow from Ohio is in favor of a Western Confederacy, & a breaking off from the New England States." Higginbotham then related the fact that "the 63rd Ohio Regt., was on picket yesterday, and said that if their officers made them charge our works they intended to surrender, and asked us not to fire on them." He affirmed, "I think now as I always have done, that we will yet gain our Independence, and I firmly believe the time is near at hand." A Virginia artilleryman spread the rumor that the governor of New York called out the militia to resist Federal conscription. Confederates expected a bloodier revolt than New York City's draft riot of the previous summer, which had claimed a thousand dead and wounded. From Mobile a rebel spread the rumor that "a good many of the Yankee prisoners whose term of service is out are taking the oath and joining our side because Lincoln will not exchange them."[33] These rumors of Union morale depicted more than despondency; they portrayed treason and mutiny at the heart of the enemy's war effort.

As the election approached, talk of financial disasters, peace movements, and Federal divisiveness intensified throughout the Confederacy. Rebels like Mississippian William L. Nugent understood that "our main hope now is the disagreement existing among the political parties North."

Troops across the South sought and swapped political rumors with an enthusiasm that matched their interest in distant battles. They read northern papers for shifts in public opinion, debated which candidate would best serve Confederate interests, and asked enemy pickets whom they were voting for. Some rebels even saw the event as the Almighty's way of ending the war in the Confederates' favor. Arkansas sergeant Edwin Fay explained, "God will work it all out for the best in some way I believe. I want to see the Yankee nation without a Govt. enjoying what they are so fond of, a state of Anarchy and confusion."[34]

But the fall of Atlanta boosted Lincoln's campaign and extinguished Confederate visions of a speedy peace. As noted, diehards first denied the facts, then spread rumors of the city being retaken, and, finally, downplayed Atlanta's strategic importance. Rebels also performed somersaults of reasoning about the presidential campaign. First, they favored a Democrat, but after Atlanta fell (and George B. McClellan announced his war policy), rebels convinced themselves that Lincoln's reelection was better for them. A Mississippi officer suspected McClellan would offer a reconstructed Constitution that would draw every Confederate state back to the Union except Virginia and South Carolina. He elaborated, "[W]e were all very much depressed when we read McClellan's letter of acceptance. He comes out so decidedly for War that the question is gravely discussed whether Lincoln would not be preferable." The officer does not mention, let alone consider, the strength of Lincoln's war platform, even though a month before he had written that Lincoln's reelection meant the war would "be continued to the bitter end regardless of loss or expense." Tennessean James Brannock concurred that McClellan was dangerous, because "he will attempt to bring about peace by a 'reconstruction of the Union' & will present terms so favorable that a great many of those in the South who are lukewarm in the Cause & tired of the War will be in favor of accepting them."[35]

When reasonable hopes for a Democratic victory and a negotiated peace disappeared, many Confederates predicted far-fetched scenarios that sustained their optimism. Some rebels reasoned that Lincoln's reelection could increase dissension and even induce other states to secede. James Brannock favored Lincoln, for "if Lincoln be elected it will probably be the cause of revolution in the North Western states & will end in securing our independence." The Tennessean's prediction gained credibility weeks later when the U.S. judge advocate general Joseph Holt accused Copperheads of designing a "Northwest Confederacy" in the heartland. Holt's scandalous report claimed that peace Democrats sought midwestern secession and an alliance with the rebels. John Walters concurred that Lincoln's reelection might cause tidal waves of disunion: "there is a possibility of the Pacific States leaving the Old Union to form a Confederacy of their own, and in this case the Northwestern States will most probably cut loose from the Eastern States, and this of itself would end the war."[36]

Foreign intervention was another scenario by which the Confederacy could gain independence without conquering its foe. In 1864 a minister in

Richmond claimed that negotiation with Europe "has become, with us, an exploded idea. It may be employed, but its repeated delusions have ceased to tempt the national expectation." He was wrong. Many Confederates still cherished the pipe dream. Rebels pointed out that America won independence through French assistance; foreign armies and armadas (or at least the threat of them) might similarly compel the Union to accept Confederate independence.[37] Whenever Great Britain's Lord Palmerston, France's Napoleon III, or Confederate emissaries squeaked about European involvement, rumors of elaborate alliances electrified the South.

In early 1864 a wave of rumors flooded the nation. General Lawrence S. Ross wrote home that a fellow officer had telegraphed him "to the effect that France had recognized the Confederacy." The next day a captain wrote from Mississippi, "startling rumors have reached us recently enlivening our hopes and brightening our prospects. It is said that France has recognized us, and Spain and Mexico & Austria." Tennessee artillerist Thomas J. Key even drafted an article that expounded "the expediency of making a commercial treaty with France and Spain, proposing to give them the exclusive transportation of cotton from the South if they would furnish the navy to open and keep unobstructed the Confederate ports." Key argued that "the colonies made similar concessions to France in 1776" and that the Confederacy was most wanting in naval power "to retake and possess the Mississippi River, and to open her harbors."[38]

Rumors of foreign intervention, however improbable they may seem, captivated rebels again in 1865. In January reports promised an imminent alliance with France or Great Britain if the Confederacy would abolish slavery. Louisiana soldier Hugh Montgomery understood that "the whole world is against Slavery," but he figured if the Confederacy called its labor system "anything else but Slavery...recognition & intervention is bound to come." From the Army of Tennessee, Captain Thomas Key announced that "France has recognized the Confederacy on condition that these States emancipate the slaves." Days later he read in the press that an "alliance between England, France, and Spain" was poised to dictate terms to the United States that would recognize Confederate independence. Meanwhile Virginian Fred Fleet told his father that a rebel emissary had "borrowed 43 millions in gold from Germany, giving cotton & tobacco as security, & that he proposes to throw 10 millions on the market and thus redeem a great proportion of the currency." An officer stationed in the Trans-Mississippi Department wrote that a friend of his "has Maximillian on the brain, and wants to get to some point in Txs where we will be in striking distance of Mexico." In 1863 Louis Napoleon proclaimed Hapsburg archduke Ferdinand Maximilian the emperor of Mexico after thirty-five thousand French troops sacked Mexico City and ousted Benito Juarez's republican government. Many Confederates envisioned a North American alliance between southern plantation owners and hacienda landlords.[39]

In February 1865 talk of foreign intervention flourished after the Hampton Roads peace conference fizzled. From his post in Texas, William Heartsill suspected that "the situation...in North America at this time is such, that foreign powers may force terms unpleasant to both the North and South." Many rumors claimed that European powers would not recognize Lincoln's second term of office, which started March 4, because the southern states did not participate in the election. Hugh Montgomery was certain that "after the 4th of March this country will be [a] separate and distinct nation from the U.S. and so recognized by one or more of the European powers." William Nugent agreed that "England & France will not recognize Lincoln as President of anything but the Northern States after the 4th of March, and a [world] war seems almost inevitable." "Let us hold on and hope," he concluded, "the day star of our Independence will soon dawn." When March 4 came and went without an eruption of world war, Virginian Charles Blackford nonetheless told his wife, "I think there is some comfort to be derived from the hope of war between France and the United States."[40]

Chatter of peace through foreign aid still filled newspaper columns in March. Captain E. D. Cheatham was "inclined to think that something will grow out of the peace rumors." In late March Edward Crenshaw spread the rumor that a member of the British Parliament promised recognition from Britain and France if the Confederacy "gained a decided success within the next two months." On March 26, a week before the fall of Richmond, Louisiana infantryman David Pierson imagined that a Federal campaign into the Trans-Mississippi Department (perhaps because it bordered Maximilian's domain) might spark foreign intercession.[41]

In April Lee's surrender challenged the optimism of the most stalwart rebels. Nevertheless, the process of denial, acceptance, and rumormongering that shrouded the fall of Atlanta and Lincoln's reelection surrounded Appomattox as well. Wish rumors circulated that offered false hopes and obscured the truth. Alabamian Samuel Pickens was captured during the evacuation of Richmond. Despite his dire circumstances, Pickens figured that "things [were] not so bad as supposed." Rumors swirled through the prison camp that Lee had captured Richmond along with most of two Union corps, General Philip H. Sheridan had been killed, and Johnston had whipped Sherman. When Union guns saluted Lee's surrender a week later, Pickens admitted, "we can't realize the truth of the astounding events that are transpiring so rapidly—crowding up on us: & we cant believe it either." True to form, rumors infected the camp that Lee had eluded surrender and fought the enemy fifteen miles from Richmond.[42]

After Appomattox, talk of foreign intervention rose from the ashes of improbability and charmed veterans in the Army of Tennessee. On April 19 cavalryman Samuel T. Foster reported that "the United States has recognized the Confederacy, and agrees to give us all our rights (and slavery) if we will help them to fight all their enemies." Rather than face their current condition, some troops preferred to imagine an imminent world war:

> Some think that the big war is about to commence, a war of some Magnitude.
> France Austria Mexico and the Confederacy on one side, against England

Russia and the US' on the other, and the great battle ground will be in the Confederacy. One plan is for the Confederacy to go back into the Union, then France will declare war with the US' and land her troops on the CS' Coast where they will have no opposition, and as the French Army advances through the CS' the people will take the oath of Allegiance to France, and our soldiers will enlist under French colors.

For days, soldiers of the Army of Tennessee sought any outcome but defeat. When Foster realized that Johnston received no terms short of "submission reunion free negroes &c," he exclaimed that "we have been fighting too long for that." He and many others could not readily let go of a cause for which they had made so many sacrifices. While negotiations for surrender were passing between the armies, Foster wrote, "I have not seen a man today but says fight on rather than submit."[43]

When news of Lee's surrender reached William Heartsill and his comrades in the Trans-Mississippi Department, they denied the report and spread hopeful rumors. Some men claimed that England and France had recognized the Confederacy. Others announced that "Emporer Napoleon has landed a large Army on the Texas coast." In Louisiana Jared Sanders heard that French ships were en route to the Gulf of Mexico and that Parisian men were enrolling in the army at a rate not seen since the Crimean War. Heartsill thought, "we should make one mighty, determined effort. For if foreign powers ever do intend to extend any aid, this is 'The auspicious moment.'" He scorned people who called for peace: "we are NOT whiped, we CAN and we MUST fight; subjugation never." On May 9 Heartsill's regiment met and resolved that they "have perfect confidence in, and will render willing obedience to our Commanding officers; and will not lay down our arms, so long as there is a Confederate soldier to vindicate the cause of Southern freedom." Their colonel urged them to "stand by their country, and if the worst comes to the worst, to stand man to man."[44]

For the sake of understanding diehard Confederates, it is important to stress how credible some rumors were. Before Atlanta fell, rebel optimism was reasonable, and wish rumors seemed plausible. In Virginia Lee's ranks inflicted roughly twice as many losses on Grant's forces while preventing them from capturing Richmond and Petersburg. Grant's campaign was a bloody mess, even by Civil War standards. In seven weeks the Army of the Potomac lost sixty-five thousand men, the equivalent of Lee's army. The carnival of death left Union men hesitant to charge Confederate defenses and more eager than ever for peace. Throughout 1864 the stalemate at Richmond and Petersburg seemed to mock Federal hopes and confirm rebel boasts that no amount of Union troops could take the capital from Lee and his veterans.[45]

For a time the Union suffered political turmoil as severe as Confederates had imagined. Before September the presidential election was a wedge that threatened to divide the United States as acutely as the 1860 contest had. In addition to heated differences between Democrats and Republicans, both parties split internally. Republicans argued over the war's prosecution and plans for reconstruction while Democrats differed over continuing the war or pursuing compromise and peace. For months Republican leaders sought another candidate. Lincoln's nomination in June did not resolve party discord, and Lincoln himself expected to lose the contest during the trying summer months. No president had served a second term since Andrew Jackson, and many Americans opposed the principle of reelection, especially during wartime.[46]

Confederates substantiated their opinion of northern morale by following U.S. finances. As Federal casualty lists lengthened in the spring and summer, rebels watched the price of gold skyrocket. A price of 100 meant that 100 U.S. dollars purchased 100 gold dollars. Rebels understood that the price rose when northern confidence fell, so they used this number to assess the impact of setbacks. In May 1864, after three weeks of carnage in Virginia and Georgia, Louisiana officer Hugh Montgomery noted that gold was 210 in New York. Though his figure was high, the price of gold did rise from 171 to 191 during the last weeks of May. Montgomery read in various New Orleans papers that "the State of New York has already commenced repudeating it[s] foreign debt by paying the interest in Greenbacks. The banks of New York City are compelled to pay off the amount that is wanting fifty thousand dollars in gold much to their regret I presume." Many rebels expected the Federal war effort would self-destruct if the Confederacy withstood (what appeared to be) the enemy's final, desperate campaigns for Richmond and Atlanta.[47]

But credibility alone cannot explain why rumors were rampant in the ranks. First, the anxieties of soldiering encouraged widespread rumors. Unable to control where or when the next battle would be fought, troops sought military information that impacted their very lives. But grand strategy was too important to trust to the discretion of thousands who wrote uncensored letters to every corner of the South. Rumors compensated for scant knowledge and relieved troops' anxiety over the future. John Walters recorded how the atmosphere of insecurity affected his unit while it waited to fight at the Wilderness. After anticipating combat for months in winter camp, the men were called to the front before daylight and waited, hunkered together, within earshot of the raging struggle. Empty ambulances passed them and shortly returned loaded with the wounded. To distract himself Walters collected rumors that swirled through the ranks and commented on their validity.[48]

Walters's account illustrates how men tried to grasp battles that enveloped them. The rumors promised good news and help from many sides. One report alleged that General Richard S. Ewell's men repulsed seven enemy assaults. "He captured some say two, some three, and others four thousand prisoners, together with several guns." Shortly thereafter rumors circulated that General George E. Pickett was bringing reinforcements from Fredericksburg and General P.G.T. Beauregard was on his way from North Carolina with twenty thousand men. Then Walters heard that General

Wade Hampton and his cavalry were "making the circuit of the Yankee army to destroy a portion of the Orange and Alexandria Railroad in their rear." According to Walters, "all these reports admitted of and received much discussion, and it is a great pity that General Lee could not hear and thus profit by the admirable plans of battle which some of our military types drew up under the inspiration of the moment." It is telling that Walters's comrades drew up "admirable plans" for the engagement—they compensated for their lack of control over events by discussing how they would command the scene. Rumormongering offered empowerment within a terrifying environment. Psychologist Ralph L. Rosnow has asserted, "the more threatening and dramatic the experience, the more likely it was to be a wellspring of rumor." In the summer months suspenseful waiting became an everyday activity as adversaries settled into prolonged trench warfare. For the rest of the war in Virginia, the enemy's activities were often heard but seldom seen. Any moment could erupt with fire.[49]

Second, ambiguity fostered gossip. If troops faced an insecure future, the present often seemed incomprehensible. Whether in combat, on the march, or at camp, soldiers lived in a confined environment—few secrets existed within the company, but ambiguities pervaded the outer world. Confederates pined for knowledge that mattered most, particularly news from home and other theaters, and they vented exasperation at not receiving enough correspondence from loved ones. From Petersburg Paul Higginbotham pleaded to his brother, "write soon and a long newsy letter." Higginbotham was trying to make sense of the presidential election, Grant's plans, and reports that Federal cavalry threatened his family. Because comrades often came from the same county, they collected and circulated letters in an attempt to piece together the situation at home. Using newspapers, speeches, and military orders, troops similarly constructed a picture of the Confederacy's fortunes in other campaigns. But the distances that veiled far-off places and events also obscured facts from fictions. Sociologist Tamotsu Shibutani appreciated this issue when be defined rumor as "a recurrent form of *communication through which men caught together in an ambiguous situation attempt to construct a meaningful interpretation of it by pooling their intellectual resources.*" In short, because physical boundaries and unreliable channels often denied rebels accurate intelligence about the subjects that interested them most, soldiers who gathered and shared information were spreading rumors.[50]

These obstacles plagued troops in the Trans-Mississippi Department. Hundreds of miles from the decisive battles in Georgia and Virginia, soldiers in the West collected and traded rumors as if they were currency. When the 1864 campaigns began across the river, William Heartsill was stuck guarding a temporary prison camp in Tyler, Texas. One day, perhaps out of sheer boredom, he critiqued some rumors that had infiltrated the stockade: Lee thrashed Grant; Johnston captured Lookout Mountain; the enemy evacuated Chattanooga; Kentucky sent eight thousand cavalrymen to the Confederacy and refused to contribute soldiers to the United States;

General Nathan Bedford Forrest took Memphis; the black Federal garrison at Vicksburg offered to surrender the city if they could return to their masters; a resolution to recognize the Confederacy failed in the U.S. Congress by only seven votes; and Lee's army numbered 280,000 men fit for duty. Heartsill mocked such news, but others accepted it as fact. In October 1864 Hugh Montgomery, an officer stationed in Shreveport, Louisiana, told a friend that "the news to day is *without exaggeration magnificent we have slaughtered* the enemy before our ranks around Petersburg & Richmond." As he understood the report, the Confederates allowed the enemy to seize the first trench and "then opened on them with small arms, light artillery & from our gunboats in the James." Distance magnified the scale and significance of the battle to the point that Montgomery proclaimed, "Such destruction of human life has never been witnessed during our struggle."[51]

Third, the media and Confederate leadership helped rather than hindered the spread of wish rumors. Across the Confederacy, soldiers found supporting evidence for rumors in newspaper columns. As the Civil War intensified and lengthened, its titanic proportions challenged the newspapermen who covered it. The difficulties of presenting an accurate picture of war plagued reporters and editors. Journalism, like the war itself, straddled modernity and an older era. Just as the war's weaponry often outran knowledge on matters that could lessen the bloodshed (e.g., military strategy and medicine), so too did advances in communication, namely the telegraph, railroads, and steam-powered presses, outpace ideas like journalistic objectivity that could responsibly handle the impact of nationwide reporting. As a result, thousands of eager readers digested highly partisan and often bogus news in their daily papers. A number of factors, including inaccurate information channels, speedy circulation, and media competition turned the nation's largest newspapers into its greatest rumor mills.[52]

Some press difficulties can be traced to the Confederacy's telegraph offices. According to scholar Ford Risley, "Wild rumors regularly found their way into news reports" because telegraph services were slow, biased, and inaccurate. Subjective reporting affected rebels' understanding of many Confederate disasters, including Gettysburg, Vicksburg, and Atlanta. While Vicksburg's citizens and soldiers desperately needed provisions, news reports reassured the rest of the Confederacy that the "Gibraltar of the South" was stocked with supplies. Dispatches transmitted false rumors that Grant lost ten thousand killed and forty thousand captured in attempts to take the city. The costliest Federal assault during the Vicksburg campaign lost just over three thousand men. The Press Association reporter in Jackson, Mississippi, spread many of these bogus reports. His only contact with Vicksburg was with people who had left the town. As for Gettysburg, only one telegraph service reporter joined Lee's invasion of Pennsylvania. The first telegraph reports reached the Confederacy on July 5. On July 6 the telegraphs claimed that Lee's men captured forty thousand enemy troops. It was not until July 9 that telegraph reports, quoting northern newspapers, admitted that the Confederates suffered defeat. Still, even those sober reports promised that "the citizens are hopeful and confident." An accurate picture of Vicksburg and Gettysburg took weeks to develop.[53]

Inaccurate reporting was worse during the Atlanta campaign. If telegrams about Vicksburg and Gettysburg were marred by incompetence, "a clear sense of morale building was evident" in the reporting on Atlanta. General Johnston ordered that the inspector general strictly censor all news from the Army of Tennessee. When Hood took command and bloodied his ranks for no gain, the wires celebrated his assaults. "Atlanta is safe. All are hopeful and in the best spirits." The telegraphs did not report Atlanta's fall until September 4. On the following day they asserted that "[w]hile the fall of Atlanta is regretted, the army and people are not at all discouraged."[54]

Weeks after the disaster, the wires circulated false rumors that Confederates cut Sherman's supply line and separated him from the body of his army. Throughout October the Army of Tennessee harassed Sherman's supply line in hopes of forcing the Federals out of Atlanta. They failed. Union soldiers pushed Hood's men into Alabama, repaired the railroad, and embarked on the March to the Sea. Nevertheless, in mid-October Richmond newsmen desperately sought good news and thought they found some. A preliminary (and false) report claimed that Hood's army had achieved a victory against Sherman in one of these brief engagements along the supply line. The news was too lean and ambiguous for even the editors to embellish, so Richmond papers informed their readers that the news from Georgia was too good to print. They insinuated that Sherman's army was completely cut off from the North and claimed that reporting the invaders' fate in Confederate papers would give Lincoln and Grant information that they could not gather otherwise.[55]

Confederates defending Richmond and Petersburg accepted this nonsense and sent word to their loved ones. Army surgeon Spencer Welch wrote his wife that "there is encouraging news from Georgia, but they will not tell us what it is, because they say they do not want Grant to find out about it." He conjectured that "Hood may have Sherman in a tight place." On the same day John W. McLure exclaimed, "there are rumors afloat about Richmond that matters are going on most prosperously in Georgia, the news is too good they say to be published to the Yankees just yet, which would be the effect of publishing in our papers, now the only mode the enemy have of ascertaining what has become of Sherman's army." David Crawford was still hopeful over a week later. "From newspaper accounts" he reported that "Hood seems to have Sherman in a pretty tight fix, I hope he may be able to put an end to that 'great General of the day.' & his army with him."[56]

Rumors and biased reporting also marked the Confederacy's religious publications. Throughout the war, Christian organizations dispatched millions of newsletters and pamphlets to rebel armies. According to historian Kurt O. Berends, the editors of these papers "created a framework of beliefs—a worldview—that sustained an unvanquished optimism for southern independence." It seems nothing could shake their confidence in ultimate victory. After the fall of Atlanta one editor argued that "there was no disaster," because General Hood's "great object was to hold it as long as be could, and to make the possession of it by the enemy cost him as much as possible. This object bas been fully attained." In February 1865 another editor reasoned that "the loss of our great cities is probable. This occurred in the Revolutionary war, and occurs in most wars; but if the heart of the people is right, never determines the result." When Richmond fell, southern columnists again compared their circumstances to Americans during the Revolution: "the taking of Richmond will have no more effect upon the final result of the war than the taking of Philadelphia, (the Capital of the Colonies) in 1777." William Norris, editor of the *Mississippi Messenger*, penned perhaps the most astounding report in March 1865, less than a month before Lee's surrender. Norris's claim that "the war shall be either closed, or its character entirely changed" within three months was not exceptional, except that he expected Confederate victory to be the result. Norris contended that Generals Grant and George Thomas "have been whipped so often that we need not take them into the calculation. In South Carolina, Sherman is confronted by an equal force with all the natural advantage on our side. Let Sherman be destroyed, and the supremacy of the Confederacy is established." "There is no reason for despondency, just the reverse," Norris concluded, for "the Confederacy controls the whole situation."[57]

When southern leaders insisted that the Confederacy was unconquerable, they reinforced wish rumors and enhanced their credibility. No politician encouraged rebels' conviction that they were invincible as strongly as Jefferson Davis. When the Confederate Congress assembled in May 1864, days before the spring campaigns began, Davis promised the statesmen, "If our arms are crowned with the success which we have so much reason to hope, we may well expect that this war cannot be prolonged beyond the current year." On the eve of Lincoln's reelection, Davis argued that nothing could deny the rebels ultimate victory and independence: "Not the fall of Richmond, nor Wilmington, nor Charleston, nor Savannah, nor Mobile, nor of all combined, can save the enemy from the constant and exhaustive drain of blood and treasure which must continue until he shall discover that no peace is attainable unless based on the recognition of our indefeasible rights." Davis went on to discuss foreign intervention, finances, and the unlikelihood of a negotiated peace with the Union "until the delusion of their ability to conquer us is dispelled." The only course to victory he identified was through persistent fighting: "Let us, then, resolutely continue to devote our united and unimpaired energies to the defense of our homes, our lives, and our liberties. This is the true path to peace. Let us tread it with confidence in the assured result."[58]

Clergymen also supported continued resistance and hopes for a northern collapse. Church leaders decried Lincoln's despotism, predicted financial catastrophe on Wall Street, hinted that masses of wretched northerners faced starvation, and labeled the Yankee press a gigantic propaganda machine that controlled a docile public. In April 1864 Episcopal bishop Stephen Elliott argued that Federal armies were not permanently occupying any vital Confederate territory and mocked the enemy's annual advance and retreat in Virginia and Tennessee. He asked his congregation, "will the people of the United States consent to be maimed and slaughtered through an indefinite series of years for the annual honor of marching from Washington to the Rappahannock, and from Nashville to Chattanooga? Impossible!" Considering the reverence thousands of rebels accorded to religious leaders, these pronouncements bolstered faith in victory and independence in profound ways.[59]

All these sources—newspapers, telegraph services, religious presses, politicians, clergymen, and the soldiers themselves—spread wish rumors, but why did they do so? Why was Confederate gossip so positive, even after the fall of Atlanta? Fear and hatred can spark the imagination and produce rumors as easily as hopes can. Why did chatter about catastrophic defeats, enemy espionage, slave revolts, or starvation on the home front not swirl through Confederate camps as the war worsened? Why did more rumors not foreshadow the nightmares of defeat: Federal domination and racial disorder? Some negative gossip did exist. Atrocity stories followed Sherman's tracks, and news occasionally announced the death of Lee or some other cherished leader; but wish rumors far outweighed despondent ones.

The phenomenon can be explained in part by soldiers' efforts to construct reality. When rebels received news of events, such as the fall of Atlanta, that threatened the very existence of the Confederacy, many of them first denied the reports and then spread positive rumors to counterbalance the disaster's impact. According to psychologist Leon Festinger, when social groups face undeniable evidence that challenges how they view themselves or foresee their future, they often band together to discuss the news and through this discourse produce rumors that support their cherished beliefs. In this manner, "a large group of people is able to maintain an opinion or belief even in the face of continual definite evidence to the contrary." Thousands of rebels committed to independence and living in uncertain times managed to deflect the significance of successive defeats and worsening conditions by unconsciously inventing good news. Thomas S. Kuhn's concept of paradigm shifts involves the same dynamic. Kuhn has argued that scientists sometimes retain long-standing theories, even when increasing evidence discredits those premises, because the older beliefs explain the universe. Instead of jettisoning how they perceive the world, scientists label contradictory facts as anomalies until those findings grow to dimensions that cannot be ignored. When Confederates deflected bad news as temporary setbacks they acted in similar ways.[60]

But cognitive dissonance was only part of Confederates' behavior; emotions also promoted the spread of wish rumors. Some soldiers questioned the validity of rumors but still circulated them because hopeful messages were too appealing to discard. Though Grant Taylor complained that "we hear so many lies we never know what to believe," he spread a report that northern prisoners were taking the Confederate oath and joining rebel armies. Paul Higginbotham remarked that newspapers "are now, as they always do, making out our prospects bright, but I believe as much of their talk as I please." Nevertheless Higginbotham frequently shared reports that bolstered his morale. Soldiers often concluded the telling of a rumor by doubting its accuracy. Statements like "it seems too good to believe," "if true this is glorious," "if that bee so," and "I hope it is true" reveal the tug-of-war between soldiers' intellects and passions. As veterans, they knew how ridiculous some of these rumors sounded. But as partisans, they could not deny the emotions that good news summoned: pride, hope, anticipation, and revenge. Charles Blackford exemplified this internal debate. In the same letter in which he told his wife that "bad rumors are always true while good ones are often false," he could not resist sharing the rumor that Grant had been killed.[61]

Patriotism and group cohesion also encouraged soldiers to spread wish rumors. By transmitting news of distant victories, northern discord, and foreign aid, troops expressed their abiding faith in the Confederacy. The most active rumormongers were diehard rebels like Hugh Montgomery, who hoped in October 1864 that positive reports would "rouse the dispondent of our land and be hailed with joy and gladness by those of us whose hope, and confidence of victory & independence has not been lost by the temporary gloom." Publicly denying the veracity of a wish rumor could seem unpatriotic or detrimental to morale. In 1865 thousands of forlorn Confederates deserted, leaving behind a more homogeneous troop of unconquered southerners. By winnowing out the disheartened, desertion created a better conduit for wish rumors. This self-selection helps to explain why bizarre rumors of European intervention swirled through the ranks in spring 1865.[62] By the end of the war, fanatics who sought any means to refute the likelihood of defeat composed a larger portion of Confederate armies.

Still, it is unclear whether rumors were a cause or an effect of homogeneity. Did positive gossip foster group cohesion, or did group cohesion foster positive gossip? The dynamic probably worked both ways. According to psychologist Ralph L. Rosnow, "As the rumors are retold, strong common interests begin to crystallize, and the loosely bound collectivity becomes more cohesive."[63] Wish rumors promoted a communal perspective on the war; they connected men who spread them, decreased disparate perceptions of events, and sparked hopeful predictions. Even rumors of Grant's death bound together those who heard them. For a week or two, thousands of rebels from Virginia to Texas wondered if a single Confederate shell had killed the tenacious general and thereby changed the course of the war. Not all individuals had the same reaction to gossip, and particular rumors were not received the same by all men. Nonetheless widespread rumors were a part of the chaotic experience that united soldiers.

Studying Civil War rumors offers both a new window into the lives of Confederates and a reflective look at the historian's craft. Nearly sixty years ago, the pioneer study of wartime rumors warned not to dismiss them as quaint deviations from otherwise rational discourse. As Allport and Postman noted, a rumor's "characteristic course of distortion in recall, forgetting, imagination, and rationalization is precisely the same course of distortion that we find in most forms of human communication," including courtroom testimony, mythology, and, yes, history. Passing gossip through a particular society assimilates stories within cultural and historical contexts. Likewise, disseminating scholarship integrates knowledge within academic assumptions and grand narratives. This is not to say that historians are rumormongers, but highlighting similarities in the processes can expose our biases. Fantastic wish rumors complemented the worldview of diehard rebels still fighting for independence; the same rumors conflict with academic histories of waning morale, desertion, and the failure of Confederate nationalism written nearly 150 years after Appomattox. When scholars stop branding false rumors as trivial, discordant information and start seeing them as true expressions of people's beliefs, fears, and hopes, mountains of evidence promise new veins of research.[64]

In some ways, however, rumors will challenge scholars just as they pestered people in 1865. The value of gossip seems fleeting, its causes and effects a riddle. But the transience of rumors offers historians a glimpse of the past as present. By showing how the flux of war must have felt to thousands, rumors illuminate the "deep contingency" of history that Edward L. Ayers has recently championed.[65] This chapter expands Ayers's concept by recounting how dense connections between Civil War events and participants linked social, cultural, political, and military issues, creating a world that was far more complicated than any epic tale. Rumors did more than mirror the times; they affected the war experiences of countless Americans. When soldiers recorded gossip in diaries and letters, the information became a part of their war narrative, their attempt to organize and understand the conflict. The Civil War, like all experience, acquired form and meaning in the stories that participants told of it. Information, true or false, contributed to these individual chronicles and to a larger story of Confederate persistence. As the rebellion faded, a stream of gossip promoted the beliefs that diehard veterans had always wanted to believe: their armies and people were unconquerable and everything would turn out right in the end. This profusion of wish rumors, spreading from Virginia to Texas and Arkansas to Georgia, helps bring to light how unvanquished southerners maintained faith through the darkest months of the war. Diehard Confederates thought and fought in ways that seem foreign, and at times unreasonable, to us. Understanding their rumors brings us one step closer to them and the world they shaped.

Looking beyond the war, the findings from research on rumors have broad implications for scholarship on the Lost Cause. Not only do pervasive wish rumors late in the war point to the final vestiges of Confederate nationalism, but they also reveal the seeds of New South legends. Scholarship on the Lost Cause often portrays it as a postwar response to defeat, Reconstruction, and corresponding social changes.[66] The legend was indeed all these things, but as recent work by David W. Blight and others suggests, it was also a continuation of warfare by other means.[67] Studying wartime gossip strengthens this point, because the similarities between widespread rumors and cultural legends are remarkably strong. As one study expressed it, "a legend is a rumor that has become part of the verbal heritage of a people."[68]

While rumors pose as news, legends masquerade as history. Confederate stories of honor, courage, and determination crystallized into postwar legends of white southern defiance. Moreover, it seems likely that diehard Confederates adept at spreading wish rumors became unreconstructed rebels skilled at disseminating Lost Cause legends. Perhaps the "heritage" that some southerners defend today stems from the same cultural mentalities and practices that created wish rumors nearly 150 years ago. Work founded upon this insight could provide valuable links between Civil War scholarship, Reconstruction history, and southern studies in general.

Notes

1. Henry G. Orr to his father, July 10, 1864, in John Q. Anderson, ed., *Campaigning with Parsons' Texas Cavalry Brigade, CSA; The War Journals and Letters of the Four Orr Brothers, 12th Texas Cavalry Regiment* (Hillsboro, Tex., 1967), 142–43. I thank the anonymous reviewers for the *Journal of Southern History* for their help.
2. Entries for July 24, 1864 (quotation), and July 28, 1864, James W. Albright diary. Folder 1, James W. Albright Books #1008 (Southern Historical Collection, Wilson Library, University of North Carolina at Chapel Hill; hereinafter SHC).
3. Entry for July 23, 1864, James B. Jones diary, Jones Family Papers #2884, SHC.
4. Abel H. Crawford to Dora, July 16, 1864, Civil War Collection, Confederate and Federal #824 (Tennessee State Library and Archives, Nashville; hereinafter TSLA), microfilm, reel 3.
5. W.R. Redding to his wife, July 18, 1864, W.R. Redding Papers #3348, SHC.
6. Leonidas Lafayette Polk to his wife, July 28, 1864, Leonidas Lafayette Polk Papers #3708, SHC.
7. Entry for October 18, 1864, Samuel Horace Hawes Diary, Mss5:lH3115:1 (Virginia Historical Society, Richmond; hereinafter VHS).
8. Social historians, particularly those who study class, race, and gender, have long identified the significance of rumors and oral culture. Southern historians have not hesitated to use rumors and oral culture to explain black southern life. In their work, hearsay illuminates the attitudes and agency of subalterns. Historians of the French Revolution and women's "gossip" have also shown how rumors demonstrate the agency of oppressed people. Important examples include Georges Lefebvre, *The Great Fear of 1789: Rural Panic in Revolutionary France*, translated by Joan White (1932; new ed., New York, 1973); Robert Darnton, *The Great Cat Massacre and Other Episodes in French Cultural History* (New York, 1984); Shema Berger Gluck and Daphne Patai, eds., *Women's Words: The Feminist Practice of Oral History* (New York, 1991); Steven Hahn, "'Extravagant Expectations' of Freedom: Rumour, Political Struggle, and the Christmas Insurrection Scare of 1865 in the American South," *Past and Present*, no. 157 (November 1997), 122–58; Bernard Capp, *When Gossips Meet: Women. Family, and Neighbourhood in Early Modern England* (New York, 2003); and Rebecca Griffin, "Courtship Contests and the Meaning of Conflict

in the Folklore of Slaves," *Journal of Southern History*, 71 (November 2005), 769–802. George C. Rable mentions Confederate rumors in "Despair, Hope, and Delusion: The Collapse of Confederate Morale Reexamined," in Mark Grimsley and Brooks D. Simpson, eds., *The Collapse of the Confederacy* (Lincoln, Neb., 2001), 129–67. Rable argues that "rationalizations and wishful thinking helped citizens hang onto hope even in the absence of any tangible reasons to do so" (p. 131). I agree that wishful thinking affected how rebels interpreted news. I disagree with the assertion that Confederates lacked any tangible evidence to bolster morale. If Confederates believed a rumor, then it was tangible to them, even if it is not to historians today. Rable also includes rumors in *Fredericksburg! Fredericksburg!* (Chapel Hill, 2002).

9. Paul D. Escott, *After Secession: Jefferson Davis and the Failure of Confederate Nationalism* (Baton Rouge, 1978), 94–134; Richard E. Beringer, Herman Hattaway, Archer Jones, and William N. Still Jr., *Why the South Lost the Civil War* (Athens, Ga., 1986). New social history has expanded our understanding of Civil War soldiers just as it has increased our knowledge of slaves, women, and working-class people. Military historians seldom compare a soldier's lot with conditions endured by racial minorities, women, and the poor. Nonetheless, army life restricted troops' power, freedom, and equality. White southern men, in particular, experienced an iron discipline that clashed with their peacetime society. Within the confines of military life, Confederates demonstrated their agency in numerous ways. Scholars who stress yeoman discontent often explain desertion as an act of empowerment—non-slaveholders "voted with their feet" to protect their interests and protest Confederate elitism. If desertion illustrates the agency of the discontented, wish rumors confirm the agency of diehard rebels, the persistent, determined Confederates who remained defiant and faithful to the end. This chapter contends that scholars should treat rumors in a manner similar to how they study desertion; both were acts of empowerment taken by men in the ranks to express their views of the war.

10. Gordon W. Allport and Leo Postman, *The Psychology of Rumor* (New York, 1947), 12–13, 8 (quotation). The final 7 percent of the rumors gathered were classified as miscellaneous. According to Allport and Postman, a Canadian psychologist, John A. Irving, found similar patterns of rumors in his country during World War II (p. 172). See Irving, "The Psychological Analysis of Wartime Rumor Patterns in Canada," *Bulletin of the Canadian Psychological Association*, 3 (1943), 40–44. It is worth noting that the American study from 1942 focused on civilian rumors. For this essay, Allport and Postman's methods and analysis matter more than their conclusions about World War II rumors.

11. Entry for May 27, 1864, John Walters diary, in Kenneth Wiley, ed., *Norfolk Blues: The Civil War Diary of the Norfolk Light Artillery Blues* (Shippensburg, Pa., 1997), 120 (first quotation); Charles Blackford to Susan Leigh Blackford, May 30, 1864, in Susan Leigh Blackford, Charles Minor Blackford, and Charles Minor Blackford III, eds., *Letters from Lee's Army; or, Memoirs of Life In and Out of the Army in Virginia during the War Between the States* (1947; new ed., Lincoln, Neb., 1998), 249 (second quotation); Charles Blackford to Susan Leigh Blackford, June 10, 1864, ibid., 254 (third quotation); Thomas Elder to Anna Fitzhugh (May) Elder, September 11, 1864, Thomas Claybrook Elder Papers, Mss2EL228b, VHS (fourth quotation).

12. Entry for June 19, 1864, William D. Alexander diary, William D. Alexander Papers #2478, SHC (quotation); George Knox Miller to unknown, fragment of undated June 1864 letter, George Knox Miller Papers #2525, SHC.

13. James M. McPherson, *For Cause and Comrades: Why Men Fought in the Civil War* (New York, 1997), 149.

14. Paul Higginbotham to Aaron Higginbotham, July 1, 1864, Paul M. Higginbotham Papers, Mss2H53588b, VHS (first and second quotations); Charles Blackford to Susan Leigh Blackford, July 11, 1864, in Blackford, Blackford, and Blackford, eds., *Letters from Lee's Army*, 266 (third and fourth quotations); entry for July 8, 1864, John Walters diary, in Wiley, ed., *Norfolk Blues*, 132 (fifth quotation). Also see J. Tracy Power, *Lee's Miserables: Life in the Army of Northern Virginia from the Wilderness to Appomattox* (Chapel Hill, 1998), 117; and Spencer Glasgow Welch to Cordelia Strother Welch, July 6, 1864, in Spencer Glasgow Welch, *A Confederate Surgeon's Letters to His Wife* (1911; new ed., Marietta, Ga., 1954), 102. Sherman's treatment of Atlanta produced a greater uproar. See James Madison Brannock to Sarah Caroline (Gwin) Brannock, September 12, 1864, James Madison Brannock Papers, Mss2B7352b, VHS; James Adams to parents, September 16, 1864, Israel L. Adams and Family Papers, Mss. 3637 (Louisiana and Lower Mississippi Valley Collections, Special Collections, Hill Memorial Library, Louisiana State University, Baton Rouge; hereinafter LSU); and entry for August 4, 1864, Thomas J. Key diary, in Wirt Armistead Cate, ed., *Two Soldiers: The Campaign Diaries of Thomas J. Key, C.S.A. and Robert J. Campbell, U.S.A.* (Chapel Hill. 1938), 108.

15. Entry for July 24, 1864, James W. Albright diary. Folder I, Albright Books.

16. Allport and Postman. *Psychology of Rumor*, 167; Walter Benjamin, "The Storyteller," in Hannah Arendt, ed., *Illuminations* (New York, 1968), 90. This hidden layer of meaning confirms the value of rumors to historians. News is ephemeral, stories are timeless, and they often reveal a culture's values, fears, and beliefs.

17. Entry for January 19, 1865, Samuel Pickens diary, in G. Ward Hubbs, ed., *Voices from Company D: Diaries by the Greensboro Guards, Fifth Alabama Infantry Regiment, Army of Northern Virginia* (Athens, Ga., 2003), 346.

18. Edward L. Ayers, *In the Presence of Mine Enemies: War in the Heart of America, 1859–1863* (New York, 2003), xvii. Studying Civil War rumors enhances Ayers's idea of "deep contingency." While other scholars, James M. McPherson most notably, have used contingency to illuminate chance and the bonds between political, social, economic, and military events, Ayers sees "deep contingency" as the "intricate connections in which lives and events are embedded" (p. xix). In other words, Civil War history should portray more than a deterministic web of factors that span the battlefront and home front; it is a humanistic endeavor to reconstruct how people's individual, emotional wars touched the distant conflict and vice versa. See McPherson, *Crossroads of Freedom: Antietam* (New York, 2002).

19. Patterns of gossip were not as apparent to Civil War participants as they are in hindsight. Rumors from all three categories affected the Confederacy throughout the war. Nonetheless, this pattern appears in my evidence, and it suggests that rebel rumors changed over time.

20. Gary W. Gallagher, *The Confederate War* (Cambridge, Mass., 1997), 58.

21. Entry for May 17, 1864, Benjamin M. Seaton diary, in Harold B. Simpson, ed., *The Bugle Softly Blows: The Confederate Diary of Benjamin M. Seaton* (Waco. Tex., 1965), 51 (first quotation); entry for May 20, 1864, William W. Heartsill diary, in Bell Irvin Wiley, ed., *Fourteen Hundred and 91 Days in the Confederate Army* (Jackson, Tenn., 1954), 205 (second quotation); Edwin H. Fay to Sarah Shields Fay, May 22, 1864, in Bell Irvin Wiley, ed., *"This Infernal War": The Confederate Letters of Sgt. Edwin H. Fay* (Austin, Tex., 1958), 397 (third through seventh quotations); James M. McPherson, *Battle Cry of Freedom: The Civil War Era* (New York, 1988), 733.

22. Henry G. Orr to his father, July 10, 1864, in Anderson, ed., *Campaigning with Parsons' Texas Cavalry Brigade*, 142 (first, second, and third quotations); James

N. Orr to his mother, July 18, 1864, ibid., 144 (fourth quotation); James C. Bates to his mother and sister, July 8, 1864, in Richard Lowe, ed., *A Texas Cavalry Officer's Civil War: The Diary and Letters of James C. Bates* (Baton Rouge, 1999), 305 (fifth quotation). For another soldier's report of the rumor that Grant was killed, see John William McLure to his wife, date uncertain but must be late July 1864, McLure Family Papers (South Caroliniana Library, University of South Carolina, Columbia; hereinafter SCL).

23. McPherson, *Battle Cry of Freedom*, 749–50; Charles Royster, *The Destructive War: William Tecumseh Sherman, Stonewall Jackson, and the Americans* (New York, 1991), 296–320; entry for June 27, 1864, William E. Sloan diary. Folder 7, Box 7, Civil War Collections, TSLA (first quotation); Grant Taylor to Malinda Taylor and children, June 26, 1864, in Ann K. Blomquist and Robert A. Taylor, eds., *This Cruel War: The Civil War Letters of Grant and Malinda Taylor, 1862–1865* (Macon, Ga., 2000), 264; John Rankin to Mrs. Leroy M. Nutt, June 21, 1864, Leroy Moncure Nutt Papers #2285, SHC (second quotation); John Cotton to his wife, July 4, 1864, in Lucille Griffith, ed., *Yours Till Death: Civil War Letters of John W. Cotton* (Birmingham, Ala., 1951), 115 (third and fourth quotations); Johnston quoted in Stanley F. Horn, *The Army of Tennessee: A Military History* (Indianapolis, 1941), 339 (fourth quotation); James Brannock to Sarah Caroline (Gwin) Brannock, July 9, 1864, Brannock Papers (fifth quotation).

24. James Blackman Ligon to his mother, June 30, 1864, James Blackman Ligon Papers, SCL (first and second quotations); entry for July 4, 1864, John Walters diary, in Wiley, ed., *Norfolk Blues*, 131 (third and fourth quotations).

25. McPherson, *Battle Cry of Freedom*, 753–55.

26. Richmond papers quoted in Adolph A. Hoehling, *Last Train from Atlanta* (New York, 1958), 167 (first quotation), 251 (second quotation); J.B. Jones, *A Rebel War Clerk's Diary at the Confederate States Capitol*, edited by Howard Swiggett (2 vols.; New York, 1935), II, 259 (third quotation); Henry Conner to his wife, August 4, 1864, Henry Calvin Conner Papers, SCL (fourth quotation); entry for July 23, 1864, James W. Albright diary. Folder 1, Albright Books (fifth quotation); Elias Davis to his wife, July 27, 1864, Elias Davis Papers #2496, SHC.

27. W.R. Redding to his wife, August 14, 1864, Redding Papers; Edwin Fay to Sarah Shields Fay, August 22, 1864, in Wiley, ed., *"This Infernal War,"* 402.

28. McPherson, *Battle Cry of Freedom*, 774.

29. Entry for September 6, 1864, Creed Thomas Davis diary, Mss5:1D2914:2, VHS; entries for September 12, October 18–19, 1864, William W. Heartsill diary, in Wiley, ed., *Fourteen Hundred and 91 Days in the Confederate Army*, 217 (quotation), 221.

30. Entry for September 7, 1864, Henry Chambers diary, Henry Alexander Chambers Papers #2260, SHC (first quotation); John W. Cotton to his wife, September 24, 1864, in Griffith, ed., *Yours Till Death*, 118; entry for October 1–2, 1864, James W, Albright diary. Folder 1, Albright Books (second quotation).

31. Entry for October 4, 1864, John Walters diary, in Wiley, ed., *Norfolk Blues*, 160; Spencer Glasgow Welch to Cordelia Strother Welch, October 25, October 2, 1864, in Welch, *Confederate Surgeon's Letters to His Wife*, 110 (first quotation), 107 (second quotation); Thomas Elder to his wife, September 11, 1864, Elder Papers (third, fourth, fifth, and sixth quotations); Thomas Dunbar Affleck to his mother, September 18, 1864, Box 5, Thomas Affleck Papers, LSU (seventh quotation).

32. Ayers, *In the Presence of Mine Enemies*, xix (first quotation); Reid Mitchell, *Civil War Soldiers* (New York, 1988), 191 (second quotation). Recent important work on soldiers' morale includes McPherson, *For Cause and Comrades*, Gallagher,

Confederate War, Stephen W. Berry II, *All That Makes a Man: Love and Ambition in the Civil War South* (New York, 2003); and Peter S. Carmichael, *The Last Generation: Young Virginians in Peace, War, and Reunion* (Chapel Hill, 2005). Robertson Davies made this point beautifully: "I try to recapture not simply the fact that people at one time believed something-or-other, but the reasons and the logic behind their belief. It doesn't matter if the belief was wrong, or seems wrong to us today: it is the fact of the belief that concerns me....I don't think people are foolish and believe wholly stupid things; they may believe what is untrue, but they have a need to believe the untruth—it fills a gap in the fabric of what they want to know, or think they ought to know. We often throw such beliefs aside without having truly understood them." Robertson Davies, *The Rebel Angels* (New York, 1982), 148–49.

33. Junius Newport Bragg to Anna Josephine (Goddard) Bragg, February 1, 1864, in Mrs, T.J, Gaughan, ed., *Letters of a Confederate Surgeon, 1861–65* (Camden, Ark., 1960), 203 (first and second quotations); Paul Higginbotham to Aaron Higginbotham, July 10, 1864, Higginbotham Papers (third, fourth, and fifth quotations); entry for July 12, 1864, James W. Albright diary, Folder 1, Albright Books; Grant Taylor to Malinda Taylor and children, December 29, 1864, in Blomquist and Taylor, eds., *This Cruel War*, 319 (sixth quotation).

34. William Nugent to Eleanor Smith Nugent, January 26, 1864, in William M. Cash and Lucy Somerville Howorth, eds., *My Dear Nellie: The Civil War Letters of William L. Nugent to Eleanor Smith Nugent* (Jackson, Miss., 1977), 203 (first quotation); Edwin Fay to Sarah Shields Fay, July 17, 1864, in Wiley, ed., *"This Infernal War,"* 399 (second quotation).

35. William Nugent to Eleanor Smith Nugent, September 17, 1864 (first quotation), August 2, 1864 (second quotation), in Cash and Howorth, eds., *My Dear Nellie*, 207–8, 193; James Brannock to Sarah Caroline (Gwin) Brannock, September 12, 1864, Brannock Papers. After McClellan's speech, Peter Guerrant admitted he could not decide between the candidates, but he seemed to lean toward Lincoln; "on the one hand I believe we [might] just as well have Lincoln, as he has already done us as much harm as he can, on the other I believe McLellan would not be so mean a man as Lincoln, yet I believe he (should he be elected) would rally more recruits than Lincoln." Peter Guerrant to his uncle, October 9, 1864, Section 3, Guerrant Family Papers, MsslG9375a, VHS. Charles Blackford was also ambivalent. See Charles Blackford to Susan Leigh Blackford, June 16, 1864, in Blackford, Blackford, and Blackford, eds., *Letters from Lee's Army*, 256.

36. James Brannock to Sarah Caroline (Gwin) Brannock, September 12, 1864, Brannock Papers; Stephen Elliott, *Vain Is the Help of Man...* (Macon, Ga., 1864), 12; William C. Harris, *Lincoln's Last Months* (Cambridge, Mass., 2004), 23 (second quotation); entry for November 7, 1864, John Walters diary, in Wiley, ed., *Norfolk Blues*, 172 (third quotation). Hugh Montgomery heard rumors that McClellan won. See Hugh Montgomery to Arthur W. Hyatt, November 19, 1864, Arthur W. Hyatt Papers, LSU.

37. D.S. Doggett, *The War and Its Close...* (Richmond, 1864), 15.

38. Lawrence Ross to Lizzie Ross, March 19, 1864, in Perry Wayne Shelton and Shelly Morrison, eds., *Personal Civil War Letters of General Lawrence Sullivan Ross; With Other Letters* (Austin, Tex., 1994), 62 (first quotation); William Nugent to Eleanor Smith Nugent, March 20, 1864, in Cash and Howorth, eds., *My Dear Nellie*, 162 (second quotation); entry for January 1, 1864, Thomas J. Key diary, in Cate, ed., *Two Soldiers*, 22 (third, fourth, and fifth quotations). Interestingly, Junius N. Bragg thought rumors of foreign intervention were lies started by the enemy: "they love to make us feel good once in a while, and it is really quite clever

of them." See Junius Newport Bragg to Anna J. Bragg, January 18, 1864, in Gaughan, ed., *Letters of a Confederate Surgeon*, 196.

39. Hugh Montgomery to Arthur W. Hyatt, January 24, 1865, Hyatt Papers (first, second, and sixth quotations); entries for January 18 and January 22, 1865, Thomas Key diary, in Cate, ed., *Two Soldiers*, 181–82 (third and fourth quotations); Fred Fleet to his mother, January 23, 1865, in Betsy Fleet and John D.P. Fuller, eds., *Green Mount: A Virginia Plantation Family during the Civil War: Being the Journal of Benjamin Robert Fleet and Letters of His Family* (Lexington, Ky., 1962), 357 (fifth quotation); McPherson, *Battle Cry of Freedom*, 683. Civilians also transmitted these rumors to men in the ranks. See Anna J. Bragg to Junius N. Bragg, January 25, 1865, in Gaughan, ed., *Letters of a Confederate Surgeon*, 265.

40. Entry for February 16, 1865, William W. Heartsill diary, in Wiley, ed., *Fourteen Hundred and 91 Days in the Confederate Army*, 230 (first quotation); Hugh Montgomery to Arthur W. Hyatt, January 24, 1865, Hyatt Papers (second quotation); William L. Nugent to Eleanor Smith Nugent, January 26, 1865, in Cash and Howorth, eds., *My Dear Nellie*, 234–35 (third, fourth, and fifth quotations); Charles Blackford to Susan Leigh Blackford, March 8, 1865, in Blackford, Blackford, and Blackford, eds., *Letters from Lee's Army*, 279 (sixth quotation).

41. E.D. Cheatham to Arthur W. Hyatt, March 20, 1865, Hyatt Papers (first quotation); entry for March 25, 1865, in Edward Crenshaw, "Diary of Captain Edward Crenshaw of the Confederate States Army," *Alabama Historical Quarterly*, 2 (Fall 1940), 384 (second quotation); David Pierson to William H. Pierson, March 26, 1865, in Thomas W. Cutrer and T. Michael Parrish, eds., *Brothers in Gray: The Civil War Letters of the Pierson Family* (Baton Rouge, 1997), 254–55.

42. Narratives of the war often treat Appomattox as the end. Indeed, scholars use "Appomattox" as a synonym for defeat. Many participants, however, saw Appomattox differently. Entries for April 7 (first quotation), April 11 (second quotation), and April 13, 1865, Samuel Pickens diary, in Hubbs, ed., *Voices from Company D*, 370–71.

43. Entries for April 19 (first quotation), April 24 (second quotation), April 22 (third, fourth, and fifth quotations), 1865, Samuel T. Foster diary, in Norman D. Brown, ed., *One of Cleburne's Command: The Civil War Reminiscences and Diary of Capt. Samuel T. Foster, Granbury's Texas Brigade, CSA* (Austin, Tex., 1980), 165–67.

44. Entries for May 7 (first and third quotations), May 13 (second quotation), May 11 (fourth and fifth quotations), 1865, William W. Heartsill diary, in Wiley, ed., *Fourteen Hundred and 91 Days in the Confederate Army*, 241–43; Jared Y. Sanders to Bessie Sanders, May 11, 1865, Jared Young Sanders Family Papers, LSU.

45. McPherson, *Battle Cry of Freedom*, 732–34, 741–42; Shelby Foote, *The Civil War. A Narrative.* Vol. III: *Red River to Appomattox* (New York, 1974), 295. According to psychologist Ralph L. Rosnow, four elements encourage the creation and diffusion of rumors: the credulity of the report, its importance or relevance, the uncertainty of the times, and personal anxiety. Confederate gossip contained all four ingredients. See Rosnow, "Rumor as Communication: A Contextualist Approach," *Journal of Communication*, 38 (Winter 1988), 19–20.

46. Phillip Shaw Paludan, *"A People's Contest": The Union and Civil War, 1861–1865* (New York, 1988), 246.

47. Hugh W. Montgomery to Arthur W. Hyatt, May 25, 1864, Hyatt Papers. Even southern ministers commented on the poor state of northern finances. See Stephen Elliott, *Gideon's Water-Lappers…* (Macon, Ga., 1864), 9.

48. Entry for May 6, 1864, John Walters diary, in Wiley, ed., *Norfolk Blues*, 113–14.

49. Ibid., (first, second, and third quotations); Rosnow, "Rumor as Communication," 20 (fourth quotation). Vernon Scannell, a British soldier in World War II, offered

a fine comparison in his memoirs when he discussed the rumors that flourished in camp while his unit waited to begin the Normandy invasion. According to Scannell, rumors flourished in an environment replete with "boredom, cold, exhaustion, squalor, lack of privacy, monotony, ugliness and a constant teasing anxiety about the future." Quoted in Paul Fussell, *Wartime: Understanding and Behavior in the Second World War* (New York, 1989), 41. Also see Tamotsu Shibutani, *Improvised News: A Sociological Study of Rumor* (Indianapolis, 1966), 39; Eric J. Leed, *No Man's Land: Combat and Identity in World War I* (Cambridge, Eng., 1979), 128; and Allport and Postman, *Psychology of Rumor*, 7–8, 31, 34. A similar scene opens Stephen Crane's *The Red Badge of Courage: An Episode of the American Civil War* (New York, 1895).

50. Paul Higginbotham to Aaron Higginbotham, August 1, 1864, Higginbotham Papers; Shibutani, *Improvised News*, 17. For more on distance and rumors in wartime, see Fussell, *Wartime*, 38; and Allport and Postman, *Psychology of Rumor*, 184. Social historians have stressed the significance of environment in shaping rumor mills and oral cultures. Life within the domestic sphere, the slave quarters, and Parisian neighborhoods shaped women's gossip, talk of slave conspiracies, and rumors of revolution, respectively. See the sources in footnote 8 for more on these examples.

51. Entry for May 5, 1864, William Heartsill diary, in Wiley, ed., *Fourteen Hundred and 91 Days in the Confederate Army*, 202–3; Hugh Montgomery to Arthur Hyatt, October 14, 1864, Hyatt Papers (quotations). Of course, soldiers who suffered most from the effects of distance and a confined world were not prison guards but prisoners themselves. For examples of how rumors affected prisoners' perceptions of the war, see Ruth Woods Dayton, ed., *The Diary of a Confederate Soldier: James E. Hall* ([Lewisburg, W.Va.?], 1961).

52. Brayton Harris, *Blue and Gray in Black and White: Newspapers in the Civil War* (Washington, D.C., 1999), x. Future research needs to examine the link between rebel rumors and Confederate newspapers more fully.

53. Ford Risley, "The Confederate Press Association: Cooperative News Reporting of the War," *Civil War History*, 47 (September 2001), 225 (first quotation), 229 (second quotation), 230 (third quotation); James R, Arnold, *Grant Wins the War: Decision at Vicksburg* (New York, 1997), 256–57.

54. Risley, "Confederate Press Association," 234 (first quotation), 235 (second and third quotations).

55. McPherson, *Battle Cry of Freedom*, 808; Risley, "Confederate Press Association," 235.

56. Spencer Welch to Cordelia Strother Welch, October 12, 1864, in Welch, *Confederate Surgeon's letters to His Wife*, 108 (first and second quotations); John McLure to his wife, October 12, 1864, McLure Family Papers, SCL (third quotation); David Crawford to his mother, October 23, 1864, Crawford Family Papers, SCL (fourth and fifth quotations).

57. Kurt O. Berends, "'Wholesome Reading Purifies and Elevates the Man': The Religious Military Press in the Confederacy," in Randall M. Miller, Harry S. Stout, and Charles Reagan Wilson, eds., *Religion and the American Civil War* (New York, 1998), 131 (first quotation), 149 (second, third, fourth, and fifth quotations), 148 (sixth, seventh, eighth, and ninth quotations). Berends's explanation for positive reporting in the so-called Religious Military Press (RMP) is similar to the argument of this essay: "Since the Confederacy lost, the optimism and bravado may seem misplaced as if editors had held onto a cause long lost. This interpretation has driven some historians, but it is mistaken; for the writers of the RMP, such optimism was the logical conclusion to their whole message." See ibid., 131–32.

58. Davis's May 2, 1864, address quoted in Lynda Lasswell Crist, Kenneth H. Williams, and Peggy L. Dillard, eds., *The Papers of Jefferson Davis*. Vol. X: *October 1863-August 1864* (Baton Rouge, 1999), 381 (first quotation); Davis's November 7, 1864, address quoted in Foote, *Civil War*, III, 624 (second, third, and fourth quotations).

59. James W. Silver, *Confederate Morale and Church Propaganda* (Tuscaloosa, Ala., 1957), 90; Elliott, *Gideon's Water-Lappers*, 9 (quotation).

60. Leon Festinger, *A Theory of Cognitive Dissonance* (Evanston, Ill., 1957), 198; Thomas S. Kuhn, *The Structure of Scientific Revolutions* (Chicago, 1962). For criticism of Festinger's theory, see Peter A. Lienhardt, "The Interpretation of Rumour," in J.H.M. Beattie and R.G. Lienhardt, eds,. *Studies in Social Anthropology: Essays in Memory of E. E. Evans-Pritchard by His Former Oxford Colleagues* (Oxford, Eng., 1975), 105–31.

61. Grant Taylor to Malinda Taylor and children, December 29, 1864, in Blomquist and Taylor, eds., *This Cruel War*, 319 (first quotation); Paul M. Higginbotham to Aaron Higginbotham, Higginbotham Papers (second quotation); Henry G. Orr to his father, July 10, 1864, in Anderson, ed., *Campaigning with Parsons' Texas Cavalry Brigade*, 143 (third quotation); Edwin Fay to Sarah Shields Fay, August 22, 1864, in Wiley, ed., *"This Infernal War,"* 402 (fourth quotation); Lafayette Orr to his brothers, April 30, 1864, in Anderson, ed., *Campaigning with Parsons' Texas Cavalry Brigade*, 136 (fifth quotation); Thomas Hampton to Jestin Hampton, December 18, 1864, Thomas B. Hampton Letters (University of Texas Center for American History, Austin) (sixth quotation); Charles Blackford to Susan Leigh Blackford, July 17, 1864, in Blackford, Blackford, and Blackford, eds., *Letters from Lee's Army*, 267 (seventh quotation).

62. Hugh Montgomery to Arthur Hyatt, October 14, 1864, Hyatt Papers.

63. Ralph L. Rosnow, "Psychology of Rumor Reconsidered," *Psychological Bulletin*, 87 (May 1980), 585.

64. Allport and Postman, *Psychology of Rumor*, viii. Future research that compares antebellum, wartime, and postwar rumors promises to link the Old South, Confederacy, and New South in new ways. Other promising comparisons are rumormongering among black and white southerners. Union and Confederate troops, the home front and battlefront, and different cultures fighting other wars.

65. Ayers, *In the Presence of Mine Enemies*, xix.

66. Charles Reagan Wilson, *Baptized in Blood: The Religion of the Lost Cause, 1865– 1920* (Athens, Ga., 1980); Gaines M. Foster, *Ghosts of the Confederacy: Defeat, the Lost Cause, and the Emergence of the New South, 1865 to 1913* (New York, 1987); W. Scott Poole, *Never Surrender: Confederate Memory and Conservatism in the South Carolina Upcountry* (Athens, Ga., 2004).

67. David W. Blight, *Race and Reunion: The Civil War in American Memory* (Cambridge, Mass., 2001); Anne Sarah Rubin, *A Shattered Nation: The Rise and Fall of the Confederacy, 1861–1868* (Chapel Hill, 2005).

68. Richard Tracy LaPiere and Paul R. Farnsworth, *Social Psychology* (New York, 1936), as quoted in Allport and Postman, *Psychology of Rumor*, 163. Rumors are stories passed from person to person during a specific period of time, and legends are stories spread from generation to generation within a particular culture. According to Allport and Postman, "In order to become legendary, a rumor must treat issues that are of importance to successive generations. Topics pertaining to national origins and honor are such," ibid., 163, Historians have often called the Lost Cause a *myth*. It is not my intention to be pedantic about word choice, but legend may be a more accurate and useful term. Myths are stories with universal themes; they explain creation, nature, and the afterlife. Legends are not cosmic.

Viewing the Lost Cause as a national legend opens new avenues of comparison. For instance, how does the Lost Cause compare in content and purpose to the accounts of King Arthur and Joan of Arc and to Sir Walter Scott's tales? Interestingly, Allport and Postman dismissed scholarship bent on debunking national legends. They wrote, "[N]o one, unless perhaps an occasional historian, extracts the kernel of truth [about legends], and no one seems to want to do so." They argued that "the poetic soul" prefers the story for its symbolism, Ibid., 165. The Lost Cause proves that some legends are not harmless stories.

10

"They are Ancestral Homelands": Race, Place, and Politics in Cold War Native America, 1945–1961

Paul C. Rosier

A nation is a soul, a spiritual principle. Two things, which in truth are but one, constitute this soul or spiritual principle. One lies in the past, one in the present. One is the posses-sion in common of a rich legacy of memories; the other is present-day consent, the desire to live together, the will to perpetuate the value of the heritage that one has received in an undivided form....A nation is therefore a large-scale solidarity, constituted by the feeling of the sacrifices that one has made in the past and of those that one is prepared to make in the future.

—*Ernest Renan, "What is a Nation," 1882*

Our land is everything to us. It is the only place in the world where Cheyennes talk the Cheyenne language to each other. It is the only place in the world where Cheyennes remem-ber the same things together. I will tell you one of the things we remember on our land. We remember our grandfathers paid for it—with their life.

—*John Woodenlegs, "Speech to the Association on American Indian Affairs," 1960*

The authors of "The International Reason" section of the October 1947 report of the President's Committee on Civil Rights noted that in the U.S. gov-ernment's battle for hearts and minds worldwide, "our domestic civil rights shortcomings are a serious obstacle.... Those with competing philosophies

From *The Journal of American History* 92 (March 2006) 1300–26. Copyright © Organization of American Historians. All rights reserved. Reprinted with permission.

have stressed and are shamelessly distorting our shortcomings. They have not only tried to create hostility toward us among specific nations, races and religious groups. They have tried to prove our democracy an empty fraud, and our nation a consistent oppressor of underprivileged people." As the historian Thomas Borstelmann has argued, "There was no greater weakness for the United States in waging the Cold War than inequality and discrimination." Indeed, the Soviet Union and its satellites offered a stream of criticism of American race relations into the 1960s and beyond. For example, a Moscow radio broadcast of February 1958 declared that American Indians, "the most underprivileged people in the United States," were forced to live on reservations that the Soviet commentator called "huge concentration camps.... Today, gradual extinction is the fate of the people in these reservations." Ironically, Soviet propagandists had much in common with U.S. officials, as they too called Indian reservations "concentration camps." But the Soviets misread U.S. officials' efforts to contain ethnic difference when they charged that the U.S. government imprisoned Native Americans on reservations against their will.[1]

During the termination era (broadly, 1944–1970), federal officials attempted to dismantle the reservation system and relocate Native Americans in "mainstream" American society. While officials' motives ranged from the criminal to the well-meaning—to strip Indians of valuable tribal property in the American West, to eliminate expensive federal programs, to end guardianship restrictions on liquor and firearms purchases, to further long-standing assimilation policies, and to adjudicate hundreds of land claims—the termination agenda serves as an example of the Cold War imperative of ethnic "integration." The discourse of termination was that of the Cold War—the avowed goal was to "liberate" the enslaved peoples of the world, who, according to American cold warriors, included Indians "confined" in concentration camps or "socialistic environments." The influential terminationist Sen. Arthur Watkins, a Republican from Utah, championed his "Indian freedom program" with an emphatic call for liberating Native Americans from their reservation prisons: "Following in the footsteps of the Emancipation Proclamation of ninety-four years ago, I see the following words embellished in letters of fire above the heads of the Indians—THESE PEOPLE SHALL BE FREE." In 1953 House Concurrent Resolution 108 codified Congress's intent to terminate "Federal supervision and control" of Indian affairs by making American Indians "subject to the same laws and entitled to the same privileges and responsibilities" as other American citizens. Federal officials subsequently attempted to terminate treaty-based federal Indian policies through legislation that unilaterally stripped individual tribes of their sovereignty, without Native Americans' consent.[2]

Recent scholarship on the intersection of race and the Cold War has studied the efforts of federal officials to ameliorate the troublesome image of American race relations that emerged internationally in the late 1940s and beyond. The scholarship has ignored Native Americans' experiences, experiences that can broaden our understanding of how domestic and international

Cold War politics evolved. While U.S. officials paid less attention to Native American issues than to African American ones, the "Indian problem" remained, as the Soviet Union reminded the world, a site of Cold War concern and competition. Mary L. Dudziak has argued that in the government's approach to mediating race relations, "the Cold War was simultaneously an agent of repression and an agent of change." In the United States, anticommunism proved a weapon of domestic "containment": African American civil rights activists, labor organizers, feminists, and others were attacked in the name of Cold War conformity. We need to add Native Americans to that list. But we also need to add them to the list of groups that used the Cold War as a vehicle for change. Reacting against a Cold War consensus that made difference un-American, college students, both black and white, women, and civil rights activists sharpened their identities. So did Native Americans.[3]

The termination movement in Congress slowed and eventually ended because it politicized Native Americans, who mobilized across tribal lines to protest termination legislation through the press and in the Congress and thus to contest what the French literary theorist Michel Foucault called "procedures of exclusion in discourse." Native American activists succeeded in blunting a well-organized campaign to divest them of sovereignty and land in part by using their own Cold War claim to an indigenous patriotism that married loyalty to the United States to Third World ethnic nationalism, challenging both American and Soviet propaganda by affirming the sacredness of the reservation. This essay examines Native Americans' engagement with the discourse and the moral and material dimensions of the Cold War, from the end of World War II to the June 1961 American Indian Chicago Conference (AICC), which helped inspire the "red power" activism that followed in the 1960s. Exploring the conflicting views of the reservation as either concentration camp or sacred space essential to Indian identity and self-determination, I contend that termination and the Cold War context fostered an international perspective among Native American activists, who drew on postwar decolonization movements and Cold War nation building and connected them to domestic concerns over treaty rights and, as Penny M. Von Eschen framed it, to "definitions of democracy, freedom, and the very meaning of American citizenship and what it entailed."[4]

Native American internationalism surfaced before World War II when activists appropriated Wilsonian language to demand their rights in a post–World War I world. The Lakota writer Gertrude Bonin (Zitkala Sa) proclaimed that "the eyes of the world are upon" the Paris peace conference, and as a result "little peoples are to be granted the right of self-determination!" Addressing the Senate Committee on Indian Affairs in 1919, the Crow politician Robert Yellowtail asserted his people's sovereignty because Woodrow Wilson had "assured...the people of the whole world, that the right of self-determination shall not be denied to any people." Post–World War II Native American internationalist perspectives differed from the post–World War I perspectives in their context, largely because the United States engaged the world differently after World War II than it had after

World War I, offering both rhetorical leadership and aid programs to further its influence.[5]

This is a story whose context is international history. An examination of Native Americans' conflation of domestic and international contexts, of local and global concerns, shows a dynamic interaction between the Cold War and decolonization that extended beyond the realm of discourse. In considering where the Cold War took place, how Native Americans made it relevant to their lives, what institutions they used to mediate its pressures, and how it shape their national and ethnic identities and thus their conceptions of patriotism and nationalism, the essay seeks to raise new questions about how struggles over material resources such as land helped define the politics of the Cold War and of decolonization.

The moral and material dimensions of the Cold War influenced both Native Americans' rhetorical strategies of resistance to termination legislation and their understanding of Marshall Plan aid for Europe and Point Four aid for "underdeveloped countries," the programmatic cornerstones of American nation building in a bipolar world, as models for reforming federal Indian policies at home. Perhaps inspired by his efforts to secure funding for the rehabilitation of Navajo and Hopi lands, President Harry S. Truman outlined an American "program for peace and freedom" during his January 1949 inaugural address; the fourth "point" called for "making the benefits of our scientific advances and industrial progress available for the improvement and growth of underdeveloped areas." A Marshall Plan–type aid package for non-European countries, the Point Four program sought to secure allies in Latin America, the Middle East, Asia, and Africa. For Native Americans, the Marshall Plan and the Point Four program became key phrases in their articulation of an internationalist perspective. And as decolonization emerged as a powerful movement, questions of race and racism became more visceral and visible. Native American activists became convinced, as Marc Gallicchio wrote about African American internationalists, "that color (or race) determined world politics." The Cold War experiences of African Americans and Native Americans mirrored each other in additional ways, including activists' responses to domestic anticommunist pressures and U.S. officials' efforts to address international criticism of American racism. But Native Americans viewed the Cold War within a different environmental, legal, and social context than African Americans did, a context shaped by the intersection of Cold War–driven termination policies and the legal legacy of America's colonial past, the national body of treaties that the Crow politician Robert Yellowtail called the "sacred covenants" of American history.[6]

For Native Americans the Cold War started on the reservation, in their own underdeveloped countries. D'Arcy McNickle, an official of Cree heritage in the Bureau of Indian Affiars (BIA) of the Interior Department and a founding member of the National Congress of American Indians (NCAI), the nation's most prominent pan-tribal organization, maintained throughout the 1950s that the solution to the "Indian problem" was not termination, but reservation development along the lines of the Point Four program. He argued that Point Four funding would invest Native Americans with the responsibility to administer development aid, rather than relegate them to being the objects of BIA programs designed and implemented by non-Indians. In 1957 the Senate debated the merits of Senate Concurrent Resolution 3 (SCR3), "An American Indian Point Four Program," drafted by the Association on American Indian Affairs, a group of predominantly non-Indian reformers based in New York City. The BIA and the Department of the Interior, the federal agencies that would have been most affected, refused to support the program, contending that it was redundant and unworkable. SCR3 died a quick death, largely because federal officials did not want to view Native American communities as nations. But the publicity generated by debates over SCR3 and McNickle's arguments for the program trickled down to the reservation level and furthered Indian nationalism, helping inspire leaders of the Apache, Colville, Northern Cheyenne, and other Indian nations to reimagine their homelands as among the world's "underdeveloped areas" and to ask the federal government to recognize them as such by extending to their people Marshall Plan or Point Four funding. By the end of the 1950s, a broad spectrum of Native American activists embraced a Cold War conception of civil rights that was based on treaties as instruments of sovereignty and thus nationhood. As the nations of "colored peoples" expanded in the 1960s, that conception made the maintenance of the national space of the reservation a symbol of a struggle for international human rights.[7]

The Ideological Roots of Termination

Although the first formal use of the term "reservation" appears in the 1825 Treaty of Prairie du Chien, negotiated with Indian nations of the upper Mississippi Valley, the commissioner of Indian affairs, Luke Lea, articulated the idea of a "reservation system" in 1850, shortly after the gold rush generated enthusiasm among Americans and Europeans for traversing Native Americans' mother earth on their way to finding the mother lode. Discussing what he called "our northern colony of Indians" (those of the northern Plains), Lea argued that "efforts should therefore be made to concentrate them within proper limits." The following year Lea announced that concentration should lead to Native Americans' "ultimate incorporation into the great body of our citizen population." Even though subsequent treaties "reserved" to Native Americans a fixed territory, white Americans viewed reservations ideologically, as a training camp for Indians' integration into the American body politic. Thus the reservation, a physical space demarcating indigenous Americans' newly circumscribed homelands, instantly became, for white Americans, *foreign* cultural space to be conquered through assimilative programs.[8]

The image of the reservation as a civilizing tool degenerated with the emergence of scientific racism, attacks on the "socialistic" and "communistic" nature of tribalism, and Native American resistance. American policy makers had always denied legitimacy to Indian land tenure because it involved communal ownership, and they had used force to convert Indians into Americans living in accord with the white political–economic imperative of laissez-faire capitalism. But the employment of anticommunist ideology to justify coercive programs became more common in the 1870s and beyond. The Paris Commune in particular fueled white Americans' conflation of Red Indians and Communist Reds. Less than a month after the commune met its violent end on May 28, 1871, the *New York World* termed Indian resistance in Texas "the Red Spectre." Contesting the label of "communism" to preserve their political sovereignty and cultural space, Cherokee politicians complained to Congress in 1880 that "the statements made to you that we, or any of the Indians, are communists...are entirely erroneous. No people are more jealous of the personal right to property than Indians." The commissioner of Indian affairs, J.D.C. Atkins, conceding that Indian resistance was "patriotic and noble," asked a fundamental question that is at the heart of modern Indian-white relations: "Is it not asking too much of the American people to permit a political paradox to exist within their midst...simply to gratify this sentimentality about a separate nationality?" In the 1880s an expanding America was not ready to embrace the political paradox of "domestic dependent nations," the term Supreme Court Justice John Marshall had employed in trying, unsuccessfully, to defend Cherokee nationalism during the removal crisis of the 1830s. Thomas Morgan, Atkins's successor, found nothing noble or patriotic in Indian nationalism, arguing in his 1889 annual report that "tribal relations should be broken up, socialism destroyed, and the family and the autonomy of the individual substituted." The discourse of "Americanization" reflected Morgan's notion that American individualism would have to replace Indian "socialism," even if the transformation required antidemocratic state intervention in the form of the federal allotment policy, which legislated the division of tribal estates into small homestead plots of 160 acres, whether Indian families wanted them or not.[9]

Native Americans' service in World War I and the first Red Scare reinforced such visceral opposition to the reservation. Shortly after the war, which had accelerated the spread of Americanization campaigns throughout the country, Rep. Melville C. Kelly of Pennsylvania attacked the reservation as "a prison pen where human beings are doomed to live amid sad memories of their ancestors and among the ghosts of the dead." Ignoring Native American religious traditions that derived from a relationship with land and ancestors, Kelly's argument both captured politicians' animus against the reservation system and reacted to new conceptions of Native American patriotism engendered by army service. Kelly and other policy makers interpreted such national service as evidence that all Native Americans considered the reservation anachronistic space.[10]

Attacks on the "communistic" nature of tribalism resurfaced in 1933, after Commissioner of Indian Affairs John Collier began promoting the

Indian New Deal, a series of initiatives related to the national New Deal and designed to ameliorate Native American poverty and strengthen tribal self-government. The Indian Reorganization Act (IRA) of 1934, the cornerstone of the Indian New Deal, not only rejected the policy and philosophy of allotment by providing federal funds to tribal governments for use in adding land to reservations but also encouraged those governments to expand sovereign powers over reservation boundaries and resources through regulations codified in tribal constitutions. Flora Warren Seymour, a lawyer and author, called the IRA "the most extreme gesture yet made by the administration in this country toward a Communistic experiment." Some Indian leaders echoed those anticommunist sentiments, forming the American Indian Federation (AIF) in 1934 to protest Collier's retribalization agenda. AIF cofounder Joseph Bruner, an Oklahoma Creek, argued that at its core was a "Russian Communistic" conception of life. Collier countered such arguments by maintaining that "white people all over the United States own land in partnerships and companies and corporations. It is not communism to allow Indians to do the same if they want to." But it was his 1939 attack on the AIF for its links to such pro-Nazi groups as the German-American Bund and Silver Shirts that prevented Congress from significantly altering or repealing the IRA; AIF member Alice Lee Jemison's later admission that the Bund paid her to incite resistance to the draft among Plains Indians further undermined the AIF's legitimacy.[11]

The Nazi regime engendered an image of the reservation more consonant with Commissioner Lea's policy of concentration. It is difficult to pinpoint the first use of the term "concentration camp" to describe a reservation, but it predated 1942, when American officials, including President Franklin D. Roosevelt, called the Japanese American detention centers concentration camps. And it was used before knowledge about the Nazi camps gave "concentration camp" its horrific connotation. In March 1940 an American politician had compared a reservation to a concentration camp. During a congressional hearing on a bill recommending "relief of needy Indians," Rep. John Schaefer of Wisconsin asked Blackfeet Nation politician Levi Burd whether the U.S. record on Indian affairs "more than parallels the atrocities and so-called concentration camps abroad." The historical record, Schaefer said, was that "the white man took the Indians' land, debauched their women, killed many of them, and herded the survivors in concentration camps which we now call Indian Reservations." Burd rejected the analogy since it painted Blackfeet as passive victims contained against their will, instead sounding a theme that would emerge in the postwar period: "If there are any people that are neglected, it is the Indians." To cite another example: in 1944 a congressional committee investigating Indian affairs explained that its goal was to "try to rehabilitate the Indians so they may be assimilated into the American way of life and not be in the reservation like a concentration camp; for, after all, a reservation is only a step or two from a concentration camp." The 1944 statement represented the reemergence of congressional critiques of the IRA, which became the foundation of the termination movement. After World War II, during an era of Cold War conformity, critics of federal Indian policy used the term concentration camp more openly to describe reservations as an oppressive space. Thus began a new stage in a long-running battle to deconstruct reservations as sites of ethnic difference.[12]

The Politics of Indian Space

Native Americans' participation in World War II campaigns at home and abroad fueled terminationists' calls for reform of Indian affairs. Native Americans volunteered for army service and purchased war bonds at rates equal to those of any other American ethnic group; roughly twenty-five thousand Native Americans, including eight hundred women, served in the armed forces. Sen. D. Worth Clark, an Idaho Democrat, remarked that Native Americans' wartime activities were "an inspiration to patriotic Americans everywhere." In addition to lives and labor, Native Americans contributed land for gunnery ranges, airfields, and camps to house Japanese Americans. The most iconic sacrifices came from Ira Hayes, one of the six Marines who hoisted the American flag on Iwo Jima in 1945, and the Navajo code talkers, who developed and used Navajo-language-based signal codes that the Japanese military never cracked. Even as Native Americans acted patriotically and heroically to defend the United States and their conception of Americanness, white commentators began calling for an end to federal Indian programs. As during World War I, non-Indians viewed Native Americans' efforts in the war as testimony to their interest in leaving the reservation and joining the American mainstream. Oswald Villard championed this position in the *Christian Century*, writing in 1944 that Native Americans "no more wish to stay at home and be confined within the reservations than did the children of the early communist settlement." Villard saw one future: eventually "the Indians themselves will tire of being considered circus exhibits, human museum pieces seeking to keep alive vestiges of a life that was picturesque." The following year, the *Reader's Digest* published O.K. Armstrong's article, "Set the American Indians Free!" Like Villard, Armstrong championed the liquidation of the Bureau of Indian Affairs, contending that the Indian New Deal forced "a collectivist system upon the Indians, with bigger doses of paternalism and regimentation," while reinforcing a policy of "racial segregation." Some Native Americans, veterans in particular, joined the attack on BIA paternalism. One Winnebago veteran told Armstrong, "When we Indian servicemen get back [from the war], we're going to see that our people are set free to live and act like American citizens." Perhaps he had read Villard's piece, as he noted to Armstrong, "We're tired of being treated like museum pieces."[13]

Villard's and Armstrong's attacks on the Indian New Deal were part of a larger anti–New Deal movement intent on cutting the federal government's bureaucracy, eliminating welfare programs, and facilitating

Americanization of the nation's diverse ethnic population. Their criticism and their promotion of a terminationist agenda fused the nineteenth-century language of the allotment era with the new language of World War II and of the emerging Cold War—anticommunism, individualism, emancipation, and liberation. Other critics used similar language to attack the idea of the reservation. Sen. George Malone of Nevada, for example, argued that the United States was "spending billions of dollars fighting Communism" while it was "perpetuating the systems of Indian reservations and tribal governments, which are natural Socialist environments." The reservation represented the literal and figurative ground for conflict between opposing conceptions of social space in Cold War America. The French philosopher Henri Lefebvre has written of "the conflicts at work within [space], conflicts which foster the explosion of abstract space and the production of a space that is *other*." In the discourse of the 1940s and 1950s, "reservation" became code for confining space, othered or racialized space, and even emasculated space. Thus Oswald Villard quoted an agency superintendent as saying, "Wardship and full manhood stature do not go together." But Malone, Villard, and other vocal anticommunists misrepresented a reservation reality: the increasingly hybrid nature of Native American political institutions and identities. To these critics, however, the reservation remained *Indian* and thus *foreign* space.[14]

The Politics of Indian Patriotism

Native Americans employed the rhetoric of World War II and the Cold War to contest the ideology of termination and to defend their institutions and identities, both American and Indian. Napoleon B. Johnson, president of the National Congress of American Indians, founded in 1944, claimed the mantle of patriotism in protesting postwar federal cuts in Native American education and health programs. Johnson, an Oklahoma supreme court justice and an enrolled Cherokee, told members of Congress in October 1947 that the "Indian people sent more than 30,000 of their boys and girls to the Colors in World War II to fight for our institutions and American way of life." Native Americans' service loomed large in postwar conversations about Indian-white relations and helped galvanize opposition to termination. Zuni veterans of World War II and the Korean War attacked termination policies by telling a congressional committee:

Gentlemen, this is supposed to be a land of freedom. We have fought side by side with other races of people whom we have looked upon as brothers to gain this freedom. We have fought for democracy and we would like to have you show us this democratic way of life.... We have served [overseas] in order to save our country, our people, our religion, our freedom of press and our freedom of speech from destruction.... We, now in the land of freedom as Americans are faced with [termination policies] which will mean total destruction of all tribes.

Johnson's linkage of "our institutions" with the "American way of life" and the Zuni veterans' suggestion that the "tribes" of America helped define the character of America reveal an important dimension of postwar Native American rhetorical defenses, a hybrid patriotism that embraced national service to strengthen both Native American identity and the "democratic way of life" that protected it: "our country" meant both the United States and the tribes; "our people" meant both the American people and the Indian people.[15]

Native Americans considered their collective sacrifices for the American nation as entitling them to basic privileges, not the least of them G.I. benefits and voting rights, hitherto denied in New Mexico and Arizona. In one important exposition of these views, Native Americans weighed in on the question of postwar race relations during an August 1947 debate aired on radio. Representatives of Navajo and Pueblo groups pointed out that injustice prevailed "so long as an Indian cannot vote for the government they must pay taxes to support and give their lives to defend." After the broadcast of "Are Indians Getting a Square Deal?" one Native American asked, in a statement reprinted in the *Washington Post:* "why do we propagate democracy abroad and suppress it at home? Why do we give millions in Europe while on an arid western desert in our own country 55,000 of our own people—though of different colored skins from those who conquered them—are slowly starving to death, because we have not kept faith with them?" Lilly J. Neil, the first woman elected to the Navajo tribal government, complained to a federal official a month later that "the government is making all these big loans to foreign countries, and bragging about what they are doing so fine and noble, for the countries who tried to ruin us....I doubt very much if there's a European or Asiatic country who are very much if any poorer than our own Navajo Indian tribe and none of them who need help any worse, and they owe their obligations to us North American Indians First."[16]

Those statements gave voice to a central critique made by Native Americans: Rather than fulfill promises made to people who shed blood for America and for the preservation of freedom around the world, the United States was instead bestowing on European nations, including former enemies, vast sums via the European Recovery Program, the Marshall Plan. Non-Indians also used the trope and the trauma of Native American poverty, especially Navajo poverty, to criticize the European focus of the Marshall Plan. A November 1947 *Los Angeles Examiner* article, part of a series called "The Citizens America Forgot," stated that "while the United States is sending billions for the relief of stricken Europe, Navajo Indians face slow starvation in the vast concentration camp of the desert." The *Examiner* article cut both ways, however, painting the Navajo as passive victims confined in a "concentration camp" against their will while capturing a difficult truth about their material conditions.[17]

Moving to head off criticism of the Marshall Plan, still under review by the Congress, the Truman administration asked Congress to provide emergency relief to the Navajo and the Hopi; Truman hoped that such aid "forecloses those who would criticize my foreign aid program on the ground that we are letting our First Americans starve." With Truman's support, Congress appropriated $500,000 in emergency relief in December 1947 and then in 1950 provided long-range funding of over $88 million in the Navajo–Hopi Rehabilitation Act, the equivalent of a Navajo–Hopi Marshall Plan. The House of Representatives fashioned the emergency relief bill in the middle of a debate on foreign aid, embedding the Navajo and Hopi question in the context of international assistance. It is important to note that Truman and the Congress first responded to the Navajo crisis in 1947, less than a month after the release of the report of the President's Committee on Civil Rights, which highlighted both the "moral" and the "international" reasons for addressing U.S. treatment of "underprivileged people." During the Cold War, American presidents and federal officials paid attention to how their resolution of domestic policies would play internationally. Emphasizing the impact of foreign criticism of federal Indian policy, Secretary of the Interior Julius Krug testified in favor of the Navajo–Hopi Rehabilitation Act in early 1949 by asserting that Congress's passage of the bill would "consequently strengthen this Nation's international prestige and moral position."[18]

The Navajo (and Hopi) alone benefited from this Cold War imperative; D'Arcy McNickle, a BIA official who championed Indian self-determination, later complained: "Possibly the other tribes did not get enough newspaper publicity; perhaps they were not near enough to starvation—though they might dispute this." In addition to stimulating federal efforts to foreclose criticism of the Marshall Plan and to improve race relations and thus America's image abroad, Navajo poverty generated aid from private charity groups, which saw the Navajo, by virtue of their wartime service, as especially deserving of their help. And the Navajo nation, given its large population and expansive lands, had the literal and figurative shape of a nation. The subcommittee of the House Committee on Indian Affairs that sanctioned the federal relief effort had noted that "this is a nation within our borders, recognized by treaty, that is actually in need of relief." Recent discoveries of uranium ore in the Colorado plateau of the four-corner area of Arizona, Colorado, New Mexico, and Utah may also have solidified federal commitments to relief, marking the Navajo reservation as an important Cold War site for material as well as moral reasons. The Navajo participated in the making of the atomic West by facilitating uranium mining, as the Navajo Tribal Council put it, "in the interest of the nation and the Navajo Reservation."[19]

The Containment of Termination

The Navajo reservation was only the first site of Cold War conflict over U.S. relations with Native Americans. As noted, the Soviet Union eagerly exploited Native Americans' deprivations, as it did African Americans'. As

Eleanor Roosevelt warned in her daily column in October 1949, "One of the Soviet attacks on the democracies, particularly in the United States, centers on racial policies. In recent months the Russians have been particularly watching our attitude toward native Indians of our country." In one such exposition, the May 14, 1949, edition of *Soviet Lithuania* called American Indian reservations "true camps of death." The article, entitled "'In the Country of the Yellow Devil': United States as It Really Is," also condemned the Marshall Plan and the exploitation of African Americans' labor.[20]

Soviet propagandists and American politicians shared the view that reservations were camps of slow cultural death. Soviet officials would have also approved of the coercive ways federal officials pushed for the termination of reservations. For example, the BIA's recommended means to "overcome obstacles" to termination of all federal Indian programs provided to the Blackfeet nation read in part: "Issue certificates of ownership to each individual for their proportionate share of tribal assets. Help to prepare necessary legislation. Insist that such legislation be mandatory and not subject to approval of local and state authorities or of Indian council and Tribes." This dictatorial approach alarmed the key architects of the Indian New Deal, in particular Felix Cohen, who had helped design IRA tribal constitutions in the late 1930s. Cohen argued in a 1949 article that "the Indian plays much the same role in our American society that the Jews played in Germany. Like the miner's canary, the Indian marks the shift from fresh air to poison gas in our political atmosphere; and our treatment of Indians, even more than our treatment of other minorities, reflects the rise and fall in our democratic faith." Cohen, influenced by his legal service to several Indian nations and his experience with anti-Semitism, expressed better and more frequently than other white critics both the dangers Native Americans faced from termination and the important place of Indian affairs in an international context of ethnic injustice.[21]

As termination pressures expanded in the early 1950s, the coercive federal policies that Cohen protested furthered nationalism among many Native American politicians, who used the language of the Cold War in their fight for civil rights. The Blackfeet, for example, confronted the BIA by contrasting its dictatorial actions with the Blackfeet's democratic aspirations. George Pambrun, the chairman of the Blackfeet Tribal Business Council, contended that the BIA used "methods of Communist dictatorship against our people.... Stalin could learn a lot about how to run a dictatorship just by watching the Indian Bureau." Walter Wetzel, Pambrun's successor, protested BIA manipulation of tribal elections by telling the secretary of the interior: "our knowledge of the principles of our Government, and our love of freedom is as great as that of any other citizen of the United States. We have proven our loyalty to the Government of the United States time and time again and we refuse to permit your employees to treat us so shamefully as to attempt to hold and run our elections for us."[22]

The strategic use of concepts of democracy, patriotism, and freedom to counter an antidemocratic and interventionist federal government became especially important for Native American politicians in early 1954 when Congress began to consider a spate of bills that proposed terminating individual Indian nations' sovereignty. In late February Native politicians traveled to Washington, D.C. to protest these termination bills at the Emergency Conference that the National Congress of American Indians organized to bring public scrutiny to the legislative blitz. When NCAI members and their attorneys entered the U.S. Capitol building to confront congressional terminationists, they passed Horatio Greenough's nineteenth-century statue (figure 10.1), which depicted a towering allegorical white figure representing civilized strength restraining a tomahawk-wielding Native American in a loincloth. Since 1945 the NCAI had complained that the statue presented an "inappropriate" image. The image it presented and its title, *The Rescue*, framed Native people as needing white intervention. The argument of terminationists followed similar lines—Native Americans needed whites to help them adopt a "civilized" and "free" mode of life, in this case through coercive termination legislation. Greenough, the sculptor of *The Rescue*, said he had wanted to show "the superiority of the white-man, and why and how civilization crowded the Indian from his soil." Members of Congress debated Indian policy in this nineteenth-century frame, perhaps influenced by Greenough's representation. In promoting termination, Sen. Arthur Watkins claimed that Congress "sought to return to the historic principles of much earlier decades." But the world, and Native Americans' engagement with it, had changed dramatically since the late nineteenth century. With the assistance of attorneys such as Felix Cohen and Norman Littell, who helped further Navajo nationalism, Native American politicians increasingly viewed themselves as leaders of nations, domestic and dependent, but nations nonetheless.[23]

Native American politicians were obligated both to defend the idea of the reservation and to attack the notion, carved in Greenough's statue, that Indianness was un-American and thus dangerous. In "A Declaration of Indian Rights," the NCAI's official response to the suite of proposed termination bills, NCAI president Joseph Garry, a Coeur d'Alene veteran of World War II and the Korean War, contested the prevailing argument that reservations were similar to concentration camps. Reflecting the hybrid patriotism dominant among 1950s Native activists, Garry argued that "some of *our fellow Americans* think that our reservations are places of confinement. Nothing could be farther from the truth. Reservations do not imprison us. They are ancestral homelands, retained by us for our perpetual use and enjoyment. We feel we must assert our right to maintain ownership in our own way, and to terminate it only by our consent." Such NCAI leaders as Garry skillfully used Cold War rhetoric in their defense of reservation "homelands," calling termination proposals "liquidation legislation" and "extermination bills." On the defensive, terminationists had to defuse not only Soviet propaganda critical of U.S Indian policy, but

Figure 10.1 Horatio Greenough's "The Rescue" (1837–1851) adorned the East Front entrance of the U.S. Capitol from 1853 to 1958, when the Capitol architect removed it for aesthetic reasons. Protests from Native American groups such as the National Congress of American Indians (NCAI) and some members of Congress, who objected to its image of Indian savagery, ensured that it would not return. Courtesy of The Honorable Alan M. Hantman, FAIA, Architect of the Capitol, U.S. Capitol, Washington, DC 20515. In storage.

comparisons with Soviet-style violence. Speaking at the NCAI Emergency Conference, the counsel for the House Committee on Interior and Insular Affairs "urged fairness," asking critics to describe termination proposals as "'terminal' legislation rather than 'liquidation legislation.'"[24]

Native American politicians also opposed termination bills by emphasizing that foreign nations paid attention to U.S. treatment of Native people. Attacking a piece of termination legislation in January 1954, the Council of the Isleta Pueblo noted: "We regret that we have to become aware of these [termination bills] when the eyes of the world are upon our nation, depending upon its integrity, its honor and its sense of intolerance [*sic:* tolerance?] and when we too seek friends among other peoples." In its Emergency Conference statement, "What Does Termination of Federal Trusteeship Mean to the Indian Peoples?", the NCAI echoed this internationalist perspective, asking the question at the heart of postwar Indian nationalism: "Shouldn't Indians have the same right of self-determination that our government has stated, often and officially, is the inalienable right of peoples in far parts of the world? Do we apply a different set of principles, of ethics, to the people within our own borders?" This perspective not only drew on bedrock notions of American foreign policy first expressed by Woodrow Wilson and Franklin Roosevelt and repeated in various guises as the Cold War evolved but also revealed an awareness of how people in other parts of the world evaluated the U.S. commitment to those ideals. Situating the struggle of Native Americans in the larger international struggle for the liberation of colonized peoples, the NCAI claimed the ideological and moral high ground.[25]

Negotiating Cold War Pressures

The 1954 Emergency Conference represented a turning point in the most visible and visceral phase of the battle against termination, the congressional effort to eliminate tribal sovereignty through legislation passed without the consent of the people involved. Assisted by the legal staff of the Association on American Indian Affairs, a white reform group, the NCAI used the Emergency Conference to mobilize Indian and non-Indian groups and to publicize the antidemocratic nature of Congress's termination agenda. Media coverage of the Emergency Conference was extensive. Jim Hayes of the American Friends Service Committee estimated that nearly four thousand newspapers, radio stations, and television stations covered the event. Hayes also cited a British Broadcasting Corporation (BBC) "analytical news broadcast." That coverage may also have found its way to European audiences that were inclined to support "the Indians" in their fight against coercive assimilation in part because of Europeans' fascination with American frontier history and traditional Indian culture.[26]

Embracing international sympathy proved problematic for the NCAI. In January 1958 Hilda Cragun, the NCAI office manager, notified Charles D. Skippon of the Department of State's Division of Security that when the

NCAI received correspondence "from individuals and organizations which we question," it hesitated to respond in order to "be sure we are not involving the organization [NCAI] in any questionable activity or corresponding with questionable organizations or individuals." Cragun forwarded a December 12, 1957, letter sent to the NCAI by a pan-German group called Interressengemeinschaft Deutschsprechender Indianerfreunde (advocacy group of German-speaking friends of the Indian), which listed members in Germany, Austria, Switzerland, and the Netherlands. Written in English, the letter noted Europeans' awareness of the "horrible wrong done to your people during centuries and we are ashamed of it....we learn that the wrong is continued today by the intention of the American Government to terminate the reservations.... Termination of the Reservations means, we understand, the extermination of your race, for when your lands are gone, your identity is lost, the Indian will be no more." In a similar letter to Congress, the group repeated this argument, adding the sentiment: "We know that the Indians, living in one of the richest countries of the world with the highest standard of life, are a neglected minority, the worst fed, the worst housed, the poorest of all Americans, as poverty stricken as the poor of Asia and Africa." The Russians could not have said it better. Reflecting the NCAI's sensitivity to the Cold War propaganda battle, Cragun told Skippon, "We are merely concerned that there may be a group of individuals in Frankfurt/Main who could *further* hurt the U.S. internationally by stirring up the 'Indian question.' We felt this should be brought to the attention of 'responsible authorities.'" In closing Cragun wrote, "Best wishes to you, Miriam, and the girls. Hope we can get together soon." This personal tone underscored the extent of their relationship.[27]

Three years after the NCAI had stirred up the Indian question with the February 1954 Emergency Conference, the NCAI was informing on groups supportive of Native American rights to the Department of State. Cragun's correspondence was not an isolated case. NCAI executive director Helen Peterson, a Cheyenne who had grown up with Oglala Sioux on the Pine Ridge Reservation, had a month earlier rebuffed an effort by the editor of *Facts for Farmers* to secure a report on the 1957 NCAI annual convention because the journal, sponsored by Farm Research, had been listed in the "Guide to Subversive Organizations and Publications" published by the House Committee on Un-American Activities (HUAC). The editor of *Facts for Farmers*, Charles Coe, had expressed interest in "the efforts made by the Indians and their friends to protect their rights." Peterson explained to Coe that "since our membership is justly very proud of its record of loyalty and our Constitution is specific in its emphasis on this aspect of our policy and operation," the NCAI was "unable and unwilling" to provide materials; she asked him to remove the NCAI from its lists. What is especially interesting, other than that the NCAI could not abide the populist, pro-small farmer rhetoric of *Facts for Farmers*, is that Peterson sent copies of the correspondence to HUAC, the National Republic, the American Legion, and Veterans of Foreign Wars. The same day, Peterson wrote Letitia Shankle of

Tulsa, Oklahoma, to reassure her that the NCAI did not get funds from the Robert Marshall Foundation, which was listed in the "Guide to Subversive Organizations and Publications," but from the Robert Marshall Civil Liberties Trust Fund, which was not. Peterson explained to Shankle, "We have always been scrupulously careful...in trying to avoid involvement with questionable groups or persons," noting that NCAI leaders routinely checked the "Guide to Subversive Organizations and Publications" as well as consulted with "three *other* groups in Washington which make it their business to keep track of un-American organizations and publications."[28]

By 1957, then, the NCAI made it its business to "keep track of un-American organizations and publications." The NCAI's association with hyperpatriotic groups, its apparently regular contact with the Department of State and HUAC, and its rejection of international critiques of federal policy that were similar to its own speaks to its moderate nature and to the *modus vivendi* with terminationist-minded federal officials that had resulted from its aggressive stand at the 1954 Emergency Conference. The NCAI leadership also took this tack to preserve its autonomy and to avoid being labeled a "subversive organization" and thus made vulnerable to federal harassment from HUAC and loss of support from both moderate Native Americans and concerned whites such as Letitia Shankle. Like their counterparts in the National Association for the Advancement of Colored People (NAACP), such NCAI leaders as Peterson as well as other Native American activists had to negotiate with institutions waging the Cold War such as the State Department and HUAC to preserve political efficacy. The NCAI remained active in fighting for Native sovereignty, but in ways circumscribed by Cold War pressures.[29]

Cold War pressures also required tribal politicians to negotiate with local institutions of power. As the termination movement gathered steam in the late 1940s, the Colville Business Council, representing the Colville of Washington State, had voted to send delegations to both the NCAI and the U.S. Congress after deciding that Native Americans "would have to enter [national] politics." Using Cold War rhetoric, local politicians and mining companies attacked the council's efforts to expand reservation sovereignty throughout the 1950s. So too did off-reservation Colvilles, who championed the terminationist agenda of dividing reservation assets on a pro rata basis. Lucy Seymour Swan, one of the most vocal opponents of reservation sovereignty, complained to the secretary of the interior in "hopes of breaking down this communistic situation." Stella Leach criticized the Colville tribe's membership in the NCAI, calling it "an organization definitely on the 'pink side.'" Colville opponents of expanded tribal sovereignty eventually formed the Colville Indian Association (CIA) and the Colville Indian Commercial Club (CICC) to protest the Colville Business Council's agenda, in particular its efforts to restore to the reservation Colville land taken in the allotment era, thus expanding the boundaries of the reservation. The CICC used the rhetorical cudgel of anticommunism in claiming that the council's proposed land-restoration legislation "would relegate the Colville

Tribe to a communist type of regimentation." And in an editorial entitled "Behind the Buckskin Curtain," President Frank Moore of the CIA contended that "the sovereign government under which Indians are forced to live does not differ from that of Russia and its satellite countries. Can we afford to fight against this form of dictatorship in foreign countries while allowing them to develop among Americans at home?" The sentiments may remind us of those of the Indian leaders George Pambrun and Joseph Garry, cited earlier. But Moore's goal was radically different from Pambrun's and Garry's—to liquidate rather than to strengthen tribal government and its control of reservation resources. Elected Colville politicians were forced to defend their actions using the language of patriotism and democracy. Frank George, an NCAI vice president and a Colville Business Council adviser, maintained that the NCAI "was not associated with any subversive groups and all its members were good Americans." George warned Colville politicians to be wary of the "ideologies" of "emancipation" and "termination." "The fact that people were not all alike in their views was the strength of our way of life," he told the council. The council's efforts to preserve the Colville reservation came at a time when "the national government was involved in a global war," as the Colville councilman Pete Gunn put it. As "loyal citizens," Gunn declared, the Colville "would help their country." In doing so, they situated patriotism within the boundaries of reservations as much as outside them, in effect erasing those boundaries.[30]

The CICC had argued that "liquidation would be the American way," by which it meant that the American end of converting assets into cash—in this case converting reservation resources into pro rata payments—justified the means used to accomplish it, even the "communistic" means of political liquidation. Non-Indians' and some Indians' efforts to force the liquidation of tribal corporate assets in the name of American values represent an example of a central contradiction of American Cold War behavior: the use of undemocratic means to further an "American" end. This campaign resonated with the federal government's late-nineteenth-century campaign to "mandate," as Alexandra Harmon argued in her study of allotment, "a measure unimaginable in U.S. society—the wholesale redistribution of property."[31]

Relocation and Resistance

By 1957 the NCAI, with the help of non-Indian groups such as the Association on American Indian Affairs, had succeeded in halting the wholesale legislative termination of reservation sovereignty. Between 1945 and 1960, about 12,000 Native Americans experienced termination, and 1,365,801 acres, about 3 percent of the Native American land base, were withdrawn from government supervision. But federal lawmakers continued to attack the integrity of Indian homelands by various means. During the same period, 1945–1960, over 30,000 Native Americans, roughly 10 percent of reservations' total population, moved to American cities via

the federal Voluntary Relocation Program, which replaced coercive legislative measures as the most effective (and purportedly "voluntary") means to
integrate "the Indian" into American society.[32]

The federal government also displaced Native communities in the name
of progress and national defense, a process begun during World War II.
Major public works, often put forth as defense measures, threatened Indian
land. The building of dams, the most notable being the Kinzua Dam in
Pennsylvania, displaced thousands of Native Americans. Opponents of
the Kinzua Dam—including a coalition of Native American groups, the
American Friends Service Committee, and prominent citizens such as
Eleanor Roosevelt—fought hard to prevent construction, which resulted in
the forced removal of seven hundred Seneca in northwestern Pennsylvania
and southwestern New York. Dam proponents justified the ostensible flood-
control project in the name of national security. A Pennsylvania congress-
man argued in 1958 that "Pittsburgh's safety from floods is one of America's
best guarantees for the survival of our democracy, for the Pittsburgh area
is one of the greatest of our arsenals of defense." A Pittsburgh businessman
claimed that the government's failure to build the dam would imperil "the
tomahawks of defense." The reference to floods was misleading. Pittsburgh
industrial interests and their congressional sponsors wanted more water,
not less; they sought the dam to facilitate expanded river traffic in the
Ohio Valley and to flush the pollutants that had become more noticeable
in Pittsburgh's rivers during the 1950s defense buildup. But they had to use
Cold War rhetoric to justify the project because engineers had developed an
alternative to removing the Seneca from their homeland, a move that abro-
gated the oldest U.S. treaty still in force, the Pickering Treaty of 1794. The
construction of the St. Lawrence Seaway in New York State also affected
the land base of the Akwesasne Mohawk and the Tuscarora. The Tuscarora
faced a traumatic relocation in 1960 after the U.S. Supreme Court rejected
their protest against state power projects that took 550 valuable acres from
their reservation.[33]

The ability of white Americans in the 1950s to pack up and relocate to
well-paying jobs and literally new communities such as the Levittowns helps
explain, especially given the conformist atmosphere of Cold War America,
why the reservation remained a symbol of confinement. In the 1950s, as in
the 1830s and the 1880s, American politicians refused to consider Native
Americans' conceptions of nation and of homeland or simply equated them
with "communistic" forms of social organization and land ownership.
They also ignored the powerful dynamic of racism, which contributed to
the failure of the Voluntary Relocation Program. Both racism and cultural
disjunction made white politicians indifferent to Native land issues. In his
dissent from the 1960 Supreme Court decision on Tuscarora land, Hugo
Black opined: "It may be hard for us to understand why these Indians cling
so tenaciously to their lands and traditional way of life.... But this is their
home—their ancestral home. There, they, their children and their forebears
were born. They, too, have their memories and their loves. Some things are

worth more than money and the costs of a new enterprise." Black ended with a sentiment that fit well with the propaganda, but not the practice, of the period: "Great nations like great men, should keep their word."[34]

In the late 1950s and beyond, Native American politicians seized on the principle that the United States should keep its word by honoring its treaties, at times defining that struggle for treaty rights as a cold war. Chippewa leaders, for example, declared in 1959 that "a state of cold war exists between the Bad River Band of Chippewa Indians and the officials of the Wisconsin Department of Conservation, and that such state shall exist until such time as the State of Wisconsin shall recognize Federal treaties and statutes affording immunity to the members of this Band from State control over hunting and fishing within the boundaries of this reservation." Clarence Wesley, a prominent activist from the San Carlos Apache community and an emerging voice in the NCAI, argued in a 1957 issue of *AmerIndian* that "real Indian issues are not generally understood by the average citizen, even by some public officials. These issues are not assimilation, integration, emancipation, or government control over the Indian person. Or even civil rights in the usual sense. The real issues are the continuing ownership of land." Wesley contended, as activists would emphasize in the 1960s, that honoring Native American civil rights involved "the protection of rights solemnly promised by treaty and law." That definition meant preserving the reservation as a legally reserved space and restoring the privileges to use resources provided in federal treaties, as the Chippewa demanded. Wesley situated this historical claim in the contemporary frame of Cold War rhetoric and nation building when he called on the federal government to offer both "an end to bureaucratic dictatorship" and "the same kind of [economic aid] program that is carried on in underdeveloped countries."[35]

Speaking for Themselves

The ideas of Native American internationalism spread by Wesley and other leaders found expression in other forums, in particular the June 1961 American Indian Chicago Conference (AICC), a seminal event that produced the Declaration of Indian Purpose, a pan-tribal statement that outlined activists' goals for the new frontier in Indian-white relations. Several months before the conference, AICC planners had distributed a draft of the proposed declaration to Native Americans around the country, asking them what they would like to see in the final statement. The conference organizer Sol Tax, an anthropologist from the University of Chicago, explained in the accompanying letter that the chance to respond to this draft represented "a rare opportunity for Indians to speak for themselves, instead of having somebody else speak for them." The responses from regional preparatory meetings reflected the diverse nature of Native America in 1961. Some embraced assimilation, rejecting what one respondent called Indians' "antiquated superannuated way of life," whereas others considered the struggle against termination a battle for Indian survival. The perspectives, while heterogeneous, articulated an Indian nationalism that conflated domestic and international contexts, demonstrating Native Americans' widespread engagement with the rhetoric of the Cold War, of decolonization, and of "the War of 1954," as a Montana writer referred to the 1954 blitz of congressional termination legislation.[36]

Many of the responses defending Indian identity drew on the rhetorical arsenal of freedom and democracy that termination opponents had employed during "the War of 1954." An activist from White Swan, Washington, protested the forced citizenship of American Indians by writing that only "a dictator nation may be able to declare an individual of another power a citizen of that government," a process he compared to the United States making "a RUSSIAN a citizen of this government." After attending a regional meeting in Haverford, Pennsylvania, Red Deer, a Mohawk–Cherokee, echoed this spirit of independence, asking that the proposed declaration "safeguard [against] the loss of our lands in what is a de facto occupation of our country." He suggested a broad public relations effort to strengthen the reservation land base. Richard Bounding Elk, from Maine's Penobscot community, supported the development of reservation lands, arguing that the government should create an "American Indian Recovery Program...a sort of Marshall Plan for Indians." Bounding Elk asked, "Why give [foreign aid] away to the world—give it away here." A respondent from Bellflower, California, reflected this nationalist theme and the belief in a program modeled on the Marshall Plan as both a panacea for Native American problems and an ethical obligation of the federal government. "We can't help but wish that the United States would treat us as well as they have some of the foreign states in the past decade."[37]

Perhaps the most comprehensive response emerged from a gathering in Orono, Maine, in April. Its summary statement recommended that "all Indians...remain separate, independent, autonomous, sovereign nations." Preaching "self-determination," it contended that Native Americans "are in great need of a 'recovery program,' much as the European nations were, in the years following the last World War...the American Indian Nations want to manage their own affairs, but need a great deal of aid. A Marshall Plan is only one possible solution. The 'Point Four' Program of aid for underdeveloped countries might be another way of extending this financial assistance to the American Indians." Maintaining that "no one is more deserving than the Indians of *foreign aid* from the U.S. government," the Orono statement noted, "One more arguing point that comes to mind is the propaganda value of such a program, particularly as far as the colored peoples of the earth are concerned, and also the existing unfavorable propaganda value of the lack of such a program."[38]

The responses, coming from Native Americans from Maine to Texas and from Alabama to the Pacific Northwest, illustrate how fully both reservation leaders and landless Indians who had no reservation home or who had relocated to cities had internalized the moral dimensions of the

Cold War and linked them to its material dimensions. And they reveal a sharpened identification with the "colored peoples of the earth" and an embrace of "self-determination," the operating principle of decolonization. A non-Indian respondent took this internationalist perspective one further step. In "An Open Letter to the American Indian Convention," L.A. Lauer of California suggested that Native Americans present their case for sovereignty by securing "a hearing in the United Nations." And if they failed, they might get a hearing "among the Bandung Conference nations, brother nations in colonial areas who also are 'unrecognized.'" Although the political and economic dynamics were not identical, Native Americans' struggle for self-determination evolved alongside the struggles of other "underdeveloped nations" facing similar Cold War pressures.[39]

More than four hundred Native Americans from sixty-seven "American Indian Nations" gathered in Chicago the week of June 13–20, 1961. The American Indian Chicago Conference did not represent the Native American version of the 1955 Bandung Conference, a gathering in Bandung, Indonesia, of twenty-nine recently decolonized nations including India, China, and Indonesia itself, though speeches at both conferences shared common themes: the need to channel precious economic resources into rebuilding postcolonial economies in order to defend political sovereignty and the importance of rediscovering or retaining individual nations' cultural attributes, which Western values and institutions had submerged in the colonial era and continued to subvert in the Cold War age. The final version of the Declaration of Indian Purpose did not reflect the nationalistic tone of Bandung statements that extolled political and cultural independence. Rather, it stayed true to the ethnic patriotism that defined the discourse of resistance to termination. Mixing its pan-tribal origins and the ancient language of American freedom, the declaration expressed the AICC delegates' belief in "the future of a greater America...where life, liberty, and the pursuit of happiness will be a reality." Still, the declaration clearly adopted an internationalist perspective, asking for federal programs "similar in operation to a Point IV plan" and insisting that "the problem we raise affects the standing which our nation sustains before world opinion."[40]

The Meaning of Home

For Native Americans in the post–World War II period "the very meaning of home change[d] with the experience of decolonization and radicalization," to borrow the words of the writer bell hooks. The Cold War and termination pressures of the 1940s and 1950s reinforced for Native Americans what the environmental scholar Devon Gerardo Pena has called "place-based identities." In the May 1961 *NCAI Bulletin*, Marie Potts reported on the work of the AICC steering committee responsible for drafting the final Declaration of Indian Purpose; a great-grandmother from the Maidu community, Potts had learned English at Carlisle Indian Industrial School, then honed her journalistic skills covering Indian affairs for NCAI publications.

Potts noted that the steering committee first resolved to address Americans' "considerable ignorance" of Indian affairs. "[One] prevalent idea is that Indian reservations are 'concentration camps'; that Indians ought, somehow, to be 'gotten off the reservations'; that Indian communities or reservations are 'rural slums.'" In this "public relations job" the steering committee felt compelled to defend the very idea of the reservation. In Potts's words,

> To the Indian his reservation is his home; it is his heritage; it is all he has. He feels a part of the land and the people who form the communities on the reservation whereas he sometimes feels unwanted in towns and cities away from the reservation. The Indian's view of the land is different from that of the non-Indian. Indians feel a *social* relationship to the land while the non-Indian regards the land in commercial terms.

The reservation, Potts concluded, "is the base of their existence, of tribal organizations and Indian identity." Beginning in late 1959 the United States Information Service (USIS) addressed the nature of Indian reservations in a report destined for distribution abroad as part of the series Discussion Papers on Minorities. It read in part: "Reservations definitely are not 'concentration camps.' They are areas of land reserved by treaty, statute, or executive order for the use and benefit of a specific Indian tribe or tribes.... Whether an individual wishes to remain on or leave a reservation is exclusively a question for that Indian to decide." Although the report proclaimed the reservation sovereign space by highlighting treaty rights, much of it denigrated the idea of the reservation as productive space, thus continuing to deny the legitimacy of the "Indianness" that defined that space. "The sum result," the report stated, "is that the reservation all too often remains a place where Indians merely continue to exist." Given that the series was designed to "counteract the racial incidents in this country," the report's paternalistic tone illustrates how little white officials comprehended the special meaning of the reservation in Native American life, a weakness that heralded other failures of cross-cultural understanding in the 1960s.[41]

Any Native American public relations campaign would have to address not just the "considerable ignorance" of white Americans, citizens and government officials alike. It would also have to persuade Native Americans to "remain on" (or return to) their homelands and fight to develop them rather than leave for the American city. The impetus for relocation stemmed not only from aggressive federal programs but also from the social realities of reservation life. Thus the campaign to defend the reservation worked two ways—first, to inhibit termination legislation and, second, to limit the appeal of federal relocation programs, which became the equivalent of a slow-moving but equally corrosive termination campaign; by 1965 the federal government was spending twice as much on relocation programs as on reservation development.[42]

Homi K. Bhabha has argued that the "nation fills the void left in the uprooting of communities and kin, and turns that loss into the language of metaphor." By 1961 Indian nationalism had strengthened in response to the deracinating effect of federal relocation policies and to lingering termi-nationist pressures from assimilated tribal groups. This new nationalism also evolved as a result of Native American leaders' growing identification with foreign nations struggling to reconstruct themselves and the leaders' related claim that the federal government should treat American Indians as members of autonomous nations and thus fight to win *their* hearts and minds as part of a worldwide struggle for the allegiance of "brother nations." Native Americans thereby showed an incipient consciousness of "a large-scale solidarity," to use Ernest Renan's term. Joining the metaphor of ancestral homelands for which their grandfathers gave their lives, as the Northern Cheyenne leader John Woodenlegs told it, with visions of the American freedom and democracy for which members of their generation had bled on World War II battlefields, Native American politicians reimag-ined American Indian nations as a middle ground between the poles of hegemonic American culture and the nascent Third World.[43]

As in African Americans' civil rights campaigns and the rise of student groups such as the Students for a Democratic Society, the 1960s brought a generational and philosophical split in the methods and mentality of Native American activists. In particular, the National Indian Youth Council (NIYC) cut its ideological teeth at the AICC. The NIYC, founded in 1961, rejected the ethnic patriotism of the AICC and the NCAI, their moderate response to coercive assimilation campaigns, to assert an ethnic national-ism. Red power embodied this ethnic nationalism, embracing the meta-phor of war that AICC delegates and NCAI leaders shunned. Mel Thom, who attended the AICC and helped found the NIYC, contended in "Indian War 1963," published in the NIYC's newsletter *American Aborigine*, that Native Americans were involved in "a different kind of war—a cold war, one might say. It's a struggle against destructive forces the Indian cannot sometimes even see, let alone understand." A new generation of activists such as Thom, politicized by the Cold War and its implications for Native American self-determination, would become radicalized when they per-ceived that Cold War–era nation building, the goal of their fathers and moth-ers, had bypassed American Indian nations. The NIYC's goal, as Thom put it, was not the AICC's "greater America" but a "greater Indian America." A "greater Indian America" was a tenuous proposition, given the heteroge-neity of Native Americans, though a greater American Indian identity was not. Both visions, however, rested on the foundation of an internationalism that emerged from the crucible of the 1950s, the product of an indigenous patriotism that crafted a version of Americanism designed to make "friends among other peoples" of the world.[44]

Notes

I want to thank *Journal of American History* reviewers, including Thomas Borstelmann, Peter Iverson, and three anonymous readers, and *JAH* editor David Nord for their invaluable comments on earlier drafts of this essay. In addition, I am grateful for the advice and assistance of the *Journal of American History* editorial staff, especially Susan Armeny, Nancy J. Croker, Bonnie Laughlin Schultz, and Donna Drucker. I also want to thank my Villanova University History Department colleagues Marc Gallicchio, Judy Giesberg, Seth Koven, Charlene Mires, and Paul Steege, who offered careful readings of the manuscript and fine suggestions for improving it. And I want to acknowledge the generous financial support provided by the Villanova University Department of History and the National Endowment for the Humanities, which made the research possible. Readers may contact Rosier at paul.rosier@villanova.edu.

1. *New York Times*, Oct. 30, 1947, p. 14; Thomas Borstelmann, *The Cold War and the Color Line: American Race Relations in the Global Arena* (Cambridge, Mass., 2001), 268; *New York Times*, Feb. 16, 1958, p. 22.
2. On "integration," see Christina Klein, *Cold War Orientalism: Asia in the Middlebrow Imagination, 1945–1961* (Berkeley, 2003), 24–29, 240–43; Arthur Watkins, "Termination of Federal Supervision: The Removal of Restrictions over Indian Property and Person," *Annals of the American Academy of Political and Social Science*, 311 (May 1957), 55. On Arthur Watkins's role in the termination movement, see R. Warren Metcalf, *Termination's Legacy: The Discarded Indians of Utah* (Lincoln, 2002), 21–48, 234–43. On HCR 108, see "House Concurrent Resolution 108," Aug. 1, 1953, in *Documents of United States Indian Policy*, ed. Francis Paul Prucha (Lincoln, 2000), 234; Donald L. Fixico, *Termination and Relocation: Federal Indian Policy, 1945–1960* (Albuquerque, 1986), 91–102; Kenneth R. Philp, *Termination Revisited* (Lincoln, 2000), 168–75; and Larry W. Burt, *Tribalism in Crisis: Federal Indian Policy, 1953–1961* (Albuquerque, 1982), 19–47.
3. Mary L. Dudziak, *Cold War Civil Rights: Race and the Image of American Democracy* (Princeton, 2000), 250. See also Mary L. Dudziak, "*Brown* as a Cold War Case," *Journal of American History*, 90 (June 2004), 32–42. On the notion of "social containment," see A. Yvette Huginnie, "Containment and Emancipation: Race, Class, and Gender in the Cold War West," in *The Cold War American West, 1945–1989*, ed. Kevin Fernlund (Albuquerque, 1998), 51–70. On the intersection of postwar domestic race policy and international affairs, see Nikhil Pal Singh, *Black Is a Country: Race and the Unfinished Struggle for Democracy* (Cambridge, Mass., 2004); Penny M. Von Eschen, *Satchmo Blows Up the World: Jazz Ambassadors Play the Cold War* (Cambridge, Mass., 2004); Brenda Gayle Plummer, ed., *Window on Freedom: Race, Civil Rights, and Foreign Affairs, 1945–1988* (Chapel Hill, 2003); and Penny M. Von Eschen, *Race against Empire: Black Americans and Anticolonialism, 1937–1957* (Ithaca, 1997). On the intersection of Native American history and Cold War popular culture, see Philip J. DeLoria, *Playing Indian* (New Haven, 1998), 128–53; and Richard Slotkin, *Gunfighter Nation: The Myth of the Frontier in Twentieth-Century America* (Norman, 1998), 347–78.
4. Michel Foucault, "The Order of Discourse," in *The Rhetorical Tradition: Readings from Classical Times to the Present*, ed. Patricia Bizzell and Bruce Herzberg (Boston, 1990), 1155; Von Eschen, *Race against Empire*, 4.
5. Gertrude Bonnin (Zitkala Sa), "Editorial Comment," in *Talking Back to Civilization: Indian Voices from the Progressive Era*, ed. Frederick E. Hoxie (Boston, 2001), 129; "Address by Robert Yellowtail in Defense of the Rights of the Crow Indians, and Indians Generally, before the Senate Subcommittee on Indian Affairs, September 9, 1919," ibid., 136, 137.
6. "Inaugural Address of Harry S. Truman," Jan. 20, 1949, in *The Avalon Project at Yale Law School* <http://www.yale.edu/lawweb/avalon/presiden/inaug/truman.htm> (Jan. 20, 2006). I borrow here from Raymond Williams's idea of "keywords."

See Raymond Williams, *Keywords: A Vocabulary of Culture and Society* (New York, 1985). Marc S. Gallicchio, *The African American Encounter with Japan and China: Black Internationalism in Asia, 1895–1945* (Chapel Hill, 2000), 2; "Address by Robert Yellowtail in Defense of the Rights of the Crow Indians," 135. See also U.S. Department of State, *Point Four: Cooperative Programs for Aid in the Development of Economically Underdeveloped Areas* (Washington, 1949).

7. See Harold Edward Fey and D'Arcy McNickle, *Indians and Other Americans: Two Ways of Life Meet* (New York, 1959), 197–200. The Association on American Indian Affairs began promoting a "Point IV program for American Indians" in late 1955. See box 151, series 2, Subject Files, subseries 1, General, Archives of the Association on American Indian Affairs (Seeley G. Mudd Manuscript Library, Princeton University, Princeton, N.J.). On Point Four funding for Native Americans, see Dorothy R. Parker, *Singing an Indian Song: A Biography of D'Arcy McNickle* (Lincoln, 1992), 175–76; Thomas W. Cowger, *The National Congress of American Indians: The Founding Years* (Lincoln, 1999), 108–9, 117–18; and Daniel Cobb, *Before Red Power: The Politics of Tribal Self-determination, 1960–1968* (Lawrence, forthcoming).

8. On the 1825 use of the term "reservation," see "Treaty of Prairie du Chien, August 19, 1825," in *Documents of United States Indian Policy*, ed. Prucha, 42–43. "Annual Report of the Commissioner of Indian Affairs," Nov. 27, 1850, ibid., 81–82; "Annual Report of the Commissioner of Indian Affairs, Nov. 27, 1851," ibid., 86.

9. The *New York World* quoted in Philip M. Katz, *From Appomattox to Montmartre: Americans and the Paris Commune* (Cambridge, Mass., 1998), 132; Cherokee politicians quoted in Alexandra Harmon, "American Indians and Land Monopolies in the Gilded Age," *Journal of American History*, 90 (June 2003), 123; "Annual Report of the Commissioner of Indian Affairs," Sept. 28, 1886, in *Documents of United States Indian Policy*, ed. Prucha, 169; "Annual Report of the Commissioner of Indian Affairs," Oct. 1, 1889, ibid., 176. On this period, see Frederick E. Hoxie, *A Final Promise: The Campaign to Assimilate the Indians, 1880–1920* (Lincoln, 1986), 115–45. On white Americans' opposition to tribal organization, see Robert A. Williams, *The American Indian in Western Legal Thought: The Discourses of Conquest* (New York, 1990), 271–80; Stephen Cornell, *The Return of the Native: American Indian Political Resurgence* (New York, 1988), 53–59, 112. For discussions of Red Indians as Communist Reds, see Katz, *From Appomattox to Montmartre*, 131–36, 188; Richard Slotkin, *The Fatal Environment: The Myth of the Frontier in the Age of Industrialization, 1800–1890* (New York, 1985), 462–63, 480–85; and Alan Trachtenberg, *The Incorporation of America: Culture and Society in the Gilded Age* (New York, 1982), 33–34.

10. Lawrence C. Kelly, *The Assault on Assimilation: John Collier and the Origins of Indian Policy Reform* (Albuquerque, 1983), 187. Estimates of the number of Native Americans who fought in the war range from 10,000 to 15,000. On this debate, see Thomas A. Britten, *American Indians in World War I: At Home and at War* (Albuquerque, 1997), 59–60. Congress passed the 1924 Indian Citizenship Act in part because of this service. See ibid., 178–81.

11. Flora Warren Seymour, "Trying It on the Indian," 1934, in *Native Americans: Opposing Viewpoints*, ed. William Dudley (San Diego, 1998), 207. For Joseph Bruner's comments, see Kenneth R. Philp, *John Collier's Crusade for Indian Reform, 1920–1954* (Tucson, 1977), 172. For John Collier's statement, see "Minutes of the Plains Congress, Rapid City Indian School, Rapid City, South Dakota, March 2–5, 1934," p. 18, file 4894–1934–066, pt. 2–AA, box 3, Records Concerning the Wheeler–Howard Act, 1933–1937, Records of the Bureau of Indian Affairs, RG 75 (National Archives, Washington, D.C.). On the American

Indian Federation and the activities of Bruner and Alice Lee Jemison, see Kenneth William Townsend, *World War II and the American Indian* (Albuquerque, 2000), 45–60; and Jere' Bishop Franco, *Crossing the Pond: The Native American Effort in World War II* (Denton, 1999), 1–33.

12. Greg Robinson, *By Order of the President: FDR and the Internment of Japanese Americans* (Cambridge, Mass., 2000), 2; U.S. Congress, House, Committee on Indian Affairs, *Relief of Needy Indians*, 76 Cong., 3 sess. (Washington, 1940), 13; U.S. Congress, House, Subcommittee of the Committee on Indian Affairs, *Investigate Indian Affairs*, pt. 3, 78 Cong., 2 sess. (Washington, 1944), 400.

13. Other Native Americans, including the Meskwaki, Comanche, and Cherokee, worked in Signal Corps detachments during the war. Although the Navajo code talkers' service remained classified until 1968, their important role during the war helped galvanize Navajos intent on securing the benefits of such service. *New York Times*, Aug. 30, 1942, p. E7; Oswald Villard, "Wardship and the Indian," *Christian Century*, March 29, 1944, 397, 398; O.K. Armstrong, "Set the American Indians Free!," *Reader's Digest*, 47 (Aug. 1945), 49, 47. On veterans' views on postwar adjustments to reservation life, see "The Problem of the Returned Indian Veterans," *NCAI Newsletter* (Oct. 1947), 5–7, American Indian Periodicals (Firestone Library, Princeton University).

14. Cornell, *Return of the Native*, 121; Henri Lefebvre, *The Production of Space* (Oxford, 1992), 271, 391. On the protean notion of hybridity, see Homi K. Bhabha, *The Location of Culture* (New York, 1994), 4. Villard, "Wardship and the Indian," 397.

15. Judge N.B. Johnson to Hon. Styles Bridges, Chairman, Senate Appropriations Committee, n.d., *NCAI Newsletter* (Oct. 1947), American Indian Periodicals; "Statement of Zuni Indian Veterans of World War II and the Korean Conflict," Feb. 17, 1954, folder "Emergency Conference Bulletin," box 257, Records of the National Congress of American Indians (National Anthropological Archives, Smithsonian Institution, Suitland, Md.).

16. "Are Indians Getting a Square Deal?," radio broadcast, Aug. 21, 1947, *NCAI Newsletter* (Oct. 1947), 5, American Indian Periodicals; "Lilly J. Neil to Mr. Beatty, General Director of Indian Education," Sept. 8, 1947, in *"For Our Navajo People": Dine Letters, Speeches, and Petitions, 1900–1960*, ed. Peter Iverson (Albuquerque, 2002), 103. My thanks to Peter Iverson for pointing me to this volume and letter. Native Americans could not vote in New Mexico and Arizona until 1948.

17. *Los Angeles Examiner*, Nov. 25, 1947, quoted in Bernstein, *American Indians and World War II*, 153.

18. For Harry S. Truman's statement, see Bernstein, *American Indians and World War II*, 155. *New York Times*, Dec. 10, 1947, p. 64; ibid., Oct. 30, 1947, p. 14; Dudziak, *Cold War Civil Rights*, 250; "Statement of Secretary of the Interior J.A. Krug before the Subcommittee on Indian Affairs of the House Public Lands Committee, April 18, 1949," folder "Navajo–Hopi Rehabilitation, 1947–1948," box 313, Archives of the Association on American Indian Affairs. In 1950 Congress passed the Navajo–Hopi Rehabilitation Act, allocating $89,946,240 for infrastructure projects. Navajo–Hopi Rehabilitation Act, Pub. L. No. 81–474, 64 Stat. 44 (1950). For details, see Peter Iverson, *The Navajo Nation* (Westport, 1981), 56–61.

19. Bernstein, *American Indians and World War II*, 156; *New York Times*, Nov. 30, 1947, p. 21; "Resolution of the Navajo Tribal Council: Advisory Committee to Draft Mining Regulations," March 22, 1951 (in Paul C. Rosier's possession). My thanks to William Chenoweth, research associate for the New Mexico Bureau of Mines and Mineral Resources, for sending me this document. The Spokane and Laguna Pueblo also contributed uranium to national defense programs. On Navajo

mining and its devastating health consequences, see Peter H. Eichstadt, *If You Poison Us: Uranium and Native Americans* (Santa Fe, 1994), 33–79.

20. Fixico, *Termination and Relocation*, 13; *New York Times*, May 20, 1949, p. 6.

21. "Listing and Description of Tasks Remaining to be Done to Effect Complete Withdrawal of Bureau Services by Termination or Transfer to Other Auspices," 1952, pp. 16–17, in "Withdrawal Programming, Schedule C, Blackfeet Agency," file 17091–1952–BF–077 part I, Records of the Bureau of Indian Affairs; Felix S. Cohen, "Indian Self-Government," 1949, in *The Legal Conscience: Selected Papers of Felix S. Cohen*, ed. Lucy Kramer Cohen (New Haven, 1960), 313–14. On Dillon Myer's regime at the Bureau of Indian Affairs (BIA), see Felix S. Cohen, "The Erosion of Indian Rights, 1950–1953: A Case Study in Bureaucracy," *Yale Law Journal*, 62 (Feb. 1953), 348–90; and Richard Drinnon, *Keeper of Concentration Camps: Dillon Myer and American Racism* (Berkeley, 1987), 163–248.

22. U.S. Congress, Senate, Subcommittee of the Committee on Appropriations, "Statement by George Pambrun," *Interior Department Appropriations for 1952: Hearings before the Subcommittee of the Committee on Appropriations*, 82 Cong., 1 sess., pt. 1, 1951, pp. 1228–29; Walter Wetzel to Secretary of the Interior, May 1, 1952, file 1141–1946–Blackfeet–068 pt. 2, Records of the Bureau of Indian Affairs. On the conflict between Blackfeet politicians and the BIA, see Paul C. Rosier, *Rebirth of the Blackfeet Nation, 1912–1954* (Lincoln, 2001), 230–64.

23. Horatio Greenough, c. 1850, quoted in Richard Drinnon, *Facing West: The Metaphysics of Indian-Hating and Empire-Building* (New York, 1980), 20; Watkins, "Termination of Federal Supervision," 55. For an analysis of the statue, see Drinnon, *Facing West*, 119–21. On the rise and literal fall of *The Rescue*, see Vivien Green Fryd, *Art and Empire: The Politics of Ethnicity in the United States Capitol, 1815–1860* (New Haven, 1992), 94–105.

24. Joseph Garry, "A Declaration of Indian Rights," folder "Emergency Conference Bulletin," 1954, box 257, Records of the National Congress of American Indians. Emphasis added. "Address by George Abbot, counsel for the House Committee on Interior and Insular Affairs," Feb. 28, 1954, ibid. On the Emergency Conference, see Cowger, *National Congress of American Indians*, 114–16. On Joseph Garry's life and times, see John Fahey, *Saving the Reservation: Joe Garry and the Battle to Be Indian* (Seattle, 2001).

25. "Statement of the Council of the Pueblo of Isleta," Jan. 27, 1954, folder "Emergency Conference Bulletin," box 257, Records of the National Congress of American Indians; "What Does Termination of Federal Trusteeship Mean to the Indian Peoples?," n.d., p. 2, folder "General Materials," ibid.

26. Jim Hayes to Lawrence Lindley, general secretary, Indian Rights Association [March 1954] folder "Hayes Correspondence," box 257, Records of the National Congress of American Indians.

27. Hilda Cragun to Charles D. Skippon, Jan. 22, 1958, folder "Subversive Organizations" Attorney General's List, 1957–1958, 1960, box 166, Records of the National Congress of American Indians. Emphasis added. M. Muller-Fricken et al. to National Congress of American Indians, Dec. 12, 1957, ibid.; Eike-M. Eckhardt et al. to the Congress of the United States of America, Dec. 21, 1957, ibid. Skippon forwarded Cragun's letter and the German group's letter to the Bureau of German Affairs. See Department of State Reference Slip, Jan. 28, 1958, ibid.

28. Charles Coe to National Congress of American Indians, n.d., folder "Subversive Organizations" Attorney General's List, 1957–1958, 1960, box 166, Records of the National Congress of American Indians; Helen Peterson to Coe, Nov. 19, 1957, ibid.; Peterson to Letitia Shankle, Nov. 19, 1957, ibid. Emphasis added.

29. On the National Association for the Advancement of Colored People (NAACP) and the Cold War, see Dudziak, *Cold War Civil Rights*, 29, 67; Von Eschen, *Race*

against Empire, 107–18; and Manning Marable, *Race, Reform, and Rebellion: The Second Reconstruction in Black America, 1945–1990* (Jackson, 1991), 24, 28, 30, 58.

30. "Minutes of the Special Meeting of the Colville Business Council," Nov. 14, 1947, file 8026–1946–Colville–054, pt. 1, box 12, Records of the Bureau of Indian Affairs; Lucy Seymour Swan to Secretary of the Interior, Feb. 23, 1953, ibid.; "Minutes of Meeting, Nespelem," March 21, 1953, ibid.; "Minutes of the Special Meeting of the Colville Business Council," Aug. 21, 1950, ibid.; Frank Moore, "Behind the Buckskin Curtain, Part 2," *Republic Independent*, April 25, 1957, file 14300–1948–Colville–054, box 18, ibid.; "Frank George talk to the Colville Business Council," Aug. 14, 1953, file 6555–1952–Colville–053, box 9, ibid.; "Minutes of the Regular Meeting of the Colville Business Council," Jan. 11, 1951, file 8026–1946–Colville–054, pt. 2, box 12, ibid.

31. "Indians Working towards Independent Status," *Republic Independent* [c. 1957], file 14300–1948–Colville–054, box 18, ibid.; Harmon, "American Indians and Land Monopolies in the Gilded Age," 109.

32. For statistics on termination, see Fixico, *Termination and Relocation*, 183. For those on relocation, see Colin Calloway, ed., *First Peoples: A Documentary Survey of American Indian History* (Boston, 2004), 409. Between 1950 and 1970, the percentage of native Americans living in cities rose from 13.4 percent to 44 percent. See ibid. See also Fixico, *Termination and Relocation*, 134–57; and Cornell, *Return of the Native*, 130–37.

33. U.S. Congress, House, Committee on Appropriations, *Public Works Appropriations for 1958*, 85 Cong., 1 sess., 1957, pp. 1036, 1049–50. On the Kinzua Dam controversy, see Joy A. Bilharz, *The Allegany Senecas and Kinzua Dam: Forced Relocation through Two Generations* (Lincoln, 1998), 24–63; Paul C. Rosier, "Dam-Building and Treaty-Breaking: The Kinzua Dam Controversy, 1936–1958," *Pennsylvania Magazine of History and Biography*, 119 (Oct. 1995), 345–68; and Laurence Hauptman, *The Iroquois Struggle for Survival: World War II to Red Power* (Syracuse, 1986), 105–22.

34. *SPA v. Tuscarora Indian Nation*, 80 S. Ct. 543 (1960), in "Tuscarora's Lose Fight for Reservation," *Race of Sorrows*, 5 (April 1960), 4, American Indian Periodicals.

35. Patty Loew, "Hidden Transcripts in the Chippewa Treaty Rights Struggle," *American Indian Quarterly*, 21 (Fall 1997), 717; Clarence Wesley, "Guest Editorial," *AmerIndian*, 5 (Sept.–Oct. 1957), 2.

36. Sol Tax, "To All American Indians," folder "American Indian Chicago Conference 'Charter Convention,'" box 148, Records of the National Congress of American Indians; Progress Report No. 4, ibid. On the American Indian Chicago Conference, see James B. LaGrand, *Indian Metropolis: Native Americans in Chicago, 1945–1975* (Urbana, 2002), 168–85; Parker, *Singing an Indian Song*, 187–93; and Cowger, *National Congress of American Indians*, 133–40.

37. Progress Report No. 4; folder "American Indian Chicago Conference 'Charter Convention,'" box 148, Records of the National Congress of American Indians; Progress Report No. 6, ibid.

38. Progress Report No. 4, ibid. Emphasis added.

39. "Letters and other Contributors to AICC from non-Indians, Reference Material 1961," folder "Other Indian Organizations," ibid.

40. "Declaration of Indian Purpose," American Indian Chicago Conference, 1961, in *Documents of United States Indian Policy*, ed. Prucha, 246, 247.

41. For bell hooks's statement, see David Harvey, *Justice, Nature, and the Geography of Difference* (Malden, 1996), 104; Devon Gerardo Pena, "Endangered Landscapes and Disappearing Peoples? Identity, Place, and Community in Ecological Politics," *The Environmental Justice Reader: Politics, Poetics, and*

Pedagogy, ed. Joni Adamson et al. (Tucson, 2002), 72–73; Marie Potts, "AICC Steering Committee Meets in Chicago, April 26–30," *NCAI Bulletin* (May 1961), American Indian Periodicals; Leonard Ware, "The American Indians: In Profile, Discussion Paper on Minorities - #5," [c. 1958], pp. 3, 5, file 811.411/12–458, box 4159, Central Decimal File, 1955–1959, Records of the Department of State, rg 59 (National Archives, College Park, Md.); Glenn G. Wolfe to Department of State, Oct. 5, 1959, "South African Comments on American Indian," memo, file 811.411/10–559, ibid.; John A. Calhoun to Gerald D. Morgan, "Request from the Civil Rights Commission," memo, Dec. 31, 1958, file 811.411/12–458, ibid. State Department archives, including the expansive File 811.411, contain little material on "the Indian problem" in contrast to the voluminous material on "the Negro problem."
42. For relocation figures, see Cornell, *Return of the Native*, 131.
43. Homi K. Bhabha, "DissemiNation: Time, Narrative, and the Margins of the Modern Nation," in *Nation and Narration*, ed. Homi Bhabha (London, 1990), 291; Ernest Renan, "What is a Nation" (1882), ibid., 19.
44. Mel Thom, "Indian War 1963," *American Aborigine*, 3 (n.d.), 2, 4, American Indian Periodicals; "Statement of the Council of the Pueblo of Isleta," 1. On red power, see Joane Nagel, *American Indian Ethnic Renewal: Red Power and the Resurgence of Identity and Culture* (New York, 1996); Troy Johnson, *The Occupation of Alcatraz Island: Indian Self-Determination and the Rise of Indian Activism* (Urbana, 1996); and Cobb, "Community, Poverty, Power."

Other Articles Nominated for the 2008 Competition

1. **Allen, Deborah J.**, "Acquiring 'Knowledge of Our Own Continent': Geopolitics, Science, and Jeffersonian Geography, 1783–1803," *Journal of American Studies* (Cambridge), 40 (Aug. 2006): 205–32.
2. **Beyer-Sherwood, Teresa**, "From Farm to Factory: Transitions in Work, Gender, and Leisure at Banning Mill, 1910–1930s," *Oral History Review* 33, no. 2 (2006): 65–94.
3. **Botts, Joshua**, "'Nothing to Seek and...Nothing to Defend': George F. Kennan's Core Values and American Foreign Policy, 1938–1993," *Diplomatic History*, 30 (November 2006): 839–66.
4. **Clayton, Nichola**, "Managing the Transition to a Free Labor Society: American Interpretations of the British West Indies during the Civil War and Reconstruction," *American Nineteenth Century History* (London), 7 (March 2006): 89–108.
5. **Cohen, Deborah**, "From Peasant to Worker: Migration, Masculinity, and the Making of Mexican Workers in the U.S.," *International Labor and Working-Class History* 69 (2006): 81–103.
6. **Cornell, Saul**, "The Early American Origins of the Modern Gun Control Debate: The Right to Bear Arms, Firearms Regulation, and the Lessons of History," *Stanford Law and Policy Review* 17, no. 3 (2006): 571–96.
7. **Curriarino, Roseanne**, "The Politics of 'More': The Labor Question and the Idea of Economic Liberty in Industrial America," *Journal of American History* (June 2006): 17–36.
8. **Doty, R.G.**, "When Money Was Different: A Look Back," *Common-Place* 6 (April 2006).
9. **Eslinger, Ellen**, "Freedom without Independence: The Story of a Former Slave and Her Family," *Virginia Magazine of History and Biography* 114, no. 2 (2006): 262–91.
10. **Frederickson, Kari**, "Confronting the Garrison State: South Carolina in the Early Cold War Era," *Journal of Southern History* LXXII, no. 2 (May 2006): 349–78.
11. **Guglielmo, Thomas A.**, "Fighting for Caucasian Rights: Mexicans, Mexican Americans, and the Transnational Struggle for Civil Rights in World War II Texas," *Journal of American History* (March 2006): 1212–37.

12. **Hodin, Stephen B.,** "The Mechanisms of Monticello: Saving Labor in Jefferson's America," *Journal of the Early Republic* 26, no. 3 (Fall 2006): 377–418.

13. **Kramer, Paul,** "Race-Making and Colonial Violence in the U.S. Empire: The Philippine-American War as Race War," *Diplomatic History* 30 (April 2006): 169–210.

14. **Lawson, Michael L.,** "'We lost our way of living': The Inundation of the White Swan Community," *South Dakota History* 36 (Summer 2006): 135–71.

15. **Latimer, Tirza True,** "The Art of Starting Over: San Franscisco Artists and the Great Quake of 1906," *American Art* 20 (Spring 2006): 96–107.

16. **Leavitt, Sarah A.,** "'Private Little Revolution': The Home Pregnancy Test in American Culture," *Bulletin of the History of Medicine* 80 (Summer 2006): 317–45.

17. **McElhinney, James L.,** "Lost in Our Own Backyard: How American Landscape Painting Lost Its Way," *American Arts Quarterly* 22 (Fall 2005): 13–18.

18. **Monkkonen, Eric,** "Homide: Explaining America's Exceptionalism," *American Historical Review* 111 (Feb. 2006).

19. **Moore, Deborah Dash,** "At Home in America? Revisiting the Second Generation," *Journal of American Ethnic History* 25 (Winter–Spring 2006): 156–68.

20. **Parr, Joy,** "Smells Like? Sources of Uncertainty in the History of the Great Lakes Environment," *Environmental History* 11 (April 2006): 269–99.

21. **Robbins, Jane,** "The 'Problem of the Gifted Student': National Research Council Efforts to Identify and Cultivate Undergraduate Talent in a New Era of Mass Education, 1919–1929," *History of Higher Education Annual* 24 (2005): 91–124.

22. **Peter Thompson,** "The Thief, the Householder, and the Commons: Languages of Class in Seventeenth-Century Virginia," *William and Mary Quarterly* 63 (April 2006): 253–80.

23. **Weinfeld, Daniel R.,** "Samuel Fleishman: Tragedy in Reconstruction-Era Florida," *Southern Jewish History* 8 (2005): 31–76.

24. **Wexler, Natalie,** "In the Beginning: The First Three Chief Justices," *University of Pennsylvania Law Review* 154 (June 2006): 1373–419.

25. **Wood, Andrew and James A. Baer,** "Strength in Numbers: Urban Rent Strikes and Political Transformation in the Americas, 1904–1925," *Journal of Urban History* 32 (September 2006): 862–84.

26. **Yeh, Sarah E.,** "'A Sink of all Filthiness': Gender, Family, and Identity in the British Atlantic, 1688–1763," *The Historian* 68 (Spring 2006): 66–88.

Index